D0683910

SEEDS
OF
MAN

*An Experience
Lived and Dreamed*

WOODY GUTHRIE

A KANGAROO BOOK
PUBLISHED BY POCKET BOOKS NEW YORK

SEEDS OF MAN:

An Experience Lived and Dreamed

POCKET BOOK edition published December, 1977

This POCKET BOOK edition includes every word contained in
the original, higher-priced edition. It is printed from brand-
new plates made from completely reset, clear, easy-to-read type.
POCKET BOOK editions are published by
POCKET BOOKS,
a Simon & Schuster Division of
GULF & WESTERN CORPORATION
1230 Avenue of the Americas,
New York, N.Y. 10020.
Trademarks registered in the United States
and other countries.

ISBN: 0-671-81658-6.
Library of Congress Catalog Card Number: 76-6556.
This POCKET BOOK edition is published by arrangement
with E. P. Dutton & Company, Inc. Copyright, ©, 1976, by
Marjorie M. Guthrie. All rights reserved. This book, or por-
tions thereof, may not be reproduced by any means without
permission of the original publisher: E. P. Dutton & Company, Inc., 201 Park Avenue South, New York, N.Y. 10003.
Printed in the U.S.A.

CONTENTS

EDITORIAL NOTE

Woody Guthrie wrote this narrative in 1947 and 1948, when he was living in Brooklyn, expanding a much shorter account, entitled *Silver Mine*, that he had written at least five years earlier. He wrote part of still another long version, under the title *Seeds of Man*, at Topanga Canyon, California, and Baluthahatchee, Florida, in 1953. The editor has done his best to coordinate the two latter manuscripts and to put the 1947–1948 version (originally called *Study Butte*) in book form. That version has been used primarily throughout, and after the first three chapters, almost exclusively. Some cutting was necessary; the original was over 800 legal-sized typed pages. All the versions, in their original form, will be kept in the archives of the Woody Guthrie Foundation.

Woody Guthrie died in 1967, at the age of fifty-five, after fifteen years' illness with Huntington's disease. Clearly the experience on which *Seeds of Man* is based had an enduring effect on Woody's life. We find him referring to it again and again in his later writings. The trip from Pampa, Texas, to the romantic Big Bend country to search for Jerry P. Guthrie's lost mine did much to crystallize that love of rambling and adventure, that sense of the beauty

of the land, that spirit of freedom, that strong social con-
sciousness and sympathy for the exploited (especially the
migratory agricultural workers) that inspired so much of
Woody's work.

The book is basically real, yet partly imagined. It is
based on an actual trip which Woody took at the age of
nineteen with three other members of the Guthrie family:
his father, Charlie; his Uncle Jeff; and his older brother,
Roy. But many of the events and characters are imagined
or embroidered. For example, Jeff Guthrie recalls that all
four men returned in the truck together, rather than split-
ting up in the Big Bend and coming back separately. In
the same way, some of the characters are either composites
(this seems to be the case with Eddie) or fictitious. Even
those who are identifiable as real people are partly invented
and often quite freely rendered. It has not been possible to
identify any real women corresponding to Helen or Riorina.
The names Helen Cliffman, Masterson, and Riorina de
Gonzales, among others, are not those of actual people. In
part, then, the book is the story of the search for the mine
as Woody imagined it might have happened, rather than as
it actually did.

The tragic experiences of Charlie Guthrie and his family
during Woody's earlier years, referred to in Chapter Two,
are described more fully in Woody's autobiography, *Bound
for Glory*.

Clearly the mountain and desert country of the Big Bend
of the Rio Grande, with its rugged grandeur and atmo-
sphere of mystery, its majestic ranges and canyons, and its
distinctive wildlife and Chihuahuan desert flora, impressed
Woody deeply. Visitors to the subsequently established Big
Bend National Park will find Terlingua and Study Butte
near Texas Ranch Road 170, a few miles west of the park
boundary. Terlingua, where at one time a quarter of the
nation's supply of quicksilver was mined, is now a ghost
town, and the population figure for Study Butte has
shrunk to 21 hospitable and friendly people in residence.
Crossing Route 118 just east of Study Butte is Rough
Run; but this is a broad, lower section. To find the wild,
rugged upper Rough Run streambed, hike up the dry bed
of Cottonwood Creek to its source in the deeper water-
course with, beyond it, the lonely mountains where lies
Jerry P. Guthrie's "backbony" vein, still lost and now never
to be developed. To the north rise the Christmas Moun-

tains, to the northeast opens the Slick Rock Gap where
only his relatives' knotted jackets and shirts saved Woody
from a hard landing on the canyon floor below as he clung
to the crumbling cliff wall. A few miles to the south you
can still walk up the path to Sam Nail's old adobe ranch
house—only its front wall, doorway and two window openings are left now—and watch his windmill still pumping a
trickle of water for the birds and small animals that come
to the desert garden the Nails cleared in 1916. Eastward
towers the purple range of the Chisos Mountains, where
the peaks and clouds look "like Ole Man Rio's face, beddin' down with a whole big batch of wimmin and pullin' a
big woolly nightgown an' flannely blankets all down
around their heads." And perhaps somewhere close to
Rough Run a diligent geologist could still locate some
traces of the mysterious vein of ore that fired the hopes and
dreams of Jerry P. Guthrie in pioneer days and of Woody
and his kinsmen during the Depression.

                                            William Doerflinger

SEEDS
OF
MAN

CHAPTER 1

DRIP GAS

"These here gas drips is always off in some dern-blamed little old cow canyon!" my uncle Jeff was telling me as we bounced loudly along in a dusty, stiff wind and driving snow in our little Model T Ford truck. The cow trail was leading us out of the city limits of Pampa, the wheat and cattle center in Gray County, Texas, that was just now turning into an oil boom town. It was the dead middle of winter on the North Plains. "Rough old sand ruts. This here wind'd cut a man plumb to pieces," Jeff swore. "Wheeooo!"

"Yeah." I hunkered down on the cushion, straining my ears to hear Jeff above the steaming noise from the truck. "Steam flyin' out of our radiator is freezin' into pure ice the minute it hits the windshield. I've heard guys tell about how to drive out to a gasoline drip in a natural-gas pipe-line an' fill up your auto tank free. Jist never did git to see one. Well, try anything once. How much didja say you paid Gus Boydstun for this here wreck?"

"Twenty-two. I give Gus twenty-two dollars for th' thing. Reckon I put out aroun' nine more dollars when I took down th' motor an' tightened it all up good. Lessee . . . them three gear bands I put in run me right

1

around four more smackers. So, I'd say she's set me back right at thirty-five dollars."

"The bands, you mean, that *we* put in! Set *us* back. You act like you done th' whole works all by yourself. Me. Me. Me. I. I. I. You talk like they's nobody else in this world but you." The fast wind blew my words Jeff's way.

"That's a dern lie, Woody, an' you know it. Don't you go tryin' to rub my hairs the wrong way. I got enough worries trottin' 'round in my brain today to drive ever'-body on these upper North Plains plumb hangdown crazy. I give up an awful easy job on that sheriff's force t' rig up this ole truck an' tear-ass off to Canady to put in fer a tract of homesteadin' land with you fellers."

This was the day we had picked to have our last big family get-together before we kissed good-bye and four of us headed our old T truck up the dust-blown highroad from the Panhandle plains of Texas to the peach-orchard country of Alberta, Canada, where we thought we might settle. While Jeff and I were getting the gas for the trip, all the rest of the bunch were, right this minute, back in Pampa cooking red beans and hamhock, cornbread and all the trimmings, down at the cabin where my father, Charlie Guthrie, and stepmother, Betty Jean Guthrie, lived at the Chippyman Tourist Court. That bunch of rickety shacks lay on the south outskirts of town, right under the over-pass where the Southern Kansas Railroad highballs through from Amarillo up towards Wichita.

Jeff was Papa's half-brother, which made him my uncle, but he was only thirty-one, twelve years older than I was. We horsed around a lot together—Jeff was always a good driver, but he drove a good bit too fast and reckless to suit me. He was a big, burly man, just about as tall and as husky as I am little and runty. Jeffie was a cross between a deputy sheriff and a blue-ribbon fiddler. He'd played in many hard-fought fiddling contests where I picked my guitar for him as a chordman. He had round, thick arms and shoulders; strong muscles just a teensy bit fat, but he moved with the quick jumps and motions of some four-footed night howler in a rocky-run canyon. Jeff knew every crack and crevice of these washout plains, anywhere and everywhere on a beeline north from Amarillo.

It always did tickle Jeff's funny rib to see that he was making you sweat cold with his driving. He looked around at me, then squinted ahead of us to try to get some little glimpse of the cow trail leading to the gas drip. My side of the windshield was dirtier and froze stiffer than his side, but neither one of us could see more than three feet ahead of our radiator. The wind howled even crazier as we stood on our nose and plunged down a steep, gravelly, rutted stretch of road. The motor groaned just about like the wind as we nosed up and stood on our tail end to hump it up over a slippery ridge. I made the sad mistake of letting Jeff see the scared look on my face. He laughed his devilish, teasing little laugh and pulled both the gas and the spark levers down as far as they would go and tore out around a sharp drop-off beside the trail. "Jest a-tryin' to get some idea if this rattle-skattle wagon's gonna run us plumb up into Canady," he yelled. "Could you cram all the gear into her?"

"Yeah, we made it, if y' ain't split it off back yonder on that hairpin twist. Papa an' all the rest of us worked at it all last evening while you was over at Elmer's swappin' for them six fruit jars of whiskey. I don't see what y'r gonna do with six half-gallon fruit jars of the stuff."

Several families of relatives and friends had helped to pack the old 2D2 truck to move ourselves and our earthly belongings away from our dusty, dried-out plains and this rough Panhandle weather on up to the north where we were hoping to be homesteaders—to plant, reap, and harvest somewhere in the bright, blossomy, orchardy land of Canada.

"Didja see anybody load my squallin' fiddle back onta that loadin' bed this mornin'?" Jeff asked.

"I seen 'em with my own damn eyes. My gittybox, too. Reenie helped Papa to load 'em on."

"I don't think I even asked ya 'bout your pore damn excuse for a gittar, did I?"

"Ya didn't ask me. I told ya anyhow!"

"Y'r lookin' like a mighty scairt rabbit over there, boy. 'Smatter with ya? Hoh?"

"Stealin' this damn gasoline out from this drip, that's what's got me so scared an' so dammable shaky," I told Jeffrey. "Them big Pampa dicky-boys catches me'n you out here in this ball-freezin' blizzard stealin' drip gas out o' this natural-gas line, they'll toss the two of us so cussed far back inside that Pampa jail that our folks'll have to shoot beans to us with a long-nose Winchesser rifle. Flurk up our whole damn trip to Canady."

"I've told you nine hundred an' ninety-nine times, Wooden Head, that not a single, solitary one of them blessed deputies will budge their fat rumps two goddamn inches out from the heatin' stove in that office on any day that's half as cold, by God, as this'n is. Anyhow"—Jeff rubbed his eyes with the backside of his dirty old pair of cotton gloves—"that line-walker man would jest blow the blame stuff all out, anyway, an' all o' that good high-test gas'd jest, by grabbers, go to waste. 'Tain't stealin'! Boy! That ole wind's a-bouncin' us every whichaway."

"Still sayin' I'd never sailed out here in the first place if I hadn't a wanted ta help out pore old Cousin Eddie Stoner Moore all that I could help 'im."

"I jest never did seem ta get the same kind o' pleasure you seem ta get outa lyin' ta yerself about makin' the trip to help Eddiereekus. I aim ta help out my own self first on my list, Mr. Woodblade."

"I reckon Eddie's down somewhere around about third place on my list of folks I'd love ta be able ta help someways if I could. I reckon I'm headin' ta Canada ta help my own self first an' my little Hell Cat gal about second; but then, too, like I said before, ta help Eddie catch onta some woman someplace, if I could."

"The war shook Eddie up too bad, I'm sad afraid," Jeff said. "Since Eddie got home, I've never heard him say so much as hello, good-bye, go ta hell, or nothin' to any blame thaing that so much as smelled jest a little bit like a she-gal, or had a pair o' titty-knockers. Eddie jest tears cold-ass away from every one we've set in his track fer th' past ten years or more, since he got back from France so damn bad shot up, shook up—"

"Gassed up—"

"Shell-shocked an' all. An' th' way he uses that old snuff ta dip, that old pluggy 'backer ta chew, makes it a little mite rough on th' gals anyhow . . ."

"Jest a little too dammable rough on 'em, if'n ya ask my opinion of it all. . . ."

Jeff's reddish, sandy head of loose, wavy hair had come through many adventures, horse swaps, arguments, and hard fiddling contests. He was born in May of 1901 and bred on a little hundred-and-sixty-acre farm down in the smoked-out timbers of the sandy Oklahoma hills near Stroud. His dad, old Jerry P. Guthrie, had cleared back the trees and dynamited the stumps and roots out. Jeff had

been a chief deputy now for the past five or six years, since
Pampa had first begun changing from a ranching cowtown
into a fast, slick-hole oil city. With thirty thousand or so
roughneck, boom-town oil-field chasers piling into a little
mudhole town of a few hundred, well, the number arrested
was enough to make the fees of the public officers a pretty
fair fistful. The fees for each arrest were split between the
arresting officer, the judge, the jailer, the county court
clerks, and several others. A rambling and restless-hearted
farm-and-fiddle boy like Jeff felt highly important when he
first walked down the street with the badge of the law on
his shirt and its gun on his hip. Driving the patrol car
around town put a good taste in his mouth. Being a fiddling
deputy sheriff was lots of wild fun, but his hours of being
on duty broke into his fiddling just as the party got warmed
up. He always had to stuff his fiddle and bow away in their
case and go back to patrol some highway, keep order in
some dancehall, or check back alleys—"to rattle old back
doorknobs," as Jeff always said disgustedly.

He was a perfect three-way cross: a farmer kid in love
with things that smell so good when they grow; a fast, bust-
down fiddler in love with the crazy gaits and paces of
dancehalls full of hot couples yelling past his elbow. He
was, third, proudly in love with his newly oiled gun and
his badge, with the folks that said a friendly word to him,
and with seeing all the inside goings-on in the public offices
and jail. He liked to smell the new paint, the creosote and
disinfectant, and the nicer smells of the parlors and back
rooms that his gun and badge got him into.

Jeff's new wife, Irene, was just nineteen turning twenty,
that juiciest of all ages for any man or any woman to be
married. She was born four months sooner than I was. She
sprung from down on a sandyland cotton farm on the
Texas South Plains, while I was born several hundred miles
away to the east on Sixth Street in Okemah, a little farming
town down in the Creek Nation, and county seat of Okfuskee County, Oklahoma. Irene's birthtown was Clarendon,
Texas, not more than fifty or sixty miles due south of
Pampa, just below the long cliff called the Caprock that
divides the higher North Plains from the lower South
Plains. Irene was born and bred on fast and fiery mustang
ponies, and rode everything that had four legs for as long
back as she could remember. She'd grown up to boss the
roost around her family, consisting of her mother, Maude,

and her daddy, Robert Boydstun, cotton and wheat farmers all of their lives. Maude married twice in her life, and Irene was born by her second husband. Jeff and Irene were some sort of relatives, since Jeff, born of Grandpa Jerry's second marriage, was Maude's half-brother. All of which stacked up to make Irene a high-headed, high-spirited, bright-eyed, shiny-haired, clear- and loud-talking young lady who had come in the past several months to be very jealous of me and my ways of handling her husband of a shorthorn year.

Jeff was so much in love with Irene that he bubbled up with it several times every day. It drifted out from him like the dust that blew and it jumped out in his wild-horse words, his funny little fast walk, and in his fiddle almost as plain as in his words. Hardly any thought could crowd its way through his mind without wheeling into Irene somewhere along its track. Jeff thought so much about Irene that he didn't just call her by her name, not even when he talked to me as man to man about her.

"My little 'Eenie gal! My little ole Reenie Weenie woman, Woodpile, she's th' pertiest one woman I believe t' my soul I ever laid my two eyes both on. But my perty, perty Reenie Macareenie's gonna be awful mad an' sore at me if she ketches me tryin' to drive off up to Canady with those six fruit jars for snootlerake bites. Says gasoline an' whiskey don't mix. Did you ever, Honest John, see any woman in your whole put-togethers that's got such perty, big, black an' brown eyes an' such perty long waves of hair like my 'Eenie woman's got, Woodsaw?" Jeff slowed down a bit to stick his head out on the driver's side and glance ahead for the road. "That dangburned, blastid, cold-hearted old wind hits me, makes me wisht I's back home already, Woody Shed, feelin' that 'Eenie gal rubbin' 'er hand over my face."

"Good thing for us," I said, "that this blue-bally blizzard's blowin' snow too dern dry to stick on the old T crate, ain't it?"

"Blows all over hell. Scatters in a right dry, flakery powder. Man's a damn fool, Woodpecker, to get out here any such day as this is, jest to chase down this dang old pipeline an' to freeze his balls off with an old inner tube wired over a blow-off valve. But these dern pipelines, y' gotta ketch 'em on a right cold day. Colder th' day, th' more gas forms in them big pipes. This ain't no oil line,

Wood Chucker, this here's the Big Inch gas line back East, itself. Saint Louis. Detroit. Chicago. New York. All back in that country. The line-walker guy totes a big wrench, see, an' he turns these valves open an' blows all this gasoline out o' the pipeline. Every time a gas line takes a low dip, then starts back up again, well, it collects all full o' this natural gasoline. 'Tain't no good for a big car motor; it tests too high. Too hot. But for a little cold-hearted motor like this old T Model truck here, well, drip gas runs the very hell out of 'em. You'll see."

Jeffrey spit past his side curtain. "I'm jest sorely afeard, Woodenpot, that I'll frizzle my damn ballicks off sa dern bad I'll not be able to top that new gal wifey of mine."

"I aim to do a little speck o' that toppin' myself," I told Jeff, "when I git that little Helen kitten of mine off up to Canady. We'll melt all the ice in Alberta quick's I talk that Hell Cat gal into tearin' off up yonder with us."

"How've you been gettin' along with her lately? She's mighty perty little picture; I'll say that much for 'er. How's ever'thing runnin' 'twixt you two?"

"I done already got her in the notion of comin' to Canady with me."

"Is that a fact!" Jeff said. "I'm sure as hell goin' to see that she jest don't ride her little fanny, as perty as it is, across no damn state lines in this T Wagon of mine! Savvy?"

"Been settin' here just waitin' for that good word to come," I told him. "I won't even ask you why."

"You awready knows why, don'cha?"

"She ain't quite seventeen yet."

"She could sure fork up th' whole works for all of us," Jeff nodded. "I ain't bein' one bit harder on you than I'm bein' on myself. I ain't lettin' that Reenie Gal ride with me on this here firs' trip up. I'm jest a-haulin' my own danged wife—perty, by grabbers, as she is—as fer as that little ole Boydstun gate."

"Thirty flat damn miles outa our way," I pointed out, "and another good thirty gettin' back."

"You've shore got that part of it figgered," Jeff fired back. "Say, you didn't let them womenfolks peep at you, didja, whilst you loaded my six half-gallon whiskey jars on the truck, didja, Squarehead?" he asked.

"Well, no," I said.

"That Reenie wife of mine has got about six dozen eyes

in the backside of her head, you know, whenever it comes to bein' able to spot a jar of liquor."

"She didn't see a damn thing this time," I told him. "I didn't load six jars in back of the truck, though. Only five."

"What? There sure had better be all six of them fruit jars aboard; that's all th't I've got to say! That stuff's the very damn best home-run likker I could get anywheres! Test right at a hunderd an' sixty-five proof!"

Jeff's daddy, old Jerry P. Guthrie, had always built his own still and run off his own whiskey all of his life, and Jeff's eye was quick to catch the signs of good or bad whiskey.

"I'm one perty shrewd little loaderman, at that, Jeffrey. I took one of them six jars out from them others, like I said, an' I sorta hid it off out away from alla them othern's. What'd you do to git a nice, big, juicymagoosey drink right now, Jeffrey?"

"Give damn near anything I've got which I've got the rights to give, boy. Jest tell me what kind of a favor it is you want me to do for ya—name 'er."

"Hell Cat."

"You cain't be talkin' about th' Hellytown Skatty Girl—"

"Shorely can. Swear that you'll let Hell Cat pile in and ride jest like that wife of yours rides that first thirty miles. Swear it? Ain't handin' you no jug of likkerjuice till you do."

"No state lines?"

"Nup. No state lines. No jails broke in. Nothin' like that."

"God a'mighty, Woodenhead," Jeff groaned, "I'm freezin' solid! Cough up that jar! I'm game to let her ride. I'm swearin' it. Fork that cussid blame jug over."

"Here's the blessid jar. Right here, idjiot. Don't go wagglin' your dammable hand around so bad. Here's th' jug. Grab 'er."

"Grabbed. Grabbed 'er. How'n holy hell come this here jug to be so damn hot, boy? Answer me that. Hot!" Jeff took a big swig and shoved the jar back to me.

"Only good reason I could think of for it bein' so hot's because I guess I had it hid out down here a little bit too close, mebbe, on top o' that 'xhaust pipe. I didn' dream it'd get that basterdly hot."

"Ya been a-settin' yer bottom here on my good truck cushion, Mister Geehawker, jest a-hopin' and jest a-prayin'" that ya'd be able, somehow or another, to boil up my whiskey till it'd be so hot I wouldn't be able to drink it. I jes' don't see, to save my pore soul from th' fiery holes of Hades, why it is your good God up in heaven lets you stay alive one minute longer! I cain't figger it!"

"Here, take the damn jar!"

But it just so happened that our good half-a-gallon fruit jar slid out of my hands when I handed it to Jeffrey; because I thought he had a good solid hold on it with his big thick mitteny gloves, but he sort of missed his grab, and I saw our jug roll and bounce off down from his steering wheel to slosh and splash all over the cushion we sat on. While the two of us tried to grab it, I saw it rolling, spinning endways, flipping mouthways, and floppering every way you could think of all down over the hard oak floorboards in under our feet, to soak our old rubbery floormat so full of rawspun home-run liquor that it made the fumes from our red-hot exhaust pipe fill our cab full of choking, burning, smoky clouds that busted up in solid firesheets of blistery flames in less than ten seconds flat. If there was one little inch of open air in that cab that wasn't jumping full of these flames, I didn't see it, I was so busy slapping and boxing and fighting at the flames.

I heard Jeffie scream. "Lookit, looky at what ya've gone an' done now! Ya damn silly idiotic moron haff-brained haffwit! Basterd! What'n th' lousy name of holy hell are ya gonna do t' me next? Grab it! Grab that jar! Whenever it rolls ov'r your way there! Grab onta 'er! Idjiot! Grab it! Op'n up your side door over there! Grab it! Now! Toss 'er out! Throw it! Kick it off out! Out!"

"You grab the damn thing over yonder on your own damn side there!" I knew, too, as I yelled, that every little word I yelled was plumb dead wrong, because Jeffrey had to hold his fingers on the wheel he steered by. I fell down on my hands and knees along the floorboards and got all tangled up in his brake and clutch pedals so bad he lost all control. Both of us were blinder than bats. We grabbed onto just any old thing, bear-hugging one another; fighting, pinching and clawing to try to save our hides from what both of us figured sure and certain would be our dead ends. Jeffrey kicked against the up and downy door handle over on my side where he saw the black paper on the door flaring up, and he hooted and he tromped till he kicked more than half our new isinglass window curtains out. The

old ruts in the road did keep our wheels heading somewheres along in what you might call the right direction.
Flaming as our cab seat was, of course, to throw our
doors wide open like we did was the worst mistake we
could make—to cause such a hard blow of icebergy wind
to puff the fiery flames higher. When the door latch over
on Jeffie's side snapped open, the cold winds blowing into
our fiery cab made Jeffrey scrabble out and jump like a
bullfrog to sink down and then to roll over and over in the
piling drifts. I did my levelest best to imitate him, parachut-
ing down into the snow driftings. Our duds had soaked so
full of that high-test whiskey that we both shot out flames
as we jumped, till we'd both rolled on through our fifth or
sixth drift of the coldest wet snow we could find on such
short danged notice.

We watched our T wagon pitch and heave and slip, slide,
and go rolly, and go smoky, and go flamery and go fiery,
on down that snow-blowedy road about another hundred
feet or so, and some few seconds later we heard a bad, sad,
awful, terrible kind of a crunch and a nice big crackup.
The two of us jumped up, brushed ourselves loose from
our snow, and walked along winking and blinkering our
eyes to look at our good T crate all stacked up.

Jeffrey threw big oversize handfuls of snow all up around
the cab on his side, puffing and grunting for air. I pulled
out a shovel we had in the cab in case we got stuck.

"Don't you jest stan' there like no damn dummy of no
kind, Woody!" Jeff panted. "Shovel, boy! Shovel that snow!
I don't have to tell you what's goin' to happen if that likker
firebally blaze takes a damn notion to make a nest down inside of our flurkin' gassyline tank! Shovel! Y' damn dumb
basterd you! Shovel! Damn your godblasted bad-luck
hide! Shovel! Shovvelll!"

"I'm off over here shovelin', cuzzin!" I yelled over towards Jeffrey's side, and tossed three or four shovel loads
into the cab. "Th' very flurkin' minute that there fireball
runs into that gas tank, it's the mortal end of the T crate,
all jest in one great big old whoooossshhh, kerwhushhhh,
blammm!"

"Shovelll! You silly-headed basterd, you, I'm still sayin'
fer you to shovel your pore hands down to their damn
bones! Hurry! Hurry! Blast you! Hurry!"

"I'm hurryin' . . . I'm a-shovelin' your damn snow—"

"*My* damn snow! Now you're callin it *my* damn snow—"

"Stuff's a-savin' our damn-ratted necks, ain't she, Jeffrey? Ri—ri—ri—right about now? I sure never did think I'd ever live to see this here damn day when I'd hafta jest up, by grabbers, an' admit that this here dern coldy-ass frozery-tail snow would be much damn good fer anything."

"Way that there snow's a-chokin' them whiskey flames down, it's a-savin' all four of our lifetime savings that we've done got tied up on 'er . . ." Jeff ran out of breath and stood there gasping.

We could see the flames was out inside the truck cab. The charred and smoking floorboards, the seat front burnt off, was the prettiest sight I ever saw because they weren't on fire no more.

We walked over to where the right front wheel of the T truck was bumped up against a little, long snow hill with something black partly showing through the snow.

"She's snowed under so damn bad," I said, "I can't quite make it out, jest which-a-ma-whatter did she whack into . . . ?"

"That there's the damn Big Inch pipeline!"

"Drap my britches!"

"The very damn pipe that runs right, keewhambo, into where that old trusty drip handle's located at!" Jeff told me. " 'Tain't too awful fer from this damn forkin' spot we're standin' on . . . Man boy! Lucky bastards! Too forkin' lucky to live . . . too damn lucky to breathe . . ."

"I'm a little mite more worried right about now, Sir Cuzzin," I said, "jest standin' here wonderin' if that sweet old T crate is gonna take a notion to run us back to Betty Jean's house . . ."

Jeff leaned his weight against the right-hand front fender and stuck his gloves down in his overalls hip pocket as he tinkered around with the snaplocks and opened the engine hood with his bare hands, telling me, as he glanced around under the hood: "Naawp. Nuppsireekus, Woodenblade, I don't rightly think that them flames done a danged bit of bad damage nowheres about this here motor . . . I'll try crankin' 'er up again; you jump up yonder under that wheel an' be dern sure that you've got that spark ear all the way up . . ."

"She's mortally all o' the way . . ."

"Gas handle jest about, oh, part of the way down . . ."

"Got 'er jest a part . . ."

"I'll choke 'er from out here . . . You flip that there

switchymajigger thing over to where she says BAT . . .
Then whenever you hear it turn over a few good licks, see,
idjiot, flip it real good 'n' fast over ta where it says MAG
. . . Got me?"

"BAT . . . gotcha. An' then . . . MAG. Gotcha . . ."

"I mean to find a foothold down in this dang slickery
snow solid enough fer me to be able to spin her like she's
gotta git spun."

Jeffie grabbed his iron crankhandle and pushed easylike
till he heard the end of the crank nose find its way up inside the hole cut out for it under the fin-blades of the fan
wheel. "I jest don't think that she's ben a-settin' here," he
said, "long enough to git what you'd call real terribly
cold . . ."

"Ought to start right off . . ."

"She ought to . . . better, anyway! Grab hold of your
damn spark handle . . . I aim to spin 'er, by grabbers, like
she's never been spun in her whole forkin' life till now . . ."

Jeffrey was right, anyhow, about spinning her like she'd
never been spun before this. He rocked that whole snowstorm and snowdrift and all those little prairie snowbushes
and our old T car and myself. I heard both of us pray in
our own ways that our old engine would kick over, would
grab a hold, would turn over a few times on her own
power. And that must be the sound I heard clacking away
back down in under her exhaust pipe, and muffler, and
engine hood. The sounds of that old T wagon thratting her
old half-rusty engine at us was more of the true sound of
angels singing to my young ears than any singing I've
heard from that day to this one.

"Started!!" I screamed out my windshield at Jeffrey in
the drifts. "She started! Whattaya know?"

"Oh, I knowed all the time she would. I jest had to sort
o' talk real nice an' sweet in 'er damn ear, an' pat her on
the hip jest a leetle bit—but I knowed she'd go all along."

"I knowed she'd better had . . . still . . . lucky that fire
didn't burn her none down in around them engine wires
like I was afraid it might have . . ."

"Me too." Jeff slapped his gloves together hard to knock
the cakedy blobs of dry snow off, and he climbed into the
cab. These few old burned-out floorboards down in under
my feet didn't amount to much. We could fix them in no
time at all.

Jeff half laughed. "Never would have got all our stuff

back into town, would we, if she hadn't took a notion to flop over, huh? Been badly screwed up, wouldn't we?"

"Sadly flurked," I told him.

Jeff backed the T truck out onto the rutted trail and we rattled on northward. It wasn't very many more jumps and humps till in a low gully we saw the big valve in the pipeline, turn-on handle and all. We stopped the 2D2 on a high place. Jeff got out an old inner tube from a truck tire and carried it down to the blow-off. The snow drove so hard I could hear Jeff's teeth popping together. Before us, by the valve, was a little pond about twenty feet from side to side, all full of slushy, gasoliney ice. Jeffrey hurried back to the truck and down again, this time carrying a pair of twenty-gallon cream cans, holding one in each hand as he skidded down his last fifteen or twenty feet.

"Need a chunk o' balin' wire next," he called, "to wire the open end of that tube around the nose end of this gasoline pipe."

I kicked around down in the snow under our feet.

"Looky here," Jeff said. "Here's a plumb good piece twice as long as yer laig."

He wired the ends of the rubber tubing and the blow-off pipe together, then skidded one of his cream cans over in my direction, telling me: "Whenever you feel me turnin' my gauger handle here, and you begin to feel that pressure on the inside of your inner tubin'—"

"Gotcha, cappy, old stud, old buddy . . ."

"All you've gotta do, see, is jest to poke the loose end of your rubber tubin' down in the open end of your creamery can—"

"Open end. Krammery cream."

"You got that?"

"Yeppy. Got that part. What's next?"

"Jest try your goddamn idjiotic best, see, not to let the end of your tube—"

"The end of my tube—"

"Fly off outta the mouth o' your can. I'm startin' in right this flurkin' minute to turn this here damn handle of mine. It's a-gonna come out from this gauger pipe here wilder'n six teams of pacin' white hosses. Y've jest mortally got, an' I do mean *got*—*gotta* hold your tube's end down on th' damn INSIDE of that flurkin' cream can—er else . . ."

Jeff commenced to turn the red handle on the valve. The

gas sung through the tube like air whizzing out of a kid's balloon. I felt the long tube flutter in my hands, like a window curtain shivering in a lost breeze. Then the humming and whining song turned into a longer scream, sounding like a fired-up riverboat with a drunken pilot. It shrieked like the Santa Fe Scout giving some little crossroad town a highball, done-gone, two-dollar whistle.

Then the natural-gas pressures jumped out at me as Jeffrey went on turning his handle, and my cream can lit out for the thorn patch and me and my traveling clothes lit out real soon thereafter. I fell down and rolled almost across that cold puddle of gasoliney ice I had been standing in. I don't think science knows any chemical on this planet able to freeze down as cold as me and this icy blast of natural gas did.

"I told you—told you to hold onto that tubin', boy, with all o' your might 'n' main. Ha yaaa! Ohhho! My pore old belly jest can't laugh no more, Woody Ducker."

I watched Jeffrey drop his gauger handle and stagger out into the thicket and carry my cream can back, laughing his bloody guts out at every step. He dragged his carcass out through the brush patch and all the way back again, so weak with laughing that he finally stumbled and fell down at my feet, like a laughing, melted-down snowman, in the slush.

"You surrender?" I stood up over him in the gasoliney ice lake, and asked him, "Surrender, man?"

"I'm surrenderin'!"

"Stand up! Stand your damself up an' hold that tube down inside that can like I done, kind uncle. You do the tube-holdin' job, an' I'll step right over here like this, an' I'll take a good handhold on this gauger wheel, and I'll jest turn it ever so gentle and ever so easy like—ah, somethin' about like this—and like *this*—and like that and like that and like these and like those and aroun' and aroun' and aroun' she goes an' where she stops at nobody knows . . ."

That natural-gas pressure shot out through that old red inner tube hard enough to knock down all of old friar's pups. Jeffrey had laughed his whole body so limber that he didn't have strength left to fight back nor to put up very much resistance. I froze him and I smeared that icicly, gasoliney snow all over his work clothes, but he had on too many thick duds for me to really be able to deal him any very long-lasting pains. Since that day, no matter how cold the weather gets, Jeffrey and myself can always say we've seen it a good bit colder. Even the very frizzyest day will always seem like a scorcher.

Our work duds took on the look of a muddy cement statue paying tribute to workhands around this world.

Jeffrey and me both figured that the score for this day in history was just about even steven. We stood off down in the deepest part of our gasoliney lake there and shook hands in sort of a treaty of peace which both of us hoped would hold water and last at least for the next ten or fifteen minutes.

"They's not gonna be no fightin'," I said, "no fightin' of any kind betwixt me an' you here, not till we get all of our gasoline drums loaded fulla this here drip gas an' hauled back to Papa's house where everybody is waitin' for us—okay by you?"

" 'S okay by me." I saw Jeffrey gasp and breathe hard a few times while he shook my hand with his work glove on.

For this next hour or so we took our turns at holding the gauger handle and the empty cream cans, to carry one full can between us each time it run and flowed and spilled over full of that fine, high-test drip gas. I kept talking about it:

"This drip gas is jest about the best kind that an old T crate like ours c'n use—ain't that right?"

" 'Bout th' bes' . . ."

"Awful good thing we thought to bring along this big galv'nized funnel to fit into them bungholes in them big steel drums, ain't it?"

When we finally got both the drums and the gas tank under the seat loaded, I said to Jeff, "You set up yonder on that cushion seat, an' let me try my hand at flippin' this engine over with the crank. Maybe I can spin 'er over fast enough to make her take off like a flyin' squirrel . . . Got yer spark all th' way upwards, Unky old man?"

"Ymmmp."

"Gas about half down . . . ?"

"Ymp."

"Wires all hitched an' tied?"

"Yp."

"Joints all oiled an' greased?"

"Yp."

I pulled the crank around with a powerful heave. The

cylinders fired and the engine started to chug along and shake the T truck.

"You do the drivin'," I told Jeff, "and me, I'll do the tourin' and the sightseein'." I climbed in. "I suppose you know how to drive this apparatus back to Papa's house."

"OK, Mister Woodenhead."

Jeffrey turned the truck around, the reverse band moaning like lost dogies. The red-hot smells blowing up from the exhaust pipe under my feet made our clothes, our soggy, soaked shoes, everything smell sour and bitter. Jeff pulled the gas and spark handles of the old truck down as fast as they would go. The open canyons and wheat country whipping past us took on a look as hungry as we both felt. Jeff's old wide-brimmed beaver hat had been a classy dude in its day and time, when he first stepped out along Cuyler Street in it, but now I laughed to myself to see how sloppy and slouchy it drooped down over his head. The way I laughed, Jeff didn't know whether I was laughing at the storm, the truck, the road, the gas drip, or at him. He had sort of lost his vinegar for a little while, till he could call up some kind of a joke to pull on me to get even with me for blowing that windy gas all over him. That was one thing that kept him quiet. Another thing that was grazing around in his brain was the way Irene would look at our messed-up clothes when we walked in.

I knew that his next words would be something about Irene. I saw it coming down across his face; it was like watching the weather drive its next herd up from the north. I watched his eyes and listened to the snorting of our Model T.

"Main thing that Irene's got against you, Woodsawyer, is, well, she's jest afraid that you're too much of a ramblin', reckless hobo to suit her. She says she sorta hates you on account o', well, you put too damn-blame many footloose, stray-dog notions inta my head. She's got 'er mind set on settlin' down here on these plains. She's born an' raised here; don't know no other part of th' country, like me an' you does. Both o' us is two foxes outa th' same damn-blame hole, me an' you is. Irene, she's like her maw, Skinny Mammy, an' like her paw Robert. Both o' them dug holes in th' groun' down here, Woody, forty solid years 'fore you or me or Irene was even born to breathe. I told her it wasn't your fault. She says ramblin's all right, long's you're jest out battin' aroun' on your own. No woman er kids er nobody hangin' onto you. Only way I could ever talk her into hitchin' onto me in th' first place wuz to swear an' promise eighteen ways sideways I'd settle down. Swore I'd help her to look out after Skinny Mammy an' Pawpaw Robert. Man'll swear to any damn-blame thing a woman spouts in his ear."

"Yeah. I know the way Reenie feels 'bout me. She's mighty afraid I'm a-gonna put that old ramblin', gamblin' bug in your head. That's what Reenie's jealous of me about. She's pounded my head full o' talk about settlin' down."

Jeff laughed out through his side of the windshield. "The more that folks talk to you about stayin' still for two minutes, Woody, the more you're gonna ramble this whole country down right under your feet. Ain't that jest about th' squeeze of it?"

"I like to roll jest the same way this old T truck likes to roll. I'm a born roller. Quick as I git in this town here I ketch my tail on fire tryin' to ramble over to the next town over yonder. Only thing I really want to know about a strip o' country is what in the heck's a-layin' right around the next little crooked bend in th' road."

" 'Tain't jest the ramblin' that Reenie's so dead set against. It's th' gamblin' end o' things. Runnin' off across the holler without a dern nickel to yer name, an' mebbe not a penny in sight."

Jeff bounced around to one side on the cushion as the truck rolled off the prairie trail, down into a splashy ditch, and up again onto the wide road covered over with last year's hot tar and this year's slick, leaky oil from the field trucks and tanker trucks and cars of all sizes and kinds. "Be drivin' in now 'bout any minute," Jeff said. "Unscrew me that lid off that there jar of lice poison, boy—that fire-starter stuff. Make yourse'f useless as well as decorational."

"Here she is. Lemme hold onto that wheel while you're guzzlin' your pore life down the drainhole. Don't slosh it so bad. Wow! That stuff smells worse 'n a buffalo waller hole full o' dead copperheads. Sheweee! Hold it still."

The Model T felt like it knew it was tearing out down the last part of the trail home. Our drip gas made the engine whine and sing as Jeff tilted the jar up to his nose again and inhaled a good liquid inch. The storm slacked off just a speck. But rattling along at a full twenty or twenty-five miles every hour made the wind blow harder and stiffer against us. The truck pulled first to the right side of the road and then over close to the left-hand bar ditch. The tires all had such big knots and boots in them that the road felt several times rougher than it really was. Jeff gulped and gagged for a minute or so and then he took the wheel out of my hand while I turned up the spirit jar.

"Drink your drink, boy. That there bug juice ain't made t' bounce along here." Jeff sped the old cart along down the last block or so home, wide open and heaving her hottest steam to the blowing wind.

I waved the jar in the air above our heads. We rattled through Pampa, and under the railroad overpass we turned into the Chippyman Tourist Court, where the whole bunch was waiting to see us off for Canada.

CHAPTER 2

DETOUR

"Hurry up and get indoors out of this blue blizzard!" Irene called through the side curtain of the truck to welcome Jeff and myself. "Well, I'll be jumpin' little hopper-grasses, Jeff, I surely never did see any two men as muddy and filthy as you both are." She pulled open the door of the cab. "Howdy, Cousin Woodrow, hurry inside and get warm. Did you gents have good luck or bad luck getting your drums of gas?"

"Two full drums," Jeff sung out. "Whole hunderd an' twenty-five gallon."

I bumped into Skinny Mammy in the kitchen. "Smells mighty good," I said as I took a few little sniffles over the pots and skillets. "Pinto beans. Ham knuckles. Greeny beanies. Beefsteak. Thickened gravy. Boys, what's comin' off around this man's joint? Looks like a store owner's banquet. Yep, got them fifty-five gallon drums full, an' our fifteen gallion tank, to boot. T truck's jest a-settin' out there boilin' hot and ready to jump."

Skinny Mammy followed me to the dining room, drying a platter with a blue-rimmed dish towel. "Ice-cold an' ready to freeze, you ought to say." She always took everything I said and twisted it around backwards. Skinny

19

Mammy was up pretty close to her sixtieth wheat crop seen blow past. Her face had more friendly wrinkles cut into it than any other face of man or woman that I ever did see. Even when she felt worried, which was all of her time, she looked sort of pleased about her worry. She worried about anything, everybody, everything. She was just as bony and skinny as she was wrinkled and worried. Real tangly gray hairs sort of waved up around her head as she smiled. And Skinny always did smile. Smiled at you, smiled all over you, smiled right on through you, smiled around at her whole world. Even when she ached and racked with her worst troubling pain, no matter how heavy it was to carry, Skinny smiled at it. She was Jeff's half-sister, born by Jeff's father's first wife. Skinny Mammy was my real aunt, my papa Charlie's own blood sister. She was always one of my favorite relatives, and just about my favorite person. No matter what she was feeling about you, good or bad, she talked right up and let you know all about it. She could cook a meal that would knock your tongue right out of your mouth when she had the meat, the flour, the eggs, the baking powder, the salt, the pepper, the sugar, the lard, the money to buy the things with. She had personally helped in the planting, reaping, threshing and hauling of more than forty running crops of cotton and wheat, yet Skinny Mammy and her man, Robert, had less than a dollar a year to call their own. Always broke. Always bogged down in debt up to their knees. Lots of crop failures and lots of bumper years shined out from Skinny Mammy's eyes. She looked at my muddy, soggy, icy, froze, gasoline-and-whiskey-soaked duds and kissed me on the forehead to get a smell of me. "Must've waded a quicksand bar to fetch those tanks of gasoline, my old crazy Mister Mud Dobber Wood Saw Wilson." Skinny Mammy, from somewhere back down her track and trail of life, had practiced and learned how to speak very polite schoolhouse English. I'd hung out around schools all of my life and couldn't speak it as correct as she could out on her six-forty wheat ranch. Her one bad habit was that she loved the stingery taste and feel of a teaspoonful of sweet snuff to be always hanging in just betwixt her lower lip and her used-to-be teeth. She motioned to me to take my hand out from behind my back and to pour her a drink of that fruit-jar juice I was trying to hide. I filled her a glass and she said, "Eddie and Charlie and Robert and all of our jellybean menfolks are right in the fourteenth parlor there playing poker for matches on the bed. Take them a little snoofter. Hurry. G'wan. Git outta my dining room."

I found Papa Charlie on one end of a little single bed dealing the poker cards out to Robert on the other end and to our cousin, Eddie Stone Moore, who was sitting on a beer case by the center of the bed. Eddie had the biggest smile of the three gamblers, because his pile of matches looked about as high as Papa's and Robert's both put together. Both of their faces looked highly puzzled and worsely worried about the sad misdoings of the poker cards. Robert wore his hat down across the front of his face, so low it hid everything but his nose and chin. Papa's hatbrim was of a much stiffer material than Robert's, and did not hide his face quite so bad. All sucked on some kind of a home-rolled cigarette. Robert rolled his out of a red-looking tin can with a fancy-dressed man on it. Eddie Moore rolled his own from an old smeary sack with a brightish yellow paper label stuck on it. Papa rolled his out of a strawy, fibery, stringy-looking tobacco with a machine he had cut and made one rainy day out of tin he found out on the vacant lot to the north of us, towards the big tool-company warehouse and the lumberyards that string up the main street towards the center of Pampa. The mixture of smoke from the rollings smelled like a mattress damply burning out under your porch. Or maybe more like our old six-weeks' trash pile out there in our back yard smoking and smudging away.

Nobody paid much more than just a slight glance of attention to me when I walked in. The house was the littlest five-roomer I'd seen in my day and time. The day was dark and the lights blinko. Counting the little boxed-in back porch, not big enough to hang your hat in, Papa and Betty Jean's tourist cabin really had six rooms, three running down the one side and three down the other side. I could stand in the middle of any room and reach out my hand and almost touch a wall. With six chairs around the dining table, your back, like everybody else's back, was rubbing against one of the walls or hanging partly out one of the windows or doors. I think every room had some kind of a two-by-nothing window in it. The cabin had a slanting shingle roof that fit nice and right and low down around your shoulders. It was raised up off of the ground on big wood blocks so as to let the north and south winds get

down in under it and fight and drink with the east wind
and the west wind.

I got a good deal more attention from the gamers when
I plunked my fingernail against the half-gallon jar in back
of me.

Eddie Moore, an old soldier and a dead shot, a veteran
with a long-time action record in the First World War, was
the first to make a nervous little sound when his ears caught
the tune of my plunking on the jar. He rubbed his eyes
with his shriveled-up, paralyzed hand that got shot in one
of the big, smoky battles. He looked around at me, laughed
a soft laugh, and said, "Hi-ho and th' mule throwed Cicero.
Whatta you got there, Mister Wood, that sounds so ding-
busted good? You pour me out a big nice glass of that
drinking whiskey and I'll just pay you off in matches. First
poker game I won since we was all a-riding back home on
that hospital train back from that battle on the Marne. I
got matches that's never been struck and I got a daughter
that's never been fucked. Git over here and pour me, boy,
pour me." Eddie had a way of poking people he liked with
his stiffened and stubby little dried-up arm. He punched
me one just above my right knee that almost sent me and
the liquor jar and all down and rolling acrost the floor.

I got him a water glass off the table and poured him a
long one, telling him, "Eddie Moore, I never did see a man
in all of my days that had as much power in a crippled
arm as you've got in that one of yours. How much more?
That's all you get. I'm a-savin' my own belly some. What's
Betty Jean doin'?"

"Betty's got her a fortune-tellin' customer," Eddie told
me as he snorted the glass half empty. "Cash customer,
too. I git up to that Canady place, I'm gonna rig me up a
cabinet shop and git *me* some cash customers."

Papa winked me one of his ornery-looking winks and I
winked back and got Papa's drinking glass. Papa tossed
half of the glass down raw, blew out a long, hard breath
of air, and cleared his throat up by singing Eddie a little
song to make him feel good. Papa kept both eyes on his
poker cards and hummed so low that everybody had to
listen hard to hear his words:

> Eddie Moore, Eddie Moore,
> Gonna build windows,
>   Gonna build doors,

Gonna build walls,
  Gonna build floors
When he crosses Canada's line,
  Eddie Moore's no friend of mine
Eddie Moore, Eddie Moore,
  Eddie ain't my friend no more.
  Eddie Moore ain't my friend no more.
  No, no more; no, no more;
  Eddie Moore ain't my friend no more.

Eddie swigged the rest of his glass while we tapped our feet and our hands and listened. Eddie wore his railroad blackbill hat and his iron-gray overalls with a dark blue jumper jacket. He had put on a couple of cheap cotton shirts, one faded yellow, one a dancehall greenish color. He carried an old pair of oil-soaked gloves in the side pocket of his jumper. He had a good many short-cropped gray hairs, but he was no older than thirty-three. Ed was built on the same hard-knot frame as Papa Charlie, but he was two inches shorter and a good bit bonier. He stood up proud with his chest out straight, like a peppy soldier in a downtown parade. Even to see Ed on his beer case here gave me the feeling that his back and shoulders didn't have to be forced to stand out square and straight, but they just grew up that way and gave Eddie enough pride to go on smiling at you when you looked down and saw his shriveled hand. He was a son of my aunt Laura Guthrie, the blood sister of Papa and Skinny Mammy, who married Trobar Moore. His older brother, Alfred Moore, had partially lost his wits when he was scared by some pranksters one dark night on a graveyard slope, between Al's sixth and seventh birthdays. Al never did pull out of the scare.

Eddie lived on his sixty-five-dollar war pension for being wounded. He chewed tobacco. He smoked all kinds. He dipped and spit bitter and sweet snuff, like most of my other relatives. Eddie had been wounded in his spirit, too, somehow, but he didn't get no pension for that. Folks said he'd been shell-shocked. From the time Ed got back home from France to 1932, twelve whole years, he'd never found any female, girl or woman, that he could get with. And he'd found he couldn't make love to a woman anymore, even when he did try. Jeff and Papa and I felt bad about this and had tried to think how we could help Eddie. In Alberta, we figured, he might shake off whatever was crip-

pling his feelings and get a fresh start. It was one big reason for going.

Thirty-some miles down the southwest spur of the Santa
Fe lines, in the wheat, oil and cowtown of Panhandle,
Texas, Laura Moore had rented a five- or six-room house
where Eddie's brother Al could rustle around town on a
donkey cart and buy and sell old junk to make or lose a
few cents each day, while their younger sister, Saralee,
held down a job in the telephone switchboard office. Eddie's
father, my Uncle Trobar, had worked as an upholsterer on
fancy railroad coaches until he died from consumption.
Eddie had put in a couple of years at this same work with
his daddy before the war took him over across the ocean
to wade through a long list of muddy and bloody woods
and bushes and rivers named Château-Thierry, Belleau
Wood, and the Marne. Eddie spent every day from sun-up
to sundown tinkering around the sawmill and workshop
he'd made in his barn. His one-lung kerosene engine pulled
a big belt that kept a dozen saws, sanders, drills and lathes
running smoky hot but only turning out a few little pieces
of furniture that he sanded and scraped and varnished and
painted and rubbed.

Eddie'd told me a hundred times, in almost the same
words each time, about 'most every single bullet that
whizzed past his ears in every single battle. Going over the
top. Tossing the hand grenade down into the Heinie dugout. Shooting thirteen Huns in a shellhole. Knocking the
tar out of the flu camp bully. Winning twenty thousand
francs in a dice game. The French ladies that waded down
into his trench to carry him a tubful of *vin roudge*. The
hill that got blasted out from under him. All the makes of
guns, grenades, tanks, and airplanes. The bugle. The parade
through the village street. The hospital. The ship and train
back home again.

Eddie's sister Saralee had helped him load a few of his
clothes and tools into their 1927 Ford Lizzie and had
drove over with him yesterday to tell us all good-bye.
Eddie stayed to help Irene, Papa Charlie, and me load
our Model T truck, and Laura and Skinny Mammy had a
few good laughs and cries before Saralee had to drive back
to fix supper for Al and to go to her switchboard, which
paid her around $11.50 a week if she was on time every
morning and did her jobs well all day.

Pawpaw Robert shook his head and told me, "No, thank

you," when I held the jar out his way. Robert was Reenie's father, and I thought every time I looked at him that he looked just like a man chopped out of a rock. His head was just like a square block, rounded at the edges, slick bald on the topside with gray frizzles around his ears. He had eyebrows that run straight across over his big nose. Thick-set lips, heavy-boned jaws, cue-ball chin, neck muscles that stood out like tight harness bands on a hard uphill pull. His shoulders and arms looked too big and burly to hang onto his frame, and his hands looked hard and heavy. Fifty or sixty years of skinned, bruised, cut, and scratched knuckles; blue and purple bruises from wheat farming, ranching, driving, lifting, carrying, and all kinds of straining had made Robert's hands like they were. Meanwhile that many years of fingering the pages of his almanac and his Bible had knocked his eyes a little bit dim, and had made his heavy hands as gentle as the easy rub of a baby rabbit's ear. He would look up or down at you through his dime-store specs and his eyes looked as deep back as a match you'd strike in a cellar cave. When he had one of his talking spells his eyebrows wiggled and danced out the full meaning of every word he told you. In this world's great big gallery of pictures where the faces come shining from life, several snapshots, statues, and sketches had ought to be hung of Robert Boydstun in his sun-up and sundown. "Too early in the day for me. Thank you," Robert told me.

Jeff and Irene walked in. "You never did pour me no firewater from your bottle, Mister Canadian Homesettler," Irene told me. I filled her glass as she held it out, and she downed it fast. In her brand-new red beady dress with white lacework around the collar and the hem, and her dress-up black leather shoes, with her thick, black waves of hair tossing as she laughed like a comedian, Irene was a sight to see. This, and her act of being a nigh-perfect lady, was about the only two happy actions she went through. I'd seen her sore and mad at the whole world lots of times when she paced the floorboards and screamed out at the solid walls. I never did meet up with anyone wilder-fired than Irene was at nineteen. She either jumped down across her bed and kicked her feet in a crying fit, or got up and dried her eyelashes with a towel and laughed at the world. She took spells of sewing, cooking, and cleaning, and could have won blue ribbons at all of those jobs. When she did

settle down to let the old pictures walk through her memory, she stayed so quiet that you couldn't help but hope
Irene's same spirits would last through your next hour.
What she done, she mortally done, and it stayed done.
She was not the wisest of folks on the plains, but the
smarter ones could have made good use of a little of her
pep and energy. When she got off on the wrong side of any
argument, after a three-hour pounding, she would switch
over onto your side and you'd always feel glad that the
argument came about. She was a stickler for anything that
was printed in the Holy Word of the Bible, even arguing
the point that all people born into this world with black
skins are born to be the beasts of burden; that the white-
skins are, by God and by Nature, born to boss the place.
She argued with me many times, too, that if you spare the
rod you spoil the child. But if Irene and myself did plough
into one another a few times every time we met, we also
tried to treat one another a little extra good, just so as to
bait and lure and keep the other one hanging around to
have another debate with. We had hotheaded and bitter
falling-outs. Irene set her foot down on more than half of
the big deals that Jeff and me cooked up together. Lots of
times she used pretty good sense, but lots of times, too, she
let her pure jealousy throw dirt in her own eye.

Jeff looked around to where he'd stood his fiddle case
in the corner. He saw Irene's little flatback, hardwood
mandolin and my guitar standing by his fiddle. "I can hear
that old squallin' panther fiddle jest a-kickin' an' a-scrootch-
in' an' a-tryin' to jump out here in my hands an' squall
out ever bust-down tune they is. Ever feel thatta way,
Reenie gal, you cute little she-devil, you?"

"Why, of course I do. And you know I do."

Irene watched Robert pick up a new card while Eddie
and Papa Charlie frowned and tossed down some bad ones
onto the blanket. Papa had to lean over in order to make
his next pickup and to bet another match. We all heard
him make a little painful groan and saw his face twist up
into a hurt, frowning smile as he lifted his back straight
again. Irene frowned as Papa had frowned and she asked
him, "You lied to me, didn't you, Mister Charlie? You told
me every day that your burns had stopped hurting you.
Lying. That's what you've been doing. Lying to me." She
stood wide-legged and rested her hands on her hips, watching Papa's face twist over into a fake and phony smile.

"Ahhh." Papa caught his breath in a short, hard jerk. "It's not bad, Reenie. It's all right. Little catchy stitch. Muscles sorta get stuck. I breathe a few times and they get to working all right again."

"If you ask me, Sir Charlie Guthrie," Reenie warned accusingly, "you had just better go back up there to that courthouse and get your office deputy job right back again. Forget this whole crazy trip to chop down trees in Canada. You're not well enough to ride from here to the Kansas line, let alone a thousand miles of bouncing from here up to Canada."

"I'm all right." Papa played another card. "Come on, you poker players. Go ahead, Reenie, you and Jeff and Woodrow play me some good music. Play me 'Tom and Jerry,' 'Done Gone,' 'Snow Bird in the Ash Bank.' Saw off 'Old Judge Parker Take Your Shackle off of Me.' All I need right now to make me feel the best in the world, Reenie, is one more little snort out of Woodrow's jar, three green aces to go with these two blue ones, and a few hours of the loudest and the prettiest fiddle music you all can make for me."

"Let's play." I stepped over towards the music corner. "We'll heal 'im up with whiskey an' music."

"You can't play any music right this minute," Skinny Mammy told us, "as long as Betty Jean is in there with her customer. And after that you've got to eat this meal I'm rattling up for you. That old Charlie Guthrie lied to me every day for eighteen months while he was laying there in my bed with the meat burnt off of his bones. I had to fight him to keep him in bed. I had to call Robert in and Irene, too, and all of us just had to set down a-straddle of him to hold him in bed. He tole me, 'Oh, Skinny, I'm just fine, let me get up. Ooo, I'm fine and dandy, Robert, hand me my pants. Oooo, Irene, I'm feeling like a fresh-born poodle dog, put my shirt on me and give me my shoes.'"

"Bed does git hard as tacks after the first month or two." Eddie tossed his card hand face up on the blanket. "I can say that an' back it up for sure. I know how you itched and twitched, Charlie. Man'd give his whole life to be able to crawl up out of that bed. Told forty lies a day to get up. I know."

"But I know one thing, myself," Robert said. "Charlie, you just cannot afford to be taking any chances of getting

out there and catching a cold. Turn into pneumony and
settle down in your burns, Charlie, and knock you out just
like a candle in the wind."

"Play cards." Papa argued. "Let me be. I feel fine. Just
a little hitch here and a little catch there. Shucks almighty,
I know and we all know I'm bound to have little crazy
kinds of jerks and pains for a while. Maybe ten years. But
as far as being healed over, Robert, I'm just as healed up
as you are. You can feel me. Lordy only know how much
I owe to all of you folks here in this room. When I make
my comeback I'll nurse all of you for eighteen months
apiece."

"Charlie's fine as frog's fuzz," Jeff laughed.

"Shore is," I put in.

"Shertainly am." Papa laughed a little, but had to stop
when his muscles got tight again. "Possitootely."

"I worked my head off for you for those eighteen
months, Uncle Charlie." Irene talked serious, like a deep
thinker. "I just got to feeling like I had your life in my
hands, like holding a little hurt bird. I didn't mind that one
little bit. I remembered how your six-room house in
Okemah burned down; how after that your little daughter,
Clara, caught fire and died when she was just fourteen;
how your wife Nora lost her mind and died in the Norman
asylum. You'd been through more kinds of hell and bad
luck than any other man or woman I ever knew of. I felt
sorry for you because you always did work so hard and
fight so hard to give your kids the best things money could
buy. I felt proud of you because you always did have the
best of everything around you. Best jobs. Best houses. Best
dogs. Best horses. Prize cattle. Blue-ribbon hogs. Best car
in your part of the country, first car in your county. Best
farms. Best of books and furniture. Then, well, when you
lost all of this, and fell down to living in those little old
dirty shacks like that hole you lived in when your cigarette
caught your Sunday papers on fire, that Sunday of your
last fire, Skinny Mammy and Robert and I got you out to
the farm here in the Panhandle, where we could feed you
and wash you and get you back on your feet. But your life
was gone when you come out there. You were a dead man.
You ached and you pained so bad you wished every day
and every night for me to let you die and go on out of your
miserable body, burnt to shreds—burnt actually into meat
and ashes.

"After a few months of this kind of howling, I saw you get a little speck of life back in your eyes, and I heard you tell me every day and night, by the holy hour, about this big comeback you're going to make. I never did see any man in my life with enough of this craving to keep on living in his tailbone to make any such a comeback as you made. Not a human among us ever did think you would live, Charlie. A pile of ashes. I never did talk to you like this, Charlie. But this might very well be our last time to see one another for some good long time, and I've just got to get this out of me. I feel like your life belongs to me.

"You've been telling me little lies? Well, I've been doing a little bit of nice fibbing my own self. Jeff has not quit his deputy job yet. He was kidding when he told you that he quit last week. He's been working every night and helping you folks to get ready to go to Canada every day. The Sheriff told Jeff that he would be more than glad to get you back up there to take back your job as the office deputy. That office is a wreck. There's not one single officer up there that knows beans from haystraws about filling out all of those docket books and papers. Why, they can't even halfway read one another's handwriting. You know office work from start to finish, from can till can't, Mister Charlie Uncle, and you taught penmanship back in Okemah. Your handwriting is still the prettiest anybody in the Panhandle ever saw. God only knows why He let your handwriting stay through your burns like it did. Maybe He wants you to go back up there to that sheriff's office and work a few more months.

"Just a few little months. You'll get well faster working in that nice warm office and eating three good hot meals every day than you'll ever be by traipsing off on that old Model T truck which, Lord knows, can't possibly haul its own weight a hundred miles without falling to pieces. I know what shape your tires are in—they'll not take you one day's run without all four of them blowing off their wheels. Sure, Jeff's got a good strong set of shoulders and a nice wide back and he's strong as a bull when it comes to fixing a car. Woodrow, your muscles don't look any too powerful to me. Eddie, you know you'd be nearly as bad as useless with your one arm in case of any kind of an accident, or even at clearing trees off your Canadian land. I know something about how much hard, backbreaking work it takes to keep a farm going after it's all cleared off and built up. Why, you three, Papa Charlie, Jeff, and Eddie here, you talk like old Santy Claus is going to ride down in his big red sled and clear you off a great big juicy peach-orchard farm without you having to shed a drop of sweat. Babies. That's just what you are. All of you. Little bitty tittysucking babies. Kids playing around with a little dreamery bubble like a balloon that's going to bust any minute right in our faces.

"I was sort of halfway ready to let Jeff go, just because I felt sorry for you, Uncle Charlie; and as for you, Cousin Woodrow, I thought the trip and the hard sweating might make you really want to settle down on some kind of a Canadian farm. It sounded good to me because, Lord knows, Skinny, you an' Robert have lost all of your footholds here on the plains, and a good chunk of land with a nice warm house and barn on it would be the saving of your lives. But you'd not make it to the first road post in your condition, Charlie; why can't you just come right out and admit it? Let's all work a few more months and save us up a little more money. I hate deputy sheriffing just as bad as you, Woody, dear Cousin, but don't you see, it's money quick. Good money. Money that will come in just as handy up across that Canadian line as it does right here.

"Go back. Go back to work. Tonight. Both of you. Let's all do it together. We'll have four or five or six months of pure dee old loving fun and big eats and lots of loud fiddlings. Let's just give Charlie a little bit of time to get to feeling better. I want to go up there as bad as you do, Cousin Woodrow, but I want to go right. Lordy Mercy little me, if it's coming down a sixty-mile ringtail whizzerd out there right this second, don't you all know it'll blow harder and colder every inch of your way up that north road? I say, go back tonight, go back up to the sheriff's office and work till the warm weather. Not a soul in all of the land of Canada is out in those tall trees staking off a homestead claim in these blizzardy months. This is the eighth of January. I'll hop in that truck and ride up there with you if you'll wait till the fourth day of July. You need a good femaler up there to cook for you and to see to it that you keep your necks clean behind your ears. What say? Go back? Back to the office tonight? Huh? What say?"

Everybody kept still and listened while Irene told her side of the case.

"Whole lots of sense in what you say, all right." Eddie shook his head up and down to agree with her.

And Robert nodded the same. "Right as a fox."

"Could very muchly be." Papa Charlie smiled and pooched up his lips to be funny. "Could certainly squirtainly be." He tossed all of his cards into a stack face up. His face and eyes lit up with old, remembered thoughts and things as he looked at the little bed with the scattered cards and matches. I knew some of the things the little bed, so tossed around, made him see in his memories. Everybody in that room knew the sad and terrible things that had wrecked our family. We all could hear wild running swarms and herds of thoughts pushing and bleating and calling out in back of each slow little word that Papa said to us. It was the shadows of the lights on his face more than his words that we watched and listened to.

"You're right about that, too, Reenie. I mean, about coming right out and talking about all of these old things. I know   had ought to be called out, called out and talked about in the clear sun. In the open air. That's where   ought to bring all of these old things. My worst pains didn't come from my old burnt skin and bones, Reenie little gally. It was a great lot more misery for me to see all of you tiptoe around me, and to hear you whisper about me off in the corner of the room. To see you sneak out to the side of the barn and talk about me. I'll tell you now, the only real pain you dealt out to me was trying to keep life some kind of a secret, secret, secret. You thought my mind was too weak to stand up and look the facts in the face—that was the pain that outburnt my burnt skin.

"You see, I often had a long dream, it kept on going along like a play. I saw a man—a man standing at a place where six roads fork and go on out in every direction. Everybody had to tell this man why he wanted to keep on going along his own special road. I watched the other people; I listened to every word they told this man at the road forks. I couldn't think fast enough when it come my time to walk up and tell him. He sent me back down my same road. I got to walking back and I bumped into all of you, everybody I ever did know. But I couldn't get anybody to open a lip and say a word to me. Nobody would talk. I wanted you to tell me a word, Woodrow; I wanted your brothers, Roy and George, to tell me some word, I even saw Nora and Clara, and they both told me to come back

here to you folks again and to try to get you to talk to me
and to make me see in my mind every little thing there is
to know back down my old lost road. That was the reason
why I burnt and fumed when I'd look at you tiptoe past
me.

"Well, I finally figured out enough to tell this man at the
crossroads. He wouldn't let me walk past him till I told
him three reasons why I wanted to keep on going. I told
him three. First was that I felt like I just had to be able to
pick my old self up again and to walk right back down
across my whole life again, to meet everybody that ever did
help me or hurt me, and to tell them how to find their own
best road to where they wanted to go. Second reason was,
I wanted to make my comeback in the real-estate business.
Third was, I told him I wanted to go down to the border
of Mexico and find that gold and silver mine that my old
daddy, Jerry P., found and had tested—the mine he covered over with flat rocks that day that he had to load up
his wagon and his wife and kids and drive back nine
hundred miles to Bristow, Oklahoma, to claim his hundred
and sixty acres of free Indian land. I told him I wanted to
give every one of my relatives a good job working that
mine, like Paw always dreamed about."

While Papa was finishing his story, I set my fruit jar
down on the old blue linoleum floor and stepped out to
the wooden bench on the washroom porch and started
washing my face and hands. "You be careful, Mister Homestead Man, out there on that wash porch," Irene called.
"You'll get too much soap in your old dirty ears. What
are you thinking about all of this cussing and discussing
we're trying to have in here?"

"Don't you worry none about me, Mistress Down Settler." I blew my words through my lather around my eyes
and mouth. "I'm a-keepin' my best ear wide open for every
word you spill in there. If I miss six years of your words I
won't be missin' out on very much. Talk's always been
perty cheap down where I come from."

My words blew high-tempered, soapy bubbles so thick
around on that wash porch that they sucked out in the drift
of the wind and went yonder fast. Maddest I'd been in
three years running.

"Don't strip a gear, Cousin," Eddie laughed out at me.

"I was just telling Irene and all of you how I feel about
things," Papa said.

"Just letting her tie you up in a little pinky baskit," I told Papa. "You'll soon git to where you cain't go piss in a bucket without somebody doin' your holdin' for you."

"Don't you get foul-mouthed about it," Jeff shot at me. "This scrap's all took place in perty good fun so far. You cain't lose a single dern-blame argument no more these days, Saw Blade, 'less you go plumb, teetotally crazy about it, an' froth off at your mouth jist like a mad dog in his summer's heat. 'Fess it up. You can see Reenie's jest as right as she can be about this here whole thing, anyhow."

"Go easy, Hack Saw," Robert told me. "This may be the last chance any of us'll get to have a good serious talk with Charlie here. I always guessed just the wrong way, Charlie, just like you told me. I didn't want to call all of those old things to your mind because I thought it'd make you that much the more miserable. Stay and work like Reenie says, and all of us will have plenty of chances to talk all of it out of us. We'll all feel better. Go back with Jeff when he drives to work tonight. Get yourself good and well and sprucey juicy before you go off anywhere. Skinny would tear every hair in her head out by its roots worrying herself sick about you if you went off without being as well as we can possibly make you. And I'm not just any too sure, Charlie, how much strained nerves your little Skinny sister can stand up under. Takes every kind of a tonic and pill in the drugstore already. For Skinny's sake, if not for my own, I ask you to do as Reenie says. Keep your office job. God only knows how I wish I could hold down as good a moneyed job as an office deputy. I wish I had that good of an education. But I'm not any good for a thing but to till that rough-root sod out there. Now, since we got kicked off for being too old to suit that banker's eye, well, I just feel like a blind mare down with a broke leg in a high drift."

"Robert is precisely right." Skinny Mammy leaned back against the side of the dining-room door and talked to us all in the bedroom. "Charlie, you know it as plain as I. I couldn't bear up to see you drive off away from here as long as I can see that you are still aching and hurting and paining every time you take a breath. You're not going to Canada to pile around in these blizzards and take your death of cold. Old Woodrow out there can just rip and snort his old, stubborn, crazy head off for all I give one little hooper-mascooper. Go on off to that snowdrifty old

Canada, Wood Mill, if you want to—go on! Go all by
your lonesome. You'll come a-running right back here to
smell of the old cookstove before the second blue blizzard
hits."

"Better retreat out of this trench," Eddie told me in his
quieter way. "Shells are busting a little too thick around
you for you to be healthy very long. Run back. Mortar fire.
Cannon fire. You're in a worse fix, Woodrow, than them
Huns was in over there in the battle of the Marne. Surrender. You're really surrounded." Eddie slapped his pants
legs and made the whole room laugh and yell out to the
washroom porch where I was drying my face on a towel.

I walked back in and looked around at them all. Jeff
was opening up his fiddle case over in the corner.

"Don't say anything you can't eat, dearly beloved
nephew," Skinny told me. "Please don't."

I started to speak, but the words got choked off somewhere in between my belly button and my upper lip. I had
so much pressure on my tongue I couldn't even get it to
going. I saw the front headlight and the red taillight of a
speech smoking through me a hundred coaches long. But
before I could grab me a hold of a handiron, the train was
gone and the fog was on. And I didn't have a word that I
could throw nor shoot back at any of them.

Jeff ran his thumb down across his four fiddle strings
and screwed his keys till every string got in haw with its
neighbor. It seemed to me that Jeff's tuning oiled my
throat up in some curious way. I reached over and took up
my guitar. I plunked down across my own strings before
Irene could walk to the corner and get her mandolin.

"Do you actually mean to stand here an' tell me to my
face, Reenie," I said, "that you'd smash this whole trip
under your shoe sole? After seein' all your relatives work
so hard to pack up an' get ready this way for so many
weeks an' months? That's all that I want to ask you,
knowin' how bad stuck down here Skinny Mammy an'
Robert is!" I looked at Irene as she lifted her mandolin up
to her bosom and felt its varnished back.

"You heard every word I said," she told me. "I know
what a sad condition my own daddy and mama are in, Sir
Wood Head. I know, and we all know, that they'd be in
seven times worse condition up there, sick or froze in under
some pine needles in Canada. Everybody here's against

you and your crazy, fool, rambling notions. Why not come over on the sensible side where we all are?"

"Sensible?" I broke out. "There's nothin' sensible about a word you said, you or any of th' rest of them. I'm a-tryin' to hold myself back, Reenie, from jist lettin' my tongue fly loose at both ends."

"Let fly." Irene tossed her head in the air. "I'm tough. I can take it."

Everybody shuffled their feet on the floor and laughed at me as Irene blew the dust off her mandolin.

"Well," I paced back and forth. "Don't go telling folks you didn't ask for it."

"Boo hooo." Reenie sniffed her nose against her arm.

"I always get made out to be the purple sheep in this family. Makes no difference which way I twist or turn. I'm always the loco bronco. I'm the careless, reckless rambler, th' don't-give-a-damn feller. I'm the wild mule in this whole big herd. The goof-off. I'm the blind-staggers man."

"Pity, pity, pity." Skinny smacked her tongue against the roof of her mouth to tease me.

"I ain't married. I ain't settled down. I ain't come to my right senses yet. Didn't grow up out o' my diapers. Still suck on my thumb."

"My, oh my," Irene shamed at me.

"I don't know how I ought to go about a-tryin' to tell you how bad an' how much I got to hatin' an' despisin' a sheriff's office, a jail window, a law office, even—I guess any kind of court house. I'll tell you now, Papa, now that all o' this stuff's comin' to its head. Been savin' the damn stuff up too long inside me, anyhow."

"Funny you didn't jest bust out a long while back." Robert leaned toward me a little.

"It's a damn good thing I got some teachin' from my folks, Robert, on how to show a little bit o' respect for folks your age. I don't guess, living on a farm like you did all o' your life, that you'd feel many of the same notions and cravin's that a guy the like of me feels. Partly 'cause I got hit over th' head with all the same things that hit Papa, here. I seen this stuff that was gonna wham into our family a good long time before it really happened. I seen what Papa's badge an' gun jobs and land-tradin' was doin' every day to Mama. My brother Roy seen it, too. George seen it 'fore he got out o' his wet diaper. My sister Mary Jo seen it while she was still a-suckin' Mama's

nipple. Clara seen it plain enough to know it had drove
Mama half out o' her wits a long time 'fore she finally got
sent off to Norman. Big guns. Big Winchesters. Big pistols.
Big billy saps. Big blackjacks. Big brassy knucks. Big fist-
fights. Gang fights. Stabbings an' cutting scrapes. Shootings,
swappings, tradings, cheating of the worst an' lowest,
fighting-an'-clawing kind. Jugs of moonshine free off o' the
bootlegger. Liquor stills caught, bought, sold again all in
the same rise an' set o' the new morning sun. Drunks beat
up. Indians whiffled out o' their good piece o' land, poor
colored farmers whipped an' drove an' swung up along
every river bridge in the county.

"Gypping an' cheating a-goin' on all around on all nine
sides. Cheating on a piece of paper. Robbing folks with a
pen an' ink. Robbing folks with a gun in their face. Doping
rich Indian girls into signing on the old dottery line.
Pressin' your Notary seal down onto the perty green an'
gray lacy papers. Scribbling your fountain pen down so
hard you can hear it scratch on the paper like dry corn
shucks. Another farm gone. Another lease run up. Another
commission rung down. Another fam'ly out. Another face
in back o' the bars. Another ruckus busted out jest down
the street. Ten more single fights chalked up on the election scoreboard. Three more gang fights from th' Third
Precinct. Two kids run over by a wild runaway team to
a wagon. Eight Indian men knocked out by drinkin' hair
tonic, vanilla extract, bay rum, rubbin' alkyhol. Black
folks singing fighting mad songs out back o' the stores on
the horse-tradin' lot. Sharecroppers in debt another hunderd dollars on account o' they couldn't make it rain
enough at the right time of the year. Two boys in the
reform school for takin' a little six-year-old girl down to
rape 'er in a den o' red ants. Three bunches o' street singers
latched up in jail for jist a-singin' along the curb without
no ten-dollar City Permit to work inside th' City Limits.
Razor Joe bleedin' from Tenth Street down to Third Street
all th' way along th' sidewalk with that big long ice pick
a-stickin' in his kidney.

"It's been stuff like this, by the day, by the hour, by the
ten or fifteen years, that's done wrecked my own family.
Mama cried with her head down a hundred spells a day,
while all of us had our eye on the money—the dough, the
long green, the coin, the last ol' bottom dollar, the deeds
to that land, that title to that property. This was what took

Clara by fire. It looked like an accident to all o' you, but I heard her say a dozen times that she jist sorta had a funny feelin' that somethin' awful bad was about to happ'n to her. She wrote in her little green leatherback diary book, about two weeks b'fore she burnt up, 'I feel like I am going to die!'

"Papa, 'bout all I can say is that you can call me your poor ramblin' son, if you're a mind to call me somethin'. I'd jest a dozen times rather be the ramblin'est ramblin' son in Oklahoma an' Texis than to ever take on a job of packin' two big thumb-busters around, an' a set o' brass knucks big enough to knock a dray horse down with.

"Cain't you see, to save your own sweet soul, how all o' us kids hid out in the weeds an' around in back o' the house when we'd see you ridin' towards us with your badges on, with your guns on, with your bloodysoaked shirt an' pants on? I'm only sayin' this one thing: I'd ruther spend th' whole rest o' my born days right out here at th' side o' this here road, the hoboin'est hobo of all o' the hoboes, the footloosest rambler of all the ramblers, the broke-downest busko musician of all the broke-down music makers, the crummiest of all o' the crummy tramps, than jest to put them two oil rods on, an' that badge, an' to go around bangin' heads in for this whole room full o' fifty dollar gold pieces.

"That sheriff's office, Irene, that you call so nice an' comfy, well, you jest oughta get out an' climb in the door of some of those patrol wagons, jest about any night, an' ride around an' watch how them high, mighty fees is took in . . . where 'bouts they roll from, an' from which syphy hands around in back of what ole greasy curtain. Jest because Jeff an' Papa's honest don't say lots of the other officers are. See th' pimps fork over. Watch a whore git vagged. See a gambler shovel out. Take a gander at a bootlegger divvyin' up. Go down to th' flats over here an' go up in them old, dark-lit stairs an' watch while the officer reaches his hand out an' grabs a fast holt on a bottle o' free likker. Ride out along th' highway towards Borger yonder an' go in while the deputy makes a little quick visit. My great God, don't this all ever turn sick an' sour an' green in your stomach? Don't you ever stand back an' look at your own self an' th' whole stinky, buzzard-pukey mess, an' don't you ever see yourself an' the whole shitty deal the way it really is? Where's your eyes at? I jist

wonder what in the world you ever do see in livin' any
such a life—how you can stand up an' ask anybody here
in this room to buckle his shooter back on an' go back to
that dammable low-down deputy sheriffing? Call it 'sheriffing,' 'officering,' 'law 'forcing.' 'Tain't much more'n helpin'
ta rob the pore damn workin' stiff out o' his last nickel jest
as fast as he can save up a dime in this high-priced, jackleg,
oil-boom town. How you ever did spend your time an'
strength thinkin' up all o' this dope dream to put Papa an'
your own husband up to be a target for the next trigger-
man to take a potshot at is more'n I can really get straight
in my head. I'd ruther spend the rest o' my days lost up a
dark holler in a one-room log cabin without no floor, than
to see my old daddy an' my best fiddlin' uncle go back to
cartin' big smoke-waggins all over again."

"To hear you talk, Woodrow," Irene put in, "nobody
ought to ever take on the job of being a peace officer in a
town."

"Don't make my donkey laugh! I ain't arguin' that you
don't need policemen. I like to see officers. But for us,
Irene, us folks right here in this room, it ain't a smart
thing to toss down our fiddle, our mandolin, our guitar, an'
our whole lives, jest to grab ahold o' the first kind o' officer
job we run onto. For plenty of people, a good law 'force
job's jest about the best damn thing they can ever hope to
stumble into. But it ain't the best thing that all o' us here
can do. We wrecked too many of our own blood kinfolks
already by jest driftin' aroun', like I said, on some kind o'
law work we never was meant to get tangled up with in the
first place. I seen Papa's law 'force work and real-estate
tradin' rip my family into nothin' but a handful o' loose
ashes. I'm jest sorta lettin' myself hope that if we throw
down our guns an' grab up our squalling fiddles, an' jest
lumber off an' out down the music road, anywheres, we
might still save the rest o' us from goin' an' dyin' where
Mama went when she died."

It was Eddie that shook his head, looking down at his
feet. "Guess all of us sees things in his own light. There
is a whole lot to what you say. Just a whole lot."

"Everything was always your poor old papa's fault."
Papa kept his eyes low. "Leastways, to hear you tell it. I
done what I done because I wanted to make things good
for you kids, for Roy, and for little Clara, for George, for
Mary Jo, and good for you, too. I had to push and shove

and fight my way to make every red little copper penny that I clothed and fed you with. That was what I swore to do, to keep the best roof over your little bushy head that money could buy, to buy you the best of books I possible could. To buy us the finest farm in Oklahoma and to raise the finest cattle, the best purebred hogs, the highest bred horses. I won every blue ribbon at our country fairs down there. You remember all of this, Woodrow. You remember how our house was always hung full of papers and pedigrees and birth papers and blue prize ribbons? All framed on every wall."

"Yeah. Sure." Irene nodded her head. "I remember when we came to visit you folks down there on Ninth Street in Okemah, Uncle Charlie. I had never seen any house half as big or half as pretty as yours and Nora's place. I just wished with all of my blood and bones that every one of my kinfolks could someday be able to build them a house just exactly like Charlie and Nora Guthrie's was. It was simply elegant."

"That's jest why, too, that all o' the kinfolks had so much pride an' respect for my fightin' brother Charlie." Jeff pointed around at us with the end of his fiddle bow. "Every single dang-blame one of 'em. Everybody admired you, Charlie, 'cause you got your start there in Okemah without a rusty nickel. You traded. You bought an' you sold. You swapped this for that. You put out a dollar an' you drug two back. You didn't only git up to be the best trader an' swapper in Okfuskee County, nor th' best livestock raiser an' breeder, nor not jest to hold down th' highest offices in the whole county, but you got to be the fistfighter for twenty towns all around Okemah. An' the' Good Lordy knows, Charlie, Oklahoma was sloppin' full o' the roughest, toughest, meanest, wildest-tailed fighters an' roughnecks from all over the whole United States. I ain't never seen a relative but what they jest nearly worshiped the ground that Charlie Guthrie walked on. I've never met up with a relative yet that feels like that about ole Woodrow . . . ever' one I ever did ask anything about you, Woodrow—well, it's jist like you said, an' you might as well know it plain. Not a livin' soul amongst 'em thinks you'll ever settle down long enough to ever make a dang-blame thing out o' your blame fool self."

"Only one," I said, "that's really on my side, only two, ruther, is Clara dead, an' Mama gone."

"You'd even call up the spirits o' the dead to help you win an argument," Robert said. "Everybody that still lives and draws a breath is solid as a rock against you, Wood. Leave Clara and Nora out of this. Let them rest in peace."

"They both got left out," I said. "Left so far out o' things that, well, neither one of 'em even wanted to go on livin'.'."

"I am very sorry, Sir Guthrie," Irene cut in on me. "Dragging your dead sister and mother into this picture just to try to make all of us get all soupy and weepy inside and bust down crying and all let you have your own dern-fool, ornery way and all run out and jump in that truck and all of us take off up into the face of a deathly blue blizzard to take down and die somewhere up yonder in Canada!"

"Mama an' Clara's not doin' no talkin' for me. I'm doin' Clara's talkin' 'cause she's . . . well, she's jest not here to talk up on her own hook. An' I'm doin' Mama's talkin', too, 'cause it so happens that nobody else I see in this here room is talkin' up for Mama. Fact is, I never did hear seven words spoke out on Mama's side while Clara an' her was both livin' right here with us."

"Ohhh, Woodrow." Papa held his face in his hands. "Please. I say to you, please, please. Please don't say a thing like that. My soul just can't stand it. There wasn't one day went by that your mama and me did not talk all of our troubles out together. Why, I sat down on the edge of her bed and talked to her every night until the sun rose in the east end of town. She just had her head set on making me give up everything there in town and retreating off out onto a farm of some kind. She hated every job I ever did hold down. She hated every office I ever rented, hated every sale and commission I ever did make. She hated everything I tried to do. She could not see that what I was doing would get all of us the very things she wanted you kids to have. Nora just didn't understand what kind of a crowd of people you had to talk and deal and fight with in a wild oil-boom town like Okemah. I told her that farmers were going hungry right and left all around us. She was just nervous. Just scared. Just afraid. Afraid of everything I done, and afraid of everybody I met.

"I hired the best of doctors I could get. They all told me the same thing. Humor Nora. Pet her. Be nice to her. Teach her not to be afraid of people. She always did beg

me to give up in town just when I was getting ahead my
fastest. I told her that the oil boom would blow over before too many years went by, and then we would take our
fifty thousand dollars and move out onto the finest farm in
Oklahoma for all the rest of our lives. What more, what
more, Woody boy, what more could I do? Nora headed me
off on every turn. She was born and raised out there on
that farm of her mother's, and she didn't know anything
else, all of her days growing up, except a farm, a river, a
creek, a holler, a timber patch, a draw, a barn, some hog-
pens, and a flock or two of turkeys and chickens. That was
what she kept on trying to pull herself back to, and she
tried to pull me, and you kids, and all of us right back out
there with her. Well, if your Mama Nora had got her own
way, we would always have been just a hungry family of
sackface farmers cropping on the shares. I saved us from
that, by the grace of God. I made something else out of
our family."

"Which else?" I asked Papa.

"I don't know, Woody. But, my God, we're not a bunch
of ragged, hungry sharecroppers, are we?" He looked
around at all of us. "Your Mama Nora was the prettiest
woman in the whole country."

"She was that, awright." Eddie nodded. "Rode th' prettiest black joker horse I ever did lay my eyes on."

"I put Nora up onto that fine horse. I wanted to see her
on the finest horse and saddle money could ever buy. The
doctors told me I had to find every possible way to try to
make Nora feel proud of all of her fine things. But—I
don't know why, and I never will know why—she just
turned mean and hateful towards every good thing I tried
to do for her," Papa said.

"I know what was going on in Mama's head," I said. "I
stood there in our house and watched her an' listened to
her talk and argue to me in the days when she commenced havin' them first nervous fits. Most all o' this here
stuff she'd talk about jest after you'd walk out o' the door
an' ride ole White Sam off to work at your office. I listened
to her every day. All o' the time that you was down there
at your office, well, Roy an' Clara an' myself seen plenty.
Plenty to let us know that our mama was having regular
fits an' spasms an' a-cussin' out at Papa all day long so
loud that everybody along our whole block'd get out onto
their porches jist to stand there 'n' listen to 'er. Beggin'

you to take off yer guns an' to throw that there big badge away, an' to move out o' your old fightin', cheatin', real-estate office in Okemah out to live on a farm of some kind. She never was afraid of people like us here. She was afraid of them shootin's, them stabbin's an' cuttin' scrapes— nervous about them killin's you never did tell 'er much about. She was scared that it'd be your body laid out on exhibit next down in some hardware store in th' black-an'-gray coffin department. That's what she talked an' sighed an' cried an' rolled down across the floor an' the bed all day long about. She had the kinda eye it takes to see the bloody kinds o' hands that your dollars an' your land titles was goin' through. I didn't jist hear her weep her soul an' her body away jest one time, nor a hunderd times, but after you'd go off to work every day an' all o' them gone nights, too, for my first twelve years till we fell down to that ole rotten East End shack where we was livin' that night that the doctors come down an' drove her off to th' asylum. I know what my mama hated an' how she hated it. An' I'm here now to tell you that I growed up hatin' th' same kinda filthy money and shootin' an' killin' that she hated right down to her last free step. This is th' reason why I'm standin' on my head an' lickin' yer hands an' askin' you to leave them guns lay an' for us to grab up our music boxes an' to take off out an' down th' bar ditch with th' rumblin', tumblin' weeds."

"You'll die in a bar ditch a good long ways before you ever get up to Canada in any truck of mine," Irene said.

"Truck of yours? Truck of whose?" I asked her.

"Truck of mine," she went on. "Truck of my husband's own money. And he bought thirty-five dollars' worth of provisions, too. Why, you never could have got your finger onto thirty-five dollars in twenty years if your very life depended on it, Sir Wood Block."

"Tell y' what I'll do, Reenie Woman, I'll jest betcha my guitar here against your mandoleen there, that even if your husband does climb in that police car when it drives up to take him to work tonight, that Papa C. E. Charlie Guthrie don't go back to work in that there sher'f's office with Jeff."

"I'll take you up on that bet. If Charlie doesn't go, well, then it might cost me a good mandolin, but it'll answer one question I always did wonder about: is this whole generation of Guthries just so loco, nitwit crazy that there never will be any little ray of hope left for any of us ever?"

There was some shuffling around in Betty Jean's front mindreading room. As the door swung open I heard Betty talking and laughing with her special cash customer. Her customers drove in from the ranches, oil fields, wheat farms, around Le Fors, Borger, McLean, Groom, Jericho, Alanreed, Mobeetie, Wheeler, Canadian, Dumas, Dalhart, Panhandle, Amarillo, and everywhere else. She would tell their fortunes, or help them make the full uses of all the hidden and buried talents and gifts of their secret, secret minds. Lots of them were not customers for cash; a pound of butter wrapped up in old magazine pages, a dozen or two of eggs in a brown sack, fruit jars of homecanned preserves, home-killed meats, sugar, candy, paints, and every other article took the place of the cash. But the family of us would not keep as quiet for a trade customer as we'd keep if you were a customer with the cash. This was why Jeff couldn't start sawing the daylights out of that squalling fiddle, and Irene could not whang into her flatback mandolin, nor me into my guitarbox, till Betty Jean had fully relieved this cash customer of all his or her worries about the cash.

Betty Jean was a big, squareheaded woman, a good seventy pounds bigger than anybody in the house. Her hair was always a frazzle; she never could comb it nor brush it up to do much good. She always wore one of her white hospital uniforms; she had been a nurse of some kind back out in California, before she came to Texas and married Papa after he left the Boydstuns' farm and got his job in Pampa. Betty Jean had read through books on Religious Faith Healing, Mental Healing, Psychology, Creative Mind, Unity, Magnetic Healing, Hypnotism, and such similar sciences, and still kept a few books on such subjects in her little front room for her customers to pick up and finger through. She had met Papa somewhere in the pages of a mail-order romance catalogue, one of those catalogues where you write love letters, swap pictures, and once in a great while, buy a bus or railroad ticket and ride to meet your lover in the flesh. There wasn't very much space left in her mindreading room for Betty Jean and a customer, cash or trade, of a very big size. I always did hear the chairs scoot back, the bed and bedslats rattle, the dresser

wiggle, the whole house vibrate a few good shivers, before
Betty and her customer could walk out.

Jeff got tired of waiting for the customer to get gone and
lit off on his fiddle. He come down on a long, high, loping
bow. I'd heard him play this tune before. He played it when
he wanted to drown everything else out with his little light-
weight, dried-out fiddle which he called his "Squalling
Panther." Sometimes he called it "Old Loud Panther" or
"Squalling Fiddle." He had three other fiddles over in the
little place Irene and him had rented on Francis Street. Two
were all unstrung and busted up, but his other two he always kept fixed with a key, a peg, a string, a neck rest, or
a neck he'd taken off of one of his old wrecks. His first-
choice fiddle was the little old reddish-back thing that we
called "Little Red." Little Red had come down through a
dozen or two of the wildest and fieriest fiddling contests in
Oklahoma and Texas. And when the contests were not already framed and decided ahead of time, Jeff always come
out with first, second, or third prize—most generally first
or second.

He had seen the little light tannish Panther fiddle one
day hung up in the window of a Pampa hock shop. He
stepped in and fixed it, tinkered with it, strung it up, tuned
it, and set the sounding post to suit him. He felt the fiddle
as it jarred his ear. He told Irene, "It squalled jist like a
big loud panther lost off somewheres down in a dark canyon, Reenie Gal."

Irene had struck her chord ahead of me on her mandolin. It was in the hardest chord for me. I was just learning how to plunk along on my guitar. It was the key of B
flat, shifting over at about the halfway mark into the key
of E minor. I didn't have time to hum it or sing it, like I
always did when I didn't know the finger positions on my
guitar. It sounded to me like my dad's best favorite knockdown, drag-out breakdown tune, old "Done Gone." What
always saved me in my guitar picking was my little steel
clamper that I clamped down across the guitar neck so I
could play some old chord I knew pretty well and could
get around with my fingers, like G, A, or just plain old D,
or C, even. I slid my clamper down across my third guitar
fret and fell in behind Irene and Jeff, whipping right on
down in just plain old G position. G, when I get it boosted
up three notches, see, turns into A flat at the first nick, just
plain old open A in my second slot, and then it whangs up

into B flat in my third nick. Everybody always hated to see me use that necker clamper. Good pickers never do use them, so they said. But I was a clamper fiend. I couldn't help myself. This clamper gave me a good chance to bluff my way along and to sound like I really knew my okra on the handle of my guitar. Otherwise I couldn't have stayed within nine miles of Jeff or Irene, because they had both been at this fiddle-and-string music now for as far back as they could remember.

I'd just set my first boot toe on the inside of these gates of high music in these past few months while I'd been working off and on as the head whiskey clerk up on Jackson Street at Little Cigar Shorty's drug and liquor store. Jeff sometimes brought his Little Red or his Loud Panther along to play after coming off duty in one of the little black county patrol cars. It made good business for Cigar Shorty to have the best fiddler and the worst guitar picker doing their loudest sawing and plinking in his place, and he was glad to have Jeff play on and on.

Jeff always had to be about half mad at the whole world before he could pitch his red sandy hair out into the wind and really buckle down to saw. He was fiddling "Done Gone" right this minute the best I'd ever heard him. I knew his fiddle sounded so good because he was mad at his dearly beloved nephew, me.

Papa Charlie slapped his hands together and patted his shoes against the floor, singing and halfway mumbling:

Done, dunnie, done gone, goney oh gone.
Dunnie dunnie done done done oh gone.
Like a turk turk turkey through th' kut kut corn.
Turkle turkle turkle in my green June corn.

C.E. "Charlie" Guthrie was lots more than just the fist-fighting land trader in our tribe. He was the speaker, the poet man, the funny-word man, and the long, sad song and ballad singer. Jeff was nearly as good as Papa, and I had a rambling, funny streak of this kind cutting up in my blood. Papa cut loose just a bit louder and funnier today, because it wasn't every day that all of his blood kinfolks met together like this in one little room.

"I hate to break in on this wonderful music." Betty Jean stood in the partition door and smiled around on all of us. "But if you all will excuse me, I would like to introduce you to one of my best and steadiest customers. Here she is. I take pleasure in giving you Helen. Miss Helen Cliffman."

"Walk right in." Eddie filled his glass one more time and filled Papa's at the same pour. "Jine the party."

"Sweet seventeen. Never been kissed." Betty Jean laughed as Helen stepped in at the door. "Prettiest little trick I guess I've seen in most of my life."

"Hi, Helen." Jeff tickled her hair in back of her head with the switch end of his fiddle bow. "Hya ben?"

"Well, Miss Helen, howdy." Irene hugged and kissed her. "I guess you know we have been having some pretty big arguments out here, and trying to keep quiet and still at the same time. Why, me, lands a-living, if I'd only known it was you that was Betty Jean's cash customer in there, I'd a talked so loud out here my tongue would have flew right out of my mouth."

"Me too," I said, still surprised that the customer was Hell Cat all the time.

The two girls hugged and kissed again. Both laughed the same way two boxers do at the end of a ten-round tie.

" 'Lo, Helen," Robert told her.

"Hi, hi, Hell Cat." Papa smiled across the room at her. Helen walked over to hug her arms around Papa's neck. She mussed his hair around over his head, and he made the most out of such a fine chance to make my britches itch and smoke. "I never did see any such a pretty-legged little Hell Cat as you are. Did you know that, Hell Cat?"

"No, Uncle Charlie." She shook her hair down to brush her shoulders. "I've not had any nice boy friend like you to tell me how nice my legs look. It makes me happy to think we finally found each other, Dear Sweet Cholly. Oh. The rest of you go on with some more nice music. Hello, Eddie, how on earth are you people in Panhandle?"

"Awww, thick's gravy." Eddie yawned and stretched. "How's yerself, Helen?"

"So so." Helen looked across the room at me. "Who could the gentle looking man over there all caked over with adobe mud, be? Is he real, or just a dummy somebody made out of mud clay?"

"He's a dummy, all right," Irene said.

I thought of a wagonload of things I should be saying, but I couldn't whistle up one single word. I just stood there and looked her up and down. Helen was the kind of a girl it was awful easy to eye up and down. She looked like a Hawaiian. Dark, thick, shiny hair the same as Irene's, only an inch or so longer. Helen's skin was smooth and the same color in the summer months as a light-tone chocolate bar. Brown big eyes that lit up her face and thick eyelashes that swept down to her cheek. She was just a speck on the skinny side around her ribs and shoulders, but her breasts stood out very full and noticeable. She moved her head the same way a high spirited horse nods, first to this side, next to that side, and had a little habit of running her fingers through her hair. She stood up straight and proud but at the same time she acted shy, sort of nervous most of the time. Her words had a sound about them like she was always bowing down her head and apologizing for being here in your way.

Helen's papa run off some years back and left her and her mama to do the best they could in an old, yellow, shacky, lopsided, fell-down tourist camp called Masterson's. In the year that I'd been going around with Helen, I never had asked her what her mama worked at. I visited her house one hot summer's afternoon, and that was the only sight I ever caught of her mama. She woke up off a little dark couch of a bed and stood in the screendoor rubbing her eyes to tell me that Helen had gone off on a hayride with a bunch of high-school kids. Her ma looked tired. All knocked out. Messed up, and stringy-haired, and drooping at her neck and shoulders. I judged that I had poked my head in at the wrong time of day, so I took my leave and walked on up through town. I had to go to work at Cigar Shorty's Liquid Store.

A big husky square-built athletic fellow rode up on a new bicycle and got off and asked me to wait up. I stopped and stood there waiting. He walked up and whaled away and slugged me in the jaw so hard I went blind for ten minutes. He said it was on account of Helen was his girl and for me to stay away from her. I told him that if he wanted her that bad he could have her with all of my best wishes. He got sorry for me and told me that he was sorry he had biffed me so hard. He said he didn't like her no more, anyway, if she would two-time him with a man as ugly as I was, and he wanted me to have her for keeps. We stood there for ten whole full minutes arguing back and forth about who in the heck was giving her to who. He gave her to me. I gave her over to him. He shot her

back to my lap. Me. Him. Her. Him. Me. My head spun
for three whole days clerking in back of my whiskey counter, and my jawbone muscles stayed sprung out of socket
for the next several weeks that Jeff and me fiddled and
sung while Cigar Shorty smoked up half of his profits and
me and Jeff sniftered away the other half.

Cigar Shorty had one of the finest fiddling liquor stores
in that whole country, and with four or five bone-dry
counties laying all around us, well, a job like I had at a
dollar a day was one to be looked up to. Not for my little
old stinking dollar-a-day salary, but for the free slugs I
could wheel and deal out over the counter and for the
half-full bottles I could toss into our trash sack and back
into our alley to be found by any such scratching and digging hands as I saw fit to have find them.

We met in high school when Helen used to take her
long hair and use it for a brush to paint the backs of my
ears with blue-black ink. We first got to fighting and then
got to walking and then got to talking and then got to feeling and then got to getting away off in the dark corner of
the moving-picture show and fishing on mud bottom.

This went on for some good time. Then she would drop
in at the whiskey store and talk me out of free cokes and
ice creams. She would read all of our new magazines and
rack them back up on the stack. We got to using our idle
hours, when customers were scarce, hugging and kissing
and trying to eat one another up all over Cigar Shorty's
store. It was a mighty good thing Cigar Shorty stayed away
so long at a time or he'd sure fired me long before he did.
As it was, he fired me about twice a day on slow days and
once on real busy days. He'd always fire me when he was
on the wagon and hire me back when he'd had another
few drinks.

I kept my eye on Helen as she tossed her light-blue
puffy-sleeved winter coat down across my little bed. She
stripped her tan, high-top Mexican gloves off and dropped
them onto her coat. She had on her thin, fancy black dress,
the one I always did like because it showed everybody
what a pretty thing she was. She lifted her hands up in the
air to do a little funny pose for all of us, and I told her,
"Hey, Hell Cat, I swan to my goodness, you git pertier 'n'
juicier every time I lay my eyes on you."

"That's nice," Helen said. "I do feel a bit dizzy, though,

with you all leaving tonight. That road to Canada is too long."

"How right you are, Helly," Irene told her. "Well, the latest twist in our sober decisions is not to go. They decided right here in this very room while Betty Jean and yourself were in there telling one another all your heart troubles and miseries. We're staying right here. Going to sit real tight till the hot weather comes and then, who knows, we might pack up again and go. And then again, well, Helly Puss, we may never go up there."

"So." Helen pulled me by my hair and laughed in my face. "So, I gotcha back. Ha."

"Never did even git rid o' me," I told her. "Ha."

Irene flipped a chord on her mandolin. Jeff got started with the first few, shuffling notes of "Old Judge Parker, Take Your Shackle off of Me." I sang the words:

> Old Jedge Parker, take y'r shackle offa me,
> Old Jedge Parker, take y'r shackle offa me.
> Turn your key an' set me free,
> Old Jedge Parker take y'r shackle offa me.

Papa knew more of the words that I knew: we all listened to him sing as he got up and done a little pattyfoot step around the floor. He acted every word out by moving his whole body.

> Ball and chain rubs hot as hell,
> Ball and chain rubs hot as hell.
> That's what makes my ankle swell,
> Ball and chain rubs hot as hell.

> One little chicky was all I stole,
> One little chicky was all I stole.
> I fed my wife and babies, ooh,
> One little chicky was all I stole.

Papa waved his drinking glass all around. "Good whiskey won't deal you one tenth the damage bad whiskey does," he told us. "My old paw used to tell me he wouldn't touch one drop of whiskey he hadn't made with his own hands—and I never did see him showing any bad signs of whiskey poisoning."

"Your paw," I put in, "made his own shoes and his kids' shoes, his own harnesses . . ."

"His own everything," Skinny told us.

"I sure would love to have known him," Helen said.

"Jerry P. was a real pioneer," I told her. "He stayed off in the mountains on the Mexican border for years. Herded cattle. Built all by himself the 'dobe house that him and his wife and kids—Jeff there and his brothers Claude and Gid—lived in."

"Prospected, too," Jeff put in. "Never went out on the range without his minin' tools."

"He sure did know about mining," Skinny Mammy put in. "Had a raft of books about mining and metals and minerals and all that."

All in one piece a big idea hit me like the sun shooting up from behind a dark mountain. I almost caught my breath. It seemed as though I could see the sunlight hitting that old, heavy-loaded Model T truck and the filled gas drums, and lighting up the open road leading out through the outskirts of Pampa towards far country.

"It's 'round about gold minin' time, Jeff!" I told him. "Tell Hell Cat a little somethin' about your paw's lost mine. Come on, Jeff. Rough Run Canyon. Terlingua. Study Butte. Slick Rock Gap."

Jeff stowed the fiddle and fiddlestick in his red alligator-skin case and I poured him a fresh glass of Gussy's Grave-yard Tonic.

"Y' see, Hell Cat," Jeff said, "Woody's grandmaw on his mother's side was named Mary Strictler. The Strictlers were neighbors of ours in Oklahoma. Mary's brother, John, left Oklahoma and went to Texas. He started a cattle ranch down in the Big Bend of the Rio Grande, near the border of Mexico. And, well, he jest naturally liked the dang-blame place. He tried to git all o' our relatives to drop every bloomin' thing, no matter what they was a-doin', and to come down there. I had an uncle by the name of Gid Guthrie. An' Gid Guthrie, he went down. Gid built up an awful big cattle ranch down there in Brewster County, right smack down near th' dern-blame Rio Grandy river, east of Terlingua and Study Butte. Built up a ranch was a hundred an' one sections—a hundred and one square miles. Fact is, Uncle Gid named his ranch th' One O One—the Hunderd an' One. Thousands an' thousands of cattle had Gid's '101' brand melted onto their hips . . . bawlin' an' squallin', wall-eyed cattle. Land belongs now to a rancher named Sam Nail."

"How about your Papa?" Helen wanted to know.

"Uncle Gid was my daddy's own blood brother," Jeff went on. "Gid got my daddy to load my Mama Ollie, an' us boys, me an' Claude and young Gid, into their big covered wagon, an' to drive off down there. Uncle Gid lived in a little mount'n town north of the ranch, up there in th' Davis Mountains chain—town by th' name of Alpine, Texas. Gid gave my dad the job of runnin' his herd o' cattle all down along the Rio Grande—very rocky an' stickery country. My dad, Jerry P. Guthrie, built his 'dobe house out in that rough mountain country, near Rough Run Canyon.

"Paw Jerry carried a prospector's pick an' axe, an' shovel, an' dipper, an' gold pan with him ever'where he'd ride his horse. You'd always find a whole miner's rig roped around on Paw's handmade saddle. Only thing Paw bought in a store was the ole limber-brim hat he always kept a-settin' right up on th' front o' his head to shade his eyes. Made them very horsehide boots he used to walk an' ride in."

"Our Paw, though, Jeff, was one big hand to take down a book and read every page back'erds and for'erds a dozen times," Skinny Mammy put in. "I guess he had just about every kind of a book about ores and min'rals that you could think of. Paw Jerry'd clean fergit to eat a meal just as long's he could turn through the pages of another book about minerals and mining."

"He could smell ores three miles before he got to them," Papa agreed with Skinny. "He knew ore and crystals just like Jeff there knows that Squalling Panther fiddle."

Jeff went on and said, "Mama Ollie camped down in the little mud-walled, adobe ranch house. She cooked, sewed, and helped to look out for the kids. Paw'd herd wild beef steers with his eye, and he'd keep a keen lookout fer mineral formations with the other eye. Like this."

"More like this," Irene joked, crossing her eyes.

"Shut up!" Jeff told Irene.

"Don't you dare to tell me to shut up, Jeff Guthrie!" Irene sassed back at Jeff. "Just who do you think that you are telling to shush up?"

Skinny stopped her by saying, "Irene, keep still. Helen wants to hear this. You know, Paw dug his head off down around there for a year or more. And then one day he was out trailing and herding some steers, and the two older boys was with him. Claude was eight years old or nine, old enough to ride his own horse. Young Gid was about six years old or seven; he hung on behind their paw. Well, that day Paw and Claude tied their saddle horses up by a spring of medicine water where they'd been stopping late every afternoon when they was out doing a little herding or passing some time prospecting.

"Paw told all of us a hundred times, I suppose, how it happened. These two kids, Claude and Gid, untied his prospecting pick off of his saddle. Paw Jerry had stepped off around the foot of the medicine-water spring and took him a big bellyful of water. He heard somebody chopping and whamming and banging away. He didn't think much about it till he'd walked back and saw Claude and Gid chopping and whopping away on a big, sharp, backbony rock outcropping. Jerry P. noticed how hard that dern-blame backbone of a rock sounded with the steel pickaxe hitting up against it. He took the pick off his boys and spent two whole hours standing there, chopping him off a sample chunk of that ore. It shined in the sun, Paw said, just like pure diamonds. He wrapped his piece of sample ore up in a box and mailed it over to the smelter they had in El Paso, and they mailed it back to him with a whole big chemical analysis—what you call an assay—and it was worth, Paw said, a hundred dollars a ton in silver, ten every ton in gold, and it also contained some other valuable minerals, copper, lead and zinc, mercury and so forth.

"But Jerry P. had to run back north to Oklahoma to put in his claim that year for some free Indian land his wife, Ollie, had coming to her . . . so he just piled some big, flat, natural-looking rocks with his name on a paper wired to one of them, right back on over that place where he had dug off that sample—or where his kids taught him, like he joked his own self about it—where them onery, bratty-headed boys of his showed him more about digging for ore rocks than he ever knew before that." Skinny Mammy shook her head in amusement and went out to the kitchen, still keeping an ear cocked to hear the talk.

"Then why didn't Jerry go back down later and open up his mine?" Helen asked.

"He just never got the money and the time it takes," Papa said, "to make the trip down and to stay down in

there long enough to do all the work necessary to get a
mine dug, a shaft blasted, a house or two built up around
the place . . . the kids were in school parts of the time;
then when they got a few years older they all moved and
scattered all over hurricane's deck—"

"Too cussed busy doin' nothing," Jeffrey told us.

"Doing nothing is correct." Reenie looked at the floor
as she spoke. "When I was a child and he was old, he
lived with us on the farm, and I remember hearing him
just fairly begging all of us—"

"Jest any of us—" Ed said to Helly.

"But not one solitary living soul could Paw Jerry ever
get to go down there long enough to dig that hole in the
ground," Skinny called out from the kitchen, "and to build
up some little shacky houses—"

"Not wood shacks like this 'un here is," I told her. "I
think Paw Jerry was always a big hand to mix that 'dobe
mud and to fix his own bricks—an' dry 'em right out 'n th'
hot sun; wasn't he, Papa?"

"Biggest hand in this world to build the sturdiest and
very longest-lasting houses every new place he moved on
to." Papa drank a longshot that set him right up even on
the old noseline with Ed and Jeffrey and me and all of us
other dark stragglers.

Skinny stood by the cookstove and dried a long stirring
spoon in the folds of her work apron. "Ladies, men, and
gentlemen, I'm just about to set my chow grub out and
I'm needing some highly attractive female girls over in my
boarding house to set dishes on table for me; pays one and
a quarter a week minus your eats, drinks, sleeps, cigarette
stubs and personal expenses—"

"I'm both of them!" Helly waved her hand, jumping up.

"And me!" Reenie jumped into the fracas around Skinny's kitchen stove. While the two youngest ladies pranked
around with big armloads of dishes to set on our eating
table, I was glad to see Papa walk over across the room
to finger at the little brassy latches of his old leather legal
briefcase. He unlocked it and took out a long lawyer's-size
envelope with a big red rubber band around it. I'd never
seen this envelope before, though I knew that for these
past few months he'd kept in there all of the free literature
the Canadian government had mailed to him, which he'd
thumbed and fingered till he had it put to memory. He
opened the envelope and pulled out some old sweat-soaked

pieces of writing paper, with some old smudged pencil marks on the blue-lined side.

When he saw how close my eyeballs hung over his old slick thin-worn papers, Papa at first tried to stick them inside his shirt, but, on a second thought, he waited for me to ask him, "What's them? Huhhhm?" Then he moved over by the south window and said, "Claude's old maps. Want to come see?"

"By damn!" I told him. I stood over back of his shoulders and rubbed my hands and fingers all around over the old codes, marks, signs, and so forth, which Claude had scribbled in old softlead pencil. "That's where th' kids found Paw's mine, ain't it, huh?"

"Nigh on about the place——" Papa told me.

"What's them words right up in that corner there say?"

"It says: 'O L D E D O B b E e E H o u s e.' It's a funny thing, Woodrow, how Claude spells out those words, 'O L D E D O B b E e E H o u s e,' to make that old house take up more miles of running space than the ranch, or the whole Rough Run Canyon, or the entire Chisos Mountain range over here; or, for that matter, this whole Big Bend of the Rio Grande river here, see?"

"I've heard Paw Jerry say there was a little dam below the spring, to make a watering pond," Jeff put in.

"It sure does make me feel awful damn funny, folks"—— I kept my eyes tight down on Papa's maps—"to think that I'm the onlyest dang one in this whole room that never laid eyes on Paw Jerry."

"Besides me, idiot," Hell Cat reminded me. "I've never seen him. I sure do wish I could. I think I've already gone and fallen head over heels in love with my dream vision I see of Jerry P. . . ."

"I always felt that same way towards that man," Irene told Helly. "He was my grampaw and I just loved him all over. He was one man that I never could hold any hard feelings against. I can see the crazy ways that he played and romped and tore around with us kids. And he was the only man that never did hold any real true deep grudges against any living person. Jerry always struck me as feeling that everything in the world was fine and dandy; and he made me feel like time to him didn't mean one snap—and, Paw Robert, I hope you'll not feel too mad at me when I say that Jerry wasn't like you are, he wasn't any kind of a big-headed religious thinker man—he didn't have even one little ready-made homemade religious idea, nor any such readings and Bible memorizings as you've got that always did keep me from knowing you, my very own daddy, quite as deep, or quite as good as I always did feel that Grampaw Jerry was to me . . . I hope I've not—not offended you too bad. But I married Jeffrey to lift myself up and out of that quicksandy lake of polite, religious apologies you and me have been stuck down in for these past few years."

I heard our back door hinges squeak with a white-hot heat as Uncle Robert brushed his clothes off and walked out into the snowstorm.

"You'd ought to be ashamed of your young proud self!" Skinny barked. "You should have waited till after supper before you tried to have it out with Robert like that, Missy Nitwit. You know he always just gets up and walks out while you're at him in that insulting, low-down way."

"Ohhh! Shut your jawbone!" Reenie screamed over in Skinny's face. "How many meals has that thick onery-headed man caused me to miss out on? Hiding in behind that sly quiet grin, that crazy devilish smile he always puts on in self-defense! I don't give one big dee how many meals I cause him to get up and to walk out on! Babyish! That's what he's acting like! He never does stop long enough to run me down in a real good hot argument. He thinks I'm always just something he can get up and walk away from, so's he won't have to waste any of his great great words of wisdom or even fatherly advice on me. Let that old grayback, grayheaded mossback go! Just let him vamoose! Just like that! I hope he never shows up in this house or in my life again as long as either one of us lives! Go! Go!"

"Reenie." Hell Cat hugged her and told her, "Don't lose control over yourself. I guess you both had this coming now for a good long time. But, my own daddy was an alcoholic drunkard—he had a sad, bad, awful, terrible disease which made his body always crave to have the feeling of whiskey in his belly; my mama didn't know what to do about him, or anything like that—and I sailed into him and railed my mouth off at him so much that he just walked out my old screendoor and he's been out and gone away now, ohhh, for these past five or six years, and I've not heard one little peek or peep, or a card or a letter or nothing from him—and if I've made any terrible, godawful mistakes in my life so far that one was mistake enough to hurt me. Remember . . . Robert's your own father—and no matter how many bad mistakes he makes, he brought you into this world. And in an hour or so, your Papa Robert will come piling back in and both of you will forget what you argued and snapped and barked about so bad . . ."

"Ohhh." Reenie snuffled her tears back. "I have been this world's biggest damn fool now for my three-hunderdth silly, idiotic time . . ."

"That's all right, ladies," I kidded over towards both of them and looked over Papa's head at his pencil maps as I talked: "Gosh sakes alive. Me'n my papa Charlie here really outscream the whole gang of you when we get to goin' real fast on some hot political argument . . . don't we, Paw?"

"Loud," Charlie said, "is the word for it."

"But, girls," I went on, "since I've so lately come to discover that my own blood father over here, Charlie Edgewood Guthrie, is one of this world's richest and most famous mine owners, I am slowly but surely deciding that for this day, at least, I'll not start any religious arguments, nor any alcoholic whiskey arguments with him like both of you have done with your old, aged, grayheaded parents. I'll try for this day, at least, to hold my tongue just to prove to my old father that I cherish and adore the many fine and upstanding memories we've got in common . . . I mean, till I can memorize these old pencil-drawn maps that lead me straight to where all his buried treasures lie . . . Ain't that about right, Sir Charles?"

"That's just about right." Papa nodded and studied his maps. "Claude, he draws a hill here and names it—or he puts it down as 'A HILL of GRAVEL R O C K Where MY PONY FELL DOWN' . . . Hmmmm."

"I reckon you know them maps of Claude's don't even match," Jeffrey reminded us.

"I'm glad to see you noticed that, Jeffrey," Papa said. "But each map shows very clearly little things that are blurred or skipped entirely in the others. And you've just got to put the three maps together in your brain to make the least ounce of living sense out of them."

"Spread 'em all down here on the floor," I told Papa, "so we can all do some first-class cranin' at 'em."

"Look out down there! You can't spread those maps

down there on that floor," Helly told us, "or you'll be in my way setting this table! And you'll get your nice pretty maps all soaked full of Skinny Mammy's very best, hot, jeewcey cornbread and black-eyed peas and ham hocks. Most of all, I want to look at those maps just as much as you men do."

"Toooot! Soak 'em with red-hot bean soup, Helly girl!" Reenie hollered. "I am so craving to look at those maps that Claudius drew, that I might send all of you workslaves down there to those old, hot, lizardy Chisos Mountains to dig me up some gold and some silver mines!"

Jeffrey made a grab for the maps, but Papa forked them up from the floor and inside his workshirt.

Skinny Mammy beat the bottom of a skillet with her wooden stirring spoon. "Break it up, you harvest hands!" she yelled. "Chow is now on! Red bean a green bean a white bean a flitter, corn bread dry bread a wheat bread fritter! Come get it before I throw it to th' hogs in th' pen! Got ham hock. Got beef steak. Come on! Come on! Slop it up and slip it down. Gotta kiss th' cook or you can't ride to town! Eats! Eats. C'mon git 'em!"

"I'll sign up!" I yelled.

"If you would be kind enough, Skinny, or Hell Cat," Papa said as we staggered up off the floor, "to twist my arm and to force me to eat just a few mouthfuls . . ."

Reenie and Helen filled all of our eating plates high and dry and soupy and droopy and all down dripping and saggling and smoking and moving and running all down over the sides; both of them forked and ladled and spooned and poured the soupy thick cementy concretey stewbrowny hamhockery stuff steamyhot from our cooking pot, and next dropped a big oversized chunk of Skinny's rusty brownish redderish goldedged yellerneck yallerback cornponey rough salty greasy cornmeal bread off down around our plates in the general direction of Skinny's black-eye peas. Both girls filled their own plates as they stood by the table's edge dumping ours full; then, whenever all of ours were ready to be claimstaked and blasted and forked and shoveled and dynamited into, they both grabbed their own burnyhot plates to forkle and gobble them down like hungry hogs.

I patted Helen's leg down in under the table and said, "I owe my apology to Skinny an' to you, both, Reenie. This is one night that you saved my life two times. Saved

from a-hittin' that north Canada trail an' a-freezin' my
balls off. Saved me from a-starvin' smack smooth to death
right here. So. Much as it pains me, I'm a-beggin' your
pardon."

"Your begging's okay by me, Cousin." Irene went on
with her eating and winked at the others.

"Rag'ler dern-gone banquet, awright," Eddie said.

"A banquet fit for th' Greenseeds," I told them.

"Fit for the Guthries." Betty Jean saluted us with a
heavy fork of beans and gravy. "Fit for the Boydstuns. Fit
for the tired, weary, sore-footed homesteaders."

"It'd have to be lots more fittener an' finer'n pinto beans
an' hammy hock an' chuck beef to fit up on top of that big
long walnut eatery table at th' Greenseed mansion." Skinny
acted the part of a lady that never had a work blister nor
never missed a meal. She moved her fork with a light easy
lift with each word she blew like bubbles from her lips:
"Greenseeds. Huhmmmph. Greenseeds wouldn't even ez
much ez slop their hogs with what all's on this table here."

"Green Seeds?" Helen asked me in my left ear. But
somebody had already started to talk again before I could
answer Helen's question.

Papa waved a knife across the table towards Skinny.
"Go ahead, Skin, give us your imitation of Patressa Greenseed. Hey, Jeff, you and Irene, Hell Cat, and you, hey,
Eddie Moore, don't eat so loud. Skinny is going to give us
her own imitation of Patsy Greenseed. Stop. Look. Listen.
I am highly pleased and greatly honored to have with us
here in our De Luxe Cafe tonight one of the most colorful
of all of our greatest showfolks, and most beloved character
actresses of both the carnival trail, the circus sideshow, the
ashcan, and the woodpile, as well as both silent and talk-
ative pictures. She has portrayed with high dignity and to
the last mighty flights of pure artistry thousands of his-
toric and fanciful personages, bringing you living human
beings back from ages and centuries long dead and forgot.
But never once in her solid-packed years has she played the
part of any person living or dead of any greater stature nor
rank than her own sweet and simple self."

Everybody broke in and clapped their hands, then sat
back in their chairs to listen. Papa talked on.

"Tonight as a special treat and privilege to us all, I have
prevailed upon this little lady to portray a scene as she
imagines it to be, a scene taken out of the book of real life.

The scene you are about to see and witness, both at the same time, is the scene of a rich lady. A very rich lady. And, thank Heavens, a very old lady. Her lands and her banks are without numbers. Her cattle are run by the untold thousands. Her oil wells are as far as the eye can see. Her mines, her mineral veins are running over. Her husband is now dead. They had no child born to them in all of their sixty-two years of buried, I mean married, life. Her mansion in the city of El Paso with its trees and hedges, its thickly painted high iron fence around its bounds, takes up no less than one whole city block. The scene is not one that this deep actress has practiced nor rehearsed before, no. No. No. And a million times no. To add to the zing and the zang and the twang and the stang of your evening here at the De Luxe De Looxe Restaurant, I mean, eating joint, God dangit, I am going to give this little lady the incident in the life of the rich old moneybag widow which I wish her to play for us."

Skinny smiled around at everybody while we all clapped and made the noises of cheering and of greeting.

"Now. For the scene. Let me see, now. Ahhh. Yesss. A dozen or so families, you see, have all been waiting with hungry eyes to see which of the two Greenseeds will die first. Will it be old man Ray D. Greenseed? Or will it be the old lady Patressa Greenseed? Nobody knows. Everybody wonders. If Patsy dies first, Ray D. wills all of his fortune over to three brothers and one lone sister, three lawyers and a schoolteacher, descending from his side of the family. But, if Ray D. dies off ahead of Patsy, she wills the whole shooting match of the fortune over to her nearest kin. As Jeffrey here told you, my first wife's mother, Nora's mother, was named Mary Strictler. Mary's own blood brother, John Strictler, left Deep Fork River bottom in Oklahoma and took up cattle ranching down along the border of Mexico. John Strictler made so good down in there that he talked his young sister, Patressa Strictler, into the notion of riding down there to get her a job as a schoolteacher. John Strictler sold out his cattle lands to a young man by the name of Ray D. Greenseed. John Strictler rode off up into New Mexico and nobody ever heard of his whereabouts again. Anyhow, Patsy Strictler stayed down along the border and married this young Ray D. Greenseed. They worked together and built up this terrible, unbelievable fortune during their years together, but they neved did have any children. If there had been children born to them, naturally enough, these children would be their legal heirs to all of their property unless it was stated in Ray's or Patsy's wills to dispose of the fortune otherwisely. Anyhow, Ray D. died first."

"One year ago, this come of June the third," Jeff put in.

"June the third. That is the day that I'm going to ask our little actress friend to portray for you. I will ask her to take the minute that people are walking past Ray's coffin paying him their last good-byes, their last respects, their last good wishes. His old and feeble widow, Patsy, has just walked down the long line of weepers. The shawl and the gown of mourning is around her from her head down to her black funeral shoes that button up one side and down the other. She walks to Ray's casket. She looks down at his fair-remembered face in the glass. She sees his hands folded pure and sweet across his chest at rest. And now. Now, may I turn you to the heart and the soul of Patressa Greenseed as portrayed for you by her eminence, Lady Skinny Mammy Boydstun."

Skinny stood up without making a sound. She tried to look as weepy and as sorrowful as she could for a bit. She touched her fingers and rubbed her funeral shawl and mourning gown. She fixed her shawl to fit her better about her head. She folded her hands across her own bosom and took on the facial twists of a holy mother. She looked down into the casket through the plate of dustproof glass and saw the face of her dead husband. After a few more seconds went past, she said as low and as doleful as her voice could speak, "Ray. Hey. Hey, Ray. My side won out. The Guthries won. Ha ha ha ha ha ha."

Everybody clapped when she sat back down. We whistled. We kicked our feet. We went back to our knives and our forks and back to our second shot at the supper table.

CHAPTER 3

LAST SUPPER

"Is all of this true?" Helen asked us. "I mean, this thing about such a rich family? The Greenseeds? The Guthries?"

"Shore it's true." Jeff stopped his eating long enough to say, "Ever' word of it's true. Jest the way Charlie an' Skinny told y'."

"Every shingle word." Eddie shook his head, so drunk he had to shake it again to keep his eyes open. "I know it's true."

"I just could not say." Irene looked over her plate with a spoon of mushed cornbread and red beany soup. "I hear so many rich tales around this little poorhouse that I never do know which from which."

Papa shook his head and told us, "Well, leastways, Jeff, you and Skinny both very well know that Ray D. and Patsy Greenseed did not bear any child, nor adopt any. Right?"

" 'At's it," Jeff said to Papa. "I checked up on it down in th' El Paso County Courthouse records."

"Truth of the whole shebang is," Papa licked his lips and wiped his mouth with the back of his hand, "John Strictler is the only legal heir, since there were no kids.

Well, then, it all would go to his next closest blood relation that is alive and kicking."

"Kicking alright." Eddie kept on jabbering every word he heard anybody say at the table.

"Eddie, hush." Skinny kicked Ed's shins under the table.

"Jest make shore y' kick th' right shinbone down in under there, Skinny." I looked at Skinny sort of halfway rough and tough. "Got lotsa nice perty laigs down in under here, Skinnyboney, don't want ya kickin' 'em any too hard. G'wan, C. E., tell it plain."

"Your mama Nora's daddy married twice," Papa begun.

"I can't recalect a dadgum relative of mine that didn't git hitched about ten dozen times. I can't see how anybody'd go 'bout figgerin' up who fell heir to what. Y' c'n see, Helly, cain't you, why I jest throw'd th' whole blame mess ov'r the pasture gate an' took off down the ramblin', reckless hobo trail?"

Helen put her hand on top of my hand on her leg under the table and told me, "Hush. Hush up. I want to hear all of this. Every little word of it. I feel like I am getting richer and richer every minute that I sit here."

"I'm a-gittin' hotter 'n' hotter," I joked in her ear.

She shushed me up again, "Shhh. Zip your lip. Here, hug me, hug me and stay still."

"Your mama Nora's daddy, I mean, yes, that's right, your mama Nora's. No, I'm tangled up. Got my right hind leg up over the single-tree."

"Shore have." Jeff laughed a little. "Your mind's a-slippin', Charlie."

"It was your mama, Nora's mother, Mary Tanner, that got married two times." Irene put us all straight. "Her first husband was John Strictler's pappy. They had two other kids, Patsy Strictler and the other Strictler boy, Luther, that got killed by a wild saddle horse, drug to death out there along the Strictler's fence line while they were stretching their first barbed wire to run cattle. Well, John Strictler, like I told you, sold out all of his lands and cattle to Ray D. Greenseed, the same year, almost, that Patsy married young Greenseed. There are no heirs living on the whole Strictler side of the fence now. Just old Mrs. Patressa, and the brother that run off up into New Mexico and never was heard from to this day."

"Why?" Helen asked Papa.

"Dunno." Jeff made a funny lost-looking face. "Nev'r knew."

"Jes' nev'r did know." Eddie shook his head.

"I never saw so many sane people in my life that don't know as much as this gang." Betty shook her fist. "If all the Strictlers were dead, part of the money would go to Nora, and through her estate to Charlie and his family. Did it not ever occur to any of you to go down there to El Paso and claim your honest share? If I had one tenth, or one one hundredth, of such a dead shot as that, you can bet your sweet shirt I would walk into that Greenseed mansion before daylight in the morning and set my foot down and stake my claims."

"I certainly would, too, Betty." Helen got nervous on her seat. "Why, goodness gracious alive, I would start out right tonight, if I thought I had a ghost of a chance to fall heir to any such a thing."

"Be no good." Papa heaved a big sigh. "Not till the day and the hour that the judges and lawyers legally declare John Strictler dead. And, in the meantime, till they do declare John Strictler dead, they tie up the whole estate in ten million knots and tangles of red tape. You go ahead down there and knock on the door of the Greenseeds. Tell them that you are the long lost legal heir to the whole works. They will tell you that if your name is John Strictler, then they are all glad to meet you and to shake your hand. But if you tell them that your name is Charlie Guthrie, or that you are the late Woodrow Guthrie, or the later Hell Cat Guthrie, they'll send down three police wagons and haul you out of there feet first, kicking and a-scratching and yelling that you are the only legal heir. And when you get down there in back of those nice rusty bars of that El Paso County jail, you'll wake up and find yourself in the same cellblock with twenty-nine legal heirs to the whole Greenseed fortune."

"That'd just about happen, all right." Irene laughed. "I am fed and stuffed fuller than a tick on a dog's ear. How long do you think it will take those lawyer fellers and judgment men, Charlie, to ever declare that John Strictler is a dead ducker?"

"If you just knew, Reenie, what big rakeoffs and take-offs, all kinds of fees, salaries, commissions, percentages, and outright pilferies, all of those dozen and one legal

geniuses draw down, so long as John Strictler does not
show up! Besides, John Strictler never will be declared
duly and soundly dead for ninety-nine years after old lady
Greenseed passes away. And, well, she's still alive and
healthy as a bull yearling."

"Well," Helen grunted, "I did feel like a very rich lady
for a few short moments. It was such a nice feeling."

I slid my hand in under her dress and rubbed her leg.
"This is lots nicer feelin', far's feelin' goes."

Jeff looked around the table. He moved his chair back
a bit to make room for Skinny Mammy to pour his cup of
coffee out of the old big-sized aluminum percolator. "Well,
Skinny, an' well, Reenie, I wanta kiss th' cooks f'r rattlin'
me up secha good fillin' meal as this is. I mean, this was."

"I was just a-waiting for that." Skinny hugged Jeff with
her free hand and kissed the backside of his neck. "Don't
hug me too rough, Jeff, you'll make me pour this perker of
scaldin' hot bug juice right down th' collar of your shirt."

"If this laig I'm a-workin' on right now don't herry up'n
git a good bit hotter'n it is," I joked out, "I'm a-goin'
right out at that back screen door, an' climb up insida the
coldest part o' that there old frozie truck an' coil up like a
rabbit an' go to sleep to keep warm."

"Silly." Helen scooted on her chair about an inch away
from me. She laughed with her hair in her face. "Crazy
thing. Talk quieter, Woody," she whispered. "Please. I
really feel exactly like you feel, hon, but you just cannot,
cannot go and scream every word we think out here across
Betty Jean's and Uncle Charlie's table. Tell me all of these
things as loud as you want to, Honey Pie, when we are
off to ourselves in some place. Goshamighty, baby, you
wouldn't ask me to spread my legs out for you right up
here in the center of this table, would you?" Helen held
her forehead against my temple and spoke in a whisper
that nobody else could hear. The table was too noisy.
Nearly too noisy to hear its own self.

I just blew my breath up my nose and sung a little old
song that sailed into my head.

> Oh, 'round th' border of Mexico,
> Hey, hey, hey, Perty Helen,
> Mexico is th' place I'll take ya,
> Oh, 'round th' border of Mexico.

Oh, 'round th' border of Mexico.
Hey, hey, hey, Perty Helen,
I'll find a leg jest warm as yours is,
Oh, 'round th' border of Mexico,

Oh, 'round that border of Mexico,
Ho, ho, ho, Perty Helen,
Dig a big hole an' pull out some gold,
Oh, 'round that border of Mexico.

Oh, 'round that border of Mexico,
Hey, hey, ho, perty Kitten Cat,
I'll rub your fur down day an' night,
Oh, 'round that border of Mexico.

Oh, 'round that border of Mexico,
Hey, ho, ho, little Helly Cat,
Rub your hair down slick as lard,
Oh, 'round that border of Mexico.

Oh, 'round that border of Mexico,
Hi, hi, hi, Helen, Babesie,
We can go in our hole if times gits hard,
Oh, 'round that border of Mexico.

Helen blushed as I sung the song, and after I finished it off.

"I'm glad," she told me, "to think that anybody would ever make up such a nice sweet song just about me. I like songs. I even like a music player man, already, in spite of my efforts to hate and despise him."

Irene was talking about Jerry P. "I still think we were a crack-headed bunch for not packing him down to the Big Bend before he died. He cried the last three days on his little old dying couch there, with his hands reaching out across the room to grab hold of us and pull us down there to his claim."

"I feel as if I already knew Jerry Guthrie," Helen said, "just like I know Charlie, Skinny, Jeff, and you, Wood Box. He sounds so nice."

"That mine sounds like some kind of an opium dream," Betty Jean said. "Too good to be true. He never was able to get any of you to go back down with him to find it?"

"We were all rigged up," Jeff told Betty, "oh, three or

four times, to go down there with him. After all of us got
growed up an' working."

"Why didn't your mother put you kids back into that
covered wagon and ride back down there with your Paw
Jerry?" Helen asked the whole bunch. "Tell me that."

"Mama Ollie never was as keen 'bout that dern-gum wild
country as Paw was," Jeff said. "Wilder it was, the finer
Paw liked it. Mama Ollie, though, she'd talk to Paw 'bout
how she hated them bugs an' she hated them there snakes,
she hated them dern-blame heely monsters, wild animals—
everything 'bout th' whole place, Mama hated it. She jest
didn't feel like she could take th' dern-blame chance,
Helen."

"I can see that," Helen said.

"I c'n see one awful perty head o' black wavery hair,"
I kidded her. "Hey, say, Hellian, know what? All o' that
there whole strip o' country down in there's like a great big
smokin' volcano full o' big hot rocks. Best place in this
world to go off to on a big three-years' honeymoon."

"Were you ever there, sir?" she asked me with her head
over on my shoulder.

"Naw. Jest heard 'em blabberin' about it all the time."

Helen brushed the side of my face with her hair and
said, "You Guthries are all pioneers in this way or that."

I nipped on her left ear. "Jest feel like I wanta take you
in th' palm o' my han' an' jist squeeze you till your jooseler
magooseler runs all down an' out."

"Y' c'n wait, cain'tcher, till you git 'er off down summers in them Cheeziz Mountains?" Eddie laughed at the
way Helen and me carried on with our flirting.

"Break that girl in good and easy, Wood Latch." Papa
didn't miss out on a good chance to tease us. "You don't
know what a wonderful little Hell Cat you took away from
me. I intend to sue you for your two parts of our gold mine.
Alienated her affections."

" 'At's bad. Guess I must be guilty, C. E. What's my
punishment gonna be?"

"Either one of two things," Papa said. "Give me my
woman back, or take this dead fruit jar somewhere out in
the alley and refill it. I cannot think if I cannot drink."

"Tell you which I'll do." I thought a bit with my head
down. "I'll go out an' fill th' jar up ag'in if you'll sign
over to my name your legal claims to th' Jerry P. Guthrie
gold mine."

"We *will* have two shares then," Helen punched me in my ribs with the sharp end of her left elbow. "One for you and one for me."

"No deal." Papa was shaking his head. "I can sell my share in that mine for enough kalex to purchase all of the whiskey in Oklahoma and Arkansas. I will promise, however, to pay you for your labors and for your efforts in my behalf. I will transfer over into your hand the first ten-dollar legal-tender note which I draw from my share of the mine on its opening night."

"Hey, Hellairious Woman," I grabbed a hold of Helen's wrist. "We done sold another jug o' snake juices. C'mon out an' help me squizzle another jug full. I wanta gitcha out here in some kinda private place. Come on."

Everybody talked louder and faster while Helen and I got up and pushed our way out of the room. Just as we walked with our arms around each other into my little bedroom, I heard Irene yell out, "Ohhh, Woodrowwww? Just where are you traveling away to, if I might ask?"

"Goin' out a-truckin'." I halfway laughed. "Gittin' your old Boney Mama's fruit jar rewound again. Gittin' a little shot o' this Hell Cat's huggin' an' kissin'."

I heard everybody talk and gab around the table. I listened for Irene to scoot her cane chair back and for her to walk into the flirting room. But no sound. She kept her seat at Jeff's left hand. Everybody laughed and joked about the whole crazy night. Canada. Drip gas. Jars of whiskey. Me and Helen. Papa's burns. Papa's comeback. The deputy car due to come any minute to take Jeff to work at the sheriff's office. Papa's deputy office job. Jerry P., the Greenseed mansion, Uncle Gid's herds of cattle. Helen said, "Let's give them time to catch up good and proper on their talking. Kiss, please. Kiss, please."

"Hurry up, Woodrow. Get a jiggle on," Papa told me through the door. "Hurry. My blood is turning off cold and windy from the north. You can chew on that Hell Cat's shoulder blade when you come back with the jug."

Helen and I stepped out on the little back washroom porch. In between kisses that stood off the cold of the blizzard, Helen asked me, "Hon, I just wonder how true all of these stories and tallish tales are? Really, tell me, Sug, are they true? Or just some big family jokes?"

"True." I kissed her some more. "True's a fiddle string."

"Wooodrooowwe! Frooot jar!" I heard Jeff yell.

"Comin' up," I yelled back. "Here. Smackereenio. Boy, you know, Hell Cat, I'm jesta natcherly burnin' up all ov'r, Honey Legs. We gotta do somethin'; I dunno what it is. Somethin'. I'm jest a-meltin' down my pants legs, Honey. We got to find some way to git t'gether, Honey. Swear to my soul we got to. Holdin' y' thisa way. Huggin' y' thisa way. Kissin' 'round over y' like this. I'm a-cravin' to slip my big slick mule, Honey Gal, into your little stable so's he won't feel so big an' so hot all the time. Hey, Hell Kit, tell me the facts, tell me this, jest this here one thing; tell me that you wanta do what I'm a-dyin' to do, jest as bad, jest as much, Honey, as I do. Tell me you want it."

And Helen held me as warm as she could and told me, "I do. Gosh, Hon, what have I got to do to prove to you that I want it just as much, if not lots more than you? I just nearly go out of my head, Woody, every time we hug each other and kiss around on each other like we are now. Don't you know I love you? Don't you know? Squeeze me. That's it. Squeeze me real good. Is there any way that we can close that little door there? Listen. Don't. Don't. You'll tear my new panties if you keep on. Honey. Listen. Here. Kiss me good. Honey. Let's close that door, Baby."

I reached out and pushed the little canvas-covered door shut. I could hear dim traces of a cold, high wind whistling and singing away over yonder in the minor keys.

"Warm?" Helen asked me.

"Uhh-hmmm. You?" I asked her. "Hot. Scorchin'. Burnin'. Simmerin'. Bubblin'. Boilin'. Runnin'. Feel me, here. Feel."

"Mmmmmm," was the only sound I heard out of her for a good bit of time. "Hmmmmm. Ummmm."

"Hmmm, yourself," I kidded in her ear. "Jest nev'r did know what a rich bunch o' fellers y' was a-minglin' an' a-manglin' 'round with, Hell, didja?"

"I guess not." She snuggled up closer. "Right at this minute I feel like it is mainly, like you say, mangling. I am getting mangled all over. But I like it. Love it. I feel so good right this minute that I could just wade along and swim in it. How do you feel, Sire Guthrie?"

"Swimmin' right along with you," I said. "Feel me?"

"What are we ever going to do? I mean, us—me and you. I know the way I feel, Woody. Want me to tell you? Well, I feel just like I have been your wife for several years already, and that you have been my real husband. I never did let any of these other boys do these things we do. I didn't even feel this way about you, not for those first few months we went around all of those places. I guess I just sort of got used to you. It just wore along and wore along and got to be kind of a habit with me to—oh, to sort of try to get your goat just the same way you always tried so hard to get mine. It even took a few weeks before I could really enjoy it when we would hug and kiss and roll around like we did. I just let you do anything you wanted to do with me—oh, just like I was getting fun out of watching a little kitten play around on the rug with a spool of thread. I always knew you loved to kiss me and to play around with my legs and my breasts and my hips and my stomach and things. I have felt now for the past month or so like I want you to take off my dress . . . like I want you to take off my slip, my bra, my stockings, my shoes, and my step-ins. I want you to take me into your bed with you and I want you to pull up the covers over us. I want you to hold me and to squeeze me all over, every inch of me, and to kiss and tickle and to bite me all over, too. I want you to stick your finger in my hairs between my legs and I want you to hold your finger in me . . . ohh, for all night long and for every night long till a hundred nights and two thousand nights go past. Ohh, I want you, I want you to, Woody. I want you to take your big, nice, hot pecker, Hon, and I want you to hold it so tight against my skin that I can feel it burn. I want you to try your very best to eat me up and don't you dare, dare, dare to leave even one crumb of me. This is the way I feel right now. All of these things. And all of our other things, Honey, Sug. I feel like the only way I can ever get any sleep or rest anymore is to hug you up on top of my belly as tight as I can with both arms. And I'm a good tight hugger, too, you will see sooner or later. I want to see the way it really does feel to have you stick your hot thing as deep in me as you can. I want you to promise me that you'll see if you can keep it up inside of my little pussyhole all night. Every night. Tell me, Baby, tell me, how deep did you go in those other times when you slipped those rubbers on? Huhh?"

"Jist about an inch, first time. Second time, 'bout two inches. Third time, three inches. Went a whole inch deeper every time. Why?"

"Ohhh. I was just reminding myself how nice it felt."

"Like it, Hell Cat?"

"I could eat it up. Please don't tear my new panties, Hon. That's the best pair that I have."

"Lemme help you to take 'em off. Ain't wantin' to wreck you."

"You'll never wreck me, Wood Chuckeroo. Here, I'm going to take them off. Here. Wait a sec. Hold me up. Brace me. Hold onto me good. Don't you let me fall, you Wood Block."

"I ain't about to letcha fall, 'less it'd be to letcha fall down over in my little bed in yunder."

"Let me roll another one of your little rubber coats on over your pecker, Hon, so we won't ruin my black best dress."

"Here 'tis. Not over there, over here."

"How does my little friend feel this cold and wintry night, huh, tell me? Here's a nice hot kiss to keep him from catching his death of cold and dampness. Roly roly roly poly poly polee."

"There is jest some certain somethin', Hell Cat 'bout the touch of your hand, that's got some kind o' warmth about it that'd knock any blizzard plumb out o' Texas. Never did know it, did'ja? Jest like y' never did know how many gold mines an' how many silver mines us Guthries had stashed away up our sleeves. Ha."

"Woooooodddrrrooowwww!"

"Froooot jarrrr!"

"Hellll Caaat! Wood Sawwww!"

"Likkkker jugggg! Remember? Rememberrrrr?"

Helen yelled, "Cooommmmmnggg."

And I yelled, "When we get damn good an' reeeady."

"Ohhhmmm." Helen grunted. "Ohhhh, Woody Chuck. Here, take off your jacket and let me put it down here under me. You won't be too cold will you, Sugar Neck? I don't want you to freeze yourself. Ohhh. You never will know how good your hand feels when you press real nice there and when you feel around inside of me like this. Tell me, what does it feel like when you feel so deep up in there?"

"Feels like glory hallelujah feels."

"How?"

"Real hot like, slickety like. I dunno. I cain't tell you. I never could tell you jest what it does feel like. I jest like to do it. 'At's all I know. Jist love to feel how hot an' how joosery my Hell Catten gets t' the feel o' my hand. Feel good t' you, good's it does t' me?"

"Better."

"Couldn't get no better. Hey, Honey. Want me t' go ahead an' slip my little man in some? Awful cold, lonesome out here 'n th' dark. He gets on a awful tantrum if I leave 'im on the outside gate for very long."

"Do you really want to come inside real good, Sugar? Do you think the rubber is all right? Mmmmm. Mmm. Tell me. What do you think? Huhhh? Keep doing what you are doing with your finger for a little . . . some more time. Ohhhh. Uhhhhm. That way. That way. What if some of the folks walk out here on this porch and see us? We are all tied up into pretty little knots. Ohhhhmmm. Uhh. Ohhhhmmnnn."

"I shore do wish that God'd take me by my hand an' show me off down to some dern wild an' rocky place where I could jest reach down with my fingers an' jiggle the gold dust around an' aroun' an' around, like this, down on th' ground. Jest so's I c'd take all o' the gold down an' pile it up all around your feet an' tell you, Hell Cat, honey, here's all o' the gold they got in this here derned, danged world. Spread your laigs, open up your perty, nice, warm laigs for me. I'm a-comin' in for the rest o' the winter."

"Ummmmm. Yummmmy yum yummm."

"Yumm yourself. Hey, Hell Cat."

"Yes, sir."

"We both'd better to make all o' the gravy run that we can tonight. I got a funny feelin' that everybody's gonna roll outta here on that there ole T truck along towards the rise of the new-day sun."

"Has some kind of an insane spell come over you, Honey? What on earth are you saying here in my ear? Mmmmm. Mmmm. You just never will know how good I feel right now. Keep your finger there some more and don't you dare to go away. Mmmm. Mm. Hhhhmm. Uhhhh. Uhh. Ohhhmmmm. Ohhhmmm. What was that idiotic remark that you just made?"

"Said that I got a feelin' everybody's gonna roll off outta here tonight on that ole rattly bangery T truck."

"The trip to Canada is off. Irene told me so."

"The trip for the borders of Mexico is jest now commencin'. This second fruit jar's gonna throw me an' Papa

an' Jeff an' Eddie so dang far down south we'll hafta back
up north again to git back up to Mexico. Yah yah."

"And how do you know? Ohhmmm. Ohhh, Baby Baby.
How?"

"Ohhh. Jest do."

"How? Pray tell?"

"I steered all the talkin' tonight down towards the
Chisos Mount'ins, six mile from the banks of the Rio
Grande."

"And why?"

"So's to keep my dad an' Jeff from a-goin' back to work
up at that there dammable ole stinkin' sheriff's office again."

"But you don't know if your daddy is going back to his
office clerking job tonight or not."

"Papa ain't goin'."

"How might you know?"

"Tell by the way his mouth's a-runnin' in there. I
knocked him plumb outta the notion of a-goin' back. Eddie,
well, Eddie'll go jest anywheres the truck goes."

"Golly. Geeee. Hon, tell me this, mmmm. How far is
this spot where your Grandpa Jerry left that mine covered
up with rocks, anyway? Just where is it on the map? And
why do you insist on getting everybody drunk tonight so
they will drive down there? Who knows that country? Nobody here would ever find that one little pile of your grandpaw's rocks. Hmmm?"

" 'Taint as hard, Heller, as you might think. We've got
Claude's maps, an' he's tol' us lotsa times how he could
always walk right back to this one little spot. Papa's got
all Claude's letters an' maps an' things right in yonder
in his suitcase."

"Mmmmmm. Bite me, Honey. Bite me on my neck. Bite
me on my shoulder. Bite me real, real hard. Make it hurt
me. Make a big black-and-blue mark on my skin so I can
walk around and feel so proud because you loved me
enough to chew me and to bite me. Hard. Harder. Ohhh.
Goddd. Mercyyy. Merrrrcyyy. Please. Woody. You can try
to put it in now, if you want to, and if you go real slow
and real easy."

"Tell me how. Like this? This?"

"You have to rub that rubber around on me real good,
Honey. Make it real good and slick like you did those last
times. Ohhhmmm. Like that. That's the way. Only, only,

ohhhhmmmm, yes, yes, yes, that's the place. That's the spot. Ohhhhhmm. Uhhh huhhmm."

"Is this dealin' you any misery, Heller Honey?"

"None whichever. It did all of those other times. I had such goofy little pains all through. But so far tonight I haven't felt any kind of a pain or anything. Ohhh, except just a good feeling of some kind. Hhhhmmm. Don't you push too hard, though. You go real good. And slow. And, Honey, be like your Papa Charlie says, be easy with your little Helly Cat. You love Hell Cat, Wood Head? How much? Tell me, how much? Oooo. Oooohh. Oooo. What if Claude drew those little maps up wrong, Baby Dolly? I never could sit down and draw you up a map of some little spot I stood on for a few minutes when I was a little girl just nine years old. Could you?"

"Dunno. Doubt it. I wish't we could lay down somewheres here on the floor, Hell Kitt'n, an' do this thing right. I cain't get it in so very good with us a-leanin' up here against this ole wall. 'Sides, whenever ya wiggle an' move all around so hot an' so fast, well, it sorta gets me all foamin' over, an' I jest cain't keep in long enough to letcha work up your best feelin's. Know what I mean, Heller? Kitty Kitten? But, I betcha my las' bottom dollar that I could set myself down at a table forty-seven years from this night here an' draw you up a nice perty map o' this one little spot here without no pile o' flat rocks anywheres 'round it. Nothin' 'ceptin' jest a little teeny handful o' nice little warm ticklin' grass."

"Things have changed, maybe, down there around the mine spot. How do you know what to look for when you get there, Sugar Lip?"

"Gonna look for jest one thing, jest one little spot, as I toldja before."

"What spot, Babe?"

"That there medicine-springs volcano waters. Spring that Paw Jerry always called the Britches Down Spring."

"Medicine water spring? Ummmm. Easy, man. There could be twenty such springs down there. Be really easy, Woodblock. What if every spring down there has got some name like Panties Down?"

"If there are that many, well, Hellicious, I guess I'll jest have to walk around an' comb my fingers around through every single dern spring till I run onto the right one. That's all. I combed my hand down in through a whole lot o' awful perty Texas females 'fore I run onto my Hellicious Cat, didn't I? Tell me that."

"I'm glad you found me, Sugar Loaf Darling. Proud and glad that you did. I want you to swear to me right here and right now, Baby, that you never will waste your time out somewhere combing through some other girl's tickly grasses. Promise? I will say one thing, Honey, that it just feels so terribly wonderful tonight that I don't care too much if we aren't laying down on your jacket on the floor and doing it any better."

"Says which?"

"I say, I don't know what I would do if it felt much better. I would just have a regular spasm. Gosh. Gee. Goshamighty whizzers. This is why I want for you and me to go down someday and get really married, Woody, Baby Boy. So that we can do this every way that you can possibly think of. And each time I want to do it some different way and feel it get better and better and better. I think I am just about to come real good this time, Honey. Do you think you can make your little man stay inside for just a little while longer? Ohhh. Please do. Please try. Talk to me some more, Hon. Tell me about some other mine, a platinum mine, a diamond mine, a ruby mine, and a sapphire mine that you found somewhere. It doesn't make me any difference where you found it. Just tell me all about it for a long long time, Sugie Sugar. Ummm."

"Got my doubts. I jest cain't. You see, whenever we do this a-standin' up this way, well, somehow or another, it jest moves aroun' so hot an' so tight every time you wiggle your tail. Sorta jest jacks me off in a right big hurry. Cain't hold out much longer. Feels too terrible good every time you move your hips an' your belly around this way. Hey. Hellicious. Listen. Listen. Whenever I do get down in there an' all of us runs onto that lost mine of Paw Jerry's, tell me this one thing, Honey Womern: tell me that you'll come down there to where I'm at, an' tell me that we're gonna do this same thing ten times every day. This feels better to me, gally, than all o' the gold an' silver mines I could ever hope to find. Say that you'll come."

"I will. Oooooo. I will, baby. You know, you know, and you just must know I will. Oooooo. Ooooo. Tell me who you love. Just tell me who it is that you love. Tell me. Oooooo. Can you come a teensie bit closer? Hold me, Woody. Oooo. Oooooo. Hold. Hold. Hold. Me. Ohhhhh.

Oooooo. Wait. God in Heaven. Woody Boy. Ooooooo. Wait some more. Please wait for me. Oooo. Just a little bit more. Honey Sugar Angel Apple Dumpling Pie. Golllly whizzzzz."

"I done already went an' done it. Helen Kitten. I shot every thing I ever did have, honey. Couldn't hold back no longer. Hey. Know what? I got it all o' the ways in that time. Didja feel it? All o' th' way. Jist for a minute or so, but I done it. We done it, Helly Cat. Every inch o' th' way."

"It just felt so good. So good."

"If we'd a-laid down here on the floor the way I first toldja, Honey, I coulda kept it in till you rolled right on down to San Antone."

"Stop worrying your poor head, Wood Chuckeroo. It felt so terribly good to me. I do not know what I would have done if it had felt any better. Now, now, is your mind convinced that I love you, love you, love you? We just have to do this more often. This, and lots of other things."

"Them other things is what I'm a-burnin' up to do. Jest which other things is it you're a-talkin' about, Heller? I wanta hear you tell me 'bout them other things. Which others?"

"Ohhhh. Those other things that both of us are going to do."

"Do? When?"

"Ohhh. When you find your gold mine and your silver mine."

"Other things, such as which? What?"

"We are going to dig up a lot of things, we are. Aren't we? Honey, listen, how long do you think it's going to take for you to go down to the border and find the mine and send for me? Where did I put my pantaloons? Oh. Here. How long do you think?"

"No way to tell about that. Don't ask me. Ask them Chisos Mountains down there."

"I just don't want us to be separated too long."

"Me neither."

"Do you really think Irene will let Jeff go down? And how do you know for sure that Jeff will go?"

"Jeffer'll go, awright. Irene'll let him go, a'right. You see, Hell Cat, I'm a-figgerin' on takin' Reenie part o' th' way down with us."

"You intend to do what?"

"To haul Reenie part o' th' way down with us. See."

"How is that?"

"Well, y'see, Uncle Robert an' Skinny Mammy left all their furniture an' stuff down at th' farm down at Jericho."

"Yes?"

"An', well, you 'n' me is a-goin' to remind Reenie Gal about Skinny's furniture still bein' down on the farm, see?"

"I see. But what then?"

"Well, Reenie's brother, Raymond Boydstun, has a Chivverlay pickup truck. An' Raymond's been wantin' for a good long time now to help Robert an' Skinny haul their stuff outta th' Jericho farmhouse an' up here to Jeff an' Irene's house in Pampa."

"I see."

"I *never* could get the whole bunch all together thisa way again in a year an' a half. Truck all loaded. 'Bout half tanked up on hosslaig liquor. 'Sides, Raymond'll haul all the stuff up here by his own self in a coupla more days, if we wait any longer. Jeff'll do whatever Papa does tonight. He's given Skinny an' Robert an' Ireenie two hundred dollars to keep 'em while we was openin' up the place in Canada. Jeff's got about forty 'er fifty dollars down in his pockets to travel on, see. Be a-thinkin' up a lot o' female ways to get this truck out onto the road, Hell Catten. Use that perty little head o' yours to help me. Heck, they's not a dern-gum thing for me here in Pampa, Helly Catter, ner not for you, neither one. Think hard. I'm goin' out to the truck an' grab another fruit jar. Kiss, please. Wheww. Air's cold. Be right back."

I humped along, down off of the back steps, out across the yard, looking at the way the little dirty shack houses of the Tourist Court shook in the night wind howling down. The houses looked dark and closed up, and the only light I had to guide my feet and hands out to the truck was the flickers of the lights that shot out from the dining room. I touched my hand in the dim light out and felt the brassy radiator cold and stiff, hanging down heavy with icicles. I felt on back along the fender to the driver's cab and listened to the side curtains flap and flip in the wind. I thought about the drip-gas drums and laughed to myself while I moved around the left-hand sideboards, all covered, wired, roped, corded, and strung like some kind of crazy old fiddle there, trembling, shaking, moaning, and wanting to warm up and go. I got two jars out from my hiding place in under the canvas. I screwed one open, undone the brassy radiator cap, and poured in about one third of the jar. I set this jar back inside the cab on what was left of the leathery spring cushion, and beat it back for the screendoor. Helen let me in, asking me, "Did you freeze yourself?"

I told her, "Nawww. Jist thinly caked over. Here. Hold this. Didja get your duds all tied back on? An' didja figger out any way for us to get this here job done?"

"I have been thinking a good deal," she told me.

"Yes'm? I'm lissenin'. I'm in a rough spot."

"You do exactly as I tell you."

"Kisser please. Hmmm. Yes'm. 'Zactly."

"You carry this jar in there and you keep them well occupied. I can't come in right now. Here. Take your jacket off and put it on me. I'll be back here in less than twenty minutes."

"Whereabouts you headin'? 'Nother feller hid off somewheres in them alleys up yonder? Where 'bouts?"

"I have to chase home and let my mother dear know that I'm going."

"Goin'?"

"Going down with Irene. I'll stay two days and help her to move her dad's and mommy's things back."

"Hey. But you'll freezle your tits off chasin' around in this here blizzard wind, Helleriner. What's come over you?"

"Telling Mother, first. Secondly, getting myself out of this dressing-up black dress of mine. I'll get into a pair of overhalls and a jacket and I'll be back here in nothing flat. You'll see. Hooppperay! Hipperee! Out of my way! Quick! Go!"

She pushed out at the door, down the steps around the northeast corner of the house, and mixed her bare head and blowing hair up into the dusty whirlingpools of the storm. Five fairly long blocks would take her from here to Masterson's yellow-orange tourist court and down the gravel driveway up to her mother's front door. I could barely make out just which part of the storm she had tore away into. I didn't know plenty of things. I didn't even know how to work my plans to get us on our way down towards that big, nice, hot, sunshiny Mexico border where Jerry piled those big heavy rocks up on top of that spot where he found his mine.

I squeezed my fruit jar as tight in my hand as I could hold it with my cold fingers. I got to clown around. Got to keep everybody occupied. I'll act a good bit drunker. And I'll see to it that all of my nice, fine, friendly kinfolks get a good bit drunker, too. Well, here goes.

I walked in, loud and blustery, with my jar and unscrewed the lid. I played like I was a fancy waiter in a white jacket. I hummed along on several old fiddling tunes while I poured each glass they held out to me. I bumped my elbow into Papa's shoulder and hummed out, " 'Shcushe me, shir. Beg your pardon, shir."

"Just so it does not occur again." Papa drank up.

I bumped Betty Jean's arm as she tried to swallow her drink, and told her, "Oh, shorry. Shorry, lady." Then I lost my balance and sat down in Irene's lap till she shoved me away.

"Get your fool self away from me. Just where is Helen at, anyhow? What did you do with her body? Stand up, nitwit. Talk."

"Here, Jeffreysh. Guzzle your geezle. Here'sh a toasht to Canaderioo."

"A toast to Canada!" Skinny lifted her glass. She kept still till we all lifted our own glasses and turned our eyes her way. "Here is a drink to the lands of Canada. Here's a shot to the T Models that freeze up and land in the big deep snowdrift to freeze everybody's toenails off. Down it."

Papa lit up all over with a long thinking smile and stood up by his plate to tell us, "But here is a toast for the Borders of Mexico."

"Hurrah! Dern right. Maixico!" Eddie lifted his glass.

" 'Ray!" was all I got said.

Papa tapped his fork against his glass to get all of us to give him our ears. "Down where the softest of breezes blow, way down to the borders of Mexico. Down where the sun chased the wind away, down where the lizard and the rattlers play. Down in the rainbow land of honey, dripping so sweet from the cactus blooming. Down in the hot volcano rockpile, down in the mesquite bush, rawbone country. Down where the ores run around in the rocks, down where gold and silver flows down along the Rio Grande, where you dig up a mine with your fingers and your hands. Down to the spring of medical waters. Down to the rockpile Jerry put there. Down to the spot where my old father cried and begged and pleaded with me, and then died asking all of us to come down. Here's to the Green-seeds in their mansion! I'll not knock at your gate like a beggar. I'll not crawl down your sidewalk asking for crumbs like a whipped little cur dog. I will go down someday or another and I'll follow my Paw Jerry's bootprints down to the cliff and down to the water hole, down to the rockpile he left there to make us Guthries just as rich here as you Greenseeds in your iron fence.

"Drink to the valleys of Rough Run Canyon. Drink to the Christmas Mountains. Drink to that big Slick Rock Wagon Gap. Drink to the Hen Egg and Niggerhead Mountains. Drink to the big hump, Study Butte. Drink to the pickaxe Claude and Gid took and pecked like baby chickies on that backbone there where Paw chopped that hunk off. Drink good! Drink those teardrops I see dripping down inside your hard, bitter glasses. Jerry P. Mama Ollie!"

"Drink." Jeff drank a long one.

Eddie said, "Ain't no man that can talk the way Charlie kin."

"Surely isn't." Skinny drank.

"If we ever do find this mine, Uncle Charlie," Irene drank and said, "I will buy you the prettiest and the longest automobile on the market just so's you can drive over to my mansion every day and drink me a whole big bunch of your toasts. Blame near makes me want to rip off this pretty red evening gown and pull on my blue cotton apron and bust off down there with all of you. Right now. Right this very minute. I have lately had a sad feeling about Jeff working up at that sheriff's office. I mean, outside of the job being too dangerous in this tough oil town, I mean . . . well, I mean the women that try to make up to him. So drink away. And this time, Mister Woodrow Waiter, please, you'll just have to come over here and pour my glass full again. Tell me this, Wood Barn: what in the world did you do with that beautiful dark-skinned little girly you used to court, by the name of Helen? Where did you shove her corpse at?"

I filled most everybody's glass and told them all. "I stuffed 'er up in under the foundation rocks o' the house. Be real still an' quiet like, an' you can hear 'er ghost howlin' 'round the house. Ha ha, ha ha!" I kept stumbling around the table. I mussed up Eddie's hair. I mussed up Papa's the same way. I patted Irene and Skinny Mammy on the back and tickled behind their ears with my cold hands. I bumped into Betty Jean and we had a big laugh at the whole crazy night, at the whole goofy crowd. I poured another round of drinks. After a bit, I told them all, "She had to go to th' gents' toilet. That's where 'bouts she's at. Theshe here wimmen aroun' this old wind-soaked Panhandle of Texas gits to feelin' like they gotta go to th' donker ever so often or jist swell up an' go bust."

Irene stood up. "I am here to announce that I fit your description perfectly. I am on my way. And I wish Betty Jean's toilet was about one mile closer to the house here tonight."

Skinny Mammy said, "I'll just slip on my old tobacco coat here and take a blow down there with you."

"If you see any traces of that there heifer gal o' mine down yunder 'round that there toilet anywheres, jest do me a favor an' shoo 'er off up thisa way. An' watch out while y'r off down there a-millin' around; you could freeze up onto that there seat perty easy."

"That, sir," Skinny told me, "is the very reason why we are going down there together. I'm waiting, Reenie."

"Coming through the June wheat, Mother dear. Come on, let's go out at this back door."

Skinny and Irene walked out onto the little back porch just at the very same minute that Hell Cat ran back out of the dark. I heard them laugh when they piled into one another, and heard Hell Cat coming into my bedroom. I left Eddie, Betty, Papa, and Jeff talking around the table, set my fruit jar up in the middle of the table, told them, "Help yourselfs," and walked into my bedroom to see Hell Cat.

After a kiss or two as warm as the jackets and shirts she had on, we talked some more.

"I have it all worked out," she told me. "Here, sit right down here on this bed and hold my hands and listen real good. Listening?"

"Yeahhhp. All ears." I sat down with her.

"I want you to know, first, that I know all of those reasons why you crave to pull your dad and your whole family here out of their deputy jobs. They have to get out of this town. God knows I hate it here, myself."

"Not's bad's I hate it. What'd you tell yer mama?"

"Simply that Irene and her Skinny mother asked me to ride down to the old farm place to help them move their furniture and things back up here to Pampa on Raymond's truck. Right?"

"Yep. I don't want to hear 'bout that there Raymond Boydstun a-bitin' on my Hell Cat Womern's naick, neither."

"My neck won't need any more biting for the next six months. Honey, did that little rubber raincoat work all right tonight? Are you sure it didn't break?"

"Naw! I looked good at it. Didn't even crack. Why?"

"I dripped so much running home and back. I was afraid. Just afraid, maybe you had squirted me full of buttermilk. It ran all down my legs. I was worried."

" 'S nothin' to worry 'bout, Helly Cat. It didn't leak out, not a drop. Y' know what's runnin' down from in 'tween your laigs? Jest honey juice, 'at's all—jest sweet little laripin' honey juice. All o' you sweety tit gals up aroun' seventeen, eighteen, nineteen, even in your early twenties, runs down with that there honey juice. Next time you feel it come a-runnin', Hell Cat, you yell an' lemme know about it, an' I lop out my ole hot tongue an' I'll lick all o' that there oozler magoozler joose down jist like likker'n draink it. Ain't no gal I ever did lay my hands on, Hell Cat, that's jest half as pretty as you look right here to me. Didja know that, huh? Didja?"

"Shhhh! Not too loud. Don't let the others in there in the dining room hear us. They don't even know I'm back yet. Where did you tell them I'd gone to?"

"To th' gentlemen's toilet."

"You are crazy. But so am I. Now listen. Here is what we're going to do. For the good of everybody here. I'm not just real certain about Skinny Mammy. This cold trip down to that farm tonight will not do her system any good. I really think we ought to see to it that Skinny stays right here with Betty Jean."

I held both of Helen's hands down in my lap to rub them warm.

"It will be lonesome with you gone." Helen lowered her eyes. "To see all of you go away just like a snap of your fingers . . . But I want you to go. I want to think that my man has this much nerve. It does take nerve. Guts. Whatever you would call it. And if you do find the mine—well, our lives will all just turn into some sort of a heaven. I'm glad to see that you want to try to pull out of Pampa and out of all of the mess things are getting in. I just want you to promise me that you're taking this lost mine of Jerry's serious. You have got to take it serious, Woody—

real, real serious. Go down there and stick it out. Stay. Stay long enough to look under every rock in Brewster County. You stick it out on your end and I'll stick it out up here on my end. You will either find it and we'll go to work on it, or else you'll not find it, and we'll all give it up for good and forever. We can find plenty of other kinds of work to get by on: Not very many people really starve to death. I hear Irene and Skinny coming back along the walk. I think the best thing we can do is just both of us to get around that table and speak our minds about it. I have a sneaking idea that Irene might not fight against this trip down to Mexico like she fought so hard against driving up to Canada in this blizzard."

Irene and Skinny said hello again to Helen while the three of them tossed their coats and jackets down onto my bed. "Nobody froze onto the seat?" I asked the pair.

"I left three good fingers out there on the handle of that old cold screen-porch door." Skinny laughed. "Now, pray tell, what are the great minds doing there hunkered down over that eating table?"

"What on earth?" Irene walked into the dining room at Skinny's heels. "Well, plague my soul! Claude's old scratchy maps. Did Claude actually draw them, as a boy, or hire somebody with a pencil?"

"Claude made 'em, awright." Jeff stood up in front of his chair and watched while Papa traced around over the maps with a red-leaded pencil.

"Well." Papa sipped some more out of his glass of liquor. He looked worried, puzzled, and wrinkled. He went on to say, "Well, dearly beloved voters, citizens, and constituents. What I done was this. I took a large size map of the Big Bend country, a regular surveyor's map—oh, this big. I laid Claude's maps down, you see, like this, side by side with the big map. Now, I am very dubious about using Claude's maps at all. Claude's hills are not correct. His canyons are named by the right names, but they're in the wrong places. I mean, here—Claude has put the name 'Rough Run Canyon' running from the general southeast, see, back along here, to the northwest, and down between this general bunch of hills, mountains, and whichnot. Actually, this canyon called Rough Run runs in the opposite direction . . . you see these red lines I've drawn here over Claude's black pencil tracks? Now, Claude tells us that from where he stood with Paw Jerry and Gid, he could throw a rock over here into this river, which just says, 'R-I-V-E-R'—oh, here is the other word, see, way back here—'T-H-E.' *The* River. Like this thing he calls 'The River' is the only river around here. Actually, even in dry times, there are two rivers, deep enough to splash water, here and over here. The Rio Grande and the Terlingua Creek that heads back here past these mountains eight thousand feet high, see, called the Chisos Mountains, which, according to brother Claude, seem to have the name of a 'Few Little Knolls'!"

"I be damn." Jeff looked some more.

"You got that figger'd right, Cholly." Eddie smiled and spit a big mouthful of snuffspit over into Skinny's tomato-can spittoon she had hid in the kitchenward corner. "Hmmmffph. I be dern."

"Mmm." Irene patted her feet against the floor so fast that I could nearly read her thoughts. "I see. In other words, you would actually be better off without Claude's maps."

"Ssshhh," Helen told her. "I am listening to Uncle Charlie."

"Listen, Helen Cat." Papa helped me to hug her some more. "I shan't tell one more word about these maps till you tell everybody around this table that you never will let another word slip out of your mouth to tell your family, apart from the Boydstuns and the Guthries, about this whole mine. Promise?"

"I promise. I throw my family in. Go ahead." Helen looked bashful and her face looked red.

"Family is now thrown in." Jeff smiled at the table. "Y' mean t' tell me, then, Charlie, th't we could jest heave Claude's maps out this winder here, an' be better off, huh?"

"Well . . ." Papa acted all of the parts of a legal advisor with a high local ranking. He fell into the old moves, the fast and the slow change of odd looks across his face. Something steamed up in him from back down the trails to the law office, to the courtroom, to the varnish on the legal and lawful desk, the pen, the ink, the stamper seal, the glue, the smells of floorsweep and disinfectant. He made biting sounds with his teeth while he rolled his eyes up to the ceiling, down to the floor, and around at the table, and looked us straight and hard in our faces. He was dignity and pride again, he was fun and he was serious again. His words rolled in on the high uplifts of the open wind, and the downdrafts of the breeze swishing through the blackjack, sumac, sycamore, elm, locust, cottonwood, post oak, hickory, tannybark, and bitterroot. He was the man that knew the questions and the answers down along the mud lips of the Canadian, the Red, the Washita, the White River, the Arkansas, the Deep Fork, the Slick City, the Oilton, the Sandy Spring, the Four Corners, the Five Crossroads, the deed, the title, the papers, the ifs and the ands, the howsomevers, the albeits, the whereases, and the therefores. I'd seen him catch this high proud breath of clear air on several occasions, when he saw some sort of a plan way back in the places of his mind. All of us remembered. None of us wanted to shake him out of his old memory. It was the speaking, not the idea, that we looked for in his face. It was the feeling of knowing that Papa was getting back into his old time and rhythms again: this was what counted most to all of us. The sense, the idea, the word, the plan—all of this would come in good time. I saw mouths drop and eyes open wider around the table while he talked.

"I would not presume to advise you people to take Brother Claude's maps out here in the wind and to throw them over the fence. No. No. Not anything like that. Because, as far as the one little spot where this medical spring trickles down the rocks, Claude seems to have done a fairly complete job of drawing this in. He has told us that this watering hole lies off to the general westerly direction from this mudwall adobe house back over here where Mama Ollie was cooking supper and waiting for Jerry and the kids to ride home with the piece of mineral rock. He has drawn several fairly big hills also over here in this same westerly direction. Claude also did a nice clear job of drawing in this big cut a few miles back over here to the north, where he writes again, 'Paw and me chocked our Wagon Up over this Gap which Paw called Old Wagon Gap.' We can tell by Claude's drawing, too, that the old mud-walled ranch house, with the windmill and water well out in back of it, did lay right down along here, due south from this Old Wagon Gap. All of this will be a big help to us when we arrive down in here. I say that Claude has done us a great favor by drawing us these little pencil maps that are fading and smearing out so fast. Claude drew them on very slickery paper and with a very soft lead pencil. The marks nearly fell off of the paper. Every time you take them out of their envelopes you can see the pencil dust sifting out like blackish iron sand.

"If we just drive down in there and walk up to Sam Nail, the old rancher who owns the land now, and we tell Sam all about our lost mine, Sam is going to demand that we sign over to him one eighth of the whole thing, because most likely the medical-water spring lays here within a few miles of Sam's ranchhouse."

"Paw Jerry spoke 'bout Sam Nail, all right," I said. "I heard Jeff'n you both tell about him, Papa."

"We have to have something except just idle words to catch the eye of Sammy Nail. He has heard a hundred, maybe a thousand tall tales about lost silver and gold mines. Well, Claude's maps will just give us something to let Sam graze his eyes over while we are making friends with him and getting him over onto our side of the pen," Papa said.

"When d' we get under way?" I know that nobody heard me say this because Hell Cat put her left hand over my lips and choked my words off.

"Makes a feller wanta crank up that there ole T truck out here an' take off." Jeff took a few deep breaths and looked around at all of us. "Huh? Don't it?"

"It's a whole lot better-soundin' than Canada ever was." My words got choked off this time by both of Helen's hands. I didn't sound like any more than a rumbling mumble.

"Shhhh," Helen whispered in my hottest ear. "Shhhh."

"If I were only a man right this minute"—Skinny still had her elbows on the table and her chin in both of her hands, looking—"if I were just half of a man! One quarter of a man! I'd be out there in that little old truck and already driving it right here, through this north ridge of mountains, here, through this Old Wagon Gap."

"How's it make you feel, Reenie? Skinny?" Jeff asked with his head and eyes as low down as he could get them. "Huhhhm?"

"Like riding. Like sniffing." Skinny wiggled both ears while she clowned over the maps. "Like digging. Like finding something. Like getting roly-poly rich."

"Reenie?" Jeff asked again with his eyes somewhere else.

"I just don't know what to say." Irene pushed her hands down in her pockets and patted her shoe soles against the floor. "I feel what you would call betwixt and betweens. Hmmm."

"A trip like this does make more sense to me than a freezy trip up to Canada in this cold weather," Helen cut in. "I sure would like to bundle up and go down to these Mexico mountains with you folks. It would make me feel five years younger."

"Hell Kitty." I tickled her rib through her shirt. "I ain't about to have you no five years younger. Too damn young awready. I'm a-tryin' my dangdest to jest git you raised up about one, two years older."

"I so far have not received your verbal reply by mouth and lip," Papa said, "if you've uttered such a reply, Miss Reenie."

"HHHmmm. Dum dum tee dum." Irene took her slow easy time on this one. "Well. Welly well well well."

"Don't stand there and 'well' all night." Skinny passed a big hot smile across the table to Papa and me. "Your well has run dry."

"Well." Irene let her eyes drift down across Claude's old pencil maps. "Canada is one awful cold place. And I suppose that Mexico is one awful warm place. Canada is full of peach trees. Mexico is loaded down with gold and silver mines."

"Quicksilver, too." Jeff reminded us.

"Up in Canada I'd always have to worry about some of those good-looking French Canadian peach-blossom girls stealing my husband. While, down in Mexico, I will have to always be worried about some real pretty suntan señorita stealing my husband. And, here in this wheat and oil town of Pampy, Texas, Lordy knows, I always have to worry about some female stealing my husband away from my bed and away from my bosom." Irene took her slow time.

"Sooo?" Jeff led her on. "Course, you're a-lyin' ever' word you let slip outta yer blame-fool mouth. Charlie's over there still a-waitin' on you to say somethin' one way 'er two ways. Talk, Reenie."

"How much could we leave Skinny and Robert and Betty with?" Irene asked Jeff. "Money, I mean."

"Two hundred," Jeff told her.

"I just don't want to be all alone tonight, Jeffrey, just to tell you the living truth. Not tonight. I feel all cocked and primed tonight to just kiss you and hug you all to pieces. I just don't want to see you leave so quickly. I was trying to think up some way by which I could go down to Mexico with you, but I see now that's not possible. I'd have to stay here with Helen and with Betty, and to help you and Robert get along, Skinny. I just couldn't go away and leave you. I'd just worry myself into a running fever about you both. Gosh. If I could think up some excuse to keep you here with me just for tonight, I'd give you half of my share in that silver mine."

"I'm a-burnin' up t' be with you, Reenie gal." Jeff squeezed his hands around her waist. "Might even git my hands on the dern-blame mine in a week, 'er coupla weeks. Dernawhizzers, Reenie, then y' could buy the fastest-runnin' dern-blame car in Pampa town here an' run down to me at a hundred mile an hour."

"May I speak in my thin and womanly voice?" Helen asked the crowd with her finger in the air. "Might I?"

"You mought. Then again, you moughtn't." Eddie drank another slug.

"I felt like you felt, Irene, I mean, about feeling so bad to see the boys leave all of us girls on such a lonesome bad night," Helen told Irene.

"I just had my heart and my soul set on it," Irene said back to Helen, being careful to speak loudly enough for every ear to hear her lonesome-sounding words. "That was all. Did you ever set your head on such a thing as that, Helen? Well, after all, you're not married, so I don't suppose you ever did."

"Our little store door hasn't exactly been nailed shut, Miss Irene. I mean, well, there have been times, two or three of these strange times come over me every day and at night, too. In fact—listen, in fact I knew that you were going to be feeling just this way tonight, Irenie. I even have it all planned out just what we are all going to do about it. Want to hear?"

"Shore," Eddie broke in.

"I've already run home and put on these old pants and things, and have also informed my mother dear of a little job of moving and hauling that you and I must assist your poor, weak brother Raymond to do. Catch on?" Helen held me as she smiled down at the maps under Irene's nose. "Catch onnn?"

"Raymond? Moving? Hauling? Raymond? My brother?" Irene had a surprised look on her face.

"Furniture?" Helen said this with a sing-songy tone. "Farm? Wheatfarm? Cattle ranch?"

"She can't think of it, Helen." Skinny talked on out louder. "I'll tell you now, Irene, what this genius of a Hell Cat girl is driving at. Well, Raymond is going to load what few odds and ends of mine and Robert's are still down in the old last house. Ray's going to haul it up here to your house. Helen is trying to say that you and her should jump in this T truck with Jeff and the rest of the tribe and drive down to Raymond's house. Stay down there a day or two, and help Ray to load our things onto his pickup and for you and Helen to ride back up to Pampa here when Ray drives back. See? Can't you see? So you can spend this cold and frizzledy night out between here and Ray's house up in under that ice-cold wagon sheet making giggle eyes at your silly loony husband there!"

CHAPTER 4

ROCKY RUN

I froze and shook with cold to my bones, and so did everybody else, feeling our way around the old truck. Most of the load had already been set on during these past few days. Betty Jean ran out in her fur collar overcoat and threw two wool blankets up to me on the back end. We put another blanket on the partly burned cab seat. I jumped fast to be the loading man because I didn't want Irene, Skinny, Betty or Hell Cat to nose around and find our four jars of moonleg whiskey. Papa and Eddie fussed around with the radiator and could not believe their eyes when they found it wasn't frozen solid like a rock. It was solid like a slush, solid like a shale of ice, but not solid like a rock. Papa took a deep smell around the little brassy radiator cap and said to the north wind: "Smells like a very expensive anti-freeze lotion to me. Just needs a few drops of lady's lilac, high-passion perfume to steam these plains from here to the Big Bend. Who poured this whiskey in this radiator, in the first place?"

Papa wore a few shirts under an old brown leathery jacket, a pair of jersey knit gloves inside a pair of big, bossy canvas work gloves, and two pairs of socks inside the same thin leather walking shoes he'd bought on the sheriff's force.

Skinny Mammy walked down the back-door steps with a steamy teakettle in her hands. She shouldered her way in between Papa and Eddie, saying, "Skatt. Skoot. You two are sure not doing me any good by standing here and snoofling around this radiator hole. Here. Let me pour a dose of this good boiling water in there. Who's got the cap to this snozzle?"

"I." Papa felt around with stiff hands and stiff fingers. "I am just wondering how a whiskey-soaked truck is going to run. Pour that scalding water on the intake manifold, Skinny."

"Skinny, don't spill water up on them spark plugs." Jeff stood across the hood and spoke with his eyes on the engine.

"You just exlax, Mister Jeffrey." Skinny poured her kettle of water down around the lower parts of the engine. The blizzard turned the water first into heavy steam, then into skinny coats of ice. "I unfroze more car engines in my day than you can stir with a broom handle. Get in the driver's seat, there. Woodhead, you mount down off from that hind end and turn that Hell Cat loose long enough to turn this thing over."

I jumped down and grunted, "Turn it over? This dern-gum crank is cemented into that engine, Skinny. I cain't ever turn 'er over fast enough to git her to fire off. Papa cain't. Eddystone cain't."

"Who'd ye shay cain't?" Ed bounced me out of the way and took a grip on the crank handle. Jeff turned the switcher key on. Papa felt his fingers along the coil box under the dashboard to see if the electricity was getting to the sparkplug wires. Skinny ran back to the house to refill her teakettle. Ed showed all of us how much power he had in his good right hand and shoulder. He let out a little quick grunting sound each time he bent up and down with the crank. He got a slow and sticky start. The cylinders sucked a draft of cold and whining wind with each turnover. Eddie picked up his speed slow and easy and then all of us grunted along with him, "Haaa Haaa Haaa Haaa Haaa haa haa haah haah haah." He tired his body out, stopped to catch a breath of air. He tried another spin. He got a bit faster this time. But no sound like a motor of any kind came out of the storm.

"Don't let it get stiff with all of Skinny's water on that motor, or she never will go in this world." Papa laid down on the floorboards, flat on his back, to keep on jiggling and flipping the coil plates.

Jeff ran around to the crank and yelled, "Woodrow, pile up in that seat'n work the gas 'n th' spark. An' always remember, she starts on th' battery an' she runs on th' mag. Flip them coils, Charlie! Hey, gittin' any spark fire through them coils?"

"Yeahhp," Papa grunted. "It ought to start with a real good fast spin. Sparkin' all right in these coils."

Jeff took Eddie's place at the crank. Skinny trotted out with her second hot water kettle.

"Stiffer'n irony glue." Jeff turned the crank a hard slow spin. He got his weight behind the turn of the crank and grunted a bit faster than Eddie. Jeff spun the crank so fast that he shook the whole truck. I felt like I was steering it down a rocky road.

Helen joked at Jeff, "Wind it up real good and tight, Jeff."

Everybody knew how strong Jeff was when he had to be. All of us watched him and all of us wished that we could throw things around the way Jeff could. He got madder and madder and hotter and redder as he turned the crank. Papa was saying, "That's her! That's her! That's it! One more. One more. Once. Just this once. Woodrow, don't pull that choker wire too much, you'll flood it out! All right. All right. Right! Right now! Now. Now. Now. She's spitting. She's spluttering!"

"She's splashin'," I laughed out.

"Puffing!" Skinny nosed around under the hood and poured her water till the warm steam clouded in her face. "Once more. Once more. This time. Now. Now."

Jeff swung his weight around and around, up and down, and moved with the turning of the crank. He sped up even faster and shook the earth beneath his feet. The spark got to the gaps in the spark plugs; it caught the gas in the cylinder afire. It fired the next cylinder, and the next one along. I stepped my foot down on the starter button, which helped turn the engine faster. Jeff helped the starter. I worked with the spark and gas levers under my steering wheel, pulling the two handles as far down as they would go till the engine commenced to run under its own fire. Then I shoved the spark lever back up to a halfway position. Skinny waltzed around the truck with her hot kettle steaming like a fog around a mountain. Jeff turned the crank loose and stumbled around to push me off the blanketed cushion, and to take over the workings of the levers and switches. And the neighbor houses for a block or so around raised up a private shady blind to look at us, to listen. We sounded like our hometown had won the big Thanksgiving Day football fight. We hooted, rooted, tooted, and we howled. We jig-danced, foxtrotted, singlefooted, and paced. We sung and we yodeled, and whistled.

"I ain't a-gon'ta ever let ya stop no more, little engine." Jeff talked at his wheel. "I'll keep ya boilin' an' a-steamin' from here all o' th' ways down into them Chisos Mountains. 'Course th' next thing t' fly loose is gon'ta be these cussed thin skin tires, all patch'd an' booted up. But we got a stack o' spares already pumped up an' loaded on. Whippeee."

The fruit jars passed around from hand to hand in the dark and in the wind. I got choked and gagged trying to drink with my nose down in the jar. I passed the jar on to Jeff at the wheel. I felt the old truck dance and shiver and asked Jeff, "Hey, d'ya want me to drive 'er first?"

"Guess I'd best to herd it," Jeff told me, "I know 'er tricks a bit better'n you know 'em."

"Yeah," I said back, "it aint th' car's tricks th't I'ma ree-ferrin' to. Reenie's gotta little trick 'er two she's a-itchin' to show ya back yonder in under that there wagon cover."

"Reenie an' me's a-gonna travel in comfort right up here in this here front seat. Motor heat'll warm us up good. I'll git Charlie t' ride up here where it's warm, till he gits sleepy. He can move back in there under th' tarp with Hell Cat an' you, ohhh, I'd say, after about th' first hour's runnin'. What we got t' do's to give Eddie Boy another big long whack so's he'll ooze off to sleep 'bout a mile down this road here."

It was hard for any of us to tell anybody good-bye. Jeff looked at everybody out milling around in the yard. He laughed a little quick one out over his steering wheel and I could tell that he was thinking several feet deeper than his actions would show. We saw two bright headlights pull up and blink three times out along the paved highway. The three blinks were the signal that his two deputy friends, Collier and Jake Sands, were out waiting to take him to his night shift. Collier was on his way home. Jake Sands would

ride around all night and work with Jeff. Jeff sat still at the
truck wheel for a bit, blinking his own eyes back at the
little black patroling sedan. We all heard Irene say, "There
is Jake and Collier, Jeff. What on earth are you going to
tell them? Go tell them something. They're out there
waiting."

We couldn't hear what Jeff said to the two deputies
when he ran out to their window and talked to them. We
kept still and tried to hear, but their motor and our truck
engine drowned out everything else except the wind.

Jeff ran back across the low ditch into the yard and
around to where the folks had stood hiding from the eyes
of Collier and Sands.

"What did you tell them?" Irene asked. "Please, Sir
Jeffries."

"I tol' 'em that I was a-drivin' Robert an' Skinny off
down t' their place t' help 'em git their stuff hauled back
up here t' Pampa. Said I might be one week. Said I might
be two weeks. An' I asked Sands if he'd hol' my job open
for me."

"And what did Sands say?" Skinny asked Jeff.

"Says that I c'n walk right back up into that office an'
buckle on my gun any ole minnit I take th' notion." Jeff
said this with his proudest smile.

"What did Sands say about me?" The wind froze Papa's
words.

"Sands says this, Charlie." Jeff hugged his arms around
Irene on his left and Papa on his right. "Says that Charlie
Guthrie's always got 'im an office-deputy job, by grape-
vines, jest any old time y' wanta walk back in. He tol' me
that."

Everybody shook their heads to make Papa feel good.
Betty Jean told him, "Well, it's nice to know that you can
always walk back in to the desk job after you miss your
gold mine."

"Ain't a-gonna miss no gold mine," I yelled.

"Hey, Wooder," Jeff stepped over to the right door curtain, "didja find a right good place fer them music boxes
so's they'll not git broke up?"

"Them fiddle gourds is fine, restin' like a dead horse."

"Reck'n I'd better styeer th' ole wrack f'r th' first few
loops." Jeff took a good slow look at Hell Cat in her
britches, then went on, "Charlie's too ole an' broke-handed
t'ever herd a T Model anywheres."

"I overheard your low remarks," Papa told us. "Who was the first man in Okfuskee County to buy and to drive a car of this very same model? I drove every day up and down trails and root roads before you were born, Jeff and Woodrow, and long years before you saw any such a thing as a concrete highway or a tarry topped byway."

"Been a long time ago," Jeff said.

"It's exactly like riding a broomytail, or learning how to swim," Papa said. "Once you learn how to do it, your mind never does forget how. It would tickle me flatly to death to show you how good I can keep this machine on its correct course from here down to the barn at that farm."

Jeff shook his head. "I'm jest-a-doubtin' jest how sober a man y' are, Charlie, after y' sucked down so much good fruit-jar juice."

Out in back of Jeff in the wind, I heard Skinny Mammy talk up. "Charlie is a safer driver than you will ever be, Mister Jeff. You always tell how sober you are, how slow you drive, but you get out onto any hog track in the country, and you get devilish, and you get to teasing everybody just to make them afraid. You drive too fast. You look backways and sideways and every other way except down the road you are driving on. If I were you people, I'd rather trust Charlie to drive that wheeler than our dear Jeffrey. I've watched the both of you operate. I say, let Charlie drive."

Betty Jean walked drom the back doorstep out to carry a double-size pot of black hot coffee steaming like a blow-off train. She had about four white cups hung along on her fingers. She poured out a cupful, first, for Papa, and Papa swiggled it down in one bite and held up his cup for Betty to refill. "Mighty pretty woman. Mighty good woman," Papa told Betty. "You may have been—who knows—as perty as Hell Cat here, or Irene over there."

"I was more the Reenie Gal type. More, Jeff?" Betty said.

"Naw." Jeff shook his head. "Thing is, Charlie, them there lamp bulbs we got ain't no brighter'n a coal fire inna duster."

"I know this turkey track road from here to that Jericho farm gate just as good as you know your own pistol, Jeff." Papa drank down his second cup of coffee. "I can find that road easier than you can find the buttons there on your

trousers. Roust yourself out from this driver's cab, Wood
Mill, Hell Cat. I am mounting to my cabin with my maps
both in my hand, and I'm taking you for a trip down to
your newfound land. Over. Out. Skat. Git."

Irene asked Papa as he pushed us out the east door and
sat down under the steering wheel, "How about me and
my husbando, Jeff, riding up here with you in the front, to
help you out with your driving?"

And Papa said, "I'm going to drive this crate so slow
and easy, Irene, that I'll meet and greet and shake hands
with every weed and every thorny bush, and get to know
every fence post. Eddie, need any help getting up here in
this engine cab? That's it. You folks clear back there and
make me a track. I'll blow my fourtime highball whistle in
one minute flat and this train will be done gone. It's the
Katydid Flyer. It's the Skeeter Buzzer. Clear back, you
folks there! You passengers. Are you passengers? No. No?
Just a bunch of hobo tramps and bums."

"Mount this hind end," I yelled in Helen's ear. "This
wind's a-howlin' down here too damn dern cold t' stan'
here'n arguefie in. C'mon, Hell Cat, gimme yer hand.
Hurry. Me'n you'll git th' best place here in under this
wagon sheet. I done got it all staked an' claimed. Boost y'r
rear end a little. Duck down. Looks perty cold back in
here. It'll warm up when we git ourselfs rolled up here.
These here ole woolly scratch blankets'll rub ya, I'll rub
ya, an' th' truck'll rub ya."

"I do believe," Helen told me. She felt her way around
in the dark under the canvas truck cover. She bumped a
beer case. She bumped into Eddie's boxes of carpenter
tools. She butted her head against one of our steel drums
of drip gas. She said, "Oops. I did it again. Same old head.
Just a different spot. Can't tell where I'm crawling to.
Here. Mmmm. Ouch. Where on earth are you?"

"I'm a-lightin' up this here lantern." I sat up against the
stack of boxes at the head end of the truck bed directly
behind the driver's cab. "Hell Cat? Y' all right? Dam
blast this here lantern globe! Sonofabitch. Bastard. Cock-
sucker. Havva helluva time ever findin' us a gold mine with
any sech a dam-burn lantern as this here thing is."

Just as I struck my match and got the kerosene wick to
light up, Hell Cat fell over onto me with her head in my
lap. "Here. Well, what do you know? It lit. And if you
didn't find any gold mine, see, you found me. That is a

nice invention, the way somebody wired the handle of this lantern up there to that top wood brace."

We got nested down and hugged and kissed a few long ones and a few more shorter ones. "Hey," I said. "I wanta speak my thanks right here in your left ear, Hell Cat, fer the way y' helped me t' git ever'body strung out down towards this here borderline of Maixico so fast. One gal as perty as my Helly Cat is, could start four big armies to marchin' off most anywheres that she'd wiggle 'er nose. Lord knows, y' done th' right thing here t'night. 'Tain't jist gittin' Papa an' Jeff out loose from these here depaty copper patroller jobs an' big oily guns. You done a whole lots more'n jist that. You helped ever' single one o' them out'n that there yard whoopin' aroun'. Y' know, Hell Cat, I think I c'n feel a little bitta heat a-hittin' down onta my face from that there dern-blasted ole lantern."

"I can feel it too," Helen said to me with her nose rubbing against my left ear. "I felt it just after you got it to burning. It's odd. Such a little flame. But, I did what I did tonight, Woody, not just to help out all of these other people. I did what I did for some other reasons of my own."

I asked her, "Which other reasons?"

"Our reasons. You. Me," she told me. "I knew—I just felt that if you went off up to Canada I would never get to see you again. I just had that feeling. But this trip to dig up Jerry's mine—well, I feel different altogether about it. Lordy knows, I don't know why. I just have a feeling that we will get back together again, somehow, if you go down to Mexico. A woman feels lots of things that she can't explain."

"Men, too," I told her. "Men feels lotsa stuff they can't never talk 'bout with half sense. Jest feelin's. Jest winds a-blowin' down. I think I hear Irenie an' Jeffereenie a-tryin' to climb up onto the back end-gate. Here, grab, fast."

Jeff climbed up over the back end-gate ahead of Irene. I saw his shape in the flicker of the lantern light. We heard Reenie teasing Jeff, Jeff teasing back at Reenie.

"Now, sir, just watch yourself. I swear, is that as strong as you are?"

" 'Smatter, Reenie gal, don't you wanta ride up here on a nice ice-cold mattress that Hell Cat 'n' Woodrow's done got all freshly het up for you?"

"I'm just as far in as I'll ever be." Irene laughed again at her husband, at the old truck, at the folks out in the

yard, and we all laughed with her. We just laughed at
the night in general. Canada. Mexico. Orchards. Mines.
Peaches. Minerals. French Canadians. Mexicans. Blizzards.
Fruit jars. Pencil maps. It all tickled my funny bone.
Every word that I tried to say came out like a laugh.

"Some hotel," Irene said. "I'm mortally glad that us
ladies fixed up this bed so nice after all, aren't you, Helen?"

Jeff and Irene dropped down onto the bedding pad and
crawled on back towards me and Helen wrapped up to our
necks and bouncing to the shots and backfirings of the
truck motor.

"Surely am," Helen said. "Ladies are good for something, you see, Wood Stitcher?"

"Okay," I told them. "Wimmen's here. I reckon they
gotta be good fer somethin' or other."

Papa threw the truck into reverse gear, his driving jerking us around so bad as he backed up it had all of us
worried. We rolled down the street, and I heard the motor
speeding up. I sat up and looked back over the end-gate
over the few vacant blocks we had already rolled in the
dark and in this high wind. Everything back there was
dark and full of odd moving cloudy shadows. Where I had
last seen the yard and the house, it was like looking back
at a dust cloud eating a wheatfield down. Like looking
backwards at nothing. All that I could say to Helen was,
"Ain't no use to wave back at nobody now. Cain't see a
dad-blame thing fer th' dark."

Helen said, "You just watch how the fur is going to fly
back in your eyes, Honey, if this trip down to the border
turns out to be a lulu."

"Yeahp." I shook my head back in my little corner
where Helen had leaned back against me to tell me her
thoughts in general. "You got that perty well figgered out.
Awright. I don't give a dadburn, Helly Cat, where'bouts
the heck I'm at. Jest me, fer my own self. Canada's fine.
Montanny's okie doke. Galveston's hunky dorie. Chisos
Mount'ins, they're *mucho bueno*. I didn't care t'night
whicha ways we drove off. Jest's long's we drove. Anywheres—to play music, to grow peaches, to work out on a
farm, to dig ditches. To find Paw's mine down yonder.
Th' minute that I set my shoe sole down anywheres within
fifty-nine miles of that there Britches Down Medicine
Spraing, well, I belong to my own self, an' to my Paw
Charlie that made me, an' to his Paw Jerry that made all

nineteen of us. Hah." All of this I kept down along in a
low, slow, highly determined whisper.

"Old truck is really traveling along, you know." Helen
rocked back and forth with her hands holding my hands
warmer inside her two cotton workshirts. "I could ride like
this from here to the end of the moon, couldn't you?"

"Ain't no breathin' human that loves to ride no better'n
me," I told her. " 'At goes fer the truck, an' fer Hell Cat
Cliffman, both. Wind's a boostin' us down this here dern
road."

"Going to be rough. I like some things rough . . . I like
you, and you're rough." Hell Cat recited a little snatch of
a song as the lantern swung on its wire hooker:

> Ride me out of the plains so cold,
> Roll me down towards Mexico

I caught the drift and helped her to finish it off:

> Down ta where th' Rio Grandie flows,
> Diggin' my Hell Cat some silv'r an' golds.

She smiled and kissed me and said, "You don't dig up
golds for your Hell Cat. You dig up gold. Gold. Just one
gold."

" 'Ass where yer dead wrong," I told her. "They's more
kinds o' gold in them there min'rul books than you can
poke yer tongue at. Yellerish gold. Red-like gold. Greeny
gold. Purple gold. Got solid gold, watery gold, flaky gold,
cakey gold, got gold that runs through the rock like spider's
web hung in a tree limb. Got gold that's thick an' gold
that's thin, gold that's good an' gold that's bad. Got old
gold, hot gold, cold gold, foolish gold. My gold and his
gold, an' her gold, an' your gold. Some gold, no gold. This
gold an' that gold. Skinny gold, fat gold, an' nugget gold.
River gold, mount'ny gold; sandy, rotten, windblew desert
gold; canyon gold, cliff-rim gold, false-teeth gold, whiskey-
mug gold, wineglass gold, weddin'-ring gold, d'vorce-mon-
ey gold, gold-dollar gold, fount'n-pen gold, gam'lin'-wheel
gold, hotel-room gold, chipped-ice gold, whore-time gold,
long-ride gold, short-timer gold, three-way gold, brassy-rail
gold, spittoon gold, sawduster gold, railroad gold, bracelet
gold, wrist-watch gold, pocket-watch gold, gold fer th'
deputy, gold fer th' cop, gold fer th' fruit jar, gold fer th'

cock, pussy-runnin' gold, cock-hound gold, cunt-lappin' gold, pecker-suckin' gold, an' jizzum-drainkin' gold, an' solid-gold gold, an' gold that's golder th'n solid pure gold. Ever' kinda gold. See, Pussymouth?"

I kissed Helen's face, ears, her hair, neck, some different spot with every word of this great long-winded rigamarole. The truck commenced to bounce around a good deal harder just as she laughed and paid me back my kisses. We tried not to make any noise. We didn't want to cause Jeff or Irene to miss up on any of their solid comfort there all rolled up and flouncing along in the hottest woolly bedroll I'd seen in all my days put together.

"There went the Le Fors turnoff," Helen told me. "And welcome to the Jericho dirt road. I suppose we had ought to get used to these dirt roads, don't you, Woody Squeetus?"

"Let 'er ripple. I ain't a-givin' one single good dadburn." I sung a little old bit of a spiritual song I remembered playing on my set of drums down in the same little church that Hell Cat sang in:

> On that Jericho road
> There's room for just two,
> No more and no less,
> Just the Savior and you.
>> Each burden he'll bear,
>> Each sorrow he'll share,
>> There's never one care, care, care,
>> When Jesus is there.

Hell Cat was a good quick-guessing harmony singer. She'd heard it sung down there a thousand times. So she tossed in a verse, and I dropped back to sing the repeating harmony, like this:

> On that Jericho Road
> (On that Jericho Road),
> Blind Patmos he sat
> (Blind Patmos he sat).
> His life was all dark
> (Yes, his life it was dark),
> It was empty and flat
> (Yes, empty and flat).
> Then God's Love appeared

(God's Love did appear),
One touch brought him light
(One touch brung th' light).
On that Jericho Road, Road, Road,
God's Love struck the light.
(Love did strike a light!)

Hell Cat had quite a quick thinking machine on her, too, for whipping up some kind of a little word or two that would fit into most any old tune you could sing—well, to tell you something about what you were doing right at this particular minute. She thought for a bit, rolling along bouncy like, and then licked her tongue out to wet her lips and sang this one to me, to the same tune:

Down this Jericho Road
(Down this Jerkwater Road),
A little truck rolled
(A cart it did roll)
Full of fathers and sons
(Fulla daddies and boys)
Hunting silver and gold
(Huntin' anythaing hot).
Jerry P. did appear
(Jerry P. did appear)
And he waved me his hand
(Sez, he waves me his hand),
Pointed his finger, finger, finger
To the stake and the claim
(Yes, the stake and the claim!)

While Hell Cat laughed along at the end of our home-made song, I held both of her breasts as warm as I could in my hands. She stopped her laughing and told me to get quiet. We listened to Papa and Eddie up in the front cab. Papa was blowing another toast out through his curtain and into the winds. We both heard his words drift back to our ears. His toast went like this:

Here is to the Mexico border,
Here is to the people up it and down it!
May the borderlines all cease to exist,
May the people crease and increase!

I squeezed my hand in between Helen's legs and said, "Papa an' Ed's gotta jug up there. I plumb forgot about it!"

"It does sound like they've found something. I feel just a little speck afraid . . . this old truck, your daddy's burned hands . . . That jar of whiskey won't make him see this crookety road on down to Jericho any plainer. What are we going to do? I just feel worried. I wish you'd stop them and take over the wheel and do the driving, Honey," Helen told me. "I really do."

I told her, "I was jest a-wishin' we could knock off another little hunk, Hellie." I had to keep my voice down to a whisper that blended in with the noises of the motor and the truck rolling. "Be jest about our las' chanct. Know that? I got all stripped down an' hot an' ready f'r it."

"We can't." She hugged onto me a little tighter. "Not here. How can we? Jeff and Irene will see us. I couldn't. These pants are hard to get off, Hon. And besides, it's too cold."

"I ain't so cold. I'll warm ya up. Jeff an' Reenie's so comfy 'tween them there blankets that they couldn't see a big red apple on a stick right square in front o' their eyes. All they're a-hearin' is jest one another's hearts a-beatin'. I can help you git outa yer britches. Gosh-a-marias, Heller Gal, ya got me plumb on fire. Meltin' clean down. Blazin'. Burnin'. 'Sides, that there little ole short-time piece that we got awhile ago back on the warshin' porch was too short ta even count. Hey, let's make this time th' longest one so far. We've not had a real good chance yet to give ya time ta git ta feelin' it yer level best." I kept my hand inside her shirt and pants and rubbed her all the time that I was talking to her. "Jist reach over here an' feela how big an' how hot this here thing is, Hellie, honey. Ya won't even notice th' cold onct we git all hugg'd up. C'mon."

"You are crazy," she told me. "That's why I like to tickle your chin. See. Like this. Like that. Do you really and truly want to with all of your heart? And with all of your soul? Really?"

"All o' my pole, Helly Cat. But wiggle fast. Then me an' you's gotta climb up there in that there cab seat an' herd this wreck. Gotta git Papa an' Eddie both back here to drink their selfs to sleep. Pantsies downy. Here, lemme help."

"How? How are we going to? I'm making enough noise

getting these trousers off to wake up the dead. Pull. There. Now, there. That's fine. Fold them up. Lay on them for a pillow right here under us. We can't get down in under the blankets with Jeff and Irene. We'll stay right here. And let's not make too much noise, Babykins. Easy. Easy this time. And quiet as we can? Huhhh? I'll unbutton my shirt, but I'm going to leave it on around my shoulders to keep me from chilling and freezing. Give me a big hug. Hold me warm. Warm me for a long time. Uhhh. We sure can't take too long, though, Babe in the Woods. I can still hear Eddie and your papa up there swigging that fruit jar down to nothing. You move. Move over a teensy speck your way. I want to make a little bed here. We've got enough old clothes on this truck to dress the king's army all in rags. Just hold onto me and keep me warm from my back. I'm laying some of these old rags down like this, see, and I'm saving back these to use for to cover us over. That's the man. Keep hugging. Hhhhmmm. Uuuhhhmmm. Honnnie pie. That little thing of yours feels as hot as a firestick when you rub it against my hips like that."

"Little thing?"

"Well, it isn't the largest thing in this world. It feels so hot that I can't hardly believe it."

"Little?"

"Bigggg. Big, then."

"Hell Cat. D'ya know somethin'? Whenever ya git me fer yer man, yer a gittin' a man that's heavy hung. Most every man ya ever run onto has got a six er a six-an'-a-half incher on 'im. But I took sech good care of mine that I done growed 'im up to be seven an' a half inches awready. An' I aim to feed 'im up to eight er eight an' a half 'fore I die. Two whole inches extry fer ya to play around with."

"I'm full-breasted and you are heavy hung. My breasts actually do measure two inches larger than nine girls out of every ten you see. My hips and my legs are just a teensy bit too plump to suit me. I've been worried about them. I don't know what to do to make them go down smaller. Maybe if you rub them real good and hard like you are right now, maybe they'll go down a bit. You're about the best rubber I've ever seen."

"How many rubbers have ya had rubbin' on ya so far? Tell th' truth, Hell Cat."

"About three. The two Kraft brothers, Timmy and Jimmy. One other fellow that took me out on a wiener roast on Sand Spring Crick. But they didn't rub me as hot as you rub me. I guess they just didn't know how it was done. Or we just didn't have a long enough time. Or I didn't know how to get my skin as hot for their hand as I'm learning to do for your hand. It does take one thing, and that one thing is lots of good practice. Like we do. Now, how do you like this for a bed, Sir Longpole Guthrie? Sir Hotrod?"

"Mighty perty bed. It's a moving bed. Ta heck with the bed. A bed made outta cactus stickers'd feel good ta me if sech a perty little, perty-titty, perty-laid Hellie Cat was all piled down on it like this."

> Little Helly's gotta gold mine,
> Hey, Helly's gotta gold mine,
> Hell Cat gotta gold mine
> Way up above her knee.
>
> Perty little gold mine,
> Perty little gold mine,
> Perty little gold mine,
> Nice and warm ta see.

"Honnieee. Let me slip little rubby raintoat on itty man."

"Ain't not."

"Not what?"

"Ain't not no itty man."

"Big man."

"Here's a raincoat. I got enough o' these here raincoats off'n old Seegar Shorty ta keep you an' me from havin' four hundert an' nineteen kids, Hellie Tatty. If ya roll th' dang thing down too hard, Kitty Catter, ya git it all rangled up in 'is hairs, an' then whenever you poosh it on down ag'in, well, it pulls th' hairs ta beat th' sights of hell. Roll it easy. Teasy. Pleasy."

Hell Cat was on her hands and knees. She fell down into the rag bed on her back and made a little pooching motion with her lips up towards the lantern burning. "Puff it out, Woody. But hurry, I'm getting all cold again. Hurry. Put it out."

I held my dad's old coat around my nakedness as I stood up to blow the lantern out. Jeff and Irene lay in my way and under my feet. They still played like they were asleep, but I knew by their extra loud breathing that they

weren't sleeping. I pushed the iron spring lever down and
blew the flame out as the globe lifted up one inch. The
truck swayed a bit and caused me to stumble and stagger
on my feet. I stepped down on Jeff's shoulder trying to
set my foot down. He grunted a bit, but kept both eyes
closed. He snorted when he moved up against Irene's
stomach, and she snorted like she was dead asleep. I
made a big step down to the foot of their pallet to keep
from stepping on them any more in the double dark of
the canvas truck tent. Down around their feet and beside
their blankets I stepped onto several bundles of extra
clothing and the suitcase that Reenie had brought along.
I held onto beer cases, boxes, chests, and all sorts of
other things till I made my way back again to where
Helen held her own arms around herself. I heard her
jigger her teeth and say, "Where on earth did you go off
to? Here. Here I am. Over to your right." Her voice
broke out a good bit louder than a whisper. She laughed
because she could not keep any quieter. "Down. Down
here. You are the silliest specimen I've ever had the
pleasure to see. This down here is me. Here. Over this
way, idiot."

"Y' mean ta say, this here's us. Hah. Me'n' you. Hey,
ya gotta awful cold-froze man here ta thaw out. This here
big raincoat feller cain't hang aroun' here on th' outside
much long'r. Ya shore gotta good warm feelin', little Missy
Hell Cat. Mighty warm woman. Even got all these here
old rags all hetted up. Perty laigs. What all didja hafta
do ta ever grow such a nice set o' laigs, anyhows, gallyo?"

"I ate cornbread rough and cornbread tough, red beans,
hamhock, cayenne pepper, and soppy gravy. I wanted my
legs to match up with this extra, extra special gentleman
here of yours. I wished for my hips to be just as pretty
as you tell me your long john is. Now, are you pleased?
Sir? Where did you lay your papa's old coat, Honey
Dover? We may have to grab something to pull over us.
My pants are under my head here. Good pillow. Excepting for that big scout knife I have in my pocket. Honey,
do you know which time this is for you and for me?"

"Lost track."

"Six."

"Hittin' a little bit more gold ev'r trip. Huh? Does this
feel as good to you as it feels f'r me? Heller?"

"Better."

"I'm still a-waitin' to jest put this here 'way up where'ts good'n warm, thissa way, an' jest ta lay down my head on yer bozum here an' go off ta sleep thissa way. Coupla three hours!"

"It never has felt this way to me ever ever before now, Woody. We never could take our own sweet plenty of time like this. Does it feel any different to you tonight, Babesies? Huhhh? Ohhm. Mmm. Mmmm."

"Hotter tonight."

"Is that all?"

"Juicier."

"Mmmmmm. Mmmm. Ohhh. Ohhhm. Ohm. Ohm."

"Pertier."

"Mmmmm."

"Hotter."

"I'm still scared about the way Charlie and Eddie are drinking and carrying forth up in that driving cab, Honey Pie. Aren't you? We had best get up there as quick as we can. We'll think up some excuse. Some way to get Charlie to stop on the road. What will we say? Mmmm?"

"Tell 'im we gotta git out an' check up on the tires. Feel o' how big the punky knots is gittin' ta be."

"Yes. Ahhhm. Mmmmhhhh. How long can you hold it in? You know. How long a time? If you try real, real hard? Oooohhhmm. Uhm. Good good good good. How long?"

"Not too awful long tonight. Worried about how drunk my dear old father at the wheel is. Truck a-jigglin' us up an' down thissa way tickles me so good that I cain't hold back my jizzum fer very much longer. How fast can ya come? We'll take 'er slower an' longer next coupla hunderd times, Hell Cat. We'll slow 'er down ta jest a slow, humpin' walk. Slow 'er down ta jest a lazy, froggy crawl. Next coupla thousand spells of it. I aim ta git myself a little fancy silver gold spoon an' I'm a-aimin' ta jest dip m'little spoon down in b'tween yer little hairs an' jest gonna eat ya smack smoothly up an' drink ya smack smoothly down. Like this. An' bing. Like this. I wanta see ya do yer best ta shoot off, Heller Cat, right here, an' right now, an' right real, real quick like. Quick."

"MMMmmm. All right, sir. If that is what you desire, then that is what you will get. I am your wife without the papers and I must get accustomed to doing the things you ask of me to do. I am your wife, am I not, Sir Wood Block?"

"Ain't nothin' previous. Come good. Big."

"This is as big as I can do. Honey. Ohhh. This is as much as I can move. I can't wiggle any higher. It can't feel any goodier. Mmmm. Any goodier. Sweetlier. It just can't. Ohhhhmm. I can't bite your neck any harder or you will have scars and bruises for everybody to see for a week."

"Ain't nothin' I hate in this here world any worser than a neck er a shoulder 'thout no scars an' blue purpeldy bruises on it. Honey. I'm a-tellin' ya fer shore. I jist cain't hold it back no long'r. It's a boirlin' up outta my ears. Cain'tcha come plumb good?"

"I ammmm. I meannn, I did. Real, real, real good. I really did. Reallly and truly good. Goodest. Ohhh. Here. Hold close. Hold warmer. Close closer. Good gooder. That's the way. I want to feel you shoot real, reallly big. Now. Now. Right this. Nowwwmmm. Big. Biggerest."

"Big as I can shoot it, Helly Catter. Feel 'er jump?"

"Jumps fine. Make it again. Some more. That is the best part for me, Hon. Honest johnest. It really is. Close. Closer. This is the best it has ever ever been for me, Hon. Was it for you?"

" 'F it's any gooder I'd die bitin' on it."

"Funny how it always goes down so little and so limber after we shoot, isn't it? Where do you suppose he runs away to? Huhhhmm?"

"Ask 'im."

"I am asking you. Where?"

"Runs off'n a panther cave to scrouge out a gold mine."

"He does?"

"Yeahhhp."

"Why does he come running back every little while, do you guess?"

"Runs back every time that he fin's 'im a little nugget. Runs back ta show ya what he's found."

"Woody, help me to slip my trousers back on, if you will, kind sir. There should be a pair of pants and a shirt here in these old clothes that you can put on. Your others are too muddy. Use them to shovel gold and silver mud with. Here's a shirt. Here. Here. These pants belong to somebody. You can get into them."

"Big enough fer me an' the north wind, both. Hug onta me. Don't lemme blow out of 'em."

"Well, sire, tell me this: how do you feel right now? And what are we going to say to your father, please?"

"Hey, Papa!" I sang out.

"Hey, Uncle Charlie!" Hell Cat called.

"Heyyy, Paaapa!"

"Hey, Ankle Charrrlllie!"

"Heyyy, Paaapa!"

"Somebody back there want me? Who?" Papa asked sideways out his door curtain. "Woodroooe?"

"Yeahh. Heyyy. Lis'n. Papa. Stop."

"Do whaaat?"

"Slow down! Stop!"

"Why?"

"We have to see about the tires. Stop! Got four bumpity tires. Le's stop an' take a feeell of 'em. Heyyy!"

"Clutch yer foot down on th' brake," Eddie spoke out.

"I have to go to the men's rest roooomm!" Helen told Papa.

"I gotta go ta th' ladies' jonick'r. Dammit! Heyy! Stop! Tire'll blow us clean off'n th' side of th' road. Le's take a look at it. Save havin' a flat! Stop!"

"I am," Papa told us.

"Hold 'er tail up, Papa. Nose 'er up ta this here post. Rope 'er down to a slow lope. Then, stop 'er dead. Left hind end tire's a-gonna blow us all ta hell an' gone. Stop."

"Grab a good hold," Papa told us. "We are now preparing to come to a stannndstilll. Hold on."

"Pull 'er out over here onta th' right han' side a little bit," I told Papa. "That's fine. That is just dandy. That's a good job o' stoppin', dear Father. Pile out back there, Hell Cat. Here. Help me ta climb down. Wheeewww! Feel that wind. Stiffer'n a doodaddy, ain't it? Colder'n a bitch." I walked around one way and Helen walked around the other. We both felt our hands along the tires with our gloves on.

Hell Cat walked over in the wind to Papa's door curtain on the opposite side of the truck from me. I heard her say to Papa and Eddie, "Howdy you doo doo?"

"I can't hear you," Papa joked out at Helen. "My engine is performing too loudly. How long have I been driving, Hell Cat?"

"For, ohh, about an hour, I would say," she told him.

"Two hours. Three hours." I walked up to Helen's back and pinched her right hip through the pocket of her pants. "Four hours."

" 'Fer'd we come?" Eddie spit down onto the red-hot exhaust pipe beneath the floorboards on his side. "Plenty heat up here a'right."

"Ohhh"—Helen squeezed her gloves in mine at her back—"I'd say that we've made almost thirty miles. Just a few more gates to where we come to Raymond's place. You did such a good job of driving that we have all decided to put a fresh pilot on the wheel." Helen talked with her head stuck in at Papa's door. "You can move out, too, Eddie. And make it fast, so we won't lose any time." I took ahold of Papa's left leathery jacket sleeve and helped him to step out the door and down onto the ground. "Right aroun' thisa way, please, sir. If this here wind don't blow ya down, well, ya jest cain't be blowed down. Tha's all there is to it."

As we walked around the truck facing into the blizzard, Papa sang a few words of this little song in my ears:

> This old wind might blow my barn down
> But it can't blow me down,
> It can't blow me down.
> This old wind might blow this world down
> But it can't blow me down,
> It can't blow me down.

"Come quick, Wood Straw," Helen said. "Let's get this crater box to rolling before our passengers fall out."

We slammed our doors to hold the engine heat in the cab. I laughed a little bit, then I dropped the clutch lever down out of neutral and into low gear. I pulled my gas ear down to pick up some speed, and I smiled again when I heard Papa, Eddie, Jeff, and Irene, flouncing around back under the covers. "See them there big tumblin' weeds rollin' off down ahead of us? Feel how that there dern wind's a-purshin' us by our hind end, Hell Cat?"

"I don't see how you see anything through this windshield. Everything seems to be drifting and rolling and melting and running together. Things look so odd out there ahead of us, don't they? Our dim lights. Everything flickers. All shimmery. Like one big dust cloud. You had sure better drive careful, Honey."

"Lotsa heat flyin' up from that there exhaust pipe down in 'tween yer shoes?"

"Plenty. What causes that exhaust pipe to stay so red-hot like this? It scorches this piece of wood flooring board under my shoe. The wood is burned loose. If it falls down just one inch onto that hot pipe there, it will blaze up and catch our whole truck on fire. This wood is turning into charcoal, Honey. Do something."

"Don't want to lose m' speed." I pulled my gas down and took a right hand curve. "Reach down there 'n' take a hold o' that there board with yer han'. Here. Slip my glove on. Lift it up. That's right. Now heave 'er out yer door. Throw. Git rid o' th' damn thing."

"Woooweee. The wind pushes this door so hard I can hardly keep it open. Throw it out? Really?"

"Throw it. Hurry. Wind's a-suckin' all o' the good heat off."

"There it goes. How do you expect to arrive down at the mine with a truck if you start throwing the pieces away before we get ten miles?"

"Fifteen! Likker, please, I ain't a-gonna drink much. Jist a little sip sap soop. Jug me, 'fore I pull out over here ta the bar ditch an' beat yer hide raw with th' butt end o' my leath'r belt."

Helen unscrewed the tin jar lid. She tilted the mouth up to her lips and sipped a sip. "Wheeewwee. Ohtchh. Hum. Oh. I never will be able to see how you drink this down without any water to wash it with. Wheew! Teach me how."

"Here. Gimme it. Be more'n glad ta teach ya. Lotsa things I'm gonna be jist too glad ta teach you, Miss Hell Skatter."

> And she says, I'll go with you
> To that cold roundup,
> And drink your hard likker
> From yore hard bitter cup.

The north wind bit us up in under our tails for another hour. I felt the sway and the rock of the truck when the wind circled on past and around us. More flying weeds

blew past. The road from Pampa south to Jericho lay
dusty flat, at first, and level with the clods along the wheat-
fields on both sides. I got a good start down the first hilly
steep road that crossed a big canyon full of cattle hiding
in little warm bunches in behind the knolls and rocks
and rises. We crossed the cement bridge at the bottom,
and pulled back up the other slope by using my low gear
pedal for about the last half of the upgrade slope. I kept
on hearing grunts and mumblings from back in the back,
but the engine and the storm and the few words I said
back and forth to Hell Cat drowned the backbed noises
out. The night did get darker. I believe that the wind
pushed harder and the cold got colder. After a few more
flat and windy miles, Helen asked me, "If you get tired
of driving, why don't we wake Jeff and Irene up?"

I told her, " 'Cause I'm a-wanting that there Jeffrey
boy ta git enough of Reenie gal's lovin' ta last 'im fer th'
next seven runnin' months."

"From my experience with you, I'd say that the more
you get, the more you want. Maybe it's that way with
Jeff, too," Helen teased at me to keep me awake.

"Could be. Could be," I told her. "Big canyon comin'
along here in jist about a mile. Might ooze down th' downside perty smartly, but I ain't so sure 'bout it humpin'
up th' steep side."

"Gollee, Honey, I sure do wish I could be going all of
the way down with you. You're crazy, but I'm sure going
to miss you bad. Are you going to miss me as bad as I
miss you?"

"Worser."

Helen watched me work with all of my handles, pedals,
springs, pulleys, levers, wires, and other things. In the far
back corner of her eyes I could see just a dim faint glimmer of a worry, first about ever making it down the first
slope with the dust and the weedystraw of this blizzard
blowing in whirlpools ahead of us down the road slope.
She said, "If you drive fast you ruin the tires. If you
drive slow you get stuck on the uphill. That's the way
things are, I suppose. Are you going to promise me one
thing?"

"What?"

"That you'll write to me. I loved those letters you wrote
to me last year while you were all snowed in for those

two or three weeks out on Skinny's wheat farm. It's a very good thing that this steep grading here's at least straight. No curves. Are you promising?"

"Feel how that wind lifts us in th' behind?"

"You never did promise me."

"Okay. Guess I can write 'em if you can stand ta read 'em. I promise. Hear them ole bunky tires a-howlin' down ag'inst th' ground? That there blizzard is a-moanin' an' a-groanin'. Hear that whine, Hell Cat? That zzaanngg? Hunnngg. Hear it? Well, I gotter eared down jist's fer's 'er ears'll pull. Jist set back now 'n' watch 'er bleed an' run."

"Mm-hmm. I think our singing and zinging and zooming and sanging is coming from somewhere else—from Irene on her mandolin, Jeff thumping on your guitar, and partly from Eddie arose from the dead and from Uncle Charlie rising up out of the tomb. Listen. Listen back there."

And I heard the guitar loping along with the mandolin, both just chording along, while all four of the rear-tent passengers sang me and Hell Cat this little old song:

> You better run, little T truck,
> You better run, little T truck,
> You better run, little T truck,
> Oh, wello, you better run.
>
> You better fly, little T truck,
> You better fly, little T truck,
> You better fly, little T truck,
> Oho, hey, ho, you better fly.
>
> You better rollll, little T truck,
> You better rollll, little T truck,
> Yo, ho, hooooe, ho ho ho,
> You better rollll.
>
> You better tear, little T truck,
> Well, well, ohhh, you better tear,
> Little T truck, trucko, trucko, T truck trucko,
> You better tearrrr.
>
> You better sail, little T truck, trucko,
> You better sail, little truckie, truckeye.

You better sail, little truck, truck, truckoe,
You better sailllll.

I couldn't always tell who it was that started off on
each verse. They sung it like a worksong holler where
you've got to come out on a loud shout to get everybody
else to keep quiet while you sing your turn. You hold up
your finger, or your hand, and you holler, "You better
flyyy little T truck," all by yourself, see. Most everybody
jumped in too soon, that is, they sung, "Little T truck" on
the very first line, which drowned the leader's voice back
down before me or Helen had a chance to guess whose
voice it could be. We got such a good feeling out of
listening to the song that both of us hated to see it come
to a stop when we hit the narrow bridge down at the bottom of the slope. I held up my hand in the cab above
Helen's head, and yelled as loud as my lungs and Windmill Creek Canyon could stand it. I yelled out,

You better diggg, little T truck, T truck,
You better diggg, little T truck, T truck,
I said, you better dig, digga digga dig,
You better digggg.

Helen shouted out as loud if not louder,

I say that you better move, little wagon,
I say that you better move, little wagon,
Moooove, mooove, moove, little wagon,
You better mooooovvve.

"That there singin's all that's a-keepin' this old engine
flippin' over right about now," I yelled over at Helen.
"Got 'er way off down in Gran'maw's low hole. Thank
yer dinner buckets that we got this here sixty-mile blizzard
pushin' up this here grade. We'd all been out along the
sides a-pushin'."

"Is that as hard as you can push on that low pedal?"
Helen kept both eyes out along the road. "We've slowed
down to less than a walk. Rabbits are hopping right past
us. See there?"

"Them's not rabbits," I kidded her, "them's brickbats
rollin' up past us. Lis'n at 'er groan an' take on. Got 'er

down jest as low's low goes. Bran' new clutch band, too. This here Windmill Creek Canyon hill's wunna th' slickest drops anywheres around this here Hanpandle country, too. Ain't a-gonna make 'er, Helly Cat. Hummy hum hum. Count them leafs on that there weed blowin' right yonder. Got plenty of time ta rent up a chunk o' this here Windmill Creek lan' an' seed us down a nice, perty wheat crop, if y'd be interested. She's a-boirlin' over. Lookit th' old steam go suckin' off up yonder, Heller Gal."

"What are we going to do? Wake up the others? I mean, yell for them to jump out and push? We're losing every bit of our speed. I can call them. Want me to?" She had been sitting with her feet crossed under her. She rocked this way and that way, she grunted to try to make the truck move another inch, spitting out the words of the little song:

> Little pretty truck, you better get along,
> Little sweety truck, you better jig along,
> Little honey wagon, you better get along,
> Little sugar car, you better move alonnng.

"Yer song's a-suckin' in around through that there motor, awright, Hell Kitten. I can hear it a-siftin' an' a-poundin' down around in them there manifolds, an' all down around amongst them there cylinder walls, an' a-soakin' inta ever' one o' them there pistons, an a-blowin' fiery blazes in around them there dern-gone old spark plugs. See it? Hear it? Yer song, I mean? Song's jest about th' only thing right this minute that's moochin' us up this Windmill Canyon Hill. Keep it up, Hell Kittie. Sing 'er onct more. Perty's ya can sing it."

I pushed against my wheel, pushed both feet against the clutch pedal, one foot on top of the other foot. I pulled the gas lever as far down as it would go and the spark lever to the same place. I guess I prayed a good prayer somewhere in the dusts of the storms flying around us as Hell Cat sang:

> You had better roll, pretty little, sweet truck,
> You had better move, pretty, pretty, pretty truck,
> Move, roll, and go, and get to moving,
> Sweetie pie, sugar wagon, you have to move.

"How is that?" Helen smiled and asked me. She had a proud little look around her eyebrows. "Did it pull us? I think it did."

"Still moving." I tried to smile. "Eddie 'n' Irene'll both git scared outta th' whole trip if they see us git stuck on th' first hill th't we come up against."

"They very likely would, at that."

"Grunt, Hell Cat. Grunt. Groan. Wiggle. Do somethin'."

"I'm cackling. I'm crowing like a rooster. I'm wiggling my pants off. What more can I do? Grunt, yourself, Sir Gerthridge. Push on that steering wheel. Ha Ha. I know it isn't funny, Woodenhead, but I just have to laugh. It seems just too crazy. Do you mean to tell me that we're still moving? We should have stopped way back down the hill. Maybe it *is* going to pull us over just to keep the others from turning back."

"Listen."

"Listen? To what? I can't listen to a thing with all of those gears screaming in my ears like this."

The truck shot steam from its brassy water cap higher into the air than a single-barrel windmill. Gassy blue smoke flew out the back exhaust pipe like a cloud that whipped over the whole truck and scattered up along across the crags and the rock-jags along Windmill Canyon in the dark. I kept the levers down and my foot on the low-gear pedal till the floorboards sweated sticky hot oil. The truck kept on the move. She groaned. She screecked. She smoked and she steamed hotter and hotter. She blocked the drift of the things in the wind even worse at such a low crawl up the hill. The upshoot and the updraft of the storm over the high side of Windmill Canyon howled louder than it had squalled back across the downside. The road was kind of a yellowish smear in the dim headlights. I couldn't make out where the deep bar ditch lay on my right or lefthand side, or see a line or fence wire on either side of my eyes. Everything was melted down into one big, dirty, coppery gold, whirling pool that I'd seen walking along in these same winds around a thousand bends and on down a thousand other roads before this one. I was seeing more than a thousand other memories out through my windshield. I saw faces of people I had met, some just to walk past or to talk a few words with. And I saw all of my hopes pretty well wash out of the rusty washpan out there in front of my mind tonight. It was out of all of this that I kept listening to Helen hum some odd and curious little tune that mixed all in with the flips and the flops of other voices.

Out of the whole tangle, and up above the roarings and backfirings of our little engine, I heard my dad's voice clear and plain. I heard him talking loud, breathing loud, straining his words out in between heavy puffs of air. And he was saying, "This is the valley of the Windmill Canyon. This is the slickoff rock, the rimrock cliff country. This is the valley of the wind and the valley of the cactus. This is that stickery bed, that thorny pallet down along the floor, this is that canyon womb and hole in the ground where the wind was born."

I looked over at Helen and asked her, "Hear that? Where's it comin' in from?"

"Your dear father, naturally. He says some very pretty things, when he gets the notion." She sat there with her legs still crossed and her shoes under her thighs, Indian fashion.

"Awful plain. Close. Think so?"

"Listen over here on my side. Listen. I hear Eddie."

Ed's voice came about as loud and as clear as Papa's had just come. He said, "If I jest had a nickel fer every truck thet I pushed up hills, I'd have nuff t' open up six gold mines. Them French hills gits all bogg'd up with that Franch mud; and ye lose a truck 'bout ever' five minitshh."

"They must be walking. Pushing." Helen smiled at me. "I'm jumping out to help. Keep everything pulled all the way down."

I watched Helen pile out at her door, and I heard Reenie's voice drift all the way from the far hind end somewhere.

"What I'm wondering"—Irene kept pushing—"is how you intend to get this thing up some of those really steep hills, if you can't make it climb this one."

"Push, Reenie! Push, Jeffie! Apusha, Papa! An' apusha, Eddie Moore! Lay y'r shoulder up ag'inst it. Hit it. Lay inta it. Don't be 'fraid of it. Heave! Tug! Dig y'r toes in. 'Tain't but about a gnat's jump to go now. 'Tain't but a flea's hop now. Push it!"

"Shee anythaing of th' Argonne Foreshtt over that

ridge, Wood?" Eddie yelled up at me. "Er Chatoe Thierrie?"

"Cain't see th' Chatoe f'r the forest. Push it up, man!" I kidded down on my right hand side towards Eddie's head. He pushed along on the right side of the truckbed just a few inches in back of the driver's cab.

"Over! Over Dover! We're up and we're over!" Helen ran up along my right side and stepped up onto the running board. Ed hopped up onto the same running board at Helen's elbow. Papa grabbed ahold and stood up on the left hand running board, laughing and howling back down the road at Irene and Jeff lost off in the dark.

"Reenie and Jeff never made her, Wood. Stop," Eddie told me.

"Cain't stop her," I yelled out. "Wind's a-blowin' too cussed hard. Wher'bouts is Jeff an' Reenie off at?"

"Can't even see them," Helen told me. "Slow down. Wait for 'em to catch up. I see them coming. Are you very cold over there, Uncle Charlie?"

"I worked too hard to get cold." Papa talked to Helen across the windshield in front of my eyes. "Nothing like a good workout to make you sweat out your cold. How far is it down to Ray's gate?"

" 'Bout a mile," I told Papa. "We turn right up onta th' paved road fer sixty mile ta Amariller."

"It'll blow somewhat windier from here to Amarillo," Papa let us know. "We gain altitude all the way. This is about thirty-five hundred feet along through here. Amarillo is thirty-nine hundred. Coldest part of the trip. The wind will be on our right instead of pushing us from the tail end. Better let Jeff take over the wheel at the turn-off. We can't haul you ladies up to Ray's door, because we'd have a hard time getting back up onto the highway again. His turn-off is too steep and too rough. Besides, we'd lose the whole morning talking, when you girls can tell him the whole story and all there is to know. Well, I swan to my goodness, I see that you finally arrived."

"Finally." Reenie tried to laugh as she stepped up onto Papa's fender. She hugged her left arm around Jeff's waist when he climbed up and stood on the same fender. "Drive on, Wood House! I can hug this fender for this last mile. I do wish you boys would ride us down to Ray's door, though. Stay just an hour or two. A good hot breakfast will get you on down the road in a whole lot finer shape, anyhow. Stella will just have one fit after the other one if all of you drive down within a rock's throw of her gate and then turn off towards old Amarillo without even dropping in to tell her howdy and hello."

"Shore would at that," Jeff agreed with Irene.

"Lose all the whole morning." Papa talked with his face straight ahead into the wind. He watched along the roadside where he knew the flat hog and cow pastures ought to be, but he could not see far in the dark. "Best part o' th' mornin' fer driving. Besides, if we stop this engine for two hours over there in front of Ray and Stella's gate, she would freeze over so tight that we'd never in our lifetimes be able to get her to firing and hitting again. We ought to get on down to Study Butte fast as we can, so we can finish up our hunting and get back up here, or I should say, send for you ladies to come down to us men as fast as we can. Savvy me?"

"Paw Gutheroo's righter'n a fox! You're dead right, Papa!" I yelled out to them through the isinglass curtain flapping about in the hardest wind we had so far pushed up against. "Me 'n' Jeff's gonna ride up here in the cab an' wheel this here pile of tin on inta Amariller 'fore ya can yell 'Britches down!' Paw Gutheride, you're right."

"You know, Reenie," Helen said, "Uncle Charlie and Woodrow *are* right about that. What if the engine froze up hard and we never were able to get it to start up and run again?"

"I'm not even caring one way or the other," Reenie answered back, "whether this little old engine ever runs again or not. I am losing a good hot husband, and that's all that I can see, Helen."

"I'm losing my good hot Woodyrow," Helen said, "but I had lots rather see him go on and get down to that mine and, like Uncle Charlie says, finish it up this way or that, and get back to me."

"I can see your point." Irene ducked her face into the wind down the road as she talked. "I guess maybe you're right."

"Here's th' paved road, folks," Eddie told all of us.

"You folks see anything out there that looks like a cement slab with a big Six Six, Sixty-Six, painted on it?" I asked everybody riding on the fenders.

"This is it," Papa told us. "The Big Sixty-Six. She goeth

from coatht to coatht. From ghost to ghost, I might add.
And this is where we come to our parting of the ways
with two of the finest little ladies in all of the plains and
canyons of Texas. Come down here on the ground, both
of you, so that I can kiss you good-bye and bid you both
a kind and a generous Fare Thee Well."

We all got out of the car and down from off our fenders.
We hugged and we kissed. We talked and we joked. We
took a few good minutes out to make each other feel good.

I left the motor running pretty fast. I left the lights on
so that all of us could see one another out in front of the
radiator. Helen gave Eddie a big hug and a big kiss. Reenie
gave Papa a big one. Jeff kissed Helen on her neck, and
Helen kissed Papa for a long time. I hugged Eddie and
Papa hugged Jeff. Jeff hugged me and I hugged Papa.
Everybody that was not kissing or hugging a girl was
kissing or hugging a man.

We laughed in the wind and the wind swung around us
lots harder. We done little goofy jig dances on the concrete slab of the Sixty-Six. Glad to hit the concrete and
glad to kiss the Sixty-Six. Glad that we had made it this
far. Glad to be here. Glad it was winter time. Glad it
was cold. Glad it was dusty and glad it was blowing dirt
in our faces while we talked. Glad to be parting. Glad to
be leaving. Glad to say good-bye and gladder to get a
little bit later on down the road. Glad that Paw Jerry was
doing such a good job of leading us through the dirt and
through this wind so far. Glad to be coming through such
a bad blizzard. Glad to be rolling. Glad to go walking
apart from one another. Glad to climb back up inside the
truck again. Glad to wave and to whoop our good-byes
again. Glad to make our promises once more to find the
mine fast and to get back together quick and warm. Glad
we always had found some way to keep warm in the
coldest northers that drifted and blew. Glad to see Helen
and Irene go walking their ways off down the little dirt
turn-off road to Ray and Stella's fence gate and to their
warm door.

Helen held her arm around Irene as they walked
away and faded out into the wind and got lost somewhere in the dust. I sat up in the cab with Jeff at the
wheel while Papa and Eddie both got back inside their
tent bed again.

Jeff drove fast. He wanted to get on away from such tender and touchy sights and scenes. He opened the gas and the spark as far as they would go. He strained to keep the truck headed due west halfway into the dead push of the blizzard. It was harder to drive it now. It was not like it had been with the wind biting us at our back. It hit us against our right side, first as hard as it could blow, then easy, then half as hard, then harder, and this kept the truck in a buck and a sway, in a jerk and in a switch, while Jeff had to keep on the cement slab of highway known about the world as Sixty-Six. Our lights got brighter and they got dimmer when Jeff drove fast or slow. He had to drive faster if he wanted to try to see something ahead of him, or out to one side a few feet. The wind did get higher and it did push us harder, but it pushed against us now, and not behind us, not with us.

I could hear above the blizzard wind, above the motor howling, above the weeds sailing past, a little song Jeff was half humming and half mumbling:

> I got a womern on Noah's Ark, an'
> I got a gal in the Arkaynesaw.
> I left a gal way down in the Ark, an'
> I lost a gal down in Arkaynesaww.

I sung this verse while Jeff listened and tilted his head to one side and the other; three verses, it was, that I put in:

> Two little Indians did strike oil
> Down in th' Ark in th' Arkansaww.
> White man came and he stoled it all, yes,
> Down in th' Ark in th' Arkansawww.

> White man kissed th' Indian girly,
> White man kissed her paw an' squarw.
> White man stoled th' long green money
> Down in th' Ark in th' Arkansawww.

> I did kiss this Indian lassie,
> I did kiss her paw an' maw.
> I did thieve th' deed an' monies
> Down in th' Ark an' th' Arkansawww.

And to the tune of the truck motor roaring, Jeff and me both sung together,

> Down in th' Ark, an' down in th' Ark, yes,
> Down in th' Ark an' th' Arkansawww.
> Down in th' Ark, an' down in th' Ark, yes,
> Down in th' Ark, in th' Arkansawww.

CHAPTER 5

WINDY ROAD

I could hear Papa and Eddie back in their tent house laughing and singing some fast-made words to one of the oldest of songs, one that Jeff had made his fiddle ring to ten thousand times over and over:

Well, I'm a-goin' down this road a-feelin' bad,
Yes, I'm a-goin' down this road a-feelin' bad,
And I'm a-goin' down this road a-feelin' bad, bad, bad,
And I ain't a-gonna be treated thissa way.

I'm a-goin' where th' gold an' silver runs,
Yes, I'm a-goin' where th' gold an' silver runs,
I'm a-goin' where th' gold an' silver runs, runs, runs,
And I ain't a-gonna be treated thissa way.

I'm a-goin' where th' gold mines grow on trees,
Rollin' down where th' gold mines grow on trees,
Law, Law, I'm a-driftin' down where th' gold mines
grows on trees, trees, trees,
And I ain't a-gonna be treated thissa way.

Papa and Ed drifted off to sleep to the sounds of the storm pushing the winds and the winds pushing our truck . . . no, not the wind pushing the truck along. Not now. We've headed off to the due west now. The wind's not pushing our truck. Our truck is pushing the winds along. Our dreams are pushing the wheels along. Our hopes are shoving the bearings and the sparkplugs along. Our songs have already pushed our hopes along against the weight and the whipping of the high wind hitting up onto the higher flats between the Jericho turn-off and Groom, in between the Groom bypass and Amarillo. Jeff missed the downtown sections of Amarillo all he could. He struck off to the outskirts. He kept down along the cutoffs and the truck routes. Amarillo looked to be as dark and as windy and as weed-blown as the farm and cattle lands we'd been wheeling acrost for the past several hours—in fact, Amarillo was even darker than the open road had been. The walls, trees, hedges, fences, and signboards along the streets made things darker.

We bounced over a railroad crossing, then hit a few streets full of rough chugholes. We laughed and talked and sung a few more songs about the road.

I don't know the numbers of the highways we come down. We left the big Sixty-Six back at Amarillo. The road ahead looked just about as dark and dusty. There wasn't much difference in the big Russian thistle tumbling weeds that rolled past us and bounced out of the ditch to blow acrost our path. I remember Jeff said, "Well, Woodsawyer, don't cuss them tumblin' weeds too much. I seen lotsa folks ketch 'em an' cook 'em an' eat 'em. Let 'em blow."

"I ain't a-stoppin' 'em," I told Jeff. "How wouldja cook 'em?"

"Bile 'em up," Jeff told me. "Bile 'em up in a kittle."

We stopped and refilled our gas tank a few miles north of Lubbock. Jeff got strangled on the rubber siphoning hose we'd brought along, while I poured the gas with a little bucket into a funnel in our tank. I froze, but Jeff got even colder than I did. He was up on the truck by the gas drum splashing gargled gas all over himself in the blizzard. He cussed me and he cussed the rolling things flying around us. He cussed his own self, the truck, and Papa and Ed back sleeping.

Lubbock went past us like Amarillo had. A town was just another thing in the night. If we had not seen some different name on hand-painted wooden signs, we never would have known town from town nor ditch from ditch. We hummed. We rolled. And we felt like turning around and going back home to the girls and to the women. Back to the hot meal and the clean table. Back to the clean sheets. Back to the warm quilts. Back to the warm stuff out of which all of our women folks were built. Back up our roads. Back where we come from. Just back. Our thoughts all pulled back on us, back on the truck, back to the north country where these weeds in the wind all tumbled from. It was these weeds that we trailed and followed on down south to Odessa. Odessa was a name on the map, but we didn't have any map, except for the little old pencil maps that Claude had drawed up for us to find that gold and silver mine by.

We blew with the wind, only a notch or so slower than the wind. On south from Odessa to Pecos. I saw the trees of mesquite take over, get bigger, higher, with shaggier bark. Mesquite was the head boss down through this Pecos County country. Mesquite was the oldest settler. Mesquite was the oldtimer. It was here before this wind rolled our truck down. The only thing that was here ahead of this mesquite was the wind, maybe. I guess there was some argument between the winds and the mesquite trees as to just which one did settle and homestead first here in Pecos County.

I talked to Jeff about the mesquite. Papa and Ed rode mostly back in the rear and under the canvas cover. I slept back in the back while somebody else drove. I drove while they slept. Somebody always drove while somebody else got their sleep in. The only one that never did get any rest at all was the little old truck itself. It never did cool off. We had a flat or two; maybe it was three. One we could patch up; the others we had to cut off the rims with our pocket knives and toss over onto the side of the road. Our spares were just as thin and papery as our other tires. Thinner, I suppose. Beat up more. Patched up worse and weaker. We got to where we could change a flat in very few minutes.

I'd been used to looking out across the country on every side back up in the Panhandle and seeing the iron grass and more iron grass. Iron grass had shot its roots down, up in the Panhandle, and had claimed every stitching inch of the Upper Plains land. Down here the mesquite rooted the iron grass out from the soil. Mesquite bushes first shot down their roots twenty feet and pushed out the iron grass. Then if the iron grass did manage to hang onto the topsoil, if the wind didn't whip it loose, if the sun didn't dry and curl it loose, and if the cattle, horses, and the people didn't pull nor chew it loose, then, well, the mesquite shot its roots on down to forty feet below the top of the ground, and on down to fifty feet to where the waters always run under, and the iron grass could not send its roots down so deep to find this water. The mesquite roots went on down as deep as sixty feet under the ground. A wrestling match down under the leaves where nobody ever saw the whole match. Roots choked one another out. Roots made one another grow bigger. Roots killed each other and they sucked from one another. Like vines you see above the ground up in the trees, loving and choking and fighting for the right to breed and the right to go to seed.

We stopped off at little filling stations and bought a sack or two of tobacco, a can or so of snuff for Eddie. We didn't have any more than ten or twelve dollars between us. Jeff had brought some money down, we knew that, but none of us asked him how much he had, and he didn't mention it.

This was a sandyland country, this Pecos County, here all around us. Sandy desert bushes. Sandy cactus of every kind, slim and long, fat and thick, wide and low, high and skinny, curly, twisty, knotty, stickery, thorny, daggery-knifed, razor sharp; hot darts, burning needles, fuzzy needles, cutting edges, stinging leaves, and blistering stems. I saw a whole world of sword and dagger weed and limb— a new world to my eyes. The feel and the breath of the air was all different, new, high, clear, clean, and light. None of the smokes and carbons, none of the charcoal smells of the oil fields. None of the sooty oil-field fires, none of the blackening slush-pond blazes, none of those big sheet-iron petroleum refineries, none of those big smoky carbon-black plants. No smells of the wild oil gusher on the breeze. No smells from that wild gas well blowing off twenty million feet into the good air every day. None of these smells drifted down this far. Odessa was the very fartherest down south that they drifted. Odessa was like the Upper Plains towns, only it was a Lower Plains oil-field town with a blacktop road that carried you over to the east towards Big Spring, Post, Brownwood, Comanche, the papershell pecan rivers that sprouted dancing trees all along back to our east, which Papa told us about by the hour. Oklahoma could get a few drinks of wild breezes under her lip and shake you down almost as many pecans as Texas could, but Oklahoma's river waters didn't give birth nor suck to the trees that rattled full of the Texas papershell pecans. No. Texas water was different, somehow. For black walnuts, maybe Oklahoma waters could beat this world down. But when it came back around to papershell pecans, well, Texas pushed you back off her map. She had the papershells. Lots of nice big fruit meat, a thin shell you can break with your fingers. A big argument about the taste: some say the harder shells have got the best flavor, because all of the good tastes leak out through the thin-skin papery shells.

This was in the river-water land to the east a few miles. Our Pecos County sandy-bush land did not have the floodwater nor the backwater, fishy rivers.

Pecos had one thing. Only one thing. The sun. It didn't have the wind like the upper North and the lower South Plains had. The wind was the stud boss up along those North and South Plains just because there wasn't a high blade of anything up there to argue back. The wind sported free up there. But down here a few miles out from the North and the South Plains, well, this mesquite told the wind it had to slow down when it blew through here on account of the little baby mesquites playing around without looking. On account of the sweetheart mesquites that were out here snorting around, planting down some newer, and burying the older mesquites. It could be wrong to say this Pecos country was the land of the mesquites, a land of lots of mesquites; maybe it was a land that was growed and sprung from just one big tangled mesquite root under its crust. Mesquite got its best meals here; its best drinks come from here; it grew here best of all, in this clear, sunny-bright air. This wasn't oil-field air, not grazing-plains air, not riverbottom air, not swamp air, not mountain air, not the winds nor the breezes off the oceans or the seas. It was pure cactus air, pure stickery air, and air that was breathed in and out by the mesquite trees. Mesquite brush sprouts and wrestles to grow in other parts, but around here it quits being a little old brushy bush and jumps up to be a fine, feathery, damp-looking, willowy tree. Hardier than your willow. Tougher than your other roots.

It was fresh and redly early in the morning of our fourth day that our little T truck rolled us on south to hit this wide, low flat of mesquite country. Papa drove. I sat by him in the cab. Ed and Jeff sang in the back end. Papa said, "It's right real funny how that blizzard turned off into a rainstorm and whipped itself out back up there around Odessa." He sounded pleased, sober, happy with his own self and satisfied with the morning. "Then how it turned around to be so sunny across this flat Pecos country. I feel fine because every turn of our wheels brings us just a few feet closer to Paw's mine. Mighty pretty country right in through here. Oh. Not to change the matter of the conversation, but tell me, when will you and Hell Cat be getting legally wedded and strung?"

"Aww. Dunno. Guess whenever'n all of us digs our faingers down inta this here mine down here. Mmmm. Awful easy ta see how 'twas that Paw Jerry loved it down here in this neck o' the timbers. Perty. Old T truck even likes it better out acrost these desert flats. Listen ta how she runs."

"Likes this mesquite country."

"Wonder what all this here damn 'skeeter brush is good fer. Anything much? Perty ta look at, anyways. Smells jest about like turpentine."

"I've seen the old cowmen use this mesquite for just about everything that you can think of. Back up in Bell County where I cowhanded in my early days, there is a good bit of the right scrubby, scrawny mesquite. Used to dig the roots up and burn them for firewood. Trunks not much good for anything. But the blossom and the bloom makes the best honey you ever did flap your lippers over. Mexicans and Indians, I've seen them lots of times, out picking off the mesquite beans and cooking them. Like your Grandma Tanner always fixed those little red beans she boiled up with good ham hock. Remember? Stiff cornbread?" Papa licked his tongue out over his lips. "Hmmmm? Recall?"

"I'll always remember Grandmaw Tanner's good cornbread. Wonder what th' secret was about it."

"Well, Mammy Ollie could dish it up just as good as your Grandma Tanner could, any old time. Main secret was that she didn't put any sugar in her batter. Maybe an egg or so, which sometimes she did have and sometimes she didn't have, but anyway, she put in lots of salt and left out the sugar. Said that the sugar made cornbread taste too much like oatmeal cookies. She greased her pan with good hot lard, bacon grease, hog lard, whatever kind of grease she had, and she heated her pan in the oven, or up on the stove before she would pour her dough-batter into the pan. She used a good bit of buttermilk."

"Likkum my slikkum. Starvin' me t' death. Keep on."

"Mainest secret, I suppose, was lots of hot lard. And she shoved it into the oven when the oven was scorching hot. And she threw the wood to the fire till she nearly burnt the whole place up, summer, winter, all of the time. She always did say that she had to chase her whole family out from the house before she could bake up good cornbread. But they always came a-running back after a bit when they got the smells of it cooking up their nose holes."

"I 'mem'er. Yeahhhm."

"Always did bake it a long time. Most of us like it good and curly brown all around the edges. Most of us would fight to get the corner piece, or at least an outside chunk."

"I remember. Me, too."

"I guess this was where I learned how to be such a good fighting hand in the first place. Fighting to get the best piece of Mommy Ollie's cornbread. Browny. Crispish. Real hot."

"Big glass o' buttermilk. Yeahhhmmmannn."

"Big slice of green onion—I mean, dry onion. No wonded that Pawpaw Jerry swung onto Mommy Ollie the way that he did. He always did say that it was her cracklin' bread that brought them together and it was this same bread that kept them together. This same cornbread that kept the whole family fighting and growing all of the time. I can just feel it sticking out of my belly button, here, right this minute. Mmmmm. Mmmm. Mmmm." Papa's face lit up with thoughts he was seeing walk acrost the places of his memory.

"Ymmm."

"She was just as crazy, though, about Pawpaw Jerry as he was about her. I don't believe that I've ever seen any two people so well matched, in my whole experiences, as they was, Wood Bean."

"Mmmm. No?"

"She lit up like a lamp, like a lantern, at just about everything he ever did say or ever did do. He lit up the same way when he would get around her. Perfectly mated. Perfectly matched. Perfect pair."

" 'Ceptin'."

"Excepting? What?"

" 'Ceptin' Mommy Ollie nev'r did wanta pack up th' kids an' drift back down here t' th' lost gold an' silver mine. She always did wanta stick up yonder onto a little ole farm. Paw Jerry didn't. He begged 'er t' pack up an' ta come back with 'im th' second time ta open up this here mine, an' Mommy Ollie always did fight back agin it."

"But she did spend, well, about three years down in here with Pawpaw. Part of it just in their covered wagon. Three kids. From the smells coming off of this mesquite brush, I'm starting in to believe I could hold out down here for three years and maybe some more."

"I'd shore like ta take a run at it. Me'n' Hell Cat. I ain't jest shore 'bout how good it'd be t' jest take off acrost this here big mesquite valley t' graze, jest by m'seff. 'Thout no womern."

Such talk went on as we drove a few more miles. Papa changed places with me on the seat cushion. I drove while he looked. He talked while I drove. It was after an hour or so of good traveling that we saw a little painted board sign that read, "Presidio." With an arrow pointing off towards our left. An arrow to our right, down the big tar highway, said, "Alpine, 90 Miles. El Paso, 250 Miles."

"We don't go to Presidio," Papa told me, "but we take the Presidio road. I often heard Paw Jerry speak about Alpine. The Strictler brothers owned that whole town of Alpine. I think there's a college there. Alpine. Yes. It is the road to Terlingua and Presidio that we take. Terlingua is a mining town—has one of the biggest quicksilver mines, Paw said, in the whole world."

Papa inhaled fresh air from off the leaves and the high, skinny, bushy-headed mesquite. I could see by the lights around his eyes that he was reaching out acrost the valley here and touching a whole new world with the tips of his fingers. I had been looking, hunting for this look to come over acrost his face and eyes for more years than one. I breathed in a lung of air every time he took a breath. He breathed in and out in time and rhythm with me.

Every breath we took was a deeper one and every little drop was a sweeter and a cleaner one.

"Just listen to this little rascal run." Papa winked and nodded out the windshield. "Knows very good and well where its little hot nose is trotting to. Do you suppose that by some odd chance this little old truck could be sort of helped along down the road by the very living spirit of Jerry P. his own self, out here somewhere in amongst all of these prickly pear and cactus, thistle, and mesquite trees that he always did love so well? Hey, see, look! Mountains coming up. Dead ahead. No way around them."

CHAPTER 6

RANCH OF THE SUN

Ahead to the south we could see the high, rocky wall of a mountain range stretching acrost the plain. There were humpy yellow foothills in front and higher peaks and ridges beyond, rising up purplish and rose-colored against the sky. The road headed straight into them.

"I seen a few low, scattered mountains out to our west 'bout th' crack o' sun-up this morning," I said. "Nothin' like those, though! Ain't they grand-lookin'? Hey. Boy. Chop me down some o' them there dern-blame clouds an' haul 'em down an' sell 'em. Half solid gold, half solid silver. See?"

"You had better try to see this road—if you could stretch your mind enough to call this dogie track a road. Mountains bigger. Road smaller. That Alpine turn-off back there was the last hard-topped road that we'll be seeing from here on in."

"How far? I wouldn't trust this here low-gear clutch band—brake, neither. How far would ya say?" I ran my eyes out ahead.

"From here to that first humpback rising up there? You can see our road bending up over it, slicing up and off over the west—shady—side. That's about seven more

miles. Hell, I don't know. Your guess is as good as mine.
I never did see such bright yellow, bright red, bright
purple—such clear rose colors. I never did smell any
such clear air in my nose as this. What's that? Right
there." Papa looked out along the trail on his side.

"Jist some feller's mail box. Seen a jillion of 'em, back
up along. Shore ain't no sign of a fence line out here
nowheres, is they? Mail box, little bit rusty, but outside
o' that it's a perty fair mail box. Name scrabbled on it.
Looks ta be Mexican." I looked back to see the sun-up
burn brighter to my left.

"El Rancho," Papa said as he read the black smears of
words. "El Rancho. El Rancho del . . . del what? There
goes his little trail running yonder, see, through the cactus
and the mesquite? El Rancho del . . . del something. I
missed it."

"I seen th' last word. It was S-O-L, *sol*. Hmmmh?
Mountain's runnin' straight at us. Watch it."

"Wonder what *sol* means in Spanish. I guess they talk
lots o' pure Spanish down in here. Paw said he learned
how to rattle it off to a fare-thee-well. El Rancho—that
means ranch."

"Monkey ranch."

"No. Means cow ranch. Cattle ranch. Hog ranch. Any
kind of a ranch except a monkey ranch. I suppose you
could raise plenty of monkeys out here, though. Sure got
plenty of room. Do just about anything you wanted to do
out here. I'm beginning to feel my old daddy Jerry's blood
steaming and juicing all around in my veins. Watch out,
there! What's that? Deer? Hold it. Don't bump him.
Watch that fat sonofagun fly. Do you suppose he's trying
to make fun of our go wagon?"

"Grass over yonder's ticklin' his belly button every
time he makes a jump. Watch 'im. Proud dickins, ain't
he? She? Whatever it is. Our T truck wouldn't run that
fast th' day that it got herded outta th' door of th' dern
factory. Heyehh! Look! They's a whole dern ocean of 'em
over in them high grasses. See 'em? Look right over here
ta my left. See?"

"Poor crazy fools, they're turning right across our trail.
Do they want to get run over and killed? I'd rather wreck
this old truck than scrape such a pretty hide as that. Be
careful. They're sure bouncing across our track. I guess
they just want to rub our radiator and nose around and

find out what our business down here might be, sir. Ohh,
you high-headed sonofagun. Ohh, you proud, proud-
hearted thing, you. I wouldn't harm you for all of that gold
and silver. Run, baby, run! Fly, baby, fly! See him go?"

"Cleared that road like it wasn't even there. Here's
another'n a-comin'. Bing! Blang! Clippity clipp! Where's
old Santy Claws at? Whinnngg! Two more. Three."

"Another one. Heyyy! Look at him go!" Papa turned
his head around to the truckbed and yelled at Jeff and
Eddie. "You get to see these deer just now? Whole army
of them."

"Yeahhhpp!" Jeff yelled back to our cab. " 'Ceptin' they
wasn't deer. Them's pronghorn antelopes. Deer runs bigger'n that. Deer's got different horns on 'em. Counted 'em!
Me'n' Eddie did."

"Thirteen we made it," Eddie yelled. "Awful perty
mornin' back here. How's it look up there in your engine
cab?"

"Fine." Papa smiled back in the breeze. "We're opening
up this front windshield to let the breeze drift in. Say,
how does that mountain there dead ahead of us look to
you navigators?"

"Dern-blame outfit gits bigger ever' time I draw my
bead on it," Jeff laughed. "We got three rims all patch'd
an' booted back here while you 'n' that Wood Shed set up
there 'n' shot the hot airs."

Papa grinned back and said, "Think we'd best let you
take the wheel, Jeff, and circle this thing up this mountain
blocking our trail. Sorry I can't order you a big, wide,
hard-top highway, but this little single-track dirt road will
just have to do you for this trip."

"Pull over and stop, Wood Pecker," Jeff said.

"Ain't no pullin' over on this here rabbit track." I
stepped down on the brake pedal and pulled back the
emergency lever at the same time. "Ya jest stop, er ya jest
go. But ya sure as heck don't do no pullin' out nor no
pullin' over."

"I am sure hoping that we won't meet a mad buffalo
bull face to face down this road." Papa watched me stop.
He stepped down onto the ground and pounded his fists
against his chest and took several sorts of fast exercises,
bending, stretching, shadow boxing, and such. His move-
ments were still as quick as any cat's. "Makes me feel

like a new man. I am going to be lots harder to get out of this country than Paw Jerry was, Jeffrey."

"Done had my extrysizes." Jeff breathed in and looked at all of us. I moved around the radiator feeling of the knots getting bigger on our two front casings. Eddie shot up his hands and fanned a few fast pokes around in my face, and said, "Yeah! Put 'em up, Wood; put 'em up there, boy! I'll jest take you on this mornin' for ten or fifteen rounds of pure ole knockdown, drag-out. I can lick you with a swiveled hand, Wooder Chuck. Gittum up! Gittum up!

> I cain't gittum up
> I cain't gittum up
> I cain't gittit up this mornin'.
> I cain't gittit up
> I cain't gittit up
> I cain't gittit up this morn."

I faked a few little lefts and rights out towards Eddie, and tried to spar with him for a bit. My eyes dropped down to his feet, where Papa had always taught me to look. I noticed what looked like a little piece of glass shining down in the middle of the road, so I swung at him and fell down on my hands and knees. I grabbed the shiny piece and looked it over. It was square in shape and the sun knocked colors of every kind out of it. I jumped up with my find. "Diamond! Diamond! Hey, everybody. I'm a diamond finder."

I skipped off the little dirt road and out onto some short grass around the rocks. Eddie chased in after me yelling, "Lemme see the diamint. Jist ta feel my finger down acrost it. I ain't a-gonna eat the dern thing. Lemme look at it."

I stopped and held out the hunk of glass. "Here. Look at it. Feel on it. Rub it."

"Gotta chunka gray, hard rock all melted down in it, ain't it?" Ed took the rock and held it up into the sun to see the sparkle. "Hmmmpf. That there's somethin'. Never did see no such blazin' fires in just one little bitty chunk o' glass. Wonder what th' devil? Charlie might know. Say, Uncle Charlie. Would you know just what sort of a chunk of glass this here dern thing is, anyhow?"

"Paw Jerry talked about how these mountains down in here are all scattered full of crystal glasses of all kinds. I don't know any too much about crystal, myself. I've seen chunks of it dug out of lead mines and zinc mines over there west of Henrietta. But I sure couldn't begin to tell you what that is Woodrow picked up. Probably look around us here on the sides of this trail and pick up a hatful of glass that will shine like a regular diamond. See if you can see some. I'm busy feeling of the knots in these tires. I want to lay back here on this mattress and look up at the sun and rest my wearies for a few miles, before we try to make it up that mountain."

Jeff looked ahead to the south where the mountain got higher, and said, "Well, all I know is, if they gotta T truck in the world th't c'n make it up 'er, this one here will. How's this here low gear been actin', Woody?"

"Perty rattledy," I told him. "Hey, looky, Ed's done found 'im a hunk o' diamond."

"Sapphire," Ed said. "Bigger'n your'n. Brighter."

"These must surely be those Glass Mountains that Uncle Gid and Paw Jerry always talked of," Papa told us. "Their name on the map is the Glass Mountains."

"This ain't a-gittin' us up over that hump yonder, men. Let's git loaded in an' make a run at it."

"Let's travel." Papa climbed the sideboard rail and lay down on the mattress.

I mounted up with Papa while Eddie trotted along the front fender and picked up one or two more chunks of the Glass Mountain crystal rocks. "I figger m'seff ta be about halfway rich even if I nev'r do lay my han's on no gold mine, ner no silver mine, neither, jest a-runnin' onta this here sapphire glass."

"I sure do get stiff if I ride up in that engine cab for too long a spell." Papa folded his hands back of his head, and looked up into the blue rosy colors of the sky. "I'd like to lay right back here and just dream my way down to the mine spot. You know I never did lay down in a car on a mattress like this and ride along to my heart's content just looking up at the great nowhere."

"How much further we gotta go?" I stood up and held onto the stack of boxes and the sideboard rails. "Got any idea?"

"I'd say a hundred more miles ought to put us down there," Papa told me. He stretched out his full length and yawned. "I'm not just certain."

"A hundred miles'll run us plumb over th' Reo Grandey an' clean inta Mexico," I said.

"I'm sure tuckered out, Wood Bine. What is Jeff doing? Trying to race with a flagtail deer along the road?"

"Jest gittin' 'im a good run at these here Glassy Mountains. An' I wisht ya'd quit callin' this here rabbit trail a road. I didn't know that we'd hit any pine down here this far south. Few jumpin' up along. Perty fair pine, too, looks like."

"Pine will grow at this altitude no matter how far north or south you go. Oh, yes, south Texas is full of pine. Pulpy pine. Call it soft pine. It will be scant and scattering, though, wherever you see it down here. Do you suppose it's necessary for Jeff to jerk and whip this thing around like he is? My burns are sticking me just a bit. I sat up in that front seat too long last stretch. My skin stayed in the same position. When I got out, that's why I had to exercise myself—to limber up a bit. Now I climb back here to lay myself down and I can feel my skin drawing up again."

"Take it easy, up there, Jeffie, Papa's burns hurts 'im." I kept standing up looking with my brush of hair whipping in the warm winds of the morning.

"Oh, let him go. The faster we travel now, the sooner we'll get there. Then it'll all be over. I'll get out and rest myself for a few weeks around my sun pool and heal up as fast as an old leatherback lizard. Let him drive. Ohhhmmm. I'll chew on my tongue. I can stand on my head, if I have to, for two more days. Go ahead, Jeff. Drive right on. Ohhhmmm."

Jeff asked us, "Talkin' ta me? Back there?" The road was steeper now and bent to the left around a cliff wall.

"Keep yer eye on this cussed blame road," Eddie told Jeff. "Not back yanner somewheres er th' other. Up thissa way. Jeff, son," he begged, "watch where ye're a-drivin', please. Fer my old mama's sake that bored me."

"See the whole cussid world from up here," I told them. "First time my britches ever did git up this high. D'ja see them two cows back yonder? Rootin' around down in under them there flat rocks? Never did see no cows a-rootin' like hawgs before this. Yonder's another. See right up along yonder?"

Papa crawled on his all fours over to look out the sideboard cracks. "I think they know what they are doing.

They are flipping those rocks over with their noses, see? They are nibbling that wet grass you find in under there. They stay as fat as a flitter on those little new root sprouts that you see when you turn a big flat rock over. Fat lookers. They're in mighty fine, slick shape. They get their water, too, out of those damp grass roots, and they can get along just fine without a river or a spring or a waterhole of any kind."

"I gotta goofy feelin' that I'm a-gonna be floppin' some ov' them there rocks over an' a-grabbin' my grub down in under 'em, 'fore sa very long, myseff." The T truck was slowing to a walk on the steep road. "I even got a sour, bitter, sweet little feelin' that I'm a-gonna be out there on th' side of this here dern trail a-pushing this here wrack up a slickwall canyon. Fall out, Eddie, an' lay yer shoulder up ag'inst 'er."

We hit the road, fell in behind the truck, and started pushing.

"You ain't a-doin' no more pushin' back there than a dead musketeer could do, Wood Horse," Eddie complained. "Throw your weight up ag'inst it. Don't be 'fraid of 'er. She'll not snap yeh. Pushh 'er! Shove 'er!"

"Don't lose any ground." Papa climbed down through the rear endgate and laid both hands on the backbed along where Eddie and myself were shoving. "Just hold what you have. If we let this thing start in to roll backwards it will roll us plumb to Fort Davis. Push! Push! Onward, gentlemen, always and forever! On and up."

I kept my back against the truckbed and shoved. I turned around and pushed with both hands. My shoes slipped on the small, gravelly rocks in the trail. I skidded over sharp stones. We all worked up a good lather of sweat. I thought we would have to grab rocks and set them down in under the backsides of the wheels to keep the truck from getting a rolling start back down our first mountain. The smoke from the exhaust made my eyes run watery. I felt the sting, too, in my nose. I felt the dust and the dirt settle down all over me, but somehow I liked the feeling of rolling around in this dirt. I slipped down a time or two, but got back up to crawl up the road and to push some more. I saw that the truck was losing its speed, that we couldn't keep it moving up. I grabbed a rock off the side of the trail and stuck it up in under the right rear wheel. My rock was not big enough to keep the truck from rolling back down over it. Papa and Ed shoved as hard frontwards as they could, and the truck was still moving back in my direction. I scrambled over on my hands and knees and grabbed one more rock the size of a brickbat, and jammed this one under the same right rear tire. But the engine would not pull it, and the emergency would not hold it. The truck rolled over my rocks in spite of all the pushing and shoving on all four sides. My piece of crystal rock fell out of my shirt pocket. I made one more fast high dive off to the weedy left side of the road and tore a bigger rock loose. I ran back to throw it down into the rut a foot or two ahead of the wheel rolling down. I pitched my weight against the truck so as to keep it from hitting down against my big rock too hard. Somebody threw a big rock in under the left tire. The truck moved back against this rock first, then pushed this rock on down till it smashed into my rock. The truck stopped for a few seconds and finally came to a dead standstill.

She stood on a steep slant. Radiator steaming over up the front. Smoke boiling out back. Jeff cut the gas and spark down to a slow idle, then he jumped out waving his arms and swearing at the truck. I heard everybody puffing, heaving, getting a fresh breath of air, talking, cursing. They all sounded worried. I could see their shoes and their legs in under the far side of the truck. Four pairs of shoes and legs—one pair too many. One extra pair from somewhere. I saw a pair of clodhopping work shoes. Ed's; two pairs of police shoes, Papa's and Jeff's. I saw one pair of sharper-toed, higher-topped, higher-heeled boots. A bigsized pair of cowman's boots. Fancy trimmed boots, but old boots. Old, dirty, fancy-cut boots. These boots looked older than our shoes. I listened while Papa talked.

"Whatever is left of us, we owe to you." Papa shook hands with the man in the boots.

"Shore do." Eddie shook hands with him.

I stood back to get a look at him. Jeff shook his hand after Eddie and Papa had finished. Jeff said, "Saved our naicks, aw'right, no gittin' aroun' that. Mucha 'blige. I never'da thought that secha a little light cowpony could ever pull a truck up a mountain."

I walked up at Jeff's back and said, "Hi."

"Buenos días." He touched his finger to a hat that was just as dusty as his pants and boots. His hat was the same color as the dirt. He stood up several inches above Papa's

head, and Papa was an inch and three quarters taller than
Jeff. He shook my hand without a squeeze. He looked
down at my hand like he was afraid he would hurt me.
He took one or two fast looks around at all of us. His
face was full and his neck set thick, with a silkish-looking
red, white, and green kerchief tied with a peach seed under
his chin. His leather hatstrap swung down past his ears
and knotted on his shirt just below his kerchief knot. The
strap from his hat ran in a little knot through a dry
cactus stem which he slid up and down as he felt of the
strap and talked. He spoke to a middle-sized paint pony
standing up the trail, snorting and looking down his lariat
rope looped around his saddle horn and tight as a fiddle-
string all the way down to the brassy knob on our radiator.
The stranger smiled in under the shadows of his hat at
the loop of his rope around our radiator cap. He'd slung
a second loopknot around our crank. His pony stood
spraddle-legged, bug-eyed, and snorty, up ahead of us,
ears straight to the clouds, nose quivering, tail-switching,
skin wiggly—prouder, maybe, than the whole gang of
us looking at our old cripply T truck.

"Good boy." I spoke out towards his pony. "Keep a
tight holt on that there dern rope. Good boy."

"No sabe inglés." The big man smiled first down on top
of my head, then up along the tight rope to the saddle
horse. *"Español."*

"Ah." Papa walked up towards the horse. "Good boy.
Cooopee. Cooopee."

"Amigo." The big man nodded at Papa. "No. You
scare. Hoss jump. Car fall. Rope slip. Nooo. You back.
Me hoss."

Papa walked back, saying, "You're right, all right."

"Me right." He looked down at his greenish, heavy
shirt, at his blue cotton britches, down to his boots, and
said, "Hoss right."

All of us laughed a bit, then we cut our laughing off.
He was rolling a sack tobacco cigarette with one hand,
licking it up its side, and looking scared as a kitten around
at our truck.

" 'Smatter?" Jeff walked over and patted the truck door
with his hand. He turned around to face the cowboy.
"What's wrong?"

"Why you truck come?"

"Why?" Eddie spoke out. "Who's gon'ta keep us out?"

"Easy, Eddie Stone," Jeff said. "Yeah, who says we cain't?"

"Jeffrey." Papa walked in between Jeff and the cowhand. "Why truck come?" He kept his eyes away from all of us.

"Truck?" Papa asked him. It was nearly impossible for any of us to make out what the man was talking about. We could understand his Mexican lingo just as good as we could his English. He spoke in such a deep chesty voice that I lost track of all of his words.

"Why come us here, he's askin' us," I told them.

"*Sabe español?*" he asked me.

"Nawp," I said. "Few words. You talk. I listen."

"You de poleezia."

"I'm one." Jeff waved his hand. "Y' need a poleece officer?"

"No. I got desert. No need poleezia." He nodded off down the side of the cliffrock. "Need cigaretta. Need tequila. Needa señorita. No need de poleezia."

"He's not. He's not a policeman." Papa smiled back at Jeff by the truck.

"He quit 'is job," Ed told the man.

"Plays th' fiddle," I told him.

"Feedle?"

"Violin. See? Like this." I acted like a man sawing a bow on some fiddle strings. "Violin. Savvy? Violin?"

"Veeoleen? Ahhh! *Sí, sí, sí.*"

"Me, see, guitar? Like you play this way. Sing thissa way."

"*Guitarra.* Ah! *Músicos.*"

"I dance, like this." Papa jigged a step for the man to look at and to smile at. "Big dancer. Me. See? You dance?"

"Ohhh!" He tilted his head back to smile some broader. "*Sí. Sí.* Ah! Why you *músicos* come here? No find people here. See? You go back. No people here. People back Alpine. People back Eagle Pass. People back El Paso del Norte. No people this place. Nooo. You truck dead here. You truck no go. *Montañas* big worse down this way. Beeg up. Beeg down. See?" He moved his hand up and down in front of his nose to show us what he meant. It didn't take any more wiggling to make all of us understand what he was getting at.

"We not look for people," Papa told him. "No people."

"No people? What you look, then?"

"We look silver," I told him.

"*Plata? Buscaráis?*" He puffed his cigarette on his lip in the dust. "*Plata? Oro.* Hah!"

"Gold, too," Papa told him.

"Hah. *Músicos? Oro? La plata? Sí, sí, sí, sí.*"

"How much do we owe you for roping us with your pony and holding us from rolling?" Papa held a greenback dollar in his hands. "Money? How much?"

"I no money." He looked at the bill in Papa's fingers. "No spend here. Beeg desert."

"Crazy fool!" Jeff felt of the tires and said, "I'm glad you cain't understan' what I'm a-callin' ya. Any man that can't find no way ta make use of money ain't got good sense. How we gonna git on up ta the top o' this here bluff's what I'm a-wantin' ta know."

"Me, too," Eddie spit out. "Shore ain't about ta make no trip nowheres on these here onionskins we got fer tars. Mebbe ya know of some way t' help us t' git on up. Huh?"

"Pony me. We tak truck you. We top road, see? You ride me frand? Road go thees way. Presidio?"

"Friend ride towards Presidio?" Papa asked him. "You get us up to the top of this mountain and we'll haul ten of your best friends to the Presidio road."

"*Bueno.*" He motioned for all of us to crank up the truck and to throw our shoulders against the sides and ends. He whistled in an odd, high way up to where his horse kept the rope tight. I thought he would walk up and mount into the saddle to help the pony pull us up the sandy grade. But he yelled some words up to the horse, and put his shoulder to the truck to push with the rest of us. Jeff sat in the cab till Ed turned the crank over and the engine started, then Jeff walked along pushing his left hand down on the clutch pedal. He held his door open and steered the wheel with his right hand, and pushed against the door hinge all he could to help.

The pony dug his hooves down and ploughed up the road as he walked up the hill. He snorted louder, he shook his head, he switched his tail, he kept that lariat as tight as one of my guitar strings. The cowboy spoke nice and easy to the horse. The horse neighed and nickered and rolled his eyes back to his master. We eased along slow, creaking like a covered wagon in a swampy mudbog. We shoved and we pushed as hard as we could, and we counted every weed and bush on up to where the road leveled off in a sharp curve around to our left.

The man was in the saddle as soon as we got to the leveling-off place. He flipped in his rope and flipped his cigarette down onto the road. Jeff yelled above the motor, "Wher'bouts d'ya say them friends o' yours is at? Hey, Charlie, hey, Wooderow, pile in back there."

"We're already aboard." Papa looked out from his back end. "Your friend? Where?"

Our cowboy rode past us and whistled over into the bushes down the west slope. "Heyyyhh! Huuyyhh!" he called.

I watched a little boy with a curly head of hair run out from the weeds and up the hill. At my first glance I thought him to be somewhere around nine or ten. A loose cotton shirt of old, faded green, the short-sleeve slipover kind, fell down over his pants, which were made of the same kind of sacking cloth a good long time ago. His pants were held around his waist by a slipstring tied in a bowknot and were dyed a dark rosy purple, faded now to no more than gray, ash-colored cloth with a little tracing of the reddish blue still in it. Around his knees these colors were rubbed and washed out even lighter. He ran to the rear end of the truck and I stood by the rod and helped him in as the cowboy lifted him up to me. The boy's hair had been cropped so close to his head that you could see the white of his skin underneath every hair. I noticed, too, that his skin was hard and tough-looking. He seemed to be all full of pep and bounce. He was making a noise like a truck engine. Then he jabbered out a long mouthful of words into the weeds and a little girl ran out of the brush. The cowhand kissed her and held her up to where I could get a good straight look into her face and her eyes.

She was younger than the boy—her brother, I guessed he was. An old bandanna handkerchief of the dime kind was tied around her hair for her shawl. Her blouse was gone, but her skirt was made to wear a blouse with some of these days, and the top part was cut out big at the arm and neck holes. The top part of this skirt looked like netting or cheesecloth—I couldn't quite made it out—while the lower half was stitched and cut out of a blackish, beat-out kind of sateen, or some kind of an old velvet. Our little lady passenger walked over, prissy and proud as she could, to sit down and hug onto her little green, raggedy dolly wrapped in a lady's fancy, lacy, white hanky. She had an ounce of fear in her eyes somewhere, but one look back at the cowman in his saddle, waving his hat in the air, washed all of this nervous, scared look out of her eyes. I saw by the damp dust sticking around her eyes and cheeks that she had been doing a good bit of crying in the last hour or so.

The saddle pony trotted back and forth acrost the road several times till the rider yelled for us to go ahead. We rolled down the next grade with our motor off to save gas. We heard Eddie and Jeff yip like coyotes up in their driving cab. It tickled the little boy and the little lady, but they didn't let loose with any more than just a wide-eyed look at one another that faded over into a smile after a time. The rider on the horse tore up alongside us to tell us, "The boy he iss Carlos. The leetle girl she iss Rosalita. You see road say Presidio, you stop; Carlos know. Rosalita know. They show you one road you get to Terlingua. They no show, you get keel."

All of us kept our eyes on him as he reined his pony up to a stop in a cloud of boiling dust. He stood close to the steep bank of a rock cliff which had no floor, no bottom, no valley, no earth in down beneath it. Desert. Clouds puffy and smeary. Purple-blue red mountains a thousand miles in back of his elbows. The colors of his hat, kerchief, shirt, pants, saddle, boots, lariat, all mixed up to blend into the same color of the little boy's finger helping his Rosalita hold her hanky around her doll. Rosalita called out first to the cowboy and his horse, *"Adiós, Jesús!"* Carlos was louder: *"Jesús, amigo, adiós!"* We watched this dusty rider on his dusty horse for the next ten or fifteen minutes standing there on the flat bend in that road, up against the sky range, waving his big hat from side to side at us. He jumped off into the brush along the lower slope to the west and we never did catch sight of him nor his rope nor his little dirty pony from that day to this.

Jeff threw the transmission into low gear and let the motor hold back the weight of the truck. We rounded a dozen or so twisty curves. Every foot of the trail got rockier and sharper. We got down to a long, straight stretch that shot ahead of us for several miles. Papa looked at Rosalita and he eyed Carlos up and down. He watched Carlos play with Eddie's big Boy Scout knife that had fell out of Ed's pocket.

"Carlos!" Sitting on Papa's mattress with her dolly, Rosalita spoke off a great long string of words to warn her brother about such a dangerous cutting weapon.

With his back to all of us, Carlos lifted his head and said a few words back to Rosalita. He spoke these words like he was talking to a bird with a broken wing in his hands. Easy. Tender-sounding. Not very loud. But the sound had a way of ringing up and out above the rattle and clatter and the puffy sounds of our smoky T truck.

Only one thing caught my ear in any special way, and that was the way Rosalita made her voice sound. Her words rang out so clear, so plain, so easy. Loud or soft had nothing to do with it. Carlos's voice had this same pitch to it. The only little difference that I noticed about Carlos and Rosalita both was that they had such an old, grownup look and sound about them. Like they had been making their own livings now for a good big number of years. Like they had been going on their own. Like they were watching and protecting us, instead of the other way around. Self-certainty. Something. I didn't know just exactly what it was that I heard in their words and saw in their eyes.

Papa put his finger up to his lips and shushed me to not make any noise, to keep quiet. He wanted to let the two kids get to know us in their own free time, when they got good and ready. Carlos played all around over the truckbed. He climbed boxes, he crawled on the floor, he mounted up to the crosswoods of our sideboards. He acted out all kinds of games in words I didn't savvy. He took spells of frowning, wrinkling up his face, then spells of busting out into big wide smiles and funny whooping laughs. He yelled acrost at Rosalita once in a while where she laid her doll down to hum it to sleep on the mattress. She rubbed, she sung, she hummed, she stroked and patted the doll, and that just about covered her play games for these first few rocky miles.

I say rocky miles, because this straight slant of good narrow clay road was full of the sharpest jaggery rocks we had run over so far in our lives, any of us. The bounce of the truck jiggled and wiggled everything so bad that my whole body felt like a pan of coldset jelly bumping down a long road. I could tell by Papa's face and hands that the bounce was dealing him misery. His burns pained him so much that he had to keep his eyes shut to keep from break-

ing out and crying. Carlos looked at Papa and his face
clouded over sad. Rosalita looked up and down at Papa,
then ducked her head down the other way towards her
doll.

I walked back to a beer case and got out a box of salty
crackers in a blue waxy wrapper. I dropped a few into
Carlos's hand and a few down between Rosalita's knees
on her lap. Carlos ate his up first, then he clumb the crosspieces of the sideboards again and looked at the box in
my hand. I handed him three or four more. I tossed the
whole box over near Rosalita's feet. Carlos climbed up
higher on the sideboards to get his chin up over the top
rail. He made all kinds of sounds in the blowing of the
wind. Just as he whooped and whistled his loudest, one
of our tires blew out, with such a loud bang that Carlos
jumped from the sideboard over onto the mattress. Rosalita
hid her face on his shoulder while he hugged both arms
around her. The truck bucked wilder and rougher for a
ways, but the grade was not any too steep. Jeff used the
reverse gear pedal for a brake and let the engine slow the
truck down to a stop.

"Think y' was shot?" I touched Carlos and Rosalita on
their heads. "Wasn't no gun."

"Don't be scared." Papa rubbed the kids on the shoulders to make them feel good. "Don't be afraid. It isn't anything. There. There, now. It wasn't anybody shooting at
you."

"No?" Carlos kept his face hid in Rosalita's long hair.

"Nooo?" Rosalita asked us. She hugged her doll.

"Tire blow'd out." I knelt down and petted them. "Tire?
You know? Big rock booomp into tire, see? Tire break
make big noise. Blooommm! We fix quick. You bring
knife, Carlos. You help fix. C'mon. Rosalita, hold y'r dolly
real warm jist a minute, see. We go fix. C'mon, Carlos.
Papa, toss a big spare tire down so's we c'n screw it on
in nothin' flat. C'mon. Jump down here, Carlioo."

Carlos jumped down barefooted and ran all around the
truck with Ed's knife in his hands. I made a motion at
Eddie to let Carlos play with the knife. The blades were
all shut. He couldn't cut his fingers or stab anybody with
it. Ed just looked at the knife and said, "Hmmmffffhhh. So.
This is where'bouts m' knife got off to. Wello, Carlio,
thank y' fer a-findin' it fer me. Guess y' c'n help us t' fix

up this here dern ole flat tar with it. How old of a man are you, anyhow, Carlos? How old?"

Ed talked while I tossed down the best of our three spare tires. Ed caught the heavy tire and rim on his shriveled hand and threw it down onto the ground by the right front wheel where Jeff had the jack slid in under the axle. Carlos looked at Eddie first in a pitying way, then his eyes turned prouder as he watched Eddie handle the heavy tire and rim. Carlos squatted down and felt the spare with his fingers while Ed and Jeff jacked up the wheel. Carlos kept his eyes on the screws and gear wheels of the jack and smiled to see how the main stem turned and went up with every turn of the cranking handle in Jeff's hands. He scraped his knife around and around on the rim of the spare and went through all of the motions of helping to get the flat off and the good tire on.

Papa put some chunks of cheese with the blue box of crackers I'd tossed down to Rosalita. I stepped back to take a quick look in at Rosalita through the sideboards. She chewed away with a big double jawful of the sticky cheese and dry crackers, and she picked up little flakes that dropped onto the floor and put them back into her mouth, talking to her doll. I had to climb up and get out the canvas water bag with the big picture of a camel printed on it. Rosalita took a long swig out of the mouth end of the wet bag, and she seemed to love the cooly cool feel and touch of the water that soaked out through the thick canvas to keep the bag cooler. She rubbed her fingers over it. She touched her cheek down against it. Then I watched her lift her doll till the water rubbed on the doll's forehead. She smiled at me and laid her doll down on Papa's mattress to change its diaper.

I swung out over the end of the truckbed and passed the bag all around. Carlos washed his mouthful of cheese and cracker crumbs down with three great long man-size swigs. He watched us work at the tire till it was all fixed. He helped Eddie to heave the flat one back up onto our stack of tires a few feet from where Rosalita sat and hummed. He made friends with all of us and we rubbed our hands on his shorty crop of hair to laugh. Jeff asked Carlos, climbing up acrost our front fender, "How old are you?"

"*Diez*," Carlos told Jeff.

"Big man," Papa said. "How old is Rosalita? Sister?"

"*Cinco*." Carlos let his feet drag down off the fender.

"Sister? Rosalita?" I asked him.

"Seestaire? *Sí*," he told me.

"Carlos," Papa asked him again, "tell us about this big place here, El Rancho del Sol. Who is this fella, Sol?"

"*Sol*. Beeg fella. Ha ha ha," Carlos laughed at us.

"Who?" I put in.

"Yeah, who's this here Sol feller?" Jeff asked. "Mighty big chunk o' land fer one feller t' be ownin'. Sol. Sol."

"*Del sol*." Carlos shook his head to try to keep from laughing and making a fool out of all of us. "*Del sol*. See? Look. Looook. Ooop. Ooop. *Sol*."

"Clouds?" Papa asked him. "The sky? The moon?"

"Nooo." Carlos pointed his finger straight into the sun and shaded his face, flat-handed, while he talked. "*Sol*. What you say? Soon. Sooone. Zune. I no talk."

"The sun," Papa nodded at Carlos.

"*Sí, sí, sí*." Carlos nodded. "*Sí, sí, sí*."

"The ranch of the sun?" Papa kept on.

"*Sí*."

"It is." Papa smiled all around at the mountains, now on all four sides of us, acrost the flats, the mesas, the slopes, the high-rock slick-off cliffs, the bright-colored shadows on the sunny valleys and the shaded sides of the cold-rock canyons. Papa repeated the words after Carlos, "It is a big place. A big ranch, Carlos. And there couldn't be a better name to suit this whole, big, fine, lost world down here."

"Gotta git a-movin'." Jeff knew that Carlos didn't understand half of the words that Papa was talking to him. "I ain't a-wantin' th' sinkin'-down sun t' ketch me out here on this dern-blame ranch."

"How fer's it to where'bouts yer Perseedio road comes in?" Eddie asked Carlos.

"Heysoos tell me almos' wan hoonder mile. I ride here? Theesa seat? You drive?" He stood by the cushion and pointed in the door as Jeff climbed in. "Me? You? Hey?"

"D'want no kids up here a-pesterin' me," Jeff said. "Need a lot o' elbow room ta make this here rattrap hang onta this here dern road. 'Sides, ya'll burn yer bare feet up here on this here red-hot 'xhaust pipe. Woodrow throwed away m' good floorin' boards. Throw m' truck away if I'd jest give 'im one half of a chanct. No. Jump on back there. Hurry. Ain't got all day an' all night ta set here. 'T won't be too many hours till dark now. Run off down one of these here dern bluffs an' kill th' whole shebootle of us."

Carlos stood back and let the truck get a pretty fair start-off down the hill. He tossed his head sideways while Rosalita screamed over the end-gate board at him. Papa sat up on his mattress and watched Carlos. I stood by Rosalita's side and looked back to where he was clowning around. He ran like a brush rabbit and caught ahold on the rear crossboard. He pulled his feet up off the road and swung down like a monkey up a tree. It was Papa's yelling that got Carlos to let Rosalita and myself pull him in by his hands.

I don't know what a railing Rosalita dished out on the head of Carlos. I know that it was the loudest and the longest bawling-out which my memory could fish up to my shores. He didn't say one single word. Not one. He crawled up to the top of our stacked boxes and lay flat on his tummy. He kept his eyes and face dead ahead into the radiator steam and facing the wind. He kept his feet folded crosswise and waved his bare toes around in the air. He made every kind of a sound that our motor made; he went like a tire blowing out; he went like the birds he saw fly and run past; he went like the deer, like the antelope, like the squalling of the cougar, like the scream of the trapped panther, like whole flocks of crows, like the hissing and the whistling sounds of every kind of a dweller in the rock and in the brushy patch. Papa drifted off to a little snatch of sleep to the tunes of Carlos on the stack of boxes. Ed and Jeff laughed and teased back and forth with Carlos because his chin rested on the topside of their driving cab straight up above both of their heads. He beat on the cab top with his hands like a wild skin drum. He kept Rosalita shaking her head and saying to her dolly in her lap, *"Carlos loco. Poco loco. Carlos loco. Loco Carlos."* And other words that I could not make out.

Our sun went towards the house in the west while we headed on to the place of the south. We saw the colors turn stronger. Lights done dances in the rocky places. I saw steeper cliffs. I smelled higher airs. I talked in the upper breezes. My ears and my head rang like Job's bells on the hills of Egypt. My eyes worked so hard that my hands got tired of pointing. I never saw any such colors as these. This was the big sunny house of the cowboy, of Rosalita, of Carlos, and of the sun itself.

Papa got him a good two-hour snatch of sleep with his eyes up towards the sky. The air felt just as light, just as

free, just as clean as the blue sky, everywhere except for
the little bubble of dust we kicked up with our truck tires
along the ruts. I didn't know the names of any of the
mountains. Every mile we drove to our south the humps
got more purple, bluer, greener, rockier, and higher. I saw
cloud rings hang up along the tops of every mountain, and
lift like your nightgown when the sun heats got hotter. The
lower peaks got their cloudy rags stripped off over their
heads like babies in the morning. But the older and higher
mamas and papas all around us kept their foggy duds on
for a few hours after the smaller humps had been undressed.

I heard Jeff telling Ed up front, "Took Mommy Ollie an'
Paw Jerry, an' Claude an' Gid an' me more'n three months
t' make it down here'n that there wagon from Bristow t'
Study Butte. Paw told me I could drive in a truck, er a
car, either one, in a day's time, over as much dern country
as him an' Mama made in a week 'n' a half. Didja ever see
sech perty canyons an' mountains as these, Eddie boy?
Cain't say that I could blame Paw Jerry fer a-likin' to live
down here as good as he did. Can you?"

"Nawp, cain't. Perty a spot as I'd ever want to set my
foot down on."

"Who d'ya think that there cowboy was back down th'
road? Had a little bit of an odd look about 'im. Think so?"
Jeff asked Eddie.

"Did, at that. I took a good look, an' couldn't see no
kinda badge er star er nuthin' on 'im. I'm a-tryin' t' guess
whose coupla brats them is we got on back yunner. Glad
whenever we let 'em off 'n' git rid of 'em. Apt t' git inta a
packa trouble a-packin' kids off down this goat road, 'thout
ever askin' who they b'long to. I wish Charlie 'n' Woodrow wouldn't of been s' damn quick t' tell 'im we'd ride
'em down t' th' Perseedeo turn-off, wherever th' heckfire
an' holy blazes th' Perseedeo turn-off is, anyhow. Have a
wreck an' ya'd have every Maixic'n in these mountains
out knifin' f'r us. They's no guarantee th't we're gon'ta be
able t' git this ole crate up that naixt steep grade yonn'r.
Stop right this minute an' set 'em both off at th' side of
this here trail's what I'd like t' see us do. They'd be bett'r
off. Some Maixic'n er some Indyun'd run onta 'em an'
pick 'em up 'n' git 'em home lots better'n we can."

Back on the backbed, we heard Jeff spit off to the dagger
weeds on his side, and say, "Ya got that figger'd out

'zactly right, Eddie Stoner. They's not a more dangerous damn thing in this world than this here old wrack of a truck. No high gear, no brakes worth a dern, no tires, no nuthin'. When we git pushed up t' th' top o' this here grade, maybe we oughta put 'em both off."

Rosalita and Carlos walked alongside the truck and piled loose rocks into the ruts back of our wheels while Jeff walked along with his left hand on the low-gear pedal and his right hand holding the driver wheel. Jeff cussed. Eddie cussed. Papa grunted and wiped off hot sweat with the back of his hand. I pushed at the back end. Carlos and Rosalita tossed their rocks; the bigger ones he handled, the littler ones that held the bigger ones, she tossed in. This made it easy for the rest of us to set our backs and shoulders against the truck and push lots harder. It took us a good half an hour to crawl like a tumbler bug up this sharp-rock, single-rut road. It wound off to the east around the hump two times, then ran off down again around the westerly side of an easterly hill, so steep and down such a long grade that, somehow, we couldn't take time out to stop at the top. Jeff jumped back in the cab and Rosalita jumped ahead of Carlos onto the driver's cushion at Jeff's side. Somehow, Jeff had the idea that everybody was on board. He let the truck coast down the straight slope for a distance of several hundred yards. Eddie made a run, but he ran too slow. Papa made a chase, but he quit too soon. I ran on ahead of Papa and Ed, but the truck traveled faster than my heavy shoes would let me.

I could see Carlos and Rosalita's hands wave and point out the cab door back up the trail to where we walked. Jeff finally got the drift of what they were trying to tell him, and stopped the truck. He shooed the kids down out of his cab telling them, "Too dangerous, too damn dangerous. Git yer tail down out o' here. Ya'll git yer feet burnt. Git her head broke in. Truck's too dangerous for them kids, Wood Saw," Jeff told me. "That's all they is to it. Ever' Maixican down here'll be a-trailin' us down with knives an' guns, too, if we miss a bend an' bust these here kids up. It's ninety more mile fr'm here down t' where they turn off. Road's a gittin' crazier by th' minute. I say they'd be better off if we left 'em out here at some ranch th<u>e</u>n up here a-climbin' all aroun' over this damn old truck, actin' up like it's a-doin'. Forty mile more'n we ain't gonna have a damn low gear ner a damn bit o' brake, neith'r one. I'm a'ready a damn good notion t' turn this here thing around an' burn 'er ass off a-gittin' back up to my dep'ty job, an' my Reenie Gal. These kids ain't a-thinkin' 'bout how dangerous this damn road is. Gittin' dangerouser ev'r foot o' the way. I can't haul 'em, Wood. I cain't. My conshence jest won't let me do it. I ain't a-wantin' to kill 'em. Dammitall. Maybe we'll run into someone that can take 'em off our hands. Rather turn 'em over to some family, with a few cans o' food in their hands than ta find th' whole mess of us off tangled up around some o' these mesquite trees at th' foot o' this here canyon. They're jest little kids, they don't know how bad this here road is, ner how bad this here truck's a-drivin', ner a damn thaing about it."

I leaned on the door by Rosalita and Carlos and said: "That cowboy back there, what was it that he told us? Said, if Carlos here an' Rosy shows us th' right road, we might by some accident roll down ta Terlingua alive an' a-snortin'. Elsewise, well, elsewise, said he couldn't swear jist what shape we would be in when th' Indians found us, like ya say, all down off acrost this here naixt big canyon like trap bait scatter'd. Ask Papa. Ask Ed. Ask these here dagger weeds out here. Which road, I mean, which trail is it that ya take ta git over inta Terlingua, an' on over into Study Butte, an' on down an' over an' a-twistin' all around off down in towards th' Medicine Springs? Ask 'em. Ask. Holler at these here weeds right over here. Holler an' ask yer one-armed cousin, here, Sir Eddie Moore. I'll ask ya, m'self, Eddie Stoner!"

"Hell's bells!" Ed told me. "Y' do talk crazy! Ship you back up t' th' insane asylum. I don't even know what th' holy blazes it is ye're a-tryin' ta make me say back ta ya."

"Rosa Reeta," Papa asked her, pointing and looking out over the valley, "which road? You know, Reeta? Which road? See, there, down yonder? Which road do we turn on down there in the valley? You tell me? Huhhhmm?"

Rosalita walked over to the west slope of the downward hill and smiled out down over the tops of the trees, bushes cactus, prickly pear, thistle, stinging weed, yucca, where no human eye could see even the faintest hint of a track nor road rut. She shook her head, "Nooo!" And she nodded her head, "Sí. Sí. Sí, sí, sí!" She opened her eyes wide when she said "Sí, sí, sí," but she squinted and frowned like she was burning with branding irons when she pointed to the

"Nooo, no, no, no" tracks and the *"No, no, no, no"* trails
and the *"No, no, no"* paths left by wild animals trotting
back and forth to fight around the mudbank of some vol-
cano-looking water hole. *"No . . . sí!" "No, no . . . Sí, sí!"*
She acted like two different girls, one very proud and
happy, the other one sad, hurt, crippled, miserable, frowning, twisting, aching, and paining. She fell down like a
dead girl when she got through with her speech. Carlos
said something and she bounced up onto her feet again
in less time than a rabbit could hop a low log.

"Ever drive a truck?" Jeff yelled out his door towards
where Carlos leaned with his arms folded, against the front
fender. "Truck like this'n?"

"No." Carlos pooched his lips and shook his head side
to side. "No. I ride truck lawts time. I no seet de seat. I
ride. Weeth my pappa. Weeth my mamma. I no seet de
seat."

Eddie and Papa helped Rosalita to climb back up into
the back bed to sing to her dolly some more. I mounted
up onto the driving cushion with Carlos in between Jeff
and me, on the side near the red-hot exhaust pipe.

"Be real careful," Jeff said to Carlos, "that ya don't
burn yer foot. Hot pipe. See?" Jeff nodded down at the pipe
and let the truck get started once more down the grade.
He made faces like your skin is blistering, burning, hurting, throbbing, and aching.

Carlos nodded and looked out the windshield. *"Sí. Sí. Sí."*

I laughed under my breath as Jeff drove along and
talked to Carlos. I could feel the double-hot heat from the
red exhaust pipe just under my shoe soles. The pipe had
not been so bad back driving through our Pampa plains
blizzard, nor even through the Lower Plains rains, but it
set up a fevery heat here on the mesquite-tree desert.

Jeff rubbed Carlos's knee and said, "Ye're shore gon'ta
make a big, fine truckdriver one of these days, Carliosa.
Ever see this road here before now?"

"Sí." Carlos rubbed his hand on Jeff's steering wheel and
talked as he looked. *"Sí.* Beeg trook she hurt my mooth-
aire. Here. Dees road."

"Truck? Yer mama?" I asked him, "How?"

"Mothaire wade. Mothaire wade de beeg wataire. I ride
de mothaire. De mothaire she ride me de her back. See?
Thees way? She poot me in de beeg trook like thees trook,
see?"

"Yeah." Jeff drove through limbs and bushes so thick on both sides that it kept all of us craning, twisting our heads, trying to see which set of running tracks to steer down.

"What about y'r mammy?" Jeff took the ruts Carlos pointed out.

"Mother?" I took a sniff out my door to taste the heavy smells of sappy breezes from out in the brushwood. I saw cactus plants and cactus trees, low, fat, high, skinny, twisty, straight, curlicue, flat, daggery, and every other shape you can call to your mind, all so thick along the ruts of sand that the thorns rubbed up against our truck fenders and backbed as we moved past each patch of it. I said, "My mommy she got hurt perty bad, too. One time. House burn. Mommy hurt bad."

"You mothaire?" he asked me. "Burrrn bad?"

"Yeah," I said.

"Me mothaire, she hurt. She ride de beeg trook." He kept still a little while, then he went on to say, "She too beega fulla. Mothaire tell me how many ride beega trooka."

"How many?" I asked him.

"She tell me. Seexistey. Seexistey-two—seexistey-nine. She say too many come in de trooka. I see de beeg crowd. See? Lika dees. Lika beega boxa fulla de, what you say, fulla de snaka, snaksas."

"Box full o' snakes?" Jeff asked. "On a truck?"

"Means they's piled in it jist like a barrel fulla rattle-snakes," I said. "Huh, Carlos?"

Carlos jabbed Jeff in the ribs, to tell him, "Hey. Theesa track. Theesa one. No theesa one. You break you trook you ride deesa one."

"What'cha gonna do, Wood Ridge?" Jeff looked out at all of the limbs tangling around our heads. "Take 'is word fer every turn o' the road? Let a dang-blame snotty-nose kid give us orders on what ta do every step o' th' way?"

"Carlosy is th' boss man right now," I laughed. "Might stop'n ask that there bunch o' wild rabbits over yonder. Mebbe them desert burros a-feedin' yonder could tell ya. Don't ask me. I'm jist a-settin' here an' a-thankin' that there cowhand back yonder fer a-sendin' these here two kids down here to show us how ta turn an' go. Hadn't of been fer him an' fer these two squirts, we'da done been piled up with th' dried bones on th' hot rocks. Ask Carlos. Go where'bouts he tells ya ta go. He's th' navygator, fer's I'm concerned."

"Kind of a truck'd y'r mommy ride on?" Jeff asked Carlos.

"Trooka she go de beega field. Beeg, beeg field. You savvy? Beetsa? Meechigan? Beetsa."

"Beat?" I thumped my finger against the back of his head two or three times, and asked him, "Beat? Beat? Thissa way?"

"No. Beetsa. Beetsa grow beeg. Beega leafa. Deega beetsa. You 'stan'?"

"Aw," Jeff said. "Beets? Red? Pickle beets? Red? Yeah. Like Skinny Mammy puts up ever' year! Why, shore! Picklin' beets."

"*Si.*"

"Red beets?" I asked him.

"*Blanco.*" Carlos nodded his head to mean, yes. "De beetsa she iss de *blanco*. White. De sam you skin. *Blanco.*"

"White beets?" I nodded. "White beets. Yeah."

"De Meechigan."

"Michigan. Yeah," I told him. "Never was up to Michigan. Jist heard of 'em. Yer mammy, she dug up th' beets, hey?"

"Two tam. T'ree tam. She ride de trook, she deega de beetsa. She come backa. See. She wade de beeg waterrr? Beeg reevaire, you say, you call de Rio Grande, Savvy?"

"What'n th' hell didjer maw wade acrost th' river fer, in th' first place?" Jeff asked Carlos. "She crazy?"

"She no stay here de Texas side." Carlos told us this with his throat choked full of tears and his words fell out over his lips as slow as waters splashing down past the big rocks. " 'Trol man, he come. Mothaire she roon. Fathaire he roon. Fathaire he fall down. Fall down de beeg wataires. Beega mud. Beega sand. Fathaire he ride my leetle seestaire opp, oop, oop on heesa backa. Lika theesa. I no see leetle seestaire more. I no see fathaire more. New fathaire he come, he keesa my mothaire. He stay weetha me. Mothaire she geeta baby, see, theesa way, baby?"

"Hhhmmm." Jeff cleared his throat and drove on. "Hmmm."

"I be dern." I tried to say something. "Mmmm."

"Yesss." Carlos talked with his eyes wet and his head down.

" 'N'en what?" Jeff asked him.

"My fathaire he geet in de beeg trook. My mothaire she

geet in de beeg trook. I lay down in de beeg trook. She go
long tam. I hear de lady she cry. De keedsa alla cry. De
papa he cry. De mothaire she cry. Man he no stoppa
trook. We cry, see, we mak de beeg sound. We singa
songa, see. We talk trooka man, we tell, 'Ohhh, stoppa.
Ohh, stoppa. I sick. You sick. Everybody she sick. I need
eata. You need eata.' Trook man he say, 'I no can stoppa
deesa trooka tella we geet de placea you calla de Meechigan.' Lang tam. Four day. Week go by. We needa wataire,
we needa cigaretta, needa fresh air, see. Alla seeka. Alla
fall down. Alla roll onna me. Mothaire she keesa me.
Mothaire she keesa fathaire. She say belly maka bad sick.
She hot. Fathaire hold weeth me my mothaire down de
trook floor. I hear trook man say, 'I stop I buy gas, you
get out de trook de p'tol man he mak you go beeg jail.'

"My fathaire tak my mothaire, my fathaire tak me, we
geet off de trook. 'Nothaire trook peeck up, tak me,
mothaire, fathaire, back to Jesús, he de *caballero de la
reata*, he de beeg hat man, savvy? Mothaire she lay down,
she cry lang, lang tam. She cry de belly she hurt bad.
Lotsa day. Lotsa night. She stop cry. De moon one night
cam down in mothaire face. She no cry more. Fathaire
deega beega hole. I feexa leaves. We poota dirta down on
my mothaire. She go. My fathaire he cry lang tam. He say
he ride nothaire trook Meechigan. Deega da beetsa. He
geeta sam money. He tak money he pay man. He geeta
papaires. He be 'Mer'cano sam day. He ask Jesús, he say,
'Jesús, I go bak da Meechigan, deega da beetsa. Jesús, you
see my son, Carlos, he geetsa back down beeg reevaire?'
Jesús, he say, 'I geet Carlos back Rio fine.' He say my
fathaire, 'No cry more, Santos, I see de Carlos back home
de Rio Grande.' You trook cam. Jesús rope you, geeva
beeg pull oop. He 'fraid you be *oficieros*. He 'fraid you
lotsa things. He tak da chance, you say you de *músicos*,
you play da mandolina, you go look finda de golda. He
laugh. He t'ink you crazy, but Jesús he say he taka da
chance. You no know deesa roada. Rosalita know. I know.
Jesús, he know. Eff Jesús laka you look, aver'body eena
Beeg Bend lika you."

"Jesús? Cowboy? That pony back there?" I asked
Carlos. "He ain't a copper, is he? P'trolman? Officer?"

"Jesús?" Carlos smiled on down ahead where the limbs
and sticker leaves parted a little to let the nose end of our
truck go past. He loved the smells and the sounds of the

old truck as good as I loved the other smells, sappy smells and crackling sounds, the sounds of the whispery leaves all down through his little Big Bend valley jungle. He went on to say, "No. Jesús, he no de 'trol man. Jesús, he what you call *caballero buscador*. Scout man. He ride de roada. He say eef you good man, you no hav beeg trabble down in beega rivaire country. Savvy?"

"Wonder what Jesús'll say 'bout us?" I said to Carlos. "Did Jesús say we good men?"

"Jesús, he say two leetle fella he looke fine. Two beega fella he see beeg hat, he see beega gun. He say you be 'trol man, you look lak. He say me fin' out. He say Rosalita fin' out."

" 'Vestigators." I laughed a little. "Where'd ya learn how to speak English so good, Carlios?"

He smiled a good bit wider, then told me, "I learn some de Meechigan. Some de Presidio. Some de Terlingua. I learn some de Mexico."

"Rosie Reeter, she speak English?" Jeff asked Carlos.

" 'Bout lak me." Carlos grinned ahead down the trail path.

"Where did ya run onta her?" Jeff asked him.

"Rosalita, she my seestaire. Not de my mothaire, not de my real fathaire, see? My new fathaire, see? He de papa de Rosalita. See? I two fathaires, see? Rosalita, she hav de two mothaires. She go sam trook one, two time weeth me. She no very old. Fi', seexa. I lots older. I *diez,* ten-a. Oh, I go de beeg trook de beetsa fielda three tam . . . ah, *cuatro,* four tam. I no lak beetsa fielda trooka. Make sick. Make cry. Make dirty. Make feela bad. You see? You savvy beetsa trook?"

"Nawp," I told him. "Ain't never seen one. What's a beet truck look like?

"Sam laka deesa one."

"Same as this'n?" I asked him again. "Yeah?"

"Seexisty she ride. You no see?"

"I'm not even cravin' ta see one." Jeff shook his head. "I'd not give a rusty penny nail ta see one. Got enough troubles on my hands right now 'thout a-sniffin' 'round ta stick my nose up inna wild truckload of Wet Mexicans. I seen 'em a-sneakin' up acrost th' little old backroads right there'n Gray County, while I'se a-patrollin' th' county roads. Gotta run like dogs an' stay hid out everywheres they go ta work. Stink like a truck loaded down with ole

salty cowhides a-headin' fer th' shoe fact'ry. Sa dern dirty
th't nobody in Gray County'll even let 'em git out an'
cook up a meal. Your folks is good folks, Carlos, jest's
long's they stay back down yonder 'crost th' banks o' that
there Reo Grandy where they belong. Jest hopin' that I
didn't hurt yer feelin's, Sonny Man. But this truck's not a-
gon'ta slow down ner stop off nowheres fer one minute to
see none o' your wetback Maixicans. I bought an' paid fer
this here truck with my own good 'Merican money. I
shore ain't a-gon'ta. I'd ten times druther'd ta side in on
th' side of law an' order than off on th' side of a bunch o'
folks that's a-breakin' th' laws.

"I'm jest a-lettin' ya know where'bouts I'm a-standin'
on this whole shebango. I'm th' boss on this here trip, till
ya git yerselves a truck of your own. I paid fer this truck.
If'n I cain't be th' boss man on it, I'll turn th' gad-blame
thaing around here right this very minute. I'll head 'er
back fer home sa fas' yer eyes'll run water. Y' soakin' all
o' this in?"

Jeff drove faster while he spoke. He made a hard turn
to the right, a little one to the left, jerking on the wheel,
with every word he said to us.

"Pore place to turn around," I told Jeff. "Jest a-prayin'
that Carlos cain't savvy Oklahoma slango lingo good
enough to understan'. Helluva way to make a friend."

"Friend?" Jeff laughed. "Kinda friends I'm a-wantin' ta
make's not a-chasin' all aroun' out here 'n this here God-
ratted cactus with their ole dirty rag clothes ripped halfway off of 'em. I'm not a-makin' no thousand-mile trip off
down through here ta make no friends, as ya say, with a
few little raggedy-ass kids with their han's an' their face
jest's, by gad, dirty as th' dirt on th' groun'. Bahhh!"

The trail ran out of the bushy trees and cactus for a few
miles. We rolled along a dry, sandy road till we got hungry.
Jeff stopped the truck and Papa opened up a big can of
pork and beans. Eddie cut open a tall can of Vienna
sausages. Rosalita helped to dump the cans out onto our
tin plates in equal heaps. I sat down on the side of the
trail with my plate on a hot rock and said to Eddie as he
sat himself on the right running board. "Good pork'n's."

"Good Vee-ennies, too. Chokes th' heck out of me.
Carliosie, wouldja han' a dyin' man th' bag o' water, there
on that there nail right at yer elbow?"

Papa watched Carlos open the mouth end of the water-bag for Eddie. "Everything is just fine," he said. "This little valley that we are in right now is something to write back to Hell Cat about, huhmm, Wood Pile? Just take a look. Look at those big canyons running off to the west. I sure do wish Skinny and Betty Jean and Pawpaw Robert could see some of this."

"Yeah. Ain'ta gonna be sa good, though, if that there Edder Stoner an' Jeffries don't talk a little bit nicer to these here k—i—d—s."

"Meanin' which?" Eddie asked me.

Jeff set his plate on the front right fender and asked with a big mouthful of beans and sausages, "Sez whooo?"

"Sez me," I told them.

"I sez, myself," Papa nodded. "Rosalita. Throw down that loaf of bread to me, will you please, Little Missy?"

"*Sí, sí, señor.*" Rosalita tossed the loaf down to Eddie on his fender.

"Le's hit th' ball, men." Jeff looked at the higher humps of sawtooth mountains away down to the southerly west, and some higher rock peaks sticking up back over to our south and east. "Wish that I only knowed what th' names of all o' them big ole sawbacks a-jumpin' up right in yonder is."

"I know." Carlos was holding Eddie's knife in one hand and an old Ford V-shaped magneto iron in the other. He kissed the magneto and rubbed it down against his pants leg. "I know de name beeg mountainios. I know de secret of de magneeto, also. You want know? You let me drive de beega wheela? I show. You say I drive leetle."

"All right," Jeff said. "Show me. Tell me. I'll letcha set right here'n my lap an' steer th' God-blessed thing. Jes' git a wiggle on. Tha'sall. Jest hurry it up. Tell me. Show me."

"Me too." I talked over Carlos's head while he looked out at the desert through the V of the magneto iron. "What's th' dern-gonned secret? Desert secret?"

"Watch." Carlos tossed the magneto out across the trail. He stood and looked where it fell by a low dagger weed and said, "That. That ees the secret of the magneto."

"Crazy idjiot!" Jeff shook his head at Carlos running to get the magneto. "Keep us holed up here fer th' naixt dern two-three days. Throw'd a good magnet clean off over'n them there stinger weeds over yonder. I jest wisht that I hadn't never run onto nobody by th' name of Carlos in th' firs' place."

"Cain't figger this'n out," I said as Jeff speeded up the engine to get ready to pull off down the trail. "Shore past me."

Carlos sniffed the magneto out of the stickery weeds and ran back to the truck to stop on Jeff's side. "Look. You see? Look de magneto. You see."

"Dern my skats!" Jeff took the magneto out of Carlos's hands and looked at it over his steering wheel. "Damn thaing's growed hairs."

"Grow'd which?" I got up onto the cushion and looked over Jeff's shoulder at the magneto. "Well, I be consarn'd!"

"Hairs!" Jeff rubbed the magneto with his fingers.

"Dern'd if it didn't!" I touched my finger to the little fine hairs along the edges of the magneto. "Blue jillion of 'em. How c'd that a-happen'd? Whatcha reckon 'tis, Jefferies?"

"What kind o' hairs is these, Carliosie boy?" Jeff kept on rubbing and talking. "What makes 'em?"

"Magneto, eet peeks op thee iron," Carlos told us. "The iron she ees all over theesa desert."

"Weellll, I be damn! Carlos, y've show'd me sech a dern good secret that I'm a-gon'ta letcha drive 'bout a mile 'n' a half. Climb right up here'n my lap, sonny boy. Yer th' best dern iron finder in all o' these here dern three counties 'round here, ole boy."

"Gimme it." I grabbed the magneto out from Jeff's hands while Carlos crawled up onto his lap to help steer the wheel. I jumped out onto the side of the road, stuck the magneto down to the ground and watched the little black and blue-gray iron hairs jump through the dirt to hang onto the two legs of the magneto iron. I stuck it down again and picked up more hairs while Jeff and Carlos got the truck to moving. They yelled for me to come on. They cursed me out and they made fun of me. I covered the magneto up with dirt and then I picked it up and made a fast run to catch up with the truck rolling off. I yelled, "Yippy yi! I'm not a awful good miner, but I'm a dang fine miner's son, an' I'll hafta do yer minin' till yer reg'lar miner comes. Yowee!"

"Crazy man," Jeff told Carlos when I sat myself down on the cushion blanket.

"Beega mine man." Carlos laughed on Jeff's lap. He held both hands on the wheel and helped Jeff steer off down the little tracky trail. "Beega shotta mina man. Hey no, Jaffie?"

The valley got narrow in between two low-size hills. A big, deep wash-out sand ditch ran along down the middle. We steered down a trail on the easterly side of this wash-out ditch. The ditch looked to be ten or fifteen feet deep, rays already shaded more than half of the bottom side of water that trickled down the ditch in the sun. The sun rays already shaded more than half of the bottom side of the ditch. We saw a cloud of dust heaving up from the south and I heard the sounds of people mixed up in the noises of a truck motor. The truck pulled up out of the floor of the ditch, up a cutout road along the west bank, till I saw it get out along the top of the ditch. We rolled along the east bank and the other truck passed us on the west bank. The ditch between the two trucks was something like fifty or sixty feet wide, like a little box canyon. The other truck was in better running condition than ours. It was roped and tied around tight with a rough brown canvas. Its paint looked fairly new—a dirty, muddy-colored black paint. It had a silvery radiator cap that looked new. Two Mexican men sat up in the cab. I yelled, "Hi! Howdy!" Carlos waved at them and called in Spanish. Jeff nodded and yelled "Hello!" I heard Papa, Eddie, Rosalita on the back saying hello.

I felt a sick chill go through me when the two men in the cab kept their eyes dead ahead to the north. They did not so much as wiggle a toenail. Their faces looked on up their road. Their truck smoked like it might be burning a little too much motor oil. Their tires had seen some wet, gray-brown mud somewhere in the past mile or so. In the whining of their motor and above the noises of our own, I did hear the sounds of several people doing some loud talking. Yelling. Some odd whistling. Crying. Wailing. More fast talking. More like begging or like pleading. Like it was something between life and death. Like something was gone bad wrong. A truckload of groans: "Oohhhee! Ahhe! Oooooeee! Ohhh!" And the truck was gone on up acrost and down through the gunny brushes before I could make out what on earth was going on.

Carlos looked ahead where he was steering. He dropped his lips down sad and told us, "That trook iss Chito's trook. He weela notta stoppa onteel they geet oop to Arisona. They weel peek the cotton. Chito weel bring them back ef they are notta dead. Chito he weela notta stoppa. Notta for waterr. Not for sick. Not for dead."

"Truck driver's not to blame, Woodyrow." Jeff kept his eyes down the side of the ditch. He drove off the topside, down the east bank, and rolled down the trickling water over pebbles and gravelly rocks about the size of green-vine peas. "If you was haulin' a load o' them goshblamed wetbacks, would you stop fer wood, water, er coal? Ya'd jes' keep yer head right straight off down th' road ahead o' yer, an' keep right on a-sailboatin'. Officers'll stop ya plenty of times 'thout y' wastin' yer good time a-campin' along th' warsh-out gullies. Truck driver does jest which-ever a way that his boss tells 'im ta. An' if'n ya don't want yer job o' herdin' that there wetback wagon—well, they's plenty of truckdrivers awaitin' fer a chance ta grab onta that there damn-blamed wheel. Boss man's orders. An' orders is orders. 'Sides, Woodrow, that there cotton cain't wait. 'S gotta be snatched when it's gotta be snatched."

"Man couldn't never pay me no kinda money to drive a truckload o' folks all a-yellin' an' a-screamin' thatta way. Don't give a big rat's ass who my bosser man was. Couldn't pay enough greenbaicks to make me take on any sech job in th' first place. I'd crawl off down here an' die in this here water ditch first, by God!"

"Eet iss verrry bad." Carlos watched the front wheels splash the rocky waters up onto both sides of the canyon walls while the truck rolled along. "This reevaire weel take us about thairty miles. Eet weel be a leetle rough sam-times, but weel cut off feefty miles of the road. And I like to drive down in the beeg deetch because nobody can see me down here."

"Makes a dern fine road, anyhow," I told him. "This is th' Carlioosie Highway, by dang."

I kept my eye skint up and down along the rocks in the water, the water splashing up and sifting down the sands on both sides of us. Jeff steered along with Carlos talking and singing. The road and the ruts turned out of the water stream and went around a rough, rocky place. But they turned back and took us down the big middle for the next hour or more. It was just turning off dark when Jeff stopped the truck on the right bank of the river that the big ditch flowed into. "Theesa place," Carlos said, "she issa the best one to go to sleep for tonighta."

He hopped down onto the flatbed of river rocks and walked along with his eyes shooting down on all sides around his feet. He splashed the water ankle deep and picked up several rocks, one here, two there. He dropped a few down inside his pants pockets and carried the others in a cup he made with both hands. He sucked two or three little pebbles into his mouth and made a grinding noise walking back to the truck and us. Jeff asked him again, "What's this?"

"Gold," Carlos told us. "Gold rocksa."

"Welll, I be gad-ratted!" Jeff said. "Jes' take a peek, woodja, Woodrow, at what this boy's dug up. 'At's gold if'n I know what gold looks like!"

"Theesa gold," Carlos told Jeff and me, "she eesa what you call, what you say, foolsa, foolsa gold. Theesa reeevaire eesa full of the foolsa gold."

"Goldest gold I ever seen anywheres." I talked up loud enough for Papa and Eddie to hear me good and plain. "Let's shovel it all up onta th' truck. Let's send a bucketful back up ta Skinny an' ta Ireenie an' back up ta Hell Cat an' Betty Jean an' a bucketful fer Pawpaw Robert."

"Oughta sack it, er box it up." Jeff put on a good act. "I'm jest afraid th' buckets'll tip over 'n' spill out on th' dern train."

"Gold she eesa found." Carlos danced around the truck whooping and yelling.

I heard Eddie say to Papa on the truck bed, "Somebody is shore 'n hell a-pullin' th' crap off on me 'n' you, Charlie."

"Unless I am having an opium dream come true," Papa said to Ed. "But I never smoked a stitch of opium in my life. Somebody is, as you say, Eddie, making you and me out to be the humorous victims of some very laughable circumstances. Look at these goldbricks here. I've seen mock trials and faked gang fights, but this fool's gold tops them all."

It was still light enough to see streaks of crazy paints the sun had kicked up over the mountain humps. I saw hazes and lights of all colors, hazes, more like dancing blazes all over my shirt, my hands, Jeff's workpants, the crossboards of the truckbed, the rocks in the water. Rosy pink, rusty purple smears, and glares that hit down off

the cliffs to the east. I had never seen such colors. Like
the trail of a drunken signpainter on a twelve-day bat.
Like fire flying from the trails of a thousand runaway
burros in the gaps and up the slopes, back over the ridge
there. It was such a bright shooting and bouncing kind of
light, I thought I was having some kind of a colored-light
dream, with colors on the hills and weeds just as bright as
I'd ever seen them in the hills and hollers of my highest
dream-walkings. These colors were rainbows splashing
against hot rock, town lights fogging and misting around
the bushy weeds. Light light. Soft light. Thin kinds of
lights, and lights in between me and the truck, where I
saw Carlos climbing down to say, "You name Woodee?
You come me. We geeta wood. We go de beeg broosh."

I followed him off to the right bank of the big ditch,
and loaded my arms full of sticks that Carlos broke down
and handed back to me.

"Hey, Carlibosio," I asked him, "does it make y' feel
bad if I try to talk yer name, an' if I cain't never say it
right?"

"No." He walked around me towards the truck and the
sounds of the voices of the rest of our outfit. "You joke
my name. I joke you name. You not mad. You say nice.
Beeg Jaffie 'fraid me. He 'fraid theesa broosha. He 'fraid
theesa beega *montañas*. He 'fraid my peepole. I mak heem
feela betta. I no know how. You say me how. You tell
me?"

"Let's make up some big, hot coffee first." I walked
along stepping down in Carlos's footprints on the dampish
night sand. "An' then, tell y' what. Ask 'im ta take out his
fiddle an' play y' some pretty music. Violin. Jeff is th'
champ fiddler."

"You play de *guitarra? Músico?*" he asked me.

"Little bit. 'Nough to git along. Ain't as good at it as my
Uncle Jeff is."

"Heyyyhhee!" Carlos hollered at the others while his
armload of wood hit the sand a few yards back from the
truck. "Me de Woodee we geeta da gooda wood. You
mak de good fire. I run de reevaire. Get de gooda
wataire. Rosalita, theesa fellas weel play for you some
nice *música*. They have a violeen. They have a *guitarra*."

Papa struck matches. Eddie blew the flames. Jeff worked
with the tin bucket of coffee grounds. I sliced some strips
of salt pork into our big black iron skillet and listened

for the sounds of the fire crackling under the limbs of wood.

We sat around and ate our supper. A can of red pinto beans with salt pork warmed in the same skillet. Eddie opened up a can of whole grain corn and stirred it in with a long stick. The lights of the fire jumped around on our faces and all of us washed our mixture down with a smoky cup of coffee.

"I feel like we are getting somewhere," Papa said, looking around. "This is the sundown of our fourth day now. The night, I should say. In the morning we'll begin our fifth day. I sure do wish that you, Rosalita, and you, too, Carlos, could stay with us all of our way down to the Rough Run Canyon."

"Gracias," Rosalita told Papa.

"Muchas gracias." Carlos nodded his head in the firelight.

"Kinda feel like I'm a-gittin' off down some'rs, but I jest don't quite know where 'tis I'm a-gittin' off down to." Jeff swallowed his coffee as he talked. "Know what I mean?"

"Same way's I felt th' first day I struck out with my regiment through that there Argonney Forrist. 'Ceptin' they's a-givin' us a good bit more of a hotter time of it over yonder," Eddie told us.

"I never was off down in no wild country like this place is," I told the crowd. "Lost world off down in here."

"It isn't so lost as you might think." Papa finished the last drops in the bottom of his cup. "Rosalita there, and Carlos, they seem to know how to find every stick and every stone in this goshdarn 'lost country,' as you call it. No. It isn't lost. Not lost to the Indians and to these Mexicans that are born and raised up down here. It's just lost to me and to you, Woodrow. Not to Carlos and not to Rosalita. I feel perfectly safe just knowing that these two are around. I'm commencing to worry about what is going to happen to all of us when our two fine partners here leave us tomorrow down here at the turn-off towards Presidio. Ohhh, welll, tomorrow can just take care of itself. Tonight is tonight. Let's all make the most of it. What can we do to stir up some stumps?"

"Feedle!" Carlos jumped to his feet. *"Guitarra."*

"Buenos músicos." Rosalita shook her fingers in the air and danced around the sand with Carlos. *"Músicos.*

Buenos músicos. Viva de los músicos. Viva de feedle. Viva de las guitarras."

Jeff walked around the opposite side of the truck and mounted up the crossboards to the backbed. He handed his fiddle case down to me while Eddie and Papa dumped more coffee into their tin cups and stirred with fresh-cut sticks. The fire burned a good deal higher now and we heard a loud snort from an animal a few feet away on the westerly side. But Carlos and Rosalita told us that it was nothing except a loose desert burro looking at our fire.

Jeff's fiddle in his hands had a dry and wide-open sound to it. My guitar sounded the same. Clear, and sort of like the music walked along on paddy feet. He tuned up with his ear close to the wood. I tuned my guitar with my head cocked sideways and watched Papa, Eddie, Carlos, and Rosalita.

Jeff made his fiddle sound like a poor boy a long ways from home. He made his chords and his discords echo and dance out in the brushy trees to sing out to all of the wild crawlers and walkers that home was not here for the fiddler. Home was back up the country. Home was here for the things that heard Jeff's music, but the music in the leaves and along the rocks, to Jeff, just didn't feel like home. I liked the outdoor ring and the rattlings of things out in the brush. I liked the smoke and the fire all stirred in with the fiddle strings and whirled around with the thomp of my guitar box. Papa liked it. I could tell by his face that he liked it. I could tell that Eddie was liking the whole trip better, with his eyes dancing off over the fire flames and past our staggering shadows, on out to the shrubbery all around him. Eddie told Papa, "Reck'n yer Paw Jerry got awf'l lonesome lotsa times, runnin' aroun' down in here 'thout no fiddle, 'thout no g'tarr. I could set back here 'n' listen ta Jeff saw that there fiddle all night long an' ev'r night ta boot. They's nuthin' in this here world th't I druther'd ta listen to than this here kind o' good fiddle music Jeff an' Woodrow plays sa perty ta my ears. Hmmm. Mmm."

"Paw Jerry brought his woman." Papa laughed past Eddie and into the fire. "And there's not a fiddle nor a guitar in this whole world that can hum to you the way a good woman can."

Carlos and Rosalita listened to the music, lights dancing in their eyes. We asked them to tell us about how the mountains got their names. The Hen Egg. The Nigger-head. The Christmas Mountains. The Cathedral Mountains. The Chisos. The Santa Rosas. The Study Butte. And we sat listening to their stories till their words drummed all of us out where the deer lay to sleep.

CHAPTER 7

OLD MAN RIO

It took us all this next day to drive the truck sixty-some miles from Fool's Gold Creek to the quicksilver mining town of Terlingua. We burnt out our gears on a dozen hills and had to push our truck up the slopes backwards, our reverse band being the only one still holding out. I was commencing to miss Hell Cat a good bit, and caught myself looking at the wild shrubbery and dreaming about her. Eddie felt better every turn of the wheels towards the mine. Papa felt even better than Eddie, and told big, long homesteading and pioneering stories to match the wild looks of this rough desert and mountain country. Jeff grabbed his fiddle out of its case, or its "coffin," as he called it, and sawed off every tune he knew with me wrastling my guitar on the backbed where Carlos and Rosa rode most of the day. The hot sun through the windshield and the red-hot exhaust pipe under our floorboards kept everybody out of that cab except one driver and one helper.

Jeff said between every fiddle tune that he was missing his 'Eenie Gal and her mandolin chording. At beantime we undone the canvas tarpaulin so that it swung loose

166

against the truck cab, but could be pulled back over our heads and bedding in case of a heavy dew or a quick rain.

We kept on playing fiddle music while Papa drove past a few mud houses. Our truck shot a stream of hot steam fifteen feet high where we pulled to a stop in front of the only store in the whole town. I stood on the backbed and looked around to see a dozen or more women, kids, and men walk out into their yards to watch us. Eddie said to Papa, wiping the coating of dust around his lips, "These folks thinks a dern circus has hit town."

He got out of the cab and spit a mouthful of snuff juice down onto the dirt. "Hi, Jeffrey, cut out that there fiddlin' sa loud; it's a-scarin' ever'body outta town."

"Which town?" Jeff ducked his head and fiddled louder. "I didn' see no town yet." He made a yipping noise up at me as I stood on a beer case and chorded my guitar.

"Down in this God-f'rsaken country," I laughed back at Jeff, "they calla matchbox a house, an' they calla house a town." I talked and chorded while I looked the place over.

Carlos and Rosa jumped to the ground and held hands as they walked around the truck. A dark-skinned girl around twenty years old dropped two bags of groceries on the porch of the store and ran down the high wooden steps to meet the two kids. She talked to them in Indian or Spanish so loud and so fast that I didn't catch a word. Rosa and Carlos danced around her and told her all about their ride in our truck, acting out all the motions of riding, driving, pushing, shoving. Carlos made a noise with his lips like the sounds of our engine and Rosa steered a make-believe wheel in her hands.

The lady thanked Papa and Eddie while they poured a canvas bag of water into our radiator. As the steam died down, she smiled up at Jeff and thanked him. She talked a few words about the kids, and said something nice about our *"música."*

"I like th' way she sez that word, *'myooseeka,'"* I said to Jeff. "I sorta like th' way she pooches up 'er lip wh'n she sez it. I keep fergittin' 'bout you bein' married only a year. Dern it all. That ole devil's a-shinin' back in your ole eyes, Jeff Davis, boy, jes' like two great big coals of red-hot fire. I'd like f'r 'Eenie Gal ta see how her new husband is a-blazin' fire outta his eyes, already, at th' first Mexican *señorita* we meet up with."

"Huntin' down these cussed gold mines is perty rough business on a new married man." Jeff rubbed his fiddle bow against his neck as he spoke. "Wonder who this young lady here is, anyways, reckon?"

"Dunno," I told him, "an' dunno how ta ax 'er."

Jeff half laughed. "But you'd like t' take her off out here'n these sticker bushes an' let 'er teach you whichever language she uses."

"No bet," I said. I had to wave good-bye to Carlos and Rosa. Their lady seemed to be in a hurry to get her two sacks of groceries and to move on. This was where the road to Presidio turned off to the west and to the sundown. It was in the early first drifts of the dust of that sundown that Papa waved a long farewell to Rosalita, to Carlos, and to their young big relative. It was not till the three of them, riding in a democrat wagon pulled by a mule and driven by a young Mexican, had rounded a high cactus clump and passed out of sight, that we stopped our waving.

Eddie screwed the radiator cap back onto its nozzle. "We gon'ta buy anything in the groc'ry store here? 'Backer? Anybody need 'backer? Snuff? Chew? Smokes?" Eddie followed Papa into the store. Jeff laid his fiddle in his case and followed them. I said I'd stay out on the truck and watch the load, and Jeff walked up the long stairs, teasing me.

"Watch th' wimmen, ya'd oughta say. What's in here ta buy, boys? What's in here ta buy?"

The store street was a wide, flat, dirt affair, twice the width of an ordinary street, covered over with small rocks as round as marbles and half the size of your thumb. It was not hot here, not like the summery heat I half-expected to find this far to the south. It was, in fact, a shade too cool for my shirtsleeves, so I slipped into an old jumper and lay my head down on a soft blanket roll. One short look up into the sky at this early hour of the sundown was enough to make me suck in a lungful of air and mumble half out loud, "Ahhh, Helly Cat. Why ain't you here ta help me dig out this gold mine?"

An old man with a blanket wrapped around him walked up to the side of the truck and knocked his knuckles against the side boards. I got up onto my knees and looked over at him. He told me, *"Buenos días,"* and I told him, "Howdy." Under his blanket he wore an old olive greenish, wore-out shirt with all the buttons off and the wind blowing against his skin. He had on a pair of old blue dungaree work britches that looked older than I was. I noticed that he was barefooted, and he was rolling a fat cigarette in some sort of a brown paper. He asked me, *"Fósforos,"* and touched his finger to his cigarette. I put a match in his hand and watched him light up.

"You go wheecha way?" He looked not at me, but at the truck.

"We go Study Butte," I told him.

"Me, I go same. Stoody Butte." He blew smoke out of his nose and mouth. "Same I go. Stoody Butte."

"Good road?" I asked him, nodding to the northeast towards the Christmas Mountains.

"No road." He shook his head with a sad look in his eye.

"Not any road?" I went on, "Study Butte is a town, ain't it? I figgered ya'd have a road."

"All road go *loco,* Terlingua, Stoody Butte. All go theesa way." He wiggled his fingers like spiders running off in different directions. "Goat path run 'way. Deer trail same way. Rabbit track same way. All go crazy."

"All wash out, huh?" I pointed to the rear end of the backbed. I helped him scramble up and to get sat down on one of our packing boxes. "Road peters out? Fades out like a rabbit trail? My name's Woody, knock on wood; what's your name?"

As he looked me and our truckload over as slow as his eyes could travel, he winked in a funny way and said, "You ask me, I tell you. I am Rio, joost Old Man Rio. You gonna beg for good rabbit trail fram Terlingua here to Stoody Butte. For why you fella here thisa place?"

"Silver," I told him. "How ya say silver in Mexican? You Mexican er you Indian?"

"I, me, I both. I all three. Hahaha." He blew on the fiery end of his cigarette and laughed soft and easy. "Me father is de Santa Rosa Montañas. Me mother she de Rio Grande. I no wear da hat, for my brother he is de sun. *El sol."*

"How ya say th' word 'silver'?" I listened to learn.

"Plata."

"How ya say, look? 'I look silver'?" I asked him.

"You mean say, you look for silvaire or you look at silvaire? Beega deeference."

"Fer silv'r."

"*Buscar*. It means you search." He grinned.

"Hunt fer?"

"*Sí.*"

"*Platty booscarr,*" I mumbled my words wrong.

"No." His voice was as soft, as easy, as smooth as the thick coats of dust over his clothing and his face and hands. "*Nosotros buscamos plata.*"

Eddie, Papa, and Jeff walked out of the store and cranked up the engine. They looked at our booted-up tires and shook the truck with their hands to see if it would fall apart. I heard Papa say, "The store man tells us that Study Butte lies right due east of here, Woody. You listening?"

"I'm lissenin'," I said.

"Not more than two terrible roads to push up," Papa kept telling me. "Flatlands, awful sandy and rutty, with some few mesquite roots in our way. He says that we can pull into Study Butte in time to throw up a camp. Lots of firewood, and a good stream of water. Want to try to make it?"

"I seen all they is of Terlinger here," I laughed back at Papa. "These Terlingwer women ain't a-treatin' me right, noway, nohow. I'll be th' guider man. I'll tell ya which rabbit trail ta foller. I'll set up here on top o' th' cab an' keep a lookout. You drive whichever way I tell ya, hey?"

By this time Eddie had mounted up into the truckbed with my old man friend and me. I put my finger to my lips and told Ed not to let Papa and Jeff know that we had a rider with us. I wanted to have some fun. "You tell me which trail ta take, see," I told Rio, "an' I'll yell it up to my papa and Jeff." I whispered to Eddie, "They'll think I'm in tech with Jerry P.'s spirit er I'm in cahoots with th' medycine men down here. Keep quiet, Eddie . . . sssshh! Don't let 'em know 'bout Rio here." I pointed to the old man.

"Hi, Ryeo," Eddie whispered. "How long you been a-runnin' loose down here'n this rough country, anyhow?"

"Long time." The old man liked our joke. He stayed down out of sight of the rear window of the cab. "You stay long time?" He smiled over towards Eddie.

"I ben here jest about five minnits," Ed said.

"Long time," the old man joked.

"Ain't that there woolly blanket perty hot an' scratchy?" Ed asked him.

"Een the winter she keeps out the cold." Rio struck a new match to relight his old, soaky cigarette. There was a whole world of bragging joshery in his words as he went on to tell Eddie, "And een de summer she keeps out the heat."

"Looks awful scratchy roun' th' neck ta me." Eddie smiled at the old man's humor. "Wanta take it off 'n' let it rest down here on th' beddin'? This limousine shore ain't a-ridin' a bit smoother, Woodrow, if ya ast me. Too rough on yer back, Ryeo? Want me ta jump out an' unroll some kind of silk carpet out here under our wheels?"

"Don't forget," the old man told Eddie, "that I was born here with all of these rocks."

I was up on top of the cab with my back to the sun going down. I never had seen any such deep, clear, fresh, clean colors as those in the sunset. I told the old man, as I looked back at the fireball in the western world, "Perty dern lucky, if ya ask me, ta be born out here under all o' these perty colors."

"*Si*," Rio answered.

"Shore lucky awright." Ed repeated my words while he bobbed up and down with his new jar of three-point snuff in his good hand. "Ever do any diggin' 'roun' in these rocks?"

"No." Rio rubbed his hand against his lip.

"Never?" I felt sort of empty when I asked him this.

"Nope?" Eddie shook his head sidewise and worried.

"No. Never," the old man said again. "My people, we have not to dig to find silver. No dig to find gold."

"No dig?" Ed asked him.

"Not even a little bit o' diggin'?" I asked Rio.

"We justa reach down with our finger like thisa. Find pocketful. Sackful. Truckful." Rio blew a cloud of peppery tobacco smoke that drifted into the fog of exhaust smoke trailing in back of our truck. By the sounds of loose rocks hitting up in under the truck frame, I could tell that the road was turning off a good bit rockier. But nothing bothered the eyes or the face of Old Man Rio. This was my first chance to get a good look at the back of his head. I saw a double strand of braids wrapped around with green yarn, dark, long, and straight, which dropped down to his hips. "I no digga like de dog."

"We're mos' likely ta dig halfa these here rock hills down fer six er eight months." I looked off over the top of his head towards a rim of darkening purple high-toppers. "An' still not even come up with a han'ful."

"Much less a pocketful," Eddie put in. "Road's a-gittin' awful rough an' rowdy 'long in here, ain't it? Bouncy."

"We have not hit the rough part," Old Man Rio told us. "In one minute we will come to the Dagger Rock Road. Tell you brother father take left rabbit trail around this next cactusa bush. Hey?"

I told Jeff which trail to take. We rolled up a slow sloping grade for a mile or so, over a road so rocky that it shook our teeth like a Panhandle blizzard. We had to get out and push up the last hundred or so yards of this slope, and the rocks stuck up like railroad spikes with the sharp ends up. Some rocks were the size of a pork-and-bean can, but none any larger. Hard, slick, crystal rocks of some kind, that stuck up their noses about three to six inches above the clay dirt of the road. Over the hump it was worse. On the downslope it got sharper, rougher, because Jeff didn't have enough brakes to hold the truck back. We got such a shaking that I could feel every bite I'd swallowed down into my stomach for the past several days.

"Too much bouncin' fer yah?" I yelled at Eddie and the old man.

"Bit my tongue a few times is about all," Eddie stuttered. "This is rougher'n th' Argonney Forrist. Y' all right, Ryeo?"

"This isa not so bad as a Chisos Mountain burro." The Old Man of the Daggery Rocks took the bounces better than Eddie or myself. "You only have to know how to get limber and how to take eet easy."

This was a road of lechuguilla, stickery things and *maravilla,* an early road here, a deer trailer, rabbit hopper, a fader-outer, an outside scouter, a skidder, a trouncer, a six-way bouncer. I unscrewed the tinny lid and tried to hand Eddie the liquor jar. I thought he looked like he needed it.

After taking down a two-finger swig, Eddie held his breath for a half a mile or so, and held out the jug to the Old Man. Eddie took the first slug to show the Old Man that the juice was not poison. The Old Man held the jar for a few more bumps, watching the whirls and dances of the bubbles in the hickory-colored whiskey. He was a fortuneteller looking at your past, present, and your front sides. He swallowed slower than Eddie had, drank longer, deeper down, stronger, and managed to hold his breath so as not to fill up his nose and lungs with the killer fumes flying out from that jug.

"Here's to Stoody Butte," the Old Man said. He took down another drink which was a good two fingers longer than Eddie had gotten down. "And to you. All of you. If you do not find any gold, any silver, than I will be sorry for you. Eef you do dig up a big bonch, I will feel sorrier for you. I willa be your friend eitherr way. Thisa whiskey it ees verra bad. I have covered many women witha tequila of every kind, but not a womawn nor any tequila that was this bad. Whoooo!"

CHAPTER 8

WINE BUCKET GIRL

The headlights threw only one or two candlelights ahead on our daggery, rocky road. The sun went on off to the western hills to chase some crazy burros up some wild trails. The last blaze of the sun's colors faded off into a night shade too dark to drive by. Old Man Rio told us to stop beside an ankle-deep bed of runny water. We all climbed out and I made Rio acquainted with Papa and Jeff. "Een de morrning," he told us, "I show you how to drive de last mile to find de Study Butte."

Eddie and Papa slept on the bed in the truck, and me and Jeff carried our bedrolls to a dry, shady spot under a rattling bush off the creek bank. Rio rolled up in his blanket in the weeds and snored almost as loud as Jeff did. Jeff snored 'most every night so loud that he woke everyone up, but this night, being so scared of the bushes, so tired from his driving and pushing, he slept but scant and little. Rio was up first and washed his face in the flowing creek. I was up second, because Jeff had dropped off at last into a sound sleep.

It was in the first warmth of the morning sun that Rio stood in the ankle-deep water and asked me, "Does your

174

uncle always make thees much noise while he ees sleeping?"

I watched the sun climb up and over the sawblade of the Chisos Mountains and told Rio, "Yeahh, always makes that racket when he's right real worried . . . scared of somethin'. Awful perty colors all aroun' this mornin', ain't they?"

"Always keep on your mind, my son, the Biga Bend world will not hurt you, just so long as you do not get to be afraid of eet, or afraid of anything. Understan'?" Rio spoke with his head down looking at the reflection of my face broken up in the whirls of the water around his feet.

"I ain't afraid o' nothin' in this whole dead rock country," I answered after a few moments. "I jest cain't think o' nothin' ta be 'fraid of down here."

He walked out onto the dry bank and lit up his morning cigarette, telling me, "The rattlesnake she will not bite me because she knows I am not afraid of her. The fly, the sick mosquito, the dagger weed, they will not hurt me, because I am not afraid of them either. The coyote, the wolf, the panther, the leopard, the cougar lion, the bobcat, I am not afraid of them, and so they leave me alone. The Indian here, the Spanish, the whites, they all treat me good, because they know I do not want what they have, and that I am never afraid of them. Eet ees not good down here," Rio moved his hands around to point over the whole Big Bend country, "to bee afraid."

"Same way 'bout lookin' a bad dog in his eye if he's a-tryin' ta bite ya." I followed Rio a few steps through the tall cactus bushes, talking to him. The smells of the limbs, twigs, leaves, roots, and seeds were strong to my nose because of the heavy coating of dew over everything. "I think I know what ye're a-talkin' about. I think I know."

"You willa thank me lots more for telling you this than if I told you where to dig for the gold and for the seelver."

"Yeah, reckon I will," I told him. I watched him rub the night's dirt and dust off his red and green blanket. I looked around at some fresh-made rabbit tracks under the tall cactus tree and asked him, "How long before we see Study Butte? How far away is it?"

"A few minutes after I drink my coffee. Here, young son, carry some of these roots for a fire. Roots burn slow." Rio loaded my arms with roots he kicked loose and our coffee boiled under our noses in short order. After his second cup Rio said, "Study Butte is so very close, I can sing a song and my people can all hear me at Study Butte." Rio hummed a little chanty song to show me what he meant. He rolled his eyes to the four hills and several winds to get me lost again in his riddling.

I really didn't mind. I wanted him to ride with us the rest of the way to the place. And somehow, the smells of the morning, the dewy leaves, the fire smoke, coffee odors, and all made me think again about the morning before, camped on a similar spot, with Rosalita and Carlos dancing around playing their jokes on all of us.

I poured another cup and asked Rio, "Hey, Rio, didja happen to see th' little boy an' th' little girl th't rode in our truck with us fr'm th' Glass Mount'ns to Terlingua?"

"Little Carlos. *Sí*. And little Rosa. Yes." His eyes lit up. He nodded his head, wrinkling his forehead. "I saw. I know. Their mother. She die." He patted his hand against his stomach. "She die with baby. She ride in little truck, pick cotton, dig beets. Roadsa rough, no water, no stop, no rest, big bounce. All day. All night bounce. She sick. Baby come. Botha die. They papa, he, I don' know; he run way, he fight de *policía*, big fight. Big trouble, somet'ing. They papa, he, I don't know."

"Who's th' perty girl that met Rosa an' Carlos back yonder at th' Terlingua store?" I asked him. I talked quiet so as not to wake up Papa, Jeff, and Eddie.

"Ooh. She name Linda. She Carlos's mother's sister."

I asked him, "Think ever'body 'roun' here knows about their mother, how she died?"

And he cut in to say, "All of the bushes are full of eyes and faces that know. *Sí*. They all know. Not how she die, no, but how she was killed. Yes. We never lose count of our people that get killed."

"Reckon folks'll think that we're down here lyin' about a silver mine jist ta git a truckload o' crop hoppers? I mean, well, I ain't a-wantin' ta rouse your folks up against us. I don't think Papa's that dumb, he can hold his tongue perty good. I got a way of sorta kiddin' Eddie along. He's got no wife—he never did much take ta any womern anywhere—an' bein' out here in this wide-open country jest about suits him fine. One that I got my doubts about's my uncle. He likes hard work, but I think he likes music better. He's got a right new wife back up in Pampa. This here truck b'longs to Jeff. He can crank th' outfit up any

time he gits good an' sore, an' drive back home. Don't
pay too much mind to whatcha hear Jeff say; he's liable
to spout off anything outta his mouth. He don't mean it.
He ain't no labor hauler. You savvy me?"

It was a wise smile that he put on to answer me with.
He turned his head slow as a wise turkey, and said, "I
savvy you. I run way off past you."

"D'ya b'lieve me?" I asked him.

He hunched his right shoulder in a funny way, drew
a clowny look onto his face, and told me, "Yes. I think
you tell me the truth. Where did the cripple fella lose his
arm?"

"World War," I said.

"Very bad." Rio sipped another sup.

"Yeah." I pointed my finger to my head. "Jesta little
bit shell shock'd. Tetched. Little bit weak up here. Cain't
go out an' do anything on his own hook, ya know? Like
a little kid. Three years overseas. They's not a mean bone
in his whole body, though. He's awful rowdy an' loud,
loves likker lika pig eatin' corn, loves all kindsa te'backer
like snuff, chewin', smokin'—all three. Funny thing,
though, I never did hear Eddie speak one single cuss word
in th' years I been a-knowin' 'im. Reckon your folks'll
know how to deal with 'im. Some o' th' time Eddie does
anything th't I want 'im to do, see? But, then, part o' th'
time, Jeff gits 'im to yellin' on his side. I know how rough
a time we're gonna have 'fore we dig up Paw Jerry's
mine. But, some people git discouraged awful quick when
th' sun gits too hot er th' rocks git too steep. Never can
tell when they'll git ideas about goin' back home to th'
women on th' plains."

"Why ees this cripple fella, Addie, afraid of de girls?
He looks to be all right, all but for his arm. He works
like two men with hees good arm. Why so full off this fear
about de women?" Rio asked me.

"He was shook up awful bad when he got home aft'r
th' Armistis got signed," I told him. "Three girls took him
up into their attic and stripped off all o' their clothes an'
tried all day to make Eddie lay 'em. Hopin' they'd rouse
his feelin's, ya know, an' bring 'im back t' bein' a natural
man ag'in. From that day ta this Eddie's never lift'd his
eye ner so much as laid 'is finger on a female girl ner a
womern either one. One fer th' odd man, huhh?"

I heard a crackling of sticks at my back, and turned

my head to see Papa listening to my story. He poured some whiskey from his fruit jar into his tin cup of coffee, then handed the jar to Rio. As Rio poured a goodly slug into his cup, Papa stretched and yawned to wake himself up.

"I overheard your story about Eddie to Rio, here," Papa said. "That is just the way it is, Rio. Ever hear of any such an odd concoction as that?"

"How old deed you say Addie was at this time when those girls made him scared?" Rio had a smack on his lips of the liquored coffee and a bit of a damp film over his eyes as he spoke. "It was when?"

"Well, he was jest about, ah . . ." I tried to think.

Papa beat me to the memory. "About twenty-two. They lived in that old shingly house there on that cotton farm on the edge of Clarendon."

"How old now is he?" Rio drank his breakfast with considerable more splash and noise. "Now. This morning."

"Eddie's thirty-three. I'm shore of that."

"Twelve years with no woman?" Rio asked us.

Papa cleared his throat to say, "Twelve or thirteen, that's about right."

"Which ees bad, very bad," Rio said.

"Which is worse than that!" Papa spoke as serious as he could. "This thing that has happened to Eddie, I honestly believe, is the worst setback, the worst injury, the worst thing that could overtake any man on this earth here. Not to be able to chase after a woman, not to be able to feel the sparks of love and passion that drives mankind to do the noble works that he does, whatever kind of works they are . . ."

I watched Rio's face as he sucked in Papa's words. He finished his coffee cocktail and I poured him another one of the same, only hotter coffee and hotter with whiskey. I listened to his words as he said, "We may be able to geev him some kind off help."

"Yeah?" I said. "Think so?"

"If we can get him to tell us who this girl is," Rio told us.

"Which girl?" Papa asked.

"This woman Addie loves," Rio went on.

"Ain't no lady in Eddie's deck. I toldja they ain't," I spoke out.

"Sure not any that I know of," Papa said, drinking.

"He has, or had one," Rio went on. "Someplace."

"Yer crazy," I argued. "None, no place."

"We can go and look for her," Rio went on.

"Go where?" Papa asked him.

"Addie will show us where to go find her," Rio said.

"Sounds batty ta me," I said to both Papa and Rio.

"Me, too." Papa poured his second cup. "What are you trying to tell us, Rio? You know some primitive method whereby you think you can arouse love and passion in this withered, crippled soldier after twelve years of complete isolation? Sounds dubious, to say the least."

"Eddie's perty tricky when ya try ta corner 'im right down an' ask 'im about th' girls an' th' women," I told Papa and Rio. "He'll ride along with ya while ye're talkin' 'bout 'em, an' he'll joke an' jorsh, an' horse aroun' some. But whenever he gits off somewheres with a she cat, he digs a big hole an' crawls off down inside it. Nothin' don't happen. Tha's all. It jest don't happ'n."

"Addie loves some one woman," Rio told us. "Not every girl he sees, the way we do—not every pair of breasts and every leetle hip which he sees. He feels so much in love weeth some one woman some tam, some place, that he had rather to live with the memory of her than to ask any other woman to try to make love with him, with a cripple arm, and everything. Here, Señor Charlie, let us, you and I, pretend that we are drunk this morning with too much wheeskey and black coffee *del negros.* You lay your head down here in my lap. Quick. Addie ees already coming from the truck. I am so drunk, and you are so drunk, also. We can't hear nawthing. And when Addie gets here for his cup of coffee, son, you try your best to make him tell you all he will about this woman which he loves. We can find out how she looks and then we can try to look around to find one that looks like her. Savvy? Hurry. Now, Señor Charlie, act very drunk. Savvy, son?"

While Papa laid his head down in Rio's lap and acted like a passed-out hobo, I nodded to Eddie as he walked up to the fire and asked myself how on earth I was going to find out who this woman was that Rio guessed about.

Eddie laughed at Papa snoring on the ground with his head in Rio's lap. I told him they drank too much liquor in their coffee. "Awful hot bre'kfust. Jest overdunnit."

Eddie looked around the cactus brush and said, "Lots o' folks cain't hold their likker, tha's all. 'Minds me o' th' day

I's a-waitin' with m' gun in m' hand fer th' bugle t' blow an' charge inta that Argonney Forrist. Guys was a-sleepin' all humped up around over one another, jest like Charlie here an' Ole Man Ryeoo! Coffee makes this whiskhey trot down a good bit eashier, don't it?"

"Where is that Arrabloney Forest?" I asked Eddie, hoping to keep him talking about France. "Germany?"

"France." He talked with his nose in his cup with the fumes bringing tears to his eyes. "I never did leave France."

"Nev'r ben ta France," I led him on. "Which battle was it where ya stopped that bullet in yer arm, Ed? Chattoe Theorie?"

"Argonney Forrist," he told me.

"Blow th' place down perty flat?" I asked him.

"Flatter'n a flitter," Ed said. "Nuthin' more'n a pile of hot rocks after them big sixteen-inchers got done with it."

" 'Bout like these rocks up and down this border, hum?" I pointed around.

Eddie rubbed the dust out of his hair. "Fact was, my Cap'n handed me a little old haffa pint o' cognac brandy that mornin'. Cap'n told me, 'Looky here, Private Moore,' he says, 'you see this here little rise of hill here?' An' I told 'im, yep, I could see th' hill—since we was awready a-standin' right up almos' ta th' top of th' derngone thing. Then he says, 'Private Moore, this here hill has got ta be guarded at th' cost of life er death, see, an', Private Moore, you're jest th' feller I figger that's damn fool enough ta stan' up here an' guard this goddamn hill.' I sez, 'Well, Cap'n, ye've got me figgered jest about right. Gimme th' haffa pint o' brandy an' promise me ya'll braing me another haff t'night when th' sun sainks down.'

"Well sir, I down'd my haffa pint th' firs' damn rattle outta th' box, an' time eight er nine o'clock come, hell's bells, my ole tongue was a-gittin' hard an' dry ag'in fer a little tetch from a bottle of some kind. Worst hell of it was, well, she commenced a-rainin' like a fresh hot cow a-pissin' on a flat rock, as Granmaw alliz used ta preach. A real, dead-down soaker. I couldn't even stand up no more. I set myself down fer about a hour er two, till my gun got so muddy it wouldn't've shot a dern fly. I waited up there in them little old limbery trees till jest about sun-down, an' I looked off down my little hill an' seein' a whole big bunch o' wimmen an' girls carryin' tubs of

Franch vin roudge down through a little trench of a thing,
belly deep with mud. So I says ta my limber tree hill,
'Y'r a mighty good little hill, but I reckon our time's
'bout come ta shake hands an' kiss good-bye.'

"I slid an' I rolled all o' th' way down th' side o' that
there hill, Woodrow, till I lit an' landed right smacker-dab
in that trench with th' rest of 'em. They wasn't any too
many soldier boys along that trench; they'd all run off ta
play poker in th' dugout ta git outta th' rain. I stopped
them ladies an' I picked up a cup o' that there wine juice,
an' I put it up ta my lips, like this, an' th' very minnit,
very secint, th't I drunk my first gulp o' that there vin
roudge, I looked up acrost my little hill an' I seen it fly
up a mile high in a big cloud o' smoke. Bango! Blingo! A
sixteen-incher hit a goshblame Heinie ammanition dump
that was dug down in under that there hill.

"It blew up like a hill, but she come down like a hole.
Loose dirt covered our trench und'r six foot o' muddy,
bloody, slickery slimery, wet, soggy dirt. Wasn't more'n
two er three of them wine-tub ladies an' girls th't ever did
make it out o' there alive, Woodrow. It blowed ever' stitch
o' clothes plumb off'n my body; lef' me naked as a jay
whopper. I woke up about two er three hours later with
m' head in a girl's lap, an' her a-pourin' big gourd dippers
of wine down me. She was hit, too. Knocked out 'bout as
bad as I was. We laid right ther in that muddy hole with
a two-gallion bucket of wine, two days an' three nights,
both of us so weak th't we couldn't lift a feather. We'd
a died in that mud bog if it'd notta been fer this here big
purple bucket of wine, boy."

"So that's where they winged yer arm?" I asked Eddie.

"My arm didn't git hit that day. Naw. It was a-goin' on
our third day. Mud was a-dryin' up an' a-gittin' harder
like a cake of concrete. Neith'r one of us could even
budge. A bunch of Heinies come along a little trail right
past us. When they walked up I says, 'Take ya a shot o'
vin roudge, then hand me a gourd.' They drunk up th'
bucket of wine, awright. Then they turn'd in loose on me'n
this crippled girl with rifles, 'sheeny guns, pistols, an'
ever'thaing else. They run off over th' road a-yellin' an'
a-gobblin', an' I had two holes right here in th' muscle of
my arm. I pulled this cripple girl over onta my lap an'
counted nine bleedin' holes in 'er. I still couldn't hardly
move. Bleedin' like a river. I held that there girl there

on my lap fer th' best part of thirty-six hours, till some stretcher bearers an' an amb'lance come along an' carted me off ta th' hospital, an' her off ta th' graveyard."

"Funny thing, Eddie boy," was all I could get my mouth to say. "I been knowin' you now, oh, fer th' past, how long? Past few years, anyhow, an' ya know, I nev'r did hear your true story till this mornin'. Funny, ain't it, how long two people can be around one another, an' think mebbe they know a little speck about each other, 'n' then find out they don't know hardly enough ta talk about? Oh, we say howdy an' good-bye, an' pull off some kind o' crazy joke 'bout th' wimmen, er 'bout the crops, an' do a little kiddin' 'round a jug o' buggy juice. But that's jest about as close to our real life, what's really burnin' down on our brains, as most of us ever do git."

"Take your own fam'ly." Eddie looked at Papa and Rio. "They've ben through hell 'n' high waters of ninety-odd kinds. But folks jest never do call up all o' this kind o' stuff ta talk about. I guess I'm jest a-tryin' ta fergit my wither'd arm an' ever'thing else connected with it."

"Even yer girl with her wine bucket?" I asked him. "Tryin' ta rub her picture outta yer mind, too, huh?"

Eddie started to say something, but the words faded out somewhere back in the places of his thoughts. Jeff, the sole owner of our old truck and most everything aboard it, walked up half awake.

He yelled one of his loudest Oklahoma creek-bottom screams to shake this dry and rattle Mexican border country out of its early-morning nakedness. He yelled about six feet at our backs, to let us know that he did not approve of our early-morning custom of pouring his homerun whiskey into such black and dirty tin coffee cups. He yelled to scare back any wild animals that might've been tracking a solid ring around our camp all night.

Rio had used his shirt for his pillow last night. He slipped into it again, wrapped and folded his blanket around his body. He watched us load our few things up onto the truck. Then he jumped into the backbed with Eddie and myself, and yelled to us in the front cab seat where I'd squeezed in with Papa and Jeff, "Only wan mile to Stoody Butte."

"Which turkey track do I follow?" Jeff yelled to Rio.

"Neither one," Rio laughed back. "There ees not any road that will take you truck from here into Stoody Butte.

Drive south up to the creekbed. Stay een de middle so as not to bomp over any roots."

Driving down the middle of the inch-deep bed of water, Jeff said, in a fairly good humor, "Well, it'll keep our tires from a-burnin' up, ta say th' least. I drove in worse floods than this back in Bristow, Oklahomy."

"I made a wild bronco swim th' South Canadian one morning while it was on a head rise, to get over to do some fast courting with Woodrow's mama," Papa said.

Papa took this chance when Eddie couldn't hear him to tell Jeff that Rio was thinking about trying to do Eddie some good with a woman. "Rio's trying to think up some way to help him. Eddie told Woodrow his whole story this morning by the fire. Rio and myself both played dog-eyed drunk, and overheard all of Eddie's story. There was a girl, all right. She got killed by some Huns while she was dragging him out of the mud. She died in his arms, in his lap."

"Whattaya 'magine Rio can do t' help Ed?" Jeff steered through the waters. "Did he say?"

"No," Papa said, "he never did say. He's rolling it all over in his mind, though. I'll bet you two dollars and one dime that Rio will have Eddie Stone Moore with a girl before that sun goes down this night."

"Us relatives, ah, I think th't we scare Eddie too bad, er his mammy's been too close on his back ever' day—sister an' ever'body," Jeff spat out the window. "Made too much of a big fuss about it. Scared 'im back in his shell faster'n he could stick 'is head out. Well, I got my doubts!"

CHAPTER 9

STUDY BUTTE

The creek got wider at a place where the truck took a slow left hand turn to the east. Jeff stopped before the turn and to see better I waded around and climbed into the back-bed. The water flowed from the humps of the mountains a few miles on farther to the east. It was rainwater, hailstone water, spring water, but no snow waters. I stood back of the truck cab, and Eddie stood at my back to look over my shoulder. Rio leaned back against the sideboard on the opposite side and pointed as he talked.

"See thee beeg rock there?" he asked us. "To the east?"

"I see a whole bunch of 'em," Eddie said. "Which'un ya talkin' about?"

"The beegest one." Rio nodded ahead.

"Looks like a young mountain ta me," I told them.

The thing that Rio called a rock was half the size of a good big mountain. It looked purple in the morning rays of the sun, because we saw it from the shady side. A few hundred feet to its top, a mile or so around its bottom, bare back and naked all over, it jumped straight up from the sandy pebbles and out of the river's bed. The sun played its riddly tricks on the river waters that bounced

and glanced like settler bullets up the slick-off sides of
the lonesome-looking rock.

Rio licked another brown-paper cigarette, and looked
as proud as if he had made that slickdown rock for us to
play with this morning. "It is what we call the Study Butte
Rock."

We made another turn to the left, at the signal from
Rio's hand. We left the river's bed, struck out under some
cactus patches high enough to scratch a man standing on
top of our truck cab. The bushes were long, dry, tall,
skinny, scraggly things, twisting and bending like dancers
over hot coals, then running up on long bumpery limbs to
grab a thin fistful of free sky.

The town of Study Butte did not look like a town to
me. The first thing I saw that looked human was the wire
fence around a cleared-off cemetery. Cleared of thorny
things and planted back with lost people. Old rotty crosses
were here, swayback sticks, little whitewashy fences, mud-
and-stick statues, dolls, sunburnt, wind-whipped, water-
soaked, cursed, spat on, loved, and cried over. I saw a
pile of flowers on every sunk or piled-up mound. Dried
rattler flowers, flowers in little cheap glasses, flowers fading
in olive-oil vases, one or two quart-size milk bottles. A
blaze of pretty ribbons, silky knots and streaming white
ribbons, green homemade ones, red, purple, bright, dull,
wiggling their hair like some kind of a ghosty visitor in
the sun.

Rio caught me looking so hard, and told me, "De place
looks cheap and sad—and eet looks foolish, yes, I know.
But tell everybody, thees burial hill is de only thing in
Study Butte which ees pretty for your eye to look at. The
quickest way out from Study Butte—on your head—ees
just you say one bad word about de place of de dead.
Savvy?"

Eddie looked back at the graveyard as we rattled by,
and told Rio, "Dern tootin'. Takes a lotta hard work ta
keep a grave up thatta way in all kindsa weath'r."

"My people they say de quickest way to get to visit our
graveyard ees to make fun of eet."

At this very instant, up on the front cushion, I heard
later, Jeff was saying to Papa, "Heck of a lookin' cemetery
back there, wasn't it? Looks kinda silly ta me, a-hangin'
out all o' them ribbons fer th' dead, 'stead o' tryin' ta

make some o' these sticky mud houses look a little bit
better."

"I'll walk back later and get a close look at the graveyard," Papa told Jeff. "I didn't get much of a look at it. I
was too busy wondering, like you say, why on earth they
don't do some work on these little mud shacks. Mud and
sticks, that's just about all I've seen so far. I wonder, to
be real truthful, where in the dickens the town of Study
Butte is. Hummm."

"Mebbe that Ole Rio feller back there can tell us." Jeff
yelled out over his shoulder: "Hey, Rio, where'n th' name
of puppydogs is yer town, Study Butte, at?"

"Eet does not belong to me, *amigo*." Rio talked back to
Jeff, "It belongs to the mining *compañía*. If Rio did own
thees town, you would see all marble and all granite, in the
place of sticks and mud."

"How many people live here, Rio?" Papa asked in the
wind.

"Oh, I don't know. I say 'round 'bouta two hundred,
three hundred. Not so sure." Rio nodded at a pair of young
boys filling a rusty barrel with water at a town trough.

"Do they all live in these mud-an'-stick houses?" Jeff
asked Rio. "Mud-smeared rabbit traps?"

"Some little bigger," Rio told us. "You see few 'dobe
ones."

"Is them 'dobe houses over yonder by th' store?" Eddie
asked. "In under them little shade trees?"

"Yes." Rio looked ahead of the truck. "They are 'dobe.
Mud brick dry in the sonn. Tal Jaff to stop as close to de
store as he can. Youp!"

As Jeff parked the truck by the hitching and watering
trough, I took the chance to ask Rio, "Hey, how old're
these 'dobe houses, anyhow?"

" 'Bout like me." Rio jumped down onto the ground,
sprang up and down on the balls of his feet, and told me as
I jumped down at his side: "These 'dobes built same time
I, Rio, got born. Bot these mud-an'-stick house, dey here
long time 'fore I, Rio, came 'long."

And looking past me at Papa and Jeff walking up the
store steps, Rio said, "You wait here de store. I go fast. I
back quick. I see friend. Heh? You wait?"

"I wait. I wisht I had a good friend somewhere in this
here town. Might be even a nice perty girl friend. I wait.
You go see. Okay."

Rio walked across the street. He nodded to several people along a dusty walk, grinned at three little girls playing dolls, patted a jinny burro on her hip as she tugged a rubber-tired two-wheeler cartload of sheet-iron oil drums being used for water barrels. Rio spoke over a small picket fence as high as his knees to a dozen faces of the family in the doors and windows of a two-room, sun-baked adobe house with a slanty tar-paper roof. He faded into the half shades and shadows along the tree lane of whiskery mesquites, and then he turned to his right around a muddy house corner. My eyes lost track of him. I felt an empty feeling come over me, a touch of something sad in my belly and in my throat. Me? Me sad? Nineteen years old and standing here feeling sad, or even halfway sad?

About who? A couple of good, long, deep breaths of this early, sunny-morning Mexican border air, and God and the devil, both, couldn't trick me into being sad. And this Old Codger, this Old Man Rio, well, him, I don't know him. Just met up with him back there along that pebble-stony street at Terlingua, where the pretty young lady had led Carlos and Rosalita away. I'll let that twenty-year-old aunt of theirs make me sad if she would like. She can pick her grounds and name her hours, her hour to make me glad to meet her, and her hour to make me sad to leave. That oversize drink of coffee whiskey so early this morning has got my gut to rippling, my brains to pounding. I don't give a hoot where you go off to, Old Man Ryeo. I'm too dizzy to worry about where you go. I'll duck my head good and deep here in this horse trough. Soak myself. Cool off some. Look at the trees and skies and clouds shining upside down here in this horse water. Hah. Bluubbble. Hmmm. What'sa matter? Outta my way! Leave me go. Heyyy!

"You weel be plenty sick, frand," somebody was saying to me, "eef you stick your bean in thees cold water. You fool."

A long-faced Mexican fellow a few years older than myself, in a white sack-cloth suit, stood with his hands on his hips looking at me. I tried to push him out of my way to soak my head in the watering tank. He stepped out of my way and boosted me off my feet, football fashion, with his shoulder. We were about the same size and weight. If I'd been my natural self, if my head had been clear, I

would have laughed out loud when he bumped me down
onto my hands and knees. Being half sick and dizzy, I got
up, looked him up and down, and tangled arms and legs
with him at the very rim of the cement water trough.

Jeff and Papa saw the whole struggle from the porch
of the general store. Jeff ran down the steps, two at a jump,
and grabbed the fellow. He jerked us loose, and was drawing back to thrash him with his fists, when Papa got there
and pulled Jeff away from the man.

"Woodrow was in the wrong," Papa told Jeff. "Dead
wrong. I saw the whole thing. This fella didn't want Woody
to soak his head in that cold horse water. Told him that it
would make him deathly sick. Woody insulted him. Tried
to push him around. I saw the whole thing. We ought to
take Woody and give his head a Dutch rubbing."

And for all of the Study Butte citizens to watch, Papa
and Jeff wrastled me down onto the ground. They rubbed
my head so hard with their knuckles that I came up with
tears in my eyes.

A dozen people stood around the truck and water
trough to watch the scuffle. A dozen more stood back in a
larger circle amidst carts, old wagons, teams of mules,
horses, and pack-loaded burros, donkeys, and long-eared
desert jinnys. The clumpy sound of the shod hoof on the
hardpan sand, the deader sound of the unshod hoofs, the
slushy sloshing of hoofs around the water troughs, was
the only noise I heard. The feet of the people were bare
and calloused, except for a handful, not more than six or
eight, who wore old, throwed-away brogan workshoes. I
saw an old woman so drawn up and bent over that her
head hung down past her knees, and her fancy-work
shawl dragged its fringe and tassels on the dirt. One tall,
halfbreed fellow stood with a twenty-year-old black cowboy
hat on his head, a purple and red rodeo ribbon around his
neck. Boys in raggledy, patched, and repatched pants
milled up to touch the truck and run back away like scared
colts. One old lady sat on the boardwalk in front of the
truck, wearing a fading pink corduroy shirt and a cottony
dress specked with little blue flowers. Everybody that I saw
had a head of coarse, shiny, heavy black hair, long or short,
straight or wavy. I saw the shine, too, of Indian and
Mexican silverwork, pins, beads, bracelets, neck yokes.
Eagles, horseshoes, rain dogs, good-luck tokens.

I could see a few hats of straw or felt, cotton or wool but most every head was bare to the weather. Born and raised amongst Indians and Mexicans, back in Oklahoma, my eye was quick to guess and to judge this crowd. They could have all been of nearly any tribe from Colorado, New Mexico, Arizona, Utah, Oklahoma, or Texas. Hopi. Apache. Seminole. Cherokee. Ute. The Creek. The Osage. Or any of the tribes. The four whites around our truck, Jeff, Papa, Eddie, and myself, could hardly be seen. The wide eyes of the young girls in the crowd sparkled with a light that asked questions. The older eyes in the crowd asked older questions. Where are you from? Why did you come here? What kind of work do you do? How many blisters do you have on your hands? Do you know how to take care of yourself out lost in the cactus hills? Can you wade through a muddy flood, and can you swim a high river with a blanket roll? What do you want from us? Are you going to help my people? Are you going to hurt my people? Are you here to carry more of us away to die on the daggery road, to die in the crops? Did you drive your truck down here to load our silver and mercury all in it, to blast down our mountains, and to leave us robbed and hungry like coyotes?

To see Papa and Jeff give my head such a knuckle-rubbing brought a short smile to most of their faces. To see me jump back up onto the bedding of our truck made them grin a little, and then, their faces got sober and long. I knew that there were several centuries of hard travels and hard fighting less than a hair's width in back of these rocky-faced grins and waiting faces.

"Folks"—I didn't know what words would come to me when I leaned over the side board to speak—"friends, I guess I'm a lot bigger fool than this feller here said I was. I feel thatta way, anyhow, right about now."

This got the whole crowd to snickering and laughing. One or two hooted and whooped at me some words I couldn't understand. The boy in the white sack-cloth suit nodded and looked around at his friends to get credit for winning the argument. The people drifted away from the truck.

"These old stick and mud dog houses," Jeff muttered, looking around. "Hell, Charlie, my cow shed's a bett'r place ta live than these pig wallers. Stinkin' mud. That Rio's supposed ta git a boy here ta show us how t' git out to the Sam Nail Ranch. Git me out o' this muddy mess of a hell hole anyway. Git me outta here. Where's Rio at?"

"Well, Jeff," Papa said, "I'm reasonably sure that these Indians and poor muddy Mexicans don't like the looks of this town any better than you like it. It's easy to criticize and to cuss about how stinky and muddy and filthy it is. You forget that our own daddy lived down in here with nothing more than a covered wagon and a lead-lined shotgun. Jerry P. was a shrewd hand, though, at holding back his lip. He could make a fencepost like him. And, remember, too, that all of Reenie Gal's folks dug mud dugouts and raised kids in them back up on those wheat plains, with no faucets to spew out hot water on your left hand and cold water on your right. This country is as rich or richer, in some ways, than our wheat and cattle plains will ever be. These Indians and Mexicans get lied to, cheated, beat up, and robbed in a hundred ways that the naked eye can't even see. I don't blame them for being sly, sneaky, odd, and suspecting. They die out here by the handfuls where you and I don't see them. They're born naked, and they die with a handful of those little ribbons. Your life is in their hands down here. You're not on the sidewalks of Pampa with a badge and two sixguns over your hip."

Papa lectured in Jeff's ear as I strained my eyes down along the street to look for Rio. "A word of high temper down here can mean that we lose this mine of Paw's and maybe lose lots more along with it. But I know you're a smart enough man to already know all these things."

"I still got my two six-shooters right back there, I mean right here in under this seat cushion"—Jeff glanced along with a dark shadow in his eye—"if it ev'r comes time ta hafta use 'em. They're still good 'n' oily, as the feller said."

"Take it easy, Jeff." Papa folded his arms. "If you want to turn this truck around and go back, I'll stay here and find Paw's mine."

Rio caught the truck moving at a slow crawl east down the only street in Study Butte. He mounted up onto the fender on Papa's side, and Jeff cussed as he pulled over to the side and jammed on the brakes. He knew better than to start a very serious argument with Rio, whose help we needed to get a guide to the Nail ranch. Jeff could not butt

his head against Rio's wall. He butted the rest of us to
let off his nervous steam. If only his Reenie Gal had been
up in that front seat with him, I thought, Jeff would have
been, as he usually was, peppy, solid, fast-working, hard-
slugging, loudmouthed, and good-natured.

Even as the truck stopped, Jeff said to Papa, "We ain't
got th' gas, Charlie, ta be racin' this motor up an' down
this road like this."

"Can I help you to save the gas?" Papa answered. "I
can't make that engine use any less, can I? I'm not the
Ford Motor Company, you know. We'll have enough to
pull us over to where Papa camped on the Sam Nail Ranch.
How far is it from here to the Sam Nail place, Rio?"

"About eighteen miles," Rio told them.

"Long or short miles?" Jeff asked Rio. "That last three
miles must've run perty close ta six."

"Jeff, if you can spare the time," Rio said, "will you
please pull 'cross this little ditch and over to that little
house there behind those cactus?"

"Which mud house? I ain't seen no other kind of dern
house. Where did you people git all o' this mud at anyhow?"

"We have a big plenty of mud. Just drive. I see that the
words from out you mouth they not any so smart this
morning."

"God's sakes alive, Jeff," Papa said. "Just drive."

"Smart?" Jeff pressed on. "Me smart? No, no siree,
Mister Rio Grandy, I'm not smart. Not a bit smart. But
I'm not ignorant enough ta live off down here like no dog
or no pig, an' ta raise my kids in no God-blamed hog pen
smeared up out o' mud an' sticks."

Rio pointed his finger towards the mud house in back of
the rough-looking cactus garden. "If you wish to remain
with the living ones very long, remember there are people
inside these muddy sticka houses lots wiser than any of us
on this truck."

"Gas aplenty in those big drums back there to pull us
over to Sam Nail's place a dozen times, if we don't blow
it up in one of our hot arguments," Papa said.

"Pish posh," Jeff answered.

Rio told them, "When you get over to the Nails ranch,
you will not be driving this truck very much, if any."

"I cain't unnerstan' a gosh damn word that ole Ryeoh

devil says." Jeff said this like it was his first early joke of
the morning. "Mebbe I better sorta try ta be halfway nice
ta th' ole geezer, anyhow, long enough ta git all th' infor-
mation out of 'im I'll need. Ryeo, *amigo*. Ryeo, my
friend."

The hard frown that froze over the face of Rio caused
Papa to nudge his elbow into Jeff's ribs.

"My truck, Charlie." Jeff acted quiet and dignified. "I'll
say anything I want ta say so long's I'm a-drivin' down
this road in my own truck. You're th' one that's actin'
like a crazy man gettin' down on your knees ta these
igner'nt Mexicans. We'll see what we shall see. Jest wait."

The truck stopped at a long row of mixed cactus shrubs.
Rio trotted up onto the porch of a little one-room mud-
and-stick house. He motioned to us to kill the engine and
to come on into the house. "Nobody ees home," he said.

There was a rusty screen door all full of holes, an old
thick wooden door all saggy and warped, an old, dank
smell of dust which had never felt the sun. I walked in after
Papa and Eddie. "Heckofa place," Eddie said, but Papa
grunted in a lazy way back and said, "Seen lots of times
back in Okfuskee County when I'd sure been powerful
glad to bump onto a house like this. Where is everybody,
Rio?"

"At some weddin'." Rio scratched his ankle as he sat
himself down on an apple crate. "They back soon."

I took a seat on a tornout Army cot by the north window. "House is always better'n an old truck, ain't it, somehow?"

Jeff stretched and yawned. His arms nearly touched the
east and westerly walls. "Everything in this whole country
down here's made outta mud. Hhhmmm."

In order to try to pass away the time without getting
lost off in the thorns of any more arguments, I asked Jeff,
"Hey, Stud Hoss, I'd shore nuff like ta hear how that ole
Squallin' Panther fiddle of yours would sound in here. My
gittar fingers are both itchin'."

Jeff blinked his eyes, like a sleepy owl, sat his hat back
on the dome of his head, and yawned again with his legs
spread all the way across the floor, "I reckon as t' how I
might. If you'll go out an' carry th' music in. Like music,
Ryeo?"

"Me? *Sí, sí.*" Rio blew a puff of smoke out his south

window. "I, what you say, grew up with *música*. Eef eet ees, what you say, good music."

I carried Jeff's fiddle case and my guitar in the screen door, and surprised them all by setting the last one third of a fruit jar down on the floor. Eddie said, "Looks mighty larrapin', Cous'n Woody, but what I'd give a left hind leg for right about now, is a big fresh gourd o' cold, cool water."

"I'm drier'n a dead bone too." Jeff rosined up his bow. We got our strings tuned up and Rio carried a wooden bucket and an aluminum dipper in from the shady side of the house.

"Don't spill a drop," he told us. "Water comes to thees door only when the boy's burro does not feel sick. Most times, this burro she pretty sick."

Jeff tapped the glass jar on the floor with his fiddle bow and said, "Heavy on th' likker, men, an' easy on th' water." He broke off into "Billy in the Lowland" and hit the high parts with a loping longbow that jarred old fifty-year-old dust down from the grease cracks. I followed him on my guitar through the "East Tennessee Wagoner" and tromped a rocking three-way bass beat.

This was a fiddling morning. It was a fiddling afternoon. I never had heard Jeff rake that tail hair any better, and I'd heard him now for a good long time. He knocked his hat off down onto the floor and tromped it under both feet on the B flat and G Minor tune, "Done Gone." Papa, Eddie, and Rio clapped hands, swayed, acted clowny, when Jeff's fingers tore into one we all sung over and over:

> I'm a-gonna kiss you, Sally Ann,
> I'm a-gonna kiss you, Sally Ann,
> I'm a-gonna kiss you, Sally Ann,
> I'm a-gonna kiss you quick's I can.
>
> Give you a lickin', Lucy Lou,
> Give you a lickin', my Lucy Lou,
> Give you a lickin', my Lucy Lou,
> Lucy, I love you, swear I do.

"East Tennessee Blues" took a fast beating. "Careless Love" got a tromping. The "Cattle Call" and "Wednesday Night" waltzes, in the key of D, both sailed easy and greasy.

While Jeff sawed off the sadder tune of "Budding Roses,"
I looked north out my window and sang some words to
tease him:

> How I miss my Little Reenie,
> How I miss my 'Eenie Gal,
> All my nights are cold and empty
> Out here in this western world.
>
> Who's gonna hug an' kiss you, 'Eenie,
> Who's gonna hold your sweet, warm breast?
> Who shall warm your bed at night, dear,
> While I'm stumbling through the West?

Jeff stopped playing the actual tune, and flumped the
strings of his fiddle on his lap, chording on it, acting like
it was a girl's head. He sang to get back at me,

> Who'll come hold yer hand, my Hell Cat?
> Who'll come rappin' on yore door?
> Who'll come creepin' in yore window
> While I'm gone six weeks or more?
>
> Who'll come kiss your lips, my Hell Cat?
> Hell Cat Gally, that's your name.
> That neighbor boy will feel your titties
> Now that Woodhead's gone away.
>
> When he finds his grampaw's gold mine,
> Woody he'll crawl back to you,
> But your hairs will turn to silver
> While he's diggin' out his gooold.

Eddie, Papa, and Rio laughed in between the words to
both of our songs. We all took a turn or two at the jar on
the floor. And when it came time for Jeff to fiddle "Make
Me a Bed Right Down on Your Floor," Papa sung with
his jaw and chin down on his chest, in a deep, lily-paddy,
froggy voice:

> Oh, set me a jar right here on the floor
> Set me a jug right here on your floor,
> And I'll go to sleep
> With my jug on the floor.

Poor lonesome boy, come a long ways today,
Poor lonesome boy, come a long ways this day,
Toss me your jug, dear.
I've not long to stay.

Eddie sang his old stand-by that went,

Good mornin', Mister Zip Zip Zippp,
With y'r hair cut jest as short as,
Hair cut jest as short as,
With y'r hair cut jest as short as mine.

Rio sang one verse of the old Revolutionary song "La Adelita." Then he turned to ask Eddie, "Soldier boy like you, he have fine tam in Study Butte. Plenty girl. Bigga bonch. Girl here like soldier fella, eh?"

"Fer who?" Eddie's face clouded over with a serious look. "Girl fer who?"

"You," Rio half-whispered in Eddie's ear. "Savvy?"

Eddie blew out a long breath, and said, "Heck fire, anyhow. I'm too dirty, cain't dress up er look halfway decent. Whiskers. Ugly. 'Sides, we gotta be trackin' on outta here 'fore so very long. Wouldn't be enough time t' do very dern much with a girl. Gosh a warriors! I don't even let 'em cross my mind, Rio. Girls jist don't mean a thing in my young life. I done forgot jest about what ta say aroun' any woman, girl. Boy, but I shore do thank yeh, Ryeo, fer off'rin' ta be so friendly with me. 'Course, now, there's Woody a-jayhawkin' over yond'r by that there north window—he's a right big lady's hand."

I looked through my guitar strings and whiskey drinks at Eddie and Rio, and told them, "I'll try t' roll any girl that'll gimme a half a chance. But I'm sure not th' biggest ladies' man runnin' in an' outta this mesquite 'roun' here— not by no sackful. Jeffrey over here was about our fastest man with a sheemale, up till—well, till he got hisself hitched up an' married."

"Trot one past Old Jefferoo"—Jeff tilted his bow in the air in a funny motion—"an' jest see how fast I snatch in after her. Trot 'er."

"Eddie here don't claim ta be no kind of a lady trimmer," I said, "but I'd bet my guitar here ag'inst a peanut hull, that he'd give a woman lots more of a goin'-over than all o' th' rest o' you gassy-mouths added up an' herded in a breedin' pen. Women, Eddie, somehow er another, well, they jest run an' fall all over th' guy that sets around sorta quietful, an' don't shoot off at his tongue, an' blow his bladder braggin'.'"

Eddie squirmed on his bucket, blushed around his face, and said, running his words together like mud pies, "I'd lots druth'r jest do my good day's carpenter work, upholstery work, er tractor work an' field work, any kinda work, Woody, than hang aroun' an' let some she-cat run it over me. I don't even like ta thaink about any womern. I feel jest as good off as all of you fellers that spends most o' yer time horsin' 'roun' the women folks."

"My cousin John," Jeff told us, "he wuzza blacksmith. Best gorsh-blame smith in our whole country back in them Oklahoma bowjack hills. He never lifted his eyelid at a girl, ner at a woman, while I was a-growin' up there aroun' his sawdust floor. He met his wife, Rachie, one week, an' married 'er th' naixt comin' week. They're bringin' up five kids t'geth'r, an' I know it fer a fact, old Smithy John never coulda slept with any other wom'n, if she'da paid 'im cash money."

"Like Jeff says," Papa told us, "everybody that ever saw John and Rachie loved them. Wasn't it John that taught you how to saw the fiddle, Jeff?"

"Yep," Jeff said, "he sawed down a bowdark tree an' built me my first fiddle, by hand, there in his old tinny shop."

"I used to flip a guitar chord or two, myself," Papa said, "before I broke my knuckles all to pieces fighting the Socialists out of Okfuskee County. I couldn't even find a string on a guitar, though, not any more. My fingers won't let me play any kind of instrument. See those bad knots there, Rio? I won't be able to have much luck, I'm afraid, out in these cattle hills with a pair of hands like those."

"Looks bad." Rio bit his lips together. "How you get? Who say you fight?"

"Socialists." Papa moved his hands. "Back up in eastern Oklahoma. You savvy Socialist? Always milling around causing trouble. Socialists. You don't savvy such a big word? Socialist?"

Rio wrinkled up his forehead, moved his tongue around in his cheeks, and told Papa, "*Sí!* I savvy. I Socialist, Rio. I been long time Socialist. I fight to let my people break down these mud an' stick house, to own de big Study Butte mine all together. *Sí*. You savvy? You want fight Rio now with your sore hands? For who you break op your hands, for what? Whatta you gotta now? Nawthing."

God and little whirlwinds! I was afraid a knockdown fight would break out between Papa and Rio. The only thing that could drag Papa into a fight was this one subject of Socialism. Rio was a few years older than Papa, but Papa's general health was not so good as Rio's. I could see Jeff was worried too. The only thing he knew to do was to try to get both of them to listen to some expert fiddle playing and forget their argument about Socialism. He tried to drown out their words with his fiddle. He struck up into the loudest key, open A. After a few strokes of his bow to feel the A chords out with his fingers and his ears, Jeff loped off acrost the notes of "Cindy," one of the loudest of his A tunes.

I looked out over the handle of my guitar and listened to the political argument. Papa swayed his head as he sat on the old, creaky apple crate. Rio had took a seat crosslegged on the floor, where he tossed and pitched while he spoke to Papa, or when he stopped talking to listen. Papa was a hard nut on the topic of capitalism, Socialism, public ownership, and free enterprise, and loved the chance to quote pages and paragraphs out of the thousand-dollar leatherback law library he had owned ten or twelve years ago, back in Okemah. Papa had tried to teach me to hate and despise, and to insult and fight the Socialists in any spot I got the time and chance. I had seen several tribes of good, healthy Indians get cheated, beaten, robbed, doped, rooked, gypped, scared, and tricked out of all of their lands and houses, their farms and orchards, pastures, and even their self-respect, their human pride, their natural lives, everything, under the slushy bucket of the rich oil companies. I felt that it was wrong to rob these good, friendly Indians in all of these ways. I felt the same way towards the black folks, and the mixed-bloods. I wasn't an expert talker, not as quick and tricky with words as Papa always was. I didn't know all there was to know about capitalists, Socialists, free enterprise, public ownership, Communists, trade unions, legal red-tapery, or naked girls. I dreamed more at night about the girls that came to my mind than I did about all the several other political and

philosophical things melted up and poured together. My
nineteen-year-old brain, though, felt as good towards Rio
as it did for Papa. I didn't see any sense to the chance
Papa was taking here, I mean, the chance of losing Rio's
friendship, and maybe Rio himself along with it. He filled
a deep hole in our blind chase to find Jerry's claimstake.
Papa had bawled Jeff out earlier this morning for just
simply getting in a few observations about ignorance and
filth in these little dog hutches made from mud rubbed
over some bark-tied sticks. Now, to see Papa pushing Rio
farther away from us by raving around about Rio's Com-
munistic ideas didn't make too much sense to me.

Jeff touched his toe against mine, and winked longjawed,
while he unstrung a few of the main depots along the
E-natural route.

"Lost Injiun." Jeff told me to grab the right chord.
"That'll bring ole Papa Charlie aroun' outta his blame
fool argermint."

"But under the capitalist system of free enterprise,"
Papa motioned his hands in Rio's face, "I've still got a
chance to make something for myself and my family."

Rio shook his head and folded his arms in his lap. "I
want to see de worker own this mine. It is built here by de
hand of de worker, while de big boss does nawthing. Nawthing."

Papa's eyes drifted over to Jeff's corner. He knew that
Jeff always played "Lost Indian" in Papa's honor, as a little
something special, like a box of things at Christmas time.
The big smile on Papa's face took the place of a truckload
of words. Papa watched my fingers while I plucked Tennessee fashion—with bare fingers, using no pick. The
chording to "Lost Indian" was not like most guitar chords;
that is, with two or three changes, or anything like that. I
held down the strings of E-natural without even making a
change anywhere in the whole song, the way you hear on a
few other specialty pieces with the fiddle, mouth harp,
organ, or leading instrument, numbers like "The Lost
Hobo," "Railroad Blues," "Runaway Train," and others
where the guitar never comes to the front. As he said,
Papa had played the guitar before I was born, with a
little cowboy ranch-house fiddle band. He always watched
me in a proud way. I felt today that his eyes were trying
to remember something from a long time ago.

"You know, Rio," Papa nodded half without knowing it, "it takes a better guitar-picker to know what not to do than it takes to bang and wham out all over the place."

"I have heard de violin and de *guitarra* every day since I was born here by this river." Rio smiled past Papa and towards Jeff and myself. In a sort of a quiet way, he said, "Champ *guitarristas* . . . López, Gómez, Juárez, Bondez, Jiménez, Odez, Romanez, Guadez, Jóquez, Jesús, Peterez, Quotrez. Champ *guitarristas*. Champ *violinistas* . . . Guadalupe, Tataye, Barquero, Honduro, Taquilla, Bonerro. But your brother, Jeff, he play this folk *música* very good, very good. I never mucha good when it comes to maka de fiddle, or play de *guitarra*. I like listen *música* all time. But I, Rio, I same like you, Señor Charlie, I no play."

"Me neither," Eddie told us. "I cain't carry a tune up over a hill in a wooden bucket."

"How 'bout a bucket full o' French wine?" I kidded Eddie. "Could'ja carry a bucket full o' that, Eddie Stoner?"

Eddie jumped to his feet and waved his arms. He sailed into me with one of the worst tongue-whippings I had ever got. "Oh, Woody, gorsh dangit, shut up! Heck fire! Leave me alone. You shore ain't got much sense in your head. Havin' fun, huh? Havin' lotsa fun, ain't ye? Well, damn yore hide, in th' first place, 'tain't no fun ta me. Keep y'r gorsh-dang trap shut about me. Jest leave me out of yer damn silly teasin's. Fun's fun, awright, yeah, but when it comes ta damn silly low-down insults like you been a-throwin' at me all mornin', they ain't funny, they jest ain't. I say, leave me out of it. That's all."

I watched Ed slam the screendoor behind him as he walked out into the front yard. There was no front window on the east side of the house, so I could not see what he was doing, where he was going. I could still hear his voice railing back at me from out in the east path. He broke down into a fit of crying which cut off his words.

"Well," I looked around at the others, "I've pulled just th' worst boner of this whole trip so far, guys. Rio, you're a Communist. Papa, you're a big rich capitalist. But me, Woody, I've just now hurt th' best damn feller in this whole bunch, f'r no good reason. I didn' aim ta hurt Eddie. I just guess I swung in a little too close to home. But I didn' wanta hurt 'im. Wonder what I did do, anyways?"

"You dug up his dream girl." Rio nodded out the screen. "You splashed moonleg whiskey on her. An' I think Addie did not wish for you to bring his girl in here to this whiskey-drinking party."

"We learned a lesson, anyhow," Papa said, "and we've found the woman in Eddie's life."

Jeff hugged his fiddle and said, "It jest looks like they's a crazy spot somewheres in all of us, don't it?"

CHAPTER 10

LEATHER BOOKS

Jeff put his fiddle into its case of red alligator leather on the floor. He told me, "Woody, my shoulders an' my arms ain't a bit tired like y' might be thinkin', but my little panther fiddle is awful mighty sleepy. That pore little fiddle has yelled his dang lungs out, a-tryin' ta out-squall these two wise men from Borneo. My bow hair's red, scorchin' hot, an' I gotta let it cool down some 'fore I play any more. I cain't understan' a blame word of what Rio an' Charlie's a-spoutin' off about. If you'll stan' here with yer shotgun an' keep guard over my panther fiddle, I'll step out here 'n th' front yard an' see if I can do any good fer Eddie. Say?"

"Fine," I said to Jeff as he walked out the door. "Any human that steals your squealin' fiddle has got ta steal me right along with it."

"But that is the way the world is run," Papa was motioning to Rio, "You can't change in three days these things that we have been doing now for several thousand years."

"The reech man," Rio told Papa, "he has geev money to thee *policía* to go anda keel my people. The Study Butte mine she own the store. If my family ees in debt a few dollar here, this Study Butte store, say, fifteen, twenty

201

dollar, my family, we stuck here in de mud stick house.
De mine she run full blast for one month, she no hire no
more than half the people here. We, other half, we stuck in
de mud, we stuck in de dirt. If I try to go work some other
town, say El Paso del Norte, I in the hole fifteen dollar
here to this store, de *policía* dey find me, Rio, dead like
rabbit under de cactus bush. You talk free enterprise—
you mean a free bullet hole. But de fife cents for de price
of de bullet, Señor Charlie? De *policía* he come my people
and he laugh, see, and he take twenty-fi' cents for another
fife-cent bullet. With this he run shoot my daughter under
same cactus bush."

"Oh!" Papa shook his head. "How many times a year
does a thing like this happen?"

"Up and down this border, every day, two, three times.
Same thing."

"As bad as the police might be, things would be twice
this bad if we did not pay the policeman to protect and
to guard our property and our lives. You'll admit that,
surely, Rio."

"Eet would be good t'ing eef this *policía* would fight on
side of de worker and not on de side of de big boss
man all off de time. De boss he right one day, mabbe so;
but de boss he not right every day."

"Well, that is the officer's job. To keep the law and to
keep the peace."

"This owner man, see, he take all my money; he not
leave me red cent. My family hongry. My brother die. My
sister she die on de floor. Why not my boss man send me
de money which is already mine? He 'fraid. He 'fraid I
run buy Winchester, I shoot him de head. You savvy me?"

"You have to fight your boss, if you do not like his
ideas, with your vote. Your state can take that mine away
from its owner in three hours, if you and enough people
like you go and vote for that law."

"What law?"

"A law that says, hereafter and commencing now, this
land, these mines, their machinery, back accounts, heirs,
assigns, and executors, shall be declared and made the
public property of the State of Texas, County of Brewster,
the Town of Study Butte, and that furthermore, the boss
doesn't own it any more, and that it is like the post office
in the town, belongs to the citizens of the town that de-
pend directly upon the products and output of the said

mine and mining machinery for employment, subsistence, and livelihood. We'll say that after six o'clock on the morning of January first, Nineteen Hundred and Thirty-Two, all incomes, moneys, valuables, goods, exchanges, profits, benefits, credits, payments, and so forth and so on and so on, that the sum total of all of these values received and accrued to the output of the Study Butte mine, be distributed to each person, male or female, according to his or her labors invested in such an enterprise, in such ranges, degrees, percentages, and proportions as are to be further agreed upon by vote of said citizens at the oncoming free and open elections."

"It does have a good sound to it."

"Clerk of the Okfuskee County Court for four terms. I memorized a stack of new leather lawbooks as high as your head, Rio. I've been a Notary Public since I was twenty-three years old."

"Than, mabbe, you can tell me how all off my people can have de vote. They no vote since they been born. They no see de vote. No read. No write. No own de property. No own this much land. No own this little mud house, Señor Charlie. Not even own their naked skin. No money for vote tax. Not feefty of us here along this Rough Run Creek voted this last time. And plenty big deputy drive up eena big new car so as to help this little handful vote for what the owner man say."

"I can't understand how a man of your age could remain such a hot-blooded revolutionary. Back while I was turning through my big leather books, yes, Woody Top, and Rio, I was not only the hottest-blooded Socialist in the state of Oklahoma, but I had the finest sets of books, the costliest library, and the best fist and footwork in the state. I yelled and made a big noise up and down a few streets. I followed the Revolution over in Russia with an honest heart and a good, clear eye. But I just did not want to be the cause of such a civil war as that breaking out over here in my country to kill my wife and to cripple my babies. You were five in those days, Woody. Big mop of real white, cottony, curly hair. Roy was eleven. Clara was thirteen. Your brother George was in your mama's belly. The more I watched the poor ignorant Russian people die by the millions just to bring all of the property into the hands of the state, well, the cooler and colder I got."

"Every country in de world she ship spies, soldiers, in to blow up the Russiana factory and to kill de kids and kill de girls, and to tell big lies say *Communista* Bolsheviky he kill everybody. Pssshht!"

"I went into the land business, real estate. I cleared fifty thousand dollars in five years' time and owned the deed and clear title to thirty farms, the smallest farm a twenty-acre hog-breeding farm, the biggest farm six hundred and forty of riverbottom pecan, walnut, and white oak timber land. I took a downspin and I lost. I ran for an office and hocked all of my properties to win the election, which I lost by less than four hundred votes. When the count came in, I had lost thirty farms in just exactly thirty days."

"De good part is, Señor Charlie, that you only lost those papers, those deeds and those titles—papers. Those farms they are still up there. De oatmeal, de pork chop, she taste just as good as when they belong to Señor Charlie. Thirty farms is too many for Señor Charlie to be de boss off, anyway. Savvy?"

I wore my neck stiff and my eye sockets raw twisting my head first to Papa and then to Rio. Both of them kept their heads cool and their tempers down as they argued. I never had heard Papa unload his beliefs in this way before. This kind of a conversation certainly could never come up between Papa and Eddie, nor between Papa and Jeff, although Papa and Jeff both had carried badges and pistols as keepers of the peace for the past dozen or so years, in Pampa and on back in my old home town. I'd hung around the stink of the jailhouse, courtroom, courthouse, Papa's offices from place to place, but never heard him tell anybody that he had been such a hotrod Socialist in his younger days.

"Funny, ain't it?" I asked Papa. "Funny we never did talk about all o' this stuff before, huh?"

"I never did know that you cared to talk about such heavy things as the world revolution," Papa told me.

"Good ta listen ta somebody that can bring it all out as plain as you here, an' Rio," I told them.

"And to which side of the debate do you so far incline?" Papa asked me, as Rio smiled.

I thought a bit and told them, "Well, from what I jest heard both of ya talkin' about, I'd say, well, this Study Butte mine would be lots better if Rio's people did own it.

But if they cain't vote on that law that ya rattled off jest now, Papa, I don't see much of a chance ta change things around, an' be any too polite about it. What I'd most like ta know is, how th' guy that owns this mine ever got ta be th' owner of it, in the first place."

"There is not but one earthly way, Woody, that the owner can get to be the owner, and that is to buy it. He can put up the money to build it or he can buy it after it's already built."

"Or he can catch it when somebody lays down to die. He can win it with a fulla house in de poker game. It is just a little scrap of paper to heem. He be dopey head, he smoke de reefer, he drunkard, whore-chaser, gambler, he be plumb crazy de head, he no like me, he hate de world, hate his own self. But de cards run in his favor just for ten minutes one night. Does that make him know 'nough about de mine, de *montañas*, de minerals, to take de life or death of my family in his hands?"

"Sounds awful bad," I said, "but how'ja know all o' this stuff about 'im? 'Bout how he hates everybody? Hates his own self? All o' that?"

"He ees bound to," Rio said, "to pay our money to his men to keep us from read de book, from having de meeting, to keep us from de vote box."

"If he does all o' that stuff, er jest half of it," I said, "he's a bastard of th' first waters. Things is jest in one hell of a twist an' a tangle, ain't they?"

Rio shook and nodded his head. "And I think de gun will be de only t'ing which will get everyt'ing out from de tangle."

"Looks thatta way," I agreed.

"As for me, Rio and Woody," Papa's words came slow as an easy wind against a rocky cliff, "I couldn't send half of your people to their deaths just to take those owner-ship deeds and titles away from that boss owner, no matter how loco he may be in the head parts. Any kind of a mine running three days a year is better than no mine at all. To you, the papers to this mine are worth more than a hundred mines like the Terlingua or the Study Butte."

"Thees owner, Charlie, Woody, he keel two hundred already, he keel two more hundred de naxta five, seex years. You no can see?" A smile was over Rio's face as he spoke about these sad and sober things. His smile had more of slow patience about it than either one of the four in my bunch. "Thees t'ing it keepa my people stuck down in de mud of de world, Woody and Charlie. We sick in de body, we sick in de soul. We no gotta doctor, we no got medicina, nor de clean bed in de hospital. We no gotta nice drugstore. We got de sleep fly. De mosquito. De bug. De dirt. De mud, de sticks. We die by de millions since we be de human race. We die under every boosh and tree, on top de every rock you touch with your fingers while you look and try to dig up your father's gold or your father's silver."

"I could tell you that the same is true of the Scotch and the Irish," Papa said. "I'm half one and half the other—Scotch-Irish. My father was Irish. His first woman was Scottish. His second had Creek Indian blood, but I come by his first wife. Jeff, out there, come by his second wife, and with his reddish hair and light complexion, you'd never guess that he had Indian blood. With my blackish hair, high cheekbones, and dark skin, I could pass as an Indian quicker than Jeff ever could. I have a great sympathy for your people, Rio, the Mexicans, the Indians, since I was born and raised with Indian and Spanish folks all around me. There aren't so many Mexicans in my part of Oklahoma. I see you don't have so many blacks down here along your border—a few camp cooks, maybe, and that's about all. I'll have to admit and agree, though, that the poor blacks in Oklahoma live lots better than your people here."

"My people live worst in de United Estados. Here on de border rim of humanity. We born here. Grow here. We no live here. This land ees full of many wonders. Many story. Every face knows a t'ousand secret, t'ousand silver, t'ousand gold, t'ousand treasure, t'ousand fortune. Eef de face no tell you, you know some of de reasons. Eef de eye look funny at you, you know why. Eef my people dey no want you dig down your rock, build op 'nother big mine dat day know kill brother, dey know kill papa, kill mama, kill seester, you not be mad, will you, Señor Charlie?"

Papa swallowed a hard lump in his throat. He thought for a bit with his eyes low along the floor, and said to Rio, "No. Me mad? I love the looks of these mountains,

Rio. This trip off down in here has done my soul a lot
of good. I'm glad, too, that Woody, my son, here, got to
lay his eyes on this country. These are the first real mountains Woody has ever seen. I don't know if Jeff will get
very much good out of the trip. But, as for Eddie Moore,
this trip and your Big Bend country may be his lifesaver.
I came down here with an open heart and empty hands,
Rio. If I never lay my finger on my daddy's claimstake,
and never touch so much as a grain of gold or an ounce
of silver, my old paw Jerry's spirit in heaven will know
that I did come here, and that I did try. I'm a hard man
when it comes to hard work, Rio, and so is Woody, here,
and so is Eddie out there in the yard. Jeff misses his new
wife so bad that he can't last very long at this, but it's
not his fault that he's restless."

Rio nodded at a blowfly on the mouth of the whiskey
jar. He blew imaginary smoke from the cigarette stuck
on his bottom lip, and said, *"Sí.* I know."

"If Jeff jumps up in his truck and drives back home
to the wheat plains, Woody," Papa asked me, "and if I
stay down in here to look for Paw's mine on foot, would
you go back to be with Hellycat, or would you stay down
here with me?"

"That's a hard 'un." I figured a moment. "I'll stay
down here with you; that is, if Rio will help me ta find
m'self a girl."

Papa laughed under his breath while Rio told me, "Me,
I, Rio, I help you find two. Two girls for you and t'ree
for Addie."

"'Fraid I got Eddie all messed up. Teasin' 'im 'bout
his wine girl. Whattaya think?"

"No, not so very bad."

"I would be glad, Rio, if we could do something to
bring Eddie around straight on the womenfolks," Papa
said.

"He's shore crackin' up fast," I told them. "He talks
all o' the time, y' notice, 'bout how he don't like fer the
women t' nag at 'im, boss 'im around, make such a big
fuss about 'im, or peck an' pick at 'im all th' time—shove
'im aroun', run his business, an' always treat 'im like he's
a-walkin' along with one foot in his grave. He don't never
git no practice at makin' up his own damn mind about
nothin'. Our womenfolks, an', yes, us menfolks, are al-

ways a-dealin' with Eddie like he's th' worst cripple in th' world. He don't ev'n git ta say 'Yes' or 'No' about how they spend his sixty-five forty on th' day that damn check hits their mailbox. Ever'thing's 'Yes, yes, uh huh.' He's not shook his head an' stood up flat-footed an' yelled 'No!' at anybody since, well, since I been a-knowin' 'im."

"And," Papa tacked on, "if you will notice, Rio, Eddie very seldom says or does anything unless some of us are doing that same thing. His head is like an open canyon, you know; it just echoes back what you yell into it. He is a real sport, and as good as gold at heart, and he'll follow you through thick or thin so long as you handle him just right. Once in a great while, he will come out with some little idea of his own, and at home, amongst all of us relatives, this one little idea of Ed's just gets run over and trampled under the push and shove of all of the rest of us, and after a bit, he really forgets what his idea was in the first place. He goes following off after any good or bad suggestion that anybody makes to him."

"That ees a varry good word. Suggestion. Eef Addie can be put straight, we weel make use off that word, suggestion. In two ways we weela try to use eet."

"That is hypnotism," Papa said. "Worth the try."

"Y' really mean it?" I asked them. "Y' mean, ah, we're a-goin' t' hipatize Eddie an' tell 'im what t' do? Be fun."

"Tell him to tell us what he would like for us to do." Rio's eyes had a fire built somewhere in their hills. His face lit up as he told us, "We have gotta make Addie be de boss. See? 'Stan'?"

"Eddie never would let you experiment on him. He's been so pushed around by his friends, Rio, that he would have a terrible fear about these mental things. They will sound spiritual and ghosty to him. It would never work. You have to get the complete faith of a person before they will go into the right state of mind for your cure and healing to take root and grow. He would have to know you several years before he would have such a complete faith in your works," Papa said.

"I weela come to Addie in de land of hees sleepa. I weel win his faith for me in less time thana one hour. I make Addie de boss man, huh? You two work with me, we do this job lots quicker, lotsa better. 'Stan'? You weetha Rio for try, say?"

Papa's face got sober like a looking-glass. He said, "I'm with you. You'll promise me that you'll not do anything to hurt Eddie any worse than he is? What am I supposed to do?"

"You weela see. You shake my han', Woody Son, do lak I, Rio, say you do?" He held out his right hand to me and we shook to make our promise good.

I said, "I'm in. Tell me what ta do."

"Do you know, did any doctor de mind ever try help Addie theesa way?"

"Not that I recall," Papa said.

"I wouldn't really know, m'seff."

"Any off Addie family ever work hard, try theesa way help Addie?"

"Never quite thought of it," Papa told Rio. "Nobody knew that much about it. His mammy and his sister did read a stack of mail-order books on magnetism, hypnotism, mental science, and creative mind. I think they used their thoughts more to create things for their own uses, however, than to pull Eddie out of this dry mudhole that his mind seems to be caught in."

"We have to go back. Back down theesa road Addie has walk down. Back. To dat day of his wine girl again. Back to dat little hill, back to thesa mud trench. Back where he tumble down theesa hill and fall down in muddy trench with girl carry vino tub. He fall in love with her the way she look, talk. Than beega gun she come, she go Buulllooommm! Ammunition dump de Huns go same like beega gun, only she go beeger. Buulllooommm! What take place?"

"Mud covers them up," Papa said.

"Knocks Eddie blind. Mebbe knocks 'im out," I said.

"Addie wake up de bed de hospital, he look 'round, he see girl she gone away. She no here. What I gon' do? I Addie? Well, I close eyes like theesa. I dream, see? See same girl. Back muddy trench, back beega gun, back beega *booom*, back de vino bucket. Back de vino cup. Back she look me. Back she laugh with me. Back she joke with me. Back listen she talk with me. Back touch little finger. Back warm finger."

"Hmmmm."

"Dern me."

"Hospital girl she come my bed. I see vino girl back

smile for me. Hospital *medico* he walk by my bed. I look see. I see vino girl joke me. Three, four, fi', sixa month, I try talk make sense to 'nother girl, 'nother man, 'nother buddy, I still see vino tub girl. I no talk too good, I hear vino girl talk me. Other friend say me theesa, say me that, I nod my head, I friendly, but I weetha girl in mud hole two, three day. For wan second I touch her finger, for one minute I see her smile. God, God, you must not wish for me, Addie, to have any woman in theesa world, or else you never would take her away from me in one leetle minute, one leetle snap, one leetle look, one leetle smile, one leetle joka. I don't want to hear any words in my ears except her words. I weela say to the other people, 'Yes, Yes,' 'Uh huhhh.' But, I weel be listening to hear that leetle joke she told me again."

"How much of an expert are you, Rio," Papa asked, "when it comes to this kind of a thing?"

"Eet does not take de expert, Charlie." Rio thought a second and touched his chest. "I just need de faith; I need for both of you to believe in what I try do. But most of all, you have gotta to believe we can help Addie come back from the grave. He ees leeving in de tomb and he ees walking with de dead.

"Eet ees de hardest job, Uncle Charlie, Sonny Wood, to hold down God's job." All of the dignity of the rock in the uplands was on Rio's face and in his words as he made us like him and trust him. "Eef all theesa Christmas Mountains, all Hen Egg Mountains, Neegerhead Mountain, Sleek Rock Gap, and every grain of dust which rolls in under your feet, eef eet was all solid gold eet would not be worth what I, de Rio, weela show to you."

My lips puckered up to whistle, Wheww! But my thoughts ran so deep and serious that I forgot how to whistle. My mind was rolling over all of the rocks in these mountains to keep up with Rio's words and the looks that chased across his face. I wondered how Jeff was going to act when he got the word about our healing experiment.

"Promise me, de Rio, that you will not tell Addie while we work with him what we do, hoh?"

"Sensible to me."

"Yeah. Fine."

"Tell Rio theesa: you weela not give up and quit until I, Rio, tell you we all done, finished. You savvy? Here.

Shake da hands. We already start feefteen minutes ago,
see? Savvy? Okay. We have to work first for see how Jeff
he feels. Ho! No?"

Rio's eyes looked like he owned the deed and title to
all of the clouds and everybody under them.

CHAPTER 11

HIGH ROCKS

I walked out the old door and stood on the footpath to
look for Jeff and Eddie. I saw them about a hundred
feet to the east of the house, and the closer I got to them,
the louder I heard them talking. Jeff's hands were both
pushed as far down in his pockets as they would push.
He jingled a few coins against some keys that tinkled. I
stretched both ears to hear what Jeff was telling Eddie; I
wanted to see if Jeff had overheard and was putting Eddie
wise to the plan Papa, Rio, and I had just agreed to in
the mud house.

"Paw always did tell me," I heard Jeff say to Eddie,
"that this here Big Bend country was a volcanic place.
Melted rocks, colored sands a-movin' all around, britches-
down waters . . . He swore that they wasn't a naked eye
in Oklahoma or Texas that had ever looked out over any
such perty-lookin' world as this'n' down here is. Funny
part is, by golly whittakers, Eddie, this place does look
mighty awful ghostery, don't it, huh?"

"Shore does." Eddie talked with both arms folded across
his overalls jumper. "I betcha they's ninety-three kinds o'
man-eaters out here in these sticker bushes. They's a

haynted look about th' whole da'gone riv'r bottom if ya ast me. Say, Jeff, how many guns y' say we got?"

Both saw me walking their path. Jeff nodded, "H'lo there, Mist'r Wise Man, did'ja git all them leath'r books memarized?"

I tried to sound jokey. "You boys dug inta any pay dirt since I last seen ya?"

Eddie nodded, with his arms still folded over his chest. "Jesta few sacks full o' eighteen-karat rocks."

"Sorry, gents," I kidded, "but my latest law an' rulin' says that it's gotta be twenty karats afore ye're allowed t' keep it. Ya'll hafta throw yer eighteen-karat stuff back so's it can grow some more."

I felt relieved to learn, at least, that Jeff and Eddie were not speaking about Rio and his efforts to do Eddie some good with the girls. After we talked awhile, Papa came out of the house and looked around. He joined us as we sucked in the late air that crawled up out of the weeds along the river.

On the road nearby, I saw a two-wheeler cart, both wheels wired up with an old automobile tire, and a desert burro with gnats in his ears. I had the feeling that this burro cart was going to show us the rabbit path, the lizard trail, the 'possum tracks, that would take us to our last stop on our road to Paw Jerry's mine. Over to the Sam Nail ranch house.

"Looks like we have company." Papa walked a step or two in the direction of the burro cart. We both heard a high, lonesome whistle like a hurt bird lost somewhere under the brush. It came in three or four short calls, and I turned all around to listen. Rio held the screendoor open with his right hand and motioned to all of us to come in.

I blinked to get my eyes used to the dark in the room, and looked around to see a family of people had moved in. A low-built man, just about Eddie's height and weight, threw a mop of heavy, straight, black hair back from his face. He had on a pair of dusty work shoes. His work pants were fairly new, but cut from the cheapest materials, and already badly shrunk. His cottony shirt had had the colors washed and faded out of its threads months ago. Broad face and forehead, sharp cheekbones, well-set mouth and lips, and eyes as sparkledy black as eyes can ever get. I shook his hand. Rio told us, "Señor Charlie, Wood, thees my good friend. He name Manuel."

"I did not get the lady's name." Papa had seen several thousand young Indian mothers dressed in this kind of a velvety dark brown blouse, with a heavy handworked necklace of silver across her bosom. There was not much of a shape to the rolly folds in her skirt of greenish yellow. She wore no stockings, only a hand-bent, home-chewed leather pair of Roman style, criss-cross moccasins. Papa kept his eyes low down on the floor, his way of acting cultured and polished in the customs of his back-home Indian tribes. He did not allow his eyes to "eat the lady up," as the old saying goes.

"She my wife. She name Estrella. Shake de han'."

"Estrella." Papa shook her hand soft, easy, dropped it as soon as he touched it. "Fine name. And a fine young lady with a fine face and a pretty smile."

When the time came for me to shake her hand, I looked down as low as I could, and I saw two young boys, one about nine and one about eleven or twelve. Before I could get a word said, the nine-year-old one told me, "I have a little seester, five years old. She die. She seek." His older brother flumped his thumb along my guitar strings and asked me, "You no mad, I play you *música?*"

Before I could quite answer him, their mother touched her fingers to her cheek, looked bashful, and told us, "Pedro loves *música*. Theesa man, mebbey he no like Pedro play his *guitarra*. No?"

"Go ahead," I told the boy. "Ya cain't hurt it much."

Both boys flipped the strings of the guitar and pushed each other back to take turns playing. They ran their fingers over the red fiddle case.

"I'll hoe somebody's behind," I heard Jeff yell out in the room. "Lettin' these two little fellers handle my good allygator skin fiddle case! God dammit, anyways. Woodrow, ain't you got jest even one brain a-workin' in that nigger-head burrheaded head of yours? Here! Outta my road! Give me my fiddle! Oh, that idjiot nephew of mine. Oh! Lemme outta here, Wood!" He slammed the screendoor so hard that the rust from the net-wires tickled our nose holes. The two brothers yelled, "Oh!" and "No!", and fell down scared on top of one another in the corner. I walked out behind Jeff just as their mother, Estrella, shot a long, loud mouthful of high, fast words at her sons, then she yelled out the door somewhat louder and faster.

Estrella waved her arms and shooed every living person

out of the room. "Shoo! Shooo! I feex sam't'ing eat. Yas, A'right. I feex suppaire."

"Y've shore made trouble now, Jeff," I told him as he laid his fiddle case up on to some bedclothes on the truck.

"Who was it started th' whole damn thaing, me? Plooey. It's you an' you know it. No earthly sense in a-lettin' them two boys beat th' holy hell outta my fiddle case, jest a-tryin' t' treat 'em nice. This fiddle's been my meal ticket more times than onct, Woody Boy. I might be a-needin' it ta make a few nickels t' git from here back t' Pampa on."

"Kids wasn't hurtin' that fiddle case. I was watching every move they made."

"Kids likely t' bang th' damn case all t' pieces. Don't stand there 'n' tell me a black lie."

I could hear the two boys talking back at the wash bench. Eddie stood and tickled the burro's ear while Papa fanned some gnats away. "What'n thund'r an' lightnin' busted loose in th' house there, Uncle Charlie?" Eddie asked.

And Papa told him, "Oh, not much of anything, Eddie. Jeff came in and found the kids with his fiddle case and carried it back out onto the truck. What can we do now to show them we didn't mean them any harm?"

"Only thing that I c'n thaink of," Eddie said, "would be, ahh—well, it'd be that glass jar we got of jerky beef, up alongside of a good can o' them pork 'n' beans, er two."

"The nail, she has been hit on the head, Eddierooster! We'll open up a real can of milk."

Eddie walked in Papa's track across the yard towards the truck. Jeff walked around to the tail end of the truck and asked Papa and Ed, "What's a-comin' off aroun' this place, anyways? Ain't cartin' my fiddle back ta that there house, are ye? I've got to take care o' that there fiddle. Truck, too, fer's thet's concern'd. Openin' up a right smart lot o' cans there, ain't ya?"

"Few f'r supper," Eddie told him.

I watched the whole squabble from beyond the truck. Papa stood on the ground while Eddie handed him the cans of pork and beans, one of milk, and the glass jar of dried beef. I heard the two boys talking, as Estrella and Manuel spoke more Indian and Spanish words in the house.

"Won't be very many suppers," Jeff said, "if you fellers

hands 'em out by th' canful that way. How much we got here? Thirty-five dollars' worth o' food, an' not a penny more. Gonna be a hungry old six weeks a-climbin' up over them volcano rocks t' dig out ole Daddy's claim, if ya open up a can o' stuff t' poke down everyone's naicks. I ain'ta needin' Mannywelly's help t' git me jest eighteen damn dern miles further, men. I can drive this here hoggle-jawed rattletrap truck this here next eighteen mile blindfolded an' hog-tied."

"Not in this country," Papa told Jeff.

"It'd be 'thout me fer yer company," Eddie joined Papa.

"Ya'd come a-wobblin' back over this very first ridge, Jeffrey!" I walked around the truck. "You'd miss th' first turn o' th' road. I vote we divvy up th' grub with them folks there'n th' house."

"We've got to make it last. I put thirty-five dollars into that grub, Woodgut; you didn't drop hardly a red penny inta that there grocery kitty, an' you know damn well y' didn't."

"I deserve more'n thirty-five dollars, Jeffwees, helpin' y' ta manipylate this truck this fer down along. I swear out a prom'sory note right now that I'll hand over ta you th' firs' thirty-fi' dollars which I dig up outta Grampaw's hole. Huhmm?"

"Stop the childhood imitations." Papa looked up toward the adobe house and said, "Woodhead, you walk up and ask them. How do you vote, say, Eddieroo?"

"Wal, 's like Jeff here says," Eddie looked around in the purply colors turning off darker. "Ah, I ain't a-sayin' fer Woodyrow t' feed them dag-nabbin' kids no thirty-five dollars' worth o' the stuff we'll need over in them Chisos Mountains. Naw. But feed 'em. Not a truckload, but, hell, go knock. Knock."

I walked to the door as quiet as I knew how. I took a peek in through a hole in the screen to see what the boys were doing now. I saw an old beat-up lantern lit up on one of the rafters, swinging over their heads in a weak gleam of shivery light.

A canvas pad, the size of a saddle blanket, was spread out down on the floor. I saw no dishes, no knives, no forks. Two old tin-plated spoons lay near a small-gauge, dime-store coffee pot of grayish graniteware. A bluer bowl of the same cheap granite was half full of what looked to be some whitish pancakes, burnt in a few places.

They looked to be hard and gummy, as each mouth bit off another bite and chewed around on it. One of the boys rolled his flapperjack around his finger, pulled on both ends of it, and bit off a mountain right out of the middle. The older boy kneeled on the table pad, like the rest of his family, but since his back was turned my way, all I could see in his fingers was a white china cup filled spilling full with black chicory coffee. The daddy's cup sat down on the pad in front of him, empty except for some dirty grounds. He looked wrinkled across his forehead kneeling down there to bite and chew his folded pancake. Estrella's eyes, like everybody else's around the canvas, fell down past her chipped granite coffee cup onto the eating pad. Did the dim light, the scant food, the old canvas padding, or the argument about the fiddle case cause every one of their faces to droop down as lowly sad as their eyelids? I did not hear them say one word, not one. But, oh, I forgot. I came to this door to knock on it, didn't I? Not to just stand here and look in.

I tapped my knuckle on the screendoor, "Helloo. Anybody home?"

Manuel came to his feet as his wife motioned the two boys to sit still. "Ahheyyy." Manuel knew it must be me. "I hope zee feedle she was not broka. Coom eena geet beeg hotta coopa caff. Hey?"

"Later," I told him. "Thanks, anyhow. Jeff's awright. Jest tetchy about his fiddle, I guess. No bad feelings over it, anyhow. Say, would y' feel mad at me if we offered yer fo'ks a part o' what we got out here fer supper? You know, dry beef? Good salty. An' some pork and beans? Cans? Savvy?"

"Oh, *sí, sí,*" the older boy piped out. And his little brother shook his head, clapped his hands and said, "*Sí, sí,* me savvy. Yummy. Yummm."

Estrella touched both boys on their knees, and said, "You must not act like the leetle peeg een thee beeg mudhole. Promise. I soopose eet ees alla right weeth me."

"My momma she crazy for Vienny sassijes," I heard the twelve-year-old boy tease her.

The younger brother yelled up to the lantern. "Geeble gooble. Me peeg. Me peeg. Oweee! Oweee! Ank annk unkunk. I de peeg!"

Manuel kicked his shoes off and pushed them under the army cot with a natural smile that came from the ringing of the boys' voices in his ears. He lowered his voice to a loud whisper to tell me, "I t'ink you name Woodachook? Sam't'ing lak?"

" 'At's my monicker," I told him. "I aim t' take a look around t' see if I can locate a can er so of them there Vye-enna sausages that y' like sa good. I go see."

"No," Manuel whispered out. "Rio say he moosta see you. Now. Queecka. Atta the sundown. Savvy?"

"Where at?"

"De Rio Grande."

"Th' Ryoe Grandey? God sakes! Sun's already sunk down. I don't know how t' find no Ryoe Grandey. Which part?"

"Sheepa trail back de house. Rio meet opp weetha you where the trail cross ov'r goata road onna reever bank. Rio there now. You ron queeck. You back queeck. I save planty dry beef, planty sassaja for Rio, for you, also. Now ron."

I ran back to the truck, puffing, out of wind, saying, "I gotta run meet Rio, boys, over here'n some other house 'crost th' town. Go ahead, open up some dried beef, pork'n's, and some cream for th' coffee. Oh, Eddie, dig out a few of them cans of doggy sausages. Save some back for me 'n' Rio. Bye-bye."

I made both legs fly. I hit that sheep trail and every root and weed along it, and from the high side of a slope I got my skin whipped raw with some kind of a long, hard-tail cat-whisker grass. But I kept on, like Manuel told me; I outrun the sun going down.

Up, down, along, and around several ditches, low hills, through goat grasses, sheep bushes, seeds that stuck in my hair and shirt collar. I hit a rolly, rocky, uphill path that twisted over itself three or four times, till it carried me up above the little feathery treetops and I stopped to grab my breath at the spot where the path started down again. I saw a long, wide, shallow, ribbony stretch of water moving at a lazy gait down its mountains, down its valleys. I figured the downhill run wouldn't take my wind so bad, so I trotted down the path in a long, muley lope, flatfoot Indian style.

I ran in under the leaves of a few trees which had the blown cottony seeds I knew belonged to the cottonwood. I stopped once more to look under and partly behind several of the oversize, papery-soft cottonwoods that grew at the edge of a bluff a hundred feet or so over a pool of the Rio's bluest waters. I caught sight of several women, girls, babies, in the pool splashing and swimming back and forth. Their voices had a sharp echo and a clear sound as they laughed, pushed, splashed, and ducked one another down under the water. I could not see any clothes on any of them. I pulled my shirt wider open and hid behind the tree trunks to see the sights. I guess my eyes got so full of pretty swimmers that my memory went dog blank on me. I forgot the old truck. Forgot all about Papa, Jeff, Eddie, and that there ever did live by these waters and rocks a man as old as the weather itself, by that very same name, yes, Rio. Gold and silver mines slipped my senses. Papa, wheat plains, oil fields, sheriff's badges, guns, jails, money, sheep yonder, cattle rooting grass out from under flat hilltop rocks. Sun gone. Light still here. Just me. Me here. Just me here. Boy, what I wouldn't give, just to be able to get that little meaty maiden down there with that long handful of black curls waving down acrost her sunburnt shoulders. How come I had to meet up with you while I'm up here, hid out in back of this old cottonwood?

That long, stringy-bean one down there, with that pair of hard-set knockers, hair all piggytailed up around over her head there, long, loose, easy-swung, limbery legs, I might have more fun playing around with her, but I'd have to climb a packing crate to ever kiss her.

Great God Almighty Lord Jesus in the High Rock! Why did you ever hate this one of your sons enough to send me off down here away from Helly Cat Cliffman, and lose me here along these old bumpy rocks; and Lord, what made you stick all these old cactus grass blades, these old devilish thorny stickers, these old bullheads, these old skin itchers, these old brushy limbs, these old cottonwoods, in between this juicy pretty little piece of pussy cat meat yonder with her legs all spread out so wide apart on that mossy flatrock? Put me where that flatrock is, Lord, turn me into that moldy green moss. Set me closer, Dear Lord, closer, and then closer, closer, closer, till I'm close as I can ever get, and then take me, Lord, and smear me just one little froggy hair closer.

Trees and skies and sundown waters. And that little way her breasts move while she ducks her head and mouth down, and she laughs that way that echoes up and down my roots and tree leaves. Now she leans back on her hands and drags her foot up like a rock seat, bends her knee and crosses both legs and her curls rub on the rock moss.

Sundown swimmer. Water's daughter. Shady sand pool hid from men's eyes. I'm the only son to suffer here to stand and kiss your tree bark and to dream this warm tree is you, but my tree can't spread its legs out and can't laugh that way you're laughing.

This feeling. It comes every time I get close to some girl I like real good. Warm-like, I guess, and blind, and dizzy, sort of blood kin to these tree vines, sorta tuned up to the berry patch, and shot full of this girl laughing.

"Thees ees where our two trails cross." I heard a voice somewhere at my back. I spun around on my heels and looked about. "Here. Over here. Do you see anyt'ing down there whicha you like?" The words drifted on the breeze, but I could not, to save me, find the spot they were coming from.

I recalled several stories about men that got killed for peep-tomming at Indian girls taking their daily baths. My neck got so tight it was hard for me to say a word. I did say, "Hmmm. Come on out."

"Gass who eet ees anda I weel walk out."

"Ole Man Rio," I laughed out.

"You right. I lose. I come." Rio's blanket hid him so well in the weaving clump of grass that my eyes could hardly see where he came out from. "I you slave. Say whata you wish, and Rio will get him and give him to your hands."

" 'Taint no him." I shook my head.

"No?" He walked over and patted my back. "Whatta could eet be, then, eef she ees not a him."

"She's a her."

"Oh. How far do I, Rio, have to walk to catch her for you, eh?"

"Not fer. She's real, real close." I pointed my finger around the cottonwood bark towards the river pool. "Right down yonder, see; take a free look."

"Mmmm." Rio looked down the slope. "I see de poola. I no see de she. You craze."

"I'm crazy? You're *loco* poconut." I motioned down at the rock pool. "Me craze? You craze. Look real close."

"You point. You show."

I pointed over his back as he squatted low and bent

over to cover his eyes and to look. "I be dam-bern," I told
Rio.

All of the women, girls, and babies were gone. The pool
did not have even a wind ripple on it. It looked as quiet
and still as Tuesday in the dead house. Gone. Took her
toes and took her legs, and took her laugh, and gone.
Curls went with her, I suppose. Wish I knew which way
she went. That silly echo of her laughing around in my
ears. That nice warm feeling, she took most of that with
her when she left.

"Craze." I pointed to my temple.

"Eet eesa very bad."

"Manuel sez ya wanted t' meet me up here."

"Eet ees about Addie."

"Go'n'ta try yer system on 'im tonight while he's on
th' truck-bed asleep, ain'tcha?"

"*Si*. I tell you how I work with Addie, and I tell you
what you can do to help Rio, sav?"

"Sav. Awful perty curls. Hung alla th' way down t' 'er
hips. Gone off away. Flooey! Talk on, Rio. Talk ahead on."

Facing away from the sun, Rio went on to tell me,
"You 'stan' when Rio say every man he's gotta two mind?
Beega Mind, Leetle Mind, 'stan'?"

I said, "Yeahp."

"Leetle Mind he hide here, he feel deesa tree, he look
down deesa hill, he smella pretty flower, he bite de red
apple, deega de deetcha, he write de letter home to friend.
He look see very nice girl she swim de pool with lotsa
other women. Sav?"

"Little? Gittin' bigger all th' time. Yeahhp."

"Leetle Mind run catch girl. Leetle Mind want touch,
rub, feel, tickle, bite de pretty girl, play, run, push down,
laugh, make de big noise pretty girl. Leetle Mind kiss girl
on de greena grass. Hot, cold, rain, shine, sun blister,
wind blow, flood roll, queeckasand try keep you back from
your girl; what you do?"

"Keep on a-huntin' 'er."

"That ees right. Your Leetle Mind, she ees always
a-honting and she ees never a-finding."

"Hmmm."

"I tal you, I have never been rested and sateesfied for
even one hour out off all of thesa days and nights of my
saventy some years. Eef I dida not have any woman, I was
always digging and looking for one. Whan I was weeth

my woman, I beg her please come do thees, please come do that. I, Rio, I was just as much lost, just as restless, as I was before she try help me."

"I bet th't you was a whing-dangler whenever you was jest about my same age. Goin' on towards twenty."

"You laka nize girl. One tam the girl she weela holda you hippa so long thata perty soon you mak leetle baby jomp outta her belly hola."

"Got a few rubbers here'n my shirt pocket. But this dry air down here's a-gon'ta dry 'em out."

"You 'stan' why Rio tak time, Woodapeck, tal you alla thesa stoff?"

"Could be that there slug o' whiskey I poured in yer coffee cup."

"You make joka. But I will notta try my words on Addie onteel we see that thesa high rocks are not any joka."

"I was jesta kiddin'. I know 'tain't so funny. This kinda mental stuff's awful deep. I'm not pokin' my fun atcha, Rio. I never would've run up that there sheep trail a mile an' a half t' set here'n listen to ya, if I didn't have some respect fer what all ye're a-sayin' to me. Is my mind in big slot 'er little slot, Rio, right now, when I'm a-seein' that naked perty gal swim up onta that flat mossy rock an' laugh th' gosh-blame way she did? Which mind am I makin' use of?"

"Your Leetle Mind eet eesa getting beegaire. Eet eesa your biggest wan that tells you that you wanta do sam't'ing good for thatta girl. See? Eet eesa your leetle wan that keeps you fram ron grab her finger nice, warm, easy. Averybody, they gotta de Beega Mind, som'place, eefa you finda queecka way for get opp eena your owna beega mountain country; than, you be able show your frand, mama, papa . . . thesa girl who sounds so pritty laughing eena your ears."

"How d'ya go about findin' yer way ta some gal's biggest mind?"

"She weela notta drop her t'ings down on de grassa, teel she t'inks she can walka with you here in thesa place where lives her Beega Mind anda her highest cleefa rock, her best place fram where she can standa opp anda look down anda see thesa whole world onna avery side off eet anda averybody's face and avery town. She weel not let you come een her world onless she can go weeth you, and you weetha her, opp her steep hill, down her worst valley.

She hate you laka de snaka, eef you try keep her back down from thesa place."

"By gollies, that shore does sound jest about right ta me, 'cept I didn't quite savvy all of it. Time I'm seventy-somethin' like you, Rio, I might ketch onta some of what ye're talkin' about. How's this hook up with Eddie Stoner?"

"I, Rio, gon' try to find sam words fram my biggest minda. I gon' try call op Addie's beegesta wan same way. You see, Addie, hees leetle wan eesa lost joost lika the baby—she yell, cry, she scareda de big weeds. Bot Addie, hees Beega Mind, eet deeda not evair geeta lost away."

"Hummm."

"Wan more t'ing, than we go eat. Addie, he not know me Rio so very long, see? Eef he deed, anda eef we be lang tam every day together, I try worka real slow weetha heem avery day. But I not gotta the lang time. I moost go to heem while he eesa not fighting me."

"Fights everybody back off his private property he's got built up all aroun' that Franch wine-dipper gal. Come jest so close, but not a damn bit closer. He's got 'er all fenced in fer his own pa'ticular use, Rio. Y' know?"

"Not even Addie's mothaire, nicest seestaire, best brothaire, has ever took Addie up de beega road, nor meet op weeth heem op een hees bast place. Addie t'inks lotsa more of you than you would guess. Thesa eesa reason why I, Rio, ask you anda not those others to meet me opp here onna my high rocks."

"Makes me feel awful proud inside myseff. Inside is a-warmin' up right smart towards you, Rio. And Rio, my ole daddy really thainks Rio's somethin' on a big long stick. Yeahp."

"You gotta good fathaire. He craze about de politeecs, bot got high mind, you papa. He do lotsa walk around op in here the place off heesa Beeg Mind. Good man."

"Reckon ye're right."

"You see, de trobble I weel have weeth Addie, ees thees: I moost ask you to follow after heem avery hour off the day and nighta. Do not letta heem get out from onder your nosa."

"Why?"

"I gon' ask Addie for me, Rio, to please throw down hisa chew 'backa, his dirty snoffa, speet run down chin. I say he love de cegarrette bot not every cegarrette he see,

joosta only thesa kind wheech Woody smoke, wheech
Woody moosta roll for Addie. I come to Addie een his
dreams; he t'ink, whan I tal heem tonight on de truck
what he eeza to do. You must go weeth heema everywhere, any place, every place. I tal Addie he no take a
drinka of water fram anybody else bot Woody. To fall
een love weeth your guitar playing. Eefa all off these
signals works, see, you can know that the rest off the
things I tal heem, ask heem, beg heem to do, he must
surely do them. I weela tal heem that the sight of Jaff's
rad hair weel geeva Addie's tongue all off the pretty words
to speak to the girl that happens to be nearest to heem. A
mothaire rabbit weel make Addie love the sun and the
wind and the birds on the fly. The whirring of the wings
of the quail will be the secret time for Addie to feel at
home with the whole world around heem. A clear drink of
spring water will send heem to ondrass the woman he love
most."

"Be fun. Fun ta watch. If he does any of it."

"The joys weel be great. To see Addie make hees way
back from hees tranch girl's ghost. I am going to try to
make heem see her eyes whan he looks in the eyes of a
certain Indian girl."

CHAPTER 12

MOON WALKING

Back at the 'dobe house, a while after dark, Rio sat across
the eating canvas from me over the two tin plates of
jerked beef, porky beans, and two-incher Vienna sausages,
with a hot pot of coffee by our cups. I ate my beans in
two or three mouthfuls, gulped down a couple of Vienna
sausages, before I caught the eyes and the mouths of the
two brothers watching every move of my elbow, hand,
spoon, and neck.

Estrella was out at the wash bench humming over a
washrag and her few little supper dishes. Manuel had gone
out to talk about trucks and burro carts with Jeff, Papa,
and Eddie. The two boys kept their eyes on Rio with the
same hungry looks that they used over me. Rio slid his
plate, still mostly full, out onto the canvas cloth and said,
"Rio he no lak. No laka de teena-can beans. No lak de
teena-can meatsa."

After the two boys had gulped his plateful down, I slid
mine out on the cloth and said, "Not a lick hongry,
m'seff." And the two boys suckled my beef and sausages
down into their guts. This was another held secret between
myself and Rio.

Jeff strolled in and helped us to drink down the coffee

in the pot. He looked on me, and acted sourly for good reasons. I heard some people singing—three, four, several of them, in good Mexican folksong tunes where the harmony grazed high and low like the cattle in the rock hills. The songs blew in at our south window over Rio's shoulder for a few minutes, then I asked him, "Phonograft records er radio, er people a-saingin' in at our window, Rio?"

"People. They seeng from that leetle house over beyond thosa treess. Laka?"

"Sounds mighty fine," I told him.

"My friends. They all go seenging, moon walking."

"Walk where?" Jeff asked Rio.

"Walking witha de moon. Eet ees joost somet'ing for tham to do. Eet passes off de time."

"Im g'n'ta git out 'n' pass off a little time with 'em." I set my coffee cup down by the rim of my tin plate. "Nothin' 'round here fer a young laddie ta do."

"Le's play right back at 'em. Sing." Jeff looked at the grounds in his cup. "Le's answer 'em back with fiddle an' gittar tunes, whut say, Woody? I'll grab my fiddle offa th' truck. Say?"

"Naw," I told Jeff. "I'm not any too much in th' music humor, somehows or t'other."

"I feel like a pore boy an' a long ole ways from home." Jeff was out the door and back again with his fiddle before I could say anything else. He jerked his fiddle up under his chin, tuned his E string a bit sharper, and struck off across his strings with his bow feeling, listening to the strings, tuning their harmony in every finger position. "C'mon. Grab y'r gittar. I'm a-goin' down where th' waters tastes like wine, boy; c'mon an' grab on an' ride with me! I'm a rip-snortin' roller an' a hub-deep mudhole hitter, an' if I miss s' much ez one mudhole er one little slick greasy string, I'll shake yer damn han', Wood Hoss, an' I'll rub out that there thirty-five dollars ye're gonna han' me on th' first day that we dig down in Paw's ole damn-dern lost mine. Grab down y'r gittybox, boy! Le's wheel on out an' down."

I strung my cord around my neck and told Jeff and Rio, "Thirty-fi' dollars is now even steven. Y' heard 'im, Rio. You're my mainest witness, Mister."

"I weetnessa." Rio nodded. "I do gooda job for savanteen feefty."

I started playing my guitar to get the notes in tune with

Jeff's strings. I nodded over to Jeff and said, "Cut one out, I'll ride 'er. I'll ride an' roll 'er till th' first break o' day in th' mornin'."

Jeff fiddled out on one of my favorites, "Sail Away Lady":

> Build my new house out of logs,
> Sail away, Lady, sail away.
> Give my old house to the hogs,
> Sail away, Lady, sail away.

> Didn't she rock 'em, daddyo?
> Didn't she shake 'em, daddyo?
> Didn't she wiggle 'em, daddyo?
> Didn't I ride 'er, daddyoooe?

> While you boys digs out yore mines,
> Sail away, Lady, sail away,
> Don't be a-diggin' this hole o' mine,
> Sail away, Lady, sail away.

Papa walked in and sat down on the floor with Eddie just in bare time to join with me to sing the chorus again:

> Didn't she rock 'em, daddyo?
> Didn't she shake 'em, daddyo?
> Didn't she jiggle 'em, daddy hoo?
> Didn't I ride 'er, daddyoooe?

After he'd worn his bow hair slick, Jeff chopped the song off and told us all, "You know somethin', fellers? I never did run up ag'inst but one damn man in all o' my put-togethers th't could saw th' gash-blanged fiddle an' sing at th' same dern time. Long old lanky, speckle-faced drunkard mule-skinner I locked up in th' Pampa jail there fer thirty days. I'd of turned him loose sooner, but he was sech a God-dernd good fiddler, hell, I jest had ta keep 'im in there as long's th' laws would allow."

"What was his best fiddle piece?" Papa asked.

The singing from the other house blew in at our window on Jeff's shoulders. "Lemme try t' think. Ah yas, I got it. It was that there tricky kind of tune, where he made his fiddle cackle jest like a blame chicken. Ah. What's its name? Ah, 'course, 'Cluck Ole Hen.' 'S in th' key of open

A, Woodstone, jest sort of a reg'lar three-way chordin', A to D, to E, to A."

Jeff clipped the strings with his front fingers to make it sound like an old hen clucking.

Papa caught his chance and sung:

> Cock-a-doodle jing-a-ling my old hen
> She lays eggs for the railroad men,
> Some days one, and some days two,
> That's enough eggs for the railroad crew.

Jeff got the tune set better in his head on the next time it went around. I picked the guitar a good bit easier and kept doing the same three chords over, like Jeff showed me. He fiddled the first part in a high range, hitting off a fast kind of jerky bounce like the scared lope and gallop of a hog-wild broomtail mare with her mane in the wind. The second part, the part where the hen cackled, was in the same chording range and rhythm, except I had to hold the tone of my guitar down as low and quiet as I could to let the old hen climb out on that panther fiddle and cluck, cackle, and sing. Now when he came around this time to the clucky-clacky part, Eddie Stone, to catch up with Papa Charlie, threw his verse onto the fire:

> Cluck ol' hin, cluck an' saing,
> Y' ain't laid an aigg since way last spraing,
> Y' ain't laid an aigg since th' middle of th' fall,
> If this keeps up, y'll starrve us all.

I closed my eyes and waited for the fiddle to whip around one more time, and I sung:

> Little Banty Roost'r, Dominecka hen
> Runna 'round t'gether, but they ain't no kin.
> Ruff up y'r feathers an' pooch up y'r hole,
> I gotta stick it in jest t' satissfy m' soul.

Rio's face lit up, he nodded with the tune, pointed his fingers in the air like a little prissy missy, and, not being able to sing the Anglo-Saxon words, he acted like the band leader, the conductor man. Jeff had to stop his bow hand to get the words out, but held his fiddle up under his chin

and sweated this verse out while I plunked my guitar in
his ear:

> My ol' hen run, she riz an' fleww,
> Up jumps th' rooster an' he run along too.
> They dunnit in th' barn, dunnit in th' lot,
> Las' time they dunnit, they dunnit in th' pot.

While Jeff touched off the last couple of go-rounds on his
fiddle, I looked out the south window. I heard the singing
of the neighbors the same as ever, but out there around
our window I saw several faces looking in. Young boys
and girls knelt down on the wild Bermuda grass, while
their older folks, three or four of them, shoved and pushed
for a ringside seat on the old family wash bench. Through
the little panes of glass it was hard for me to see the
grown-up faces very clear or plain; the wood strips and
crosspieces marked them out. One pair of knees I saw
caused both my eyes to stick like glue on a short, sporty
skirt of thick, ruffly, blue cotton cloth. I let my eyes lift
up along her hips and waistline till I came to a strip of
new territory where I saw signs of a brownish blouse
covered all up and down with splashings of reds and
yellows.

I pitched my head back like the king of the timber
wolves yelping somewhere up towards his old moon. I
yelped out ahead of Jeff's fiddle, partly to show him which
tune I intended to sing, partly to help him fish out the
right key, but mostly, I guess, to show that girl out there
on that wash bench what I thought about her blouse,
sporty skirt, and such a pretty pair of knees and thighs.

I sung this verse after the guitar and fiddle died down
with all their noises:

> Ohh, my sugar tit, you look so sweet to me,
> Yes, my honey bee, you look so sweet to me,
> Apple dumplin', you look so sweet to me, me, me,
> Up an' down jest fer's my eye can see.

A dozen verses of this old song caused everyone to
shake, talk, jabber along, play around with my words. This
brought on that old, slow, hugger-kisser one, "Birming-
ham's Jail." And that one called up "Red River Valley,"

which made room for a zippier one, "Don't Give a Hang if
I Do Die, Doo Dye Day."

This brought on some tickly laughing out along the wash
bench, while a little crowd out there sang a long waily
one. I nudged Rio with my elbow and asked him, "What's
them words mean? Sounds awful perty."

Rio bent his head side to side in beat with their song,
then told me, "Eet means in you Gringo lingo, Why are
your eyes full with tears like de moon of cold winter?
Why must you cry ona your pillow alone? Come climb
outta you weendow and walk and I show you my new
moon. My warm summer moon she doess not let anyone
cry. Teedle tumm, tumm, tummty, tum, tommm, tommm,
tommm."

They sang along with us here through the window, I
guess, an hour or two. The younger kids fell down asleep
in the house, on the floor, around the wash bench, on the
grass, on laps, hugged up in arms, and any other place
where the powers of sleep overtook them.

Whispered in at the window, I heard a rough-looking
young boy tell me, "My seesateer she say shee show you
how play thatt *guitarra*."

I heard somebody's open hand give him a slap across
the seat of his britches, laugh out, and say, "She deeda
notta. I deed notta say thees."

"Why shore, shore." I carried the guitar out the door
as Jeff clicked his fiddle case closed and locked. Out in
the dark on the grass, I held out my guitar and told them,
"Where is yer sister, boy?"

A crowd of nine or ten boys and girls rolled around on
the grass, laughed, giggled, and put on silly faces to tease
me. A boy stood, dressed in a pair of ragged overalls
wearing no shirt and no socks, only a pair of whitewashed
tennis shoes on his feet. "Here. Thees wan. She woulda
love for to try play onna yourr *guitarra*." He had to dodge
around over the grass to run out from under the slaps,
whacks, and pokings his sister dealt out to him.

"Here 'tis." I tossed the guitar down on the grass. "Play
on it all y' wanta. I'll stan' up here 'n' listen."

The brother crawled around on the grass to play with
the gang of young folks while his sister walked over. She
dropped to her knees, felt the strings of the guitar, hummed
a little note, then she sat down cross-legged to hold the
music box on her lap. This was the first good chance I

had to see any of her sunburn above the knees, or to take my good look at the way her long twisty curls dropped around her face and cheeks, on down to brush the guitar and the grass.

"Plunka bloonka kleenka bleenk." She threw all kinds of silly sounding words down in the guitar's sounding hole. I saw that she played the whole C chord, from C to F, from F to G seventh, and on back again to the C position with her fingers. "Heenka deenka doe dee day, hoe dee, doe dee, rattle my ray." She flipped the strings with the tip end of her thumb, and I very quickly saw that she was acting the fool more than she was taking the guitar very seriously. She laughed and smiled back over her shoulder towards the gang of kids scattered in the dark, and I thought of ten thousand words that I could not say nor call onto my lips. With this open air, this clear fine night, and the kids goofing around, the folks blowing out the lantern in Estrella's house to climb into bed, my folks over there by the truck talking more gold mines, the whole night of music playing and our loud singing games, I felt choky in around my throat, somehow or another. I had to shake the snakes out of my eyes while I coughed and cleared my throat several times. I did snag onto two words, two only: "Awful perty."

"*Sí, no?* Oh, you speak of my *música?*"

"Well, I mean, yeah."

The rosy rose had time to sprout and bud, to bloom, to blossom, and so wild to blow, before I scared the next words out of my weeds. "Th' music, too. I mean, both."

"Botha? Wheecha you talk?"

"Music's a-runnin' second, from where I'm a-standin'."

She tilted her face in a cocky smile, then said, "My older broother teecha me few leetle t'ings onna the *guitarra.*"

"I'd like ta teach ya some little thaings yer brother never was able to. Who was it that taught yer hair ta be so curly? 'At's what I'm a-wantin' ta know." I watched her pet the wood of the guitar. "Huh?"

"My mama papa geev me de peegsa tail. My older broother he was to be here tonighta so he could show your truck de Sam Nail roads. My broother he have de fight, de trroble, he no come Study Butte tonighta. Tomorra nighta my broother come."

I sat myself down on the grassy mat a few inches from

her sandal toes and touched my finger to the guitar strings to see if the night air had got it out of tune. I studied about life in general and things in the broad a few seconds, then asked her, "You know Ole Man Rio?"

"*Si.*"

"How long?"

"He come. He stay. He go 'way. He talka deesa house, talka datta housse, speek dees man, dees woman, even speak de leetle keeds. He joke me, poola my curls. He always calls me Riorina. Savvy Riorina?"

I shook my head to tell her, No.

"Eet means Leetle River Girrl. Or, lak, mebbe you say, Leetle Girl off the River."

"Off th' riv'r. In th' riv'r. I'd like t' run jump in yore riv'r, an' jest see how long I could stretch m' arms an' my laigs out, an' do th' dead-log float. How old didja say that ya was?"

"I wass wance thirrteen."

I swallowed a lump down my throat as big as a baseball. "Hmmm. Thirteen?"

"Than I wass feefteena for a few years."

"How many?"

"Two years."

"Well, them two's gonna help a lot. You know much about Sam Nail?"

"Two three times I see heem. He has de beeg, beeg rancha grande. Hoonderd miles square. I was marri'd for almost all of last yearr."

"Hundred miles which? What? Married? Last year? How 'n th' name of th' holy cow d'ya 'spect me ta chase all over a ranch that's a hundred miles square? Married to who? Why?"

"The Sam Nail Rancho eesa named the Hoonderred and One. One Oh One."

"Yeah. My papa's papa—called 'im Jerry—talked about that there Hunderd an' One Ranch a lotta times. Yes, ma'am. He didn't ever know I'd come off down in here an' see no such of a perty little married pigtail gal as you are. Married? What'n th' holy beejesus did ya ever go an' pull a thaing like that fer? Anyhow? Where'bouts is yer husband at now?"

"He ron way."

"Run? How come?"

"He alla tam fight. Make de trobble. Every day he get de

fights with samboddy. He home, he fighta me. He speet inna my face, slappa me downa, keecka me. He joosta the baby, nervous, he smoke de reefer weeds too mucha. I breaka everyt'ing over hees had one night."

"Hooo?"

"So, he go, I stay. I steela here, see?"

"Both of us."

"Anda so eesa my sweeta leetle broother. He eesa now running over to tella me thatta he eesa tired, anda he eesa sleepy, anda seester, seester, you have to joompa op anda taka me home to bed. See?"

Her kid brother wrapped his arms around her neck from the back side before she finished telling me. He gave her curls a tug and a pull, and told her, "Seesie, seesie, I tired, I hongery, I want playy de *guitarra*, I want go home."

"Yes, broother. Bot, how can I letta you play onna *guitarra* anda taka you homa de same time?"

"Hey, Spudder," I told the boy, "I'll walk along with Rina here, an' you c'n walk along in back of us, 'an play my git-fiddle, hey?"

"I want de strring over my shoulder sam laka my seester. Geev me."

Riorina stood up to fit the neck cord around his neck. "Eet eesa good lang waya fram theesa place over to our house, did you know?"

I patted her kid brother on the head, and said, "Further th' better, huh, Studder? Gotta meet Rio here 'round about midnight sometime, but he'll be waitin', I'm a-thinkin'."

Walking past Manuel's water cart, the brother a step or so behind us thumping my guitar, Riorina asked me, "Meeta weeth who?"

"Rio," I told her.

"To do whatta? Meedanight?"

"Big secret. Cain't let a dead horse know about it." We stepped out onto a wider wagon road and turned off to the south away from the lantern lights and trucks and people.

"Woulda you say thata I am a deada horrse?"

"I didn' say that."

"Tal me, than, theesa beega seecret between you anda Rio."

I told her, "Okay. If you'll lemme hold yer hand all o' the ways home an' kiss me at yer gate, I'll bust open my secret fer ya. Deal? Good 'n' dark out aroun' here, ain't it?"

"Yes, vary."

"Meanin' yes, I can warm my hand in yours all of th' road home? Yes, very what?"

"Vary, vary dark. The road turrns here. Look outa! Ohhe, what deeda you do? Where deeda you fall to?"

I stuck the top of my head up above the dry seed stems of a high weed patch. As I got to my feet to pick the itchy seed hulls out of my shirt and overalls, I said, "Why'n th' name of holy hell don't ya say which way ya want me t' turn? I ain't no dang mind reader."

I heard her giggle and laugh somewhere out in the night air. "Most fellas would know," she told me, "which way a girl wants tham to turn."

I saw in the moonlight her whitish-blue, short-cut skirt, her checkery blouse, her black curls and sunnytan skin.

"I jest ain't like yer oth'r men, I don't guess, Reety. I get th' blind staggers sa bad whenev'r I set my eyes on your little flapper skirt, here, that—well, heck, ye've gotta push on me, whichev'r way that ya want me ta go. I cain't guess as good as lotsa fellers."

She said, "Your hair eesa fuller off de stickers thana your clothes are. I feela tham. Wheeeoo! I never deeda see soocha stuck-up man."

"Gonna take you 'n' that little brat bruther of yores jesta 'bout a week an' a half t' pick me outta these here stickers. Where's he at?"

"When he see you dive in de weedsa he run find you. Whann he no see you come-a up, he run for home, papa, mama."

"Papa, mama my guitar, y' mean ta say."

"I run heem two, three week, I catch heem for you."

"Two weeks? You're gonna be a-pickin' sticker seeds outta me fer a whole lots longer than two or three weeks."

Her curls fell down towards the dirt on the road as she did a little knee bend now, and said, "I your slave? No? Yass. De firsta t'ing tomorra morning I start. Where do you say me come-a?"

"Come-a? Y' know what that means back in th' dry leaves of Oklahomer, Reety Rinio? Come-a?"

"Somet'ing bad?" She bit her fingernail walking along.

"Somethin' too good ta talk about, I reckon."

"You never deeda tal me"—Riorina danced a little circle

on the dirt—"whatta de deepa, darka seecret ees between Rio and yourself. Here eesa the hand wheecha you weeshed to hold to maka you tongue talk fast, speak truth."

I stuck her hand down in my overalls pocket, squeezed it till I could feel the heat, and told her, "Well, truth is, if you an' me was a-walkin' down th' streets of my old hometown, an' you was a-holdin' yer hand down inside o' my overhalls pocket, ya'd learn perty soon what my folks means 'never they say, 'I come. You come. We both come together.' "

She slacked her gait and swung her weight against my right shoulder. I felt her curls now brush against my cheek as they had brushed my guitar box back on that adobe house grass. "You say Riorina to come-a eet ees notta bad. We walk alonga now, I say we go, you say we come-a. I no know."

"Well, d'ya remember back, say, what you done when you first climbed up in yer bed with yer husband? Whenever he laid up on top of ya, what was it that you done?"

"He teeckle. I weegle. I tired, I stop-a, I no weegle no more."

"Well, jest 'fore ya quit a-wigglin', it got ta feelin' better 'n' better, didn't it? Whenever yer wigglin' gets ta feelin' its very level best, well, my people say, ya come. See?"

"Oh, I see. Yas. Ees my hand inna your pocket going to make you weegle good-a? I take hand out you letta me."

"No let," I told her.

"How does theesa all feet eento the beega seecret your frand Rio and you are cooking op?"

"I dunno, 'xactly, how ta 'splain it. Didja git a chance ta see my cousin Eddie's crippled arm?"

"Yes, een at de weendow. Addie aska Rio finda heem girl maka heem weegle? No? *Si?*"

"Eddie cain't make no girl wiggle."

"No? Why notta? He craze?"

"Eddie was in the war for over three years. Big German dump blowed up while he was down in a trench dugout with 'is girl friend. Some more Huns come along and shot Eddie and his girl with pistols, 'sheeny guns, rifles— killed the girl, and sent Eddie up to th' hospital f'r a year 'er two. He never did wanta make any girl wiggle no more since that day in that trench with his girl."

"That ees bad. Anda Rio?"

"Rio jest wants ta have a little talk with Eddie t'night at midnight, while Eddie's a-sleepin' on our truck bed."

"Talk? How? Wheecha?"

I stopped walking and stood spraddle-legged in the road, and asked her, "It'll jest cost ya one kiss, Missie Pigtails, right here, right now, ta find out what Rio's gonna talk in Eddie's ear. Midnight."

"Eef I kees you here in de road, I mighta weegle a beeg bonch. I kees lotsa fella, but I holda back, I no weegle weetha tham so vera mucha. *Sí, no?* Sav?"

"I'll promise ta pay ya back, Sugar Titty, wiggle fer wiggle, hug fer hug, kiss fer a kiss, an' a rub fer a rub."

It must have been for the best parts of an hour that I held her up as tight against me as two people can stand. We moved on along the road in the dark, sort of by side steps, and by long pushes, rocking, swaying, weavering, and shuffling our feet. The feel of her hips and her thighs against mine, that windly smell of her hair curling down around both of us, the smell and hot feeling of her sweat as she soaked her fancy blouse around her arm holes, and the soft petal press of her breasts and her nipples up foamy and starchy against my body, those ways she lifted her eyes up to my face, then let them droop closed and shut again on my chest, the feelings of my lips nibbling around her ears, caused both of my hands to commence slipping her silkery fancy blouse down from around off her shoulders. I lost my powers over words. I lost my power to remember time. I lost my name somewhere, my hat, my shoes, my overalls, my people, my relatives, all of my good and bad friends—everything floated along on the waves of some big muddy backwater. I felt her whole shape, and the shapes of every muscle in her body. I combed my fingers through her curls till the oily heats came. The harder I pulled her hips against mine, the harder she would move and go through her hot little wiggling. I asked her, I guess, a few silly questions, the same kind she asked me. And when I dropped down onto my hands and knees at the grassy place alongside the road, I tried to pull her down with me. She had tears in her eyes when she told me, "Honey. Notta now. I can no do noth-inng. Notta now. Notta tonighta. I weesha for eet lotsa more de you. You 'stan'?"

And I asked her why not. "Why cain'tcha?"

"Riorina, see, Hon, her Leetle Reever ees ronning tonighta. I havva no more gooda clothes een thesa world, Hon, besides these I havva on. They are getting all dirty wrinkle. I weesha for thesa wan night I deedn't have thesa pretty things on. And I wass notta seek."

"Well, considerin' we done some perty fair wiggling"— I patted the flat grass with the palms of my hands—"an' considerin' as ta how yer th' pertiest gal I ever did wiggle with, an' as ta how most ain't got no sech perty head o' curls as you got, an' as ta how yer mouth an' lips know a dernsight more'n any other gal's tongue that I ever did suck on, an' as ta how you are dressed up in yer finest riggin', I ain't a-gonna jerk yer clo'es off an stick no brandin' iron in yer belly hole. Ain't even gonna strip y' naked an' beat y' down with my bull whip. Ain't even gonna shoot ya more'n seven er eight times with my six-shooter. Likey?"

She stood with her fingers in my hair, telling me, "Oh. I feela vary lucky, and you are vary kind. My prittee skirt anda blouse eesa not a-goinng to be torn op."

"Down. Neither. Sorry if I bungl'd ya up sa much. Shucks, fer a spell there, Reety, I never even knowed what I was a-doin'. Y' felt sa hot that ya've melted me all down ta nothin'. Heckfires, I couldn' give ya a frailin' no matter if I was ta try my best."

"Deeda you weegle niza good?"

"Finest I ever did do. An' all o' my folks is knowed aroun' as perty dern good wigglers, whenever it comes right smack-dab down to it. How 'bout you? Good?"

"Yes. So good."

"Hummm. 'S funny."

"I woulda lika to tear my owna clothes off and weegle all over thesa grrass weetha you righta now."

"My knees is both hot an' ready. We c'n dig this dirt up aroun' here, Reeoritty, fer 'leven miles frontways an' backwards, if y' sa much as lemme undo that little blue majigger skirt. These ole slouchy overhalls drops away perty easy. I got about sev'n inches, Honey."

"Eesa savan incha theesa longa? Laka thees?"

"Jesta 'bout like that. Hey, Riorita, wanta—wanta reach yer hand down here 'n' feel with yer fingers? Hey? Hmm?"

"Down where?"

"Down here inside my overhalls. Nice an' warm. Hot."

"I gass mabbe."

"Kneel down here, thataway, that's m' lady."

"Where eesa he hiding at? Eena here? No? *Si?*"

"Mmmm, mmmm. Yeahh."

"He feel so hotta. Why?"

"Been a-doin' some hard labors, I reckon. How da I know? Ask 'im how come he's sa hot. Warm."

"Hees head ees so very very smootha; for why?"

"So's he c'n slick in home real nice an' greazledy, I'd bet."

"So sleeka that he can-a come eenside my leetle secret cave nize anda notta hurt very mocha. You sleeka heem opp de very many girls' pussies?"

"Few."

"Hmmm. He fonny fella. Alla time sneak eena de sneak outta. Eet eesa always fonny to me, how deesa fella he get so beega, so harda, so longa, I no canna see how he slips op een my leetle hairsa so easy when he eesa theesa hard anda theesa beeg anda theesa long. I gass mabbe I weela have to weegle my belly de beega bonch, Honey, whan I try to make 'nougha rooma for theesa fella here. Hoh?"

"When's that?"

"You breenga de fella friend here to thesa same-a spot in the morning weeth the sonn-op, promise? I no can take heem een my housa tonighta. You keepa heema niza warm, niza beeg, niza cleana. I weela letta you curl my curls anda kees me onna my belly button while he comes eenside to veesit weetha me. Whatta eesa he doing now?"

"I dunno."

"What eena de worrld?"

"Mmmm."

"Whatta deed he do, theesa beega lug head? I guess he ees crying, crying because I cannota letta heem come de eenaside tonight, hoh? He ees alla wetta, wetta laka de baby. Now, now, no cry, beega fella. I open op for you een de morning firsta thing. I wear my olda yelloww cheepa dress, no hatta, no stockings, no shoes. I come de barefoot de bare arms. I come with no step-ins onder my drassa. I lay down, Honey, my legs, I spread tham for you theesa wide aparta? Look see. I hold you so tighta you melta weetha my heat. I show you both my tittee, Honey, both verry verry prittee. You suck my neepple alla day lang tomorra, Honey, they are laka prittee leetle acorn nut. You see me, Riorina, weeth no clothes onna. I prittee. I dance for you barefoota, anda de no dress. You canna

keesa me all over whan you weesha. Tomorra. I fly home
now. I fly home."

She tore loose and ran off away into the dark so fast I
could never catch her.

I got up onto my feet in the little cart road and walked
my way back to the truck. Everybody must be asleep
around here. No sounds of life. Couple of snores. One's
Jeffrey's. But who's this other guy sawing off the logs?
Ohh. I remember, I remember that snore from last night.
That's old friend Rio's. Jeff and Rio don't see much alike
while they're awake, but they sure get together when it
comes to this snoring. It's so loud it sounds to me like
they're both awake, but I know that they're sacked up
asleep, just like everybody else around here. Guess I'll
catch a short nap too.

And if that old lobo alligator, Old Man Rio, asks me
where I've been off to and up to, when I wake him up,
I'm gonna tell him, "Well, Ole Man, I been out moon
walkin'."

CHAPTER 13

SALTY LAKE

I woke up wondering what time of night it was getting to be. The walking moon stood out a good bit brighter, so Manuel's mud-and-stick house looked plainer than it had by daylight. The weeds and brushy trees caught little sprigs of moony foam and threw it back at the sky. Our old truck was parked in back of the cactus garden windbreak, looking as much like an old pile of grayed ashes as like a factory-made thing you call a truck.

This moon is really strutting her stuff along these rocky ridges here tonight. I feel the same damp, cool air on my skin that, I guess, jumps up around midnight out across anybody's desert. Not a moving wind, not what I'd call a good high breeze, just a circle-dance of fresh air out of the night leaves. I started to whistle like a night bird as a signal to Rio at the truck, but I bit my lip and kept it still. If I was running late, maybe my noise would disrupt the work Rio was doing.

A dry cactus limb cracked under the sole of my shoe. I saw somebody walk towards me from the truck.

"Whissfft." He whistled in the roof of his mouth so as to make very little noise. "That you? Woodhead?"

"Yeah," I whispered out. "Who's this?"

"Your flesh-and-blood father." He got close enough for me to see. "Where on earth have you been off to? We have trotted our legs off looking for you. Jeff is about mad enough to turn that truck around and drive it home."

"Jest walked home with that there, that there girl. I was gonna meet Rio here at th' truck at midnight. I thought you knew." I could see that Papa was pretty sore.

"How did you expect us to know? Did you let any of us know? Why didn't you just come over to any one of us and tell us that you were walking home with a girl?"

"Hell, I dunno. Jest fergot it."

"Country like this, Woody, trip of this kind, it's a dangerous thing when every man doesn't try his best to be careful. There are just about a hundred kinds of death waiting here to catch all of us, no matter how hard we try to work together and to help one another. How would you feel if Jeff or Eddie, or me, any one of us, just took a notion to disappear out here in the dark? Not say one word to anybody? How would that make you feel?"

"Pretty bad, I reckon." I rubbed my chin and told him, "I'll try ta letcha know next time. I'm sorry. How mad you say Jeff is?"

"I'd not be at all surprised to see him crank up and turn that truck towards that little wife of his the first break of dawn in the morning. Where is your guitar?"

I swung around in my tracks feeling for my guitar strap. "Hmmm? What say? Ohh. Kid's a-gonna braing it back in th' mornin'. His daddy's gonna glue it, fix it up a little fer me. Why? Where's Rio at?"

"I feel pretty dubious, to say the least, considering that you were born into a long line of fiddle-makers. Pretty handy man at a glue can, yourself." Seven years of loud doubts ran through Papa's face and eyes. "Jeff will really and truly have something to razzle us about now."

"Gittar's gonna be right here'n my hands, I'm a-tellin' ya, first thing in th' cracklin' daylight. He's a good kid."

Rio jumped out from a tall spot of weeds and gave a low whistle. He fanned his blanket like a bigtail bird.

"Hey!" I kept my voice low. "What time is it now? Time t' go t' Eddie?"

"Allamosta."

"I'm anxious to see," Papa told Rio. "Is there some special hour?"

"Firsta hour Addie sleepa, she no so deepa, savvy? He

sleep deep second hour. Fourth hour he starrt back op again, every hour he wake op de leetle beeta more. Joosta de enda off de second hour seems to be best time. Who thesa?"

"Me. Don'ta poola de treegair." It was Rina's voice. "I come bring de *guitarra* back. My leetle brother he was sleepa weeth eet een heez bed."

I said to Rina, "I see you made a quick change of yer dress. An' ye've lost ya'r moccasins somewheres back down th' weeds."

"My fancy blouse and my flapper skirt, they are verra prittee bot verra warrm. Thisa old one-piece yellow dress, eeta speens out laka this when I do my leetle spider-web dance, like so." She tossed her curls about, held her fingers out, and spun a few circles in slow, droopy waltz time. Her eyes looked at the grass around her bare toes, feet, and legs, and the moon sprinkled over her yellowish polky-dotted one-piece air-conditioned cotton dress.

She ran to hug Rio's neck and asked him, "Here eesa beega keesa! Now, I aska you—beg you, Rio—please letta me halpa you tonight when you talk weeth Addie."

Rio's thumbs were down in his trouser cord, his blanket mostly over his shoulders and down his back, as he asked her, "And what could soch a leetle señorita fram the reever bed do for Addie? Say? What?"

Rina kissed Rio again, a longer one. "I canna do planty. You see. You let-a me. Ho?"

"How you find out I, we meet here de truck at meednight? Tal me." Rio studied Rina's face in the moon. "Pleesa."

"He. Heem." She nodded towards me. "Tonight."

Rio studied a bit and said, "Eefa Rina willa keepa verra steel. Eef Reeta weela get a girl friend tomorrow for Addie. Hey?"

She nodded her head. "Planty off tham. But I am wonndering, willa Addie need a girl laka me, or weela he need a woman, laka, say, Luisa?"

"Luisa Martínez? Ho?" Rio bit his bottom lip to think. "Leev een de mud house on de reevair? Pappa mamma die sick de stomach? Who leev een de house weetha Luisa now? I see planty fella cam, go. Cam. Go. Ho?"

"Her older seesater, Cleo. Tequila Cleo."

"How olda you say de botha seester?"

"Oh, Luisa she closa de twanty-fife. Cleo looksa mabbe

old as de Study Butte. Don' for sure know. Luisa she
gooda keed, but we ron eento trobles weetha Cleo. Canna
wee get samplace a leetle boddle of tequila?"

"For Luisa?" Rio wrinkled his face.

"No. For Cleo."

"Sure." Papa nodded at Rina. "Our truck. Fruit jars.
Rattlesnake medicine."

"Them gals bite a fell'r very bad?" I asked Riorina.

"That ees joosta de reesk you weela haf to ron." She
smiled up at me. "I will try to see thatta she weel notta
bite you, notta so varra bad. Ha."

"Riorina," Rio said to her, "you pappa mamma, they
know you go tomorra these house, de Cleo, de Luisa?"

"They know. I tal tham I go weetha Luisa, op de Goatsa
Rancha to cry for that olda lady thata fell down dead.
Savvy? I hated de dust on 'er feet. She was always mean
to us keeds. I glad she die down. I taka de boddle tequila
over to Cleo. I am sure we cann work eet, Uncle Rio.
Pleasa, pleasa, let-a me stay de trock anda halp. I quiet
like mouse."

"No laugha?" Rio asked her. "Not cut de jaybird?"

"No." She shook her curls. "You be planty glad eef you
letta me halpa you. I hear alla my life, Rio, how you go
deesa house, dat-a house, do de good for lotsa sick people.
I see you, I leesten, I be stilla, I learn, I feela mabby I be
smart laka you. I learn de way Rio say de word halpa sick
people. Ho, no, Rio?"

Rina's words came as smooth as the skin of her bare
arms in her old rough-and-tumble yellow dress. The moon
sparked a new glint and glimmer of lights that jumped
around amongst her candystick curls and shone where she
licked her lips with the end of her tongue.

"Oncle Rio. My Oncle Rio." Rina spoke each word in
some different way to give it a different catchy sound. She
never pronounced her words in any set way. She had that
streak of young cockiness in her, that kind of a limber
twist in her words that I'd seen in her fingers while she
talked, in the motions of her arms and hands, the tilt and
nod of her neck and head. She seemed to me to be imitat-
ing a whole crowd of imaginary people in her walk, talk,
ways and actions. She spread her *rrr*'s out long and wide
in one sentence, and skipped over those same *rrr*'s in her
very next breath. She held her *s*'s long like a snake hissing, then in her next word and movement, skipped out

over these same *s* sounds or made them sound like a
trashpile nest of bumbling bees, zzz, zzz, zzzz, zzz. It all
had to do with how much of a hurry she was in, and if
she felt high or low, happy or sad, gay or muddly, jumpy
or lazy. I wondered where she learned to speak in English
as plain and as well as she did. But, by her look, her way
of moving around so easy and limber-like, by her skin
color and hair, I judged that she did not act in the exact
typical ways of most full-blood Mexicanos or Indians. It
seemed to fill her now with fun of some sort to talk in
English.

Rio told us, "*Sí. Sí.* Yas, Riorina, you de smart head,
we needa your woman's finger. You came along joosta de
righta time. Mebbe eet was your Beeg Mind that told you
to jump and run down here, geev usa four olda men
beega halp."

"*Sí, sí.*"

"Could be possible," Papa said.

"Anyhow," I told them, "I'm awready a-feelin' a good
bit better 'bout th' whole damn thaing. Rina, I don' know
how t' tell y' very plain 'bout how I feel. It jest sorta makes
thaings feel, well, not so ghosty an' haynted an' spookerish
anymore."

"No go de truck," Rio said. "I go de first. Me." He
trotted away in the dark. I heard his words fade out as
he ran: "I wheestle. You come."

We squatted and sat down on the grass. The moon
moved into a brighter stretch of sky. I'd seen some bright
nights of moon on the flat plains of snow in the dead of
winter cold back up to our north. These border nights had
been as bright in other ways, not so glaring as the blinding
sun and moon on the wheat plains, but with more of a
fuzzy touch across pure patches of red, yellow, or blue
that kept some of their colors in the moonlight. The fires
of the hot sun touched these fresh, warm heaps of volcanic ashes, crystal rocks, crystal dust, mineral dumps,
chemical pilings and combed and fluted cliffs, and made
their colors wiggle and jiggle by daylight, and the moon's
own blazing lit them by night.

By the day's rays of light this world was afire, it glowed,
boiled, and shimmied. But here all around me tonight, I
noticed how the moon came a-dancing in with its nose
turned up and told you, "Pooh, today you only watched the
daily Sun and his wild-ass crew of clumsy splashers, rock-

dashers, and silly wasters of paints and powders. Now I, the Moon, me and my crews of other moons, stars and planets, friends, kinsmen, and relations, will show you another kind of glory dance which the Sun's gang cannot produce. Look at my Moon-Rock World, my Moon-Water Country, my Moon-Tree Spot, my moon faces and moony eyes, and moony splashing grasses, my lit-up weeds and my bushes, and tell me the truth I know is lying in your heart. Now are you not glad and proud that the noisy, clattering, wild and stumbling crew of the Sun has ridden on out over the westerly hill for tonight? I, the Moon, I am to the universes the same thing that Riorina here is to the work you are working, to the dreams you are now hoping and hatching. I am the Girl Woman, with storms and floods in both of my eyes, but by my blue lamp of night, I can let you look into the outermost parts of the sky-blue ocean, farther than you can see by that braggart Sun of the blinding day. Hoy! I admit, well and true, that my brother Sol, the Sun, can heal your worst diseases, but he is too rough about it. He makes your skin blister and your clothing an oven. I make your naked skin pretty and the colors run in the threads of your clothes even prettier than they really are. It has always been a woman's job to come along after the man and to clean up, to fix up, to put things, mountains, rivers, cities, papers, and dirty dusts back where they really belong. I come by the night because I am too busy every day doing this same work around on earth's other side."

After several minutes of waiting, Papa told Rina and me, "Think I'll take a little gander down around the truck, see what goes on. I've heard about this kind of thing all of my life, but never got to see how it worked. Makes me itchy and anxious to see what happens. I suppose my son will be comparatively safe here in your hands, Miss Rina. Maybe you can help him more than we can Eddie."

"Yes. *Sí, sí.* He needs planty of halp allaright. I holda you son-a so he no ron away." Papa went out towards the truck. She folded her fingers in my hand and told me, "Riorina she itch like Señor Charlie. You?"

"Derndist itchin' I ever did have. I'm shakin' all over like a wet rabbit on a cold mornin'. Wonder jest what that there old Rio Dickens is up to an' a-doin' t' Eddie right now. You?" I pulled her head over on my shoulder, just to see if she would let me. We kept our eyes off down the

trail, and I asked her through the twists of her curls,
"Change yer mind yet, I mean about tomorrow mornin'?
Ah, thank ya for the guitar."

She told me, "No. This is my old drass. I went to my
house; I take my good drass off, I jomp in my bed, I maka
de noise. Mama, Papa t'ink I sleepa. But I look outta my
weendow, and I see de moona, fly so bright I t'ink eet was
de sun. I say, 'Oh, looka, eet eesa morning!' I taka your
guitarra from de brroother's bed, I out de door. Bom!
Lika dees! Com."

"Bom! Coom! I'm a-pickin' up Mexican perty fast, hey,
ain't I, keed?"

I heard Papa run up the path all out of breath, saying,
"All right, all right, you two love eagles. Rio says for you
to come on, but not to make a sound." And he walked
back in such long steps that we had to trot along to keep
up with him.

The truck in the light of this moon looked quiet and
still, and even like a newer truck. Everything around it lay
quiet. My brogan shoes scraped as I held onto Rina's
hand and ran up to the truck. Her bare feet made no
sound and she held her breath. Rio could not have asked
the Mexico border to mix him up a finer night, or a
quieter one. Tiptoeing around the radiator, Rina led me to a
foot or two behind Papa's back. Then, to bust up the peace
and quiet of the whole night, we heard a real loud snort, a
bubbling sneeze, sort of like a night animal blowing at us
from somewhere out in the cactus patch. The sound turned
out to be Jeff snoring. He lay stretched on the bed of the
truck on the north side. Eddie, I saw by Papa's nod, lay
on quilts and blankets on my left hand, or southerly side,
closer to the moon. Jeff had on his work pants and the
same old shirt. Eddie lay like a dead man in a thin suit
of longhandle underwear. He held his back straight and
stiff like he'd learned to do in the army, with both hands
folded under the back of his head, his bare feet near the
rear end of the truckbed. His face looked tight, stiff, hard-
jawed, and troubled, where the full light of the moon
touched on him.

Papa walked around the truck and motioned to tell us,
"Sssshh. Don't touch the truck."

"Jaff he snorre anda keep Addie from de gooda sleepa.
Sssh," she whispered to me. "Ohh, jossta whatta ees these?
These two hands? Say?"

I kept my hands around her tighter and told her in a low whisper, "It's th' only thing that c'n keep me quiet. Little snuggle huggin'. Hurt? Too tight on ya?"

Rina wiggled back against me and whispered, "Oh, no. But for what Rio ees doing, we moosta keepa quiet."

Rio hung his blanket on the two-by-four corner brace of the truckbed, clicked his tongue around in his mouth, rubbed his hands together. His blanket hanging from the post hid the truckbed from us. We stood by the cab door and front fender, listened through the blanket at Jeff's fits of rattling snores. He snored so loud that he shook his head and gritted his teeth. Jeff would wake Eddie. Rio walked barefoot past Eddie Stone, and stopped close to Jeff's ear as the snoring got louder. We ducked our heads to listen.

"Jaff!" We heard Rio talking low. "Jaffrey! Thees ees your olda frand Rio. Hallo. Hallo, Jaffrey. I be you frand. You mada weeth Rio. I no care. I be your frand anyhow. My people laka Jaff play hees feedle. Jaff no gotta his woman here de truck blanket. I mada, too, Jaff, I no gotta niza woman in de blanket. You laka hear niza perty *música*, hey? Leesten. Leesten."

"Ain't sawin' no logs, is he?" I blew my breath under the twistings of Rina's curls. "Ssssh! Listen."

"Your feedle, Jaff, you nama heem, what you say, Squalling Pantherr. That ees good."

"Wiggle," I told Rina.

"Eef Rio tals me de weegle, I weegle."

"Listen." I tried to talk Mexicanly. "Shush, squash!"

"I leesten." She squirmed back some more, trying to act bashful. She rested her right toes on top of her left toes. She watched my hand while I fingered her nipple and asked, "Too beega? T'ink?"

"Jest right. Listen."

Rio told Jeff, "Eefa you geev me your ears I tak you and show you where de cave ees of de panther. Be still. No sound. Tip-a-toe. Easy. Here, follow me, Rio. Cam lang. Not a sounda. Easy. Een thesa beeg darka hole, see, een thesa beeg sleeka rock cave. You can hear de pantherr breathing. No sound. Quiet. Stay here and leesten. I go 'nother side. I go find pantherr. Jaff stay. Wait. Ho? You canna steel hearr Rio's words, see, but they bounce on de rocks, so you Jaff, can'ta quite tal de word wheecha I, Rio, say. Leesten. Ears theesa way, and leesten. Leesten."

"Jaff hee ees no weegle."

"I'll wiggle fer 'im," I told her.

From beside us under the moon, I heard Papa whisper, "This, friends, is one kind of a miracle. Jeff is quiet."

I nodded at Papa, but kept my lips quiet so as to listen to Rio and to Eddie.

Rio talked to himself as he kept his ear tuned to see how Jeff would act. He looked out over the radiator past us, and told us, "Jeff weela not give usa any morre trouble thesa night. And, now, you keeds, Woodachok, Rina, eef your hands can untie each other long enough, Rina, singa for me and for Eddie, soft, your leetle song—'Ron Off Down Passt Mexico.' Jaff no wake up. Addie he needa pretty girl sing. I go now. You sinng. Pretty."

Rina started to sing by herself. She moved out from the bearhug I had on her, and leaned back against the cab with one ear against Rio's blanket. Rio gave her time enough to sing,

> Take a ron down around Maxico,
> Take a ron down around Maxico,
> Take a ron down around Maxico,
> Take a ron down around Maxico.

I looked at her head up against the green blanket. I did not feel like singing. I did feel, though, like listening. Rina stopped singing when she heard this first word that Rio spoke a few inches from Eddie's face.

"Addie, my frand, hallo Addie. You know me, Rio. Gooda place for us meet op, Addie, here deesa place. You dream, you notta dream. You sleep and you notta sleep. You wake and you notta wake.

"Thesa place, Addie, ees where the Truth builds de house to raise big family in. I see Addie here de way Addie really wants to be—lika Addie really ees. Een thesa True Contry, Addie, I cannot tal you de lie, you no tal me de lie. Every word thesa whole country she tals only de truth, Addie. You been tella de beeg lie to your mother, Addie. To your seesterr. Uncle Charlie, you lie same way; to Jaff, Woody, and even to your own self, Addie.

"Thesa beeg lie she like da snake 'rounda your neck. She choke your life half away, Addie, half away.

"You soldier fella, Addie. Proud when you sent your family your picture, before de big blow-up. You stand niza straight, Addie, proud fella, you know you look good to thata leetle Franchey girrl, hay?

"I see, Addie, here you gotta stuck down de muddy hole with your *vino* girl for three, four days. De mud she get hard, Addie, you say she hold you, so you no canna climb out. I say no, you lie me; Addie he no want for climb out. Wantsa go back de same hole, stay stuck down de same mud, Addie, de same girl, same *vino* bucket. I hear you tell me now, I no laka de looks of any other girl wheech walks on two feet. De bullet kill my only woman here, de blood soak my naked skin for two, three nights een de mud bog. No. You lie me, Addie. You notta stuck down that muddy hole, you stuck down different kinda hole. You stilla stuck here de crazy lake, here in my country, een my lake I call my Salt Lake.

"I say Addie can see feefty lakes anda pools 'round Utah, Nevada, Texas, in de hot rocks and sand. Salt lakes.

"No joke, Addie, de salt lakes witha my people, my birds, and my animals. These lakes arre lots worse than-a de graveyard you saw there, riding past eet in de truck.

"Nothing, Addie, grows een de salt lake. Nothing even moves down een eet. Nothing stays alive een your salt lake. Not a stick, not any tree, not one little weed thesa big, Addie, there ees not a root living anywhere around thesa lake.

"Addie cannot fool my people, cannot fool Rio. I know nice girl come geegle, come smile, make hair stan' op on de salt block's back. Make dead stick get beega rise on. Make de blood ron to both of my heads, hay? A man, Addie, feels thesa tickle for the weemen a long time after he has turned away to the blowing dust.

"Tomorra Riorina's brother, José, will show you de way de old 'dobe house onna de Sam Nail ranch. I no see Addie more after thees. Addie no see me, Rio, more after that.

"I giva my words over to your frands, to Uncle Charlie, to Wooderstone, to Riorina, to nice look girl you see, name Luisa—you say Louise. Luisa fine girl, Addie, she halp me, Rio, t'ousand times. More, mebbe. Luisa like Addie, Addie he lika Luisa. She had a hard pull, but Luisa she jump up niza girl. You like her face, eyes; she talk good sanse, walk straight lika de soldier. You wisha for touch her skin, her hand, her hair. You can always leesten to Rina, and to Wood, and to Luisa, and to Uncle Charlie, Addie, eef you would lika to hear my words.

"I, Rio, have to speak to a leetle meetinng of my people about working down de mines, Addie, and how my children can fight to get some money for build lotsa beeg house, Addie. I have gotta go and meet them. I tella them they are stuck down een their little muddy steeck house-a, joosta same way Addie down de mud and the *vino* anda the salt lake. I tella them go fight for get out. I tella you, my frand, Addie, go fighta same way, kick your way outta here to where de open air blows.

"You willa no tella any of your frands, Addie, thatta you hadda thesa talka with Rio. No. Whan you feela like you woulda love to hear Rio's word to show your own feet where to walk, or to talk, Addie, I, Rio will be gone. I willa be hiding een some little mud stick house from de *policía*. I willa be geeving my words eento some other ear. 'Stan'? My words you will hear lika your own words. My word eet willa sound and feel joosta like Addie's. Sav?

"Eef you weesh to let me know that you thanka me for thesa leetle word or two, Addie Stone, tell eet to me by thesa secret seegnal.

"Throw down onna the dirt you jar of de snuff. You plugs of de dirty chew 'backer. Aska Woody, ask Luisa, halp you roll op de cigarette. They crave for to halp you, Addie; they itch and burn to halp you. Letta them halp you, anda letta their half start, say, by de roll for you de cigarette. You will know that thesa ees only de seegnal.

"Avery time you see de rabbit hop, Addie, the hair of thesa rabbit moosta blow in-a de weend the same to your eyes, Addie, as your girl tamorrow, Luisa. Some leetle word of hers willa come-a to your tongue, and you willa speak op your own feelings about how Luisa makes you think of all de other women everywherre, Addie.

"I not-a force you do lak Rio say, Addie. I helpa your own words to grow. I not-a tal you what I make Addie do; no, I tal Addie whata Addie hees own salff weesh to do.

"You will not forget thesa wine girl, Addie, no; that would be no good. You will hear your wine girl in the words anda the smiles of every girl and every woman whicha you see. She will talk for you and she will tella you to be proud of your own salf, to maka jokes, to laugh.

"You will wake op whanaver de daylight hits your face. You will show me how proud you are of your creeple arm, Addie, whan you see Tequila Cleo. You willa pour a pint boddle of Jaff's leeker op anda take eet over for Cleo anda Luisa.

"Anda all of your lifetam, Addie, whan your eye feels de lights of de son, whan your nose smells de honeys of de flower, whan your ear hears de talking of my peoples, and your eye flies op to de moon anda down with de stars, eet willa make Addie Moore feela like he ees de finest man een thesa worlda for any of you ladies to hold onto.

"Rina, Woody, Uncle Charlie, anda Jaff, they can show Addie planty about the woman, but tomorra, Luisa anda Tequila Cleo can teacha you lots more than any of the others. Leesten to Luisa alla you can.

"I, me, Rio, I go way now. I no come-a back. You lie to yourself anda say nobody likes Addie. I talka de truth, averybody likes Addie, same way I, me, Rio, love Addie.

"I go now, Addie. I no be here de truck whan you wake op weeth-a the sun. You love Addie joost as-a moch as we love Addie, and all of us willa jump op all right.

"*Adiós*, Addie. I meet you here sometime whanever you catch me in your thoughts. Bye-bye, Addie. Taka gooda care off my people anda they will always taka good care of you. You maka tham be gooda to each other while I, me, Rio, am gone away."

Rio left without taking his blanket. I hid behind it to wait for him to walk up and get it, but after five or six minutes, we knew that he had gone. I told Rina, "I don't believe it. Rio's not so loco in th' poconos as ta run off like that an' leave sech a good blanket."

"Rio wants for you to have eet," Rina told me. "He does odd t'ings samtimes."

I yanked the blanket off its post and held it up above my head. I ran and waved it, yelling my loudest, "Rio! Rio! Ya left y'r blanket!" I caught the toe of my shoe in some ankle-high cactus daggers and fell down on my shoulder in another bed of its relatives. Rina dropped down on her knees to see how bad I was hurt. She ran her eyes over Rio's blanket wrinkled along the grass, and asked me, "Are you dead, say?"

"Nope. Not quite." I squinched my face at her. "That ole crazy alligator. What made 'im, d'ya s'pose, pull a stunt like that?"

"Rio is a strange man. I t'ink he weesh to geeve you

somet'ing; he not know what you lika, he not know how to tall you, so he josta leave de blanket. He go way off to 'nother world whan he talka weeth Addie. Rio not even know hees own name for two t'ree days."

"Funny dern thaing." I looked at the blanket.

"He wants the finder to be the keeper. See? That ees what I, me, Rina, t'ink."

"Well, I, me, Woody, I reckon as how yer jest 'bout right. If'n I ever do lose my blanket, Rina, I shore do hope that you're th' one that finds it." I watched her eyes. "Rio'd shore wanta see his blanket kept warm an' nice, wouldn't he?"

"Rio would." She rubbed a wrinkle out of the corner.

"I couldn't keep that there blanket very warm tonight, now, jest me by myself." I rolled over onto the blanket and hugged her down alongside me. "We don't need no blanket on top of us, Rina. Moon up yonder's warm enough. Huhm?"

She wiggled out of my arms and rolled off onto the grass, telling me, "No. No. *Mi amigo,* that wasa not een our bargain."

I was saying, "Huh, 's matter? Why not? Why sa uppity?"

"I am op beecause I am notta down. See? What you t'ink you are, my hosbond? Anda whatta you t'ink I am, your wife? I no see you till thees very night, anda you try roll me t'ree times. Speewey over you. I spitta in your eye eef you insulta me wan more word. I de whore, de bitch whore, you see, you look, you smacka, you t'ink you poosh lika deesa onna de blanket? Phooey doowey onna you!" She stuck her nose, tongue, chin out at me to make me see what she meant. She stuck her hips, elbows, legs, backside out at me from her other end to make her feelings as plain to me as she could.

"What 'n th' holy cow's eatin' on ya now?" I lay on my back, face up to the moon, and asked her. "Some of Ole Man Rio's salt lake water snuffin' up yer nose holes?"

"Blahh!" She stomped her feet around and around my blanket, spitting down into my face. "Blahhh on you! You are joost asa seeck as Addie ees, anda seecker. I hadda rather be weeth any bashful fella thanna weetha you to bang on my head lika you own me anda my soul."

"Aww, Rina. What n' th' heck's come over ya, anyway?" I stretched out my full length on the blanket. "Ya shorely must've been off down yunder drainkin' outta that there ole salty lake."

"Anda my gooda frand, for all I care about you, you cana go and falla down dead and I, me, Rina, willa notta come anda cry where you fall downa. Good-bye, Meestairre Ponk Head. *Adiós*." And her words trailed out like a long, thick cloud of northbound blackbirds as Rina trotted like a wild horse off into some bushes and away.

And there I lay to listen to the pounding sounds of every word Rio had said to Eddie tonight while I had hugged Rina up against our truck cab and listened through Rio's old green blanket with the three broad black stripes around and around and around its borders.

Borders.

Borderlines.

Pull up these old crazy boundary borders and toss them over into the mouth of the first good volcano you run acrost. If you lose your boundary line and I find it, well, finders are to be keepers just as long as I'm the head stud on this damn pasture. Huhhmm. Helluva note.

CHAPTER 14

BIG NEW BOSS

If I snore and beat my gums as loud as Jeffrey all night, it's because I've got good reasons—because I'm sore at that little eighteen-year-old girl of a thing that goes by the name of Riorina.

I feel like a wild-toothed hyena yellering over a skeleton of runny bone meat. I feel worse than that. I had that little Rina girl all hot and ready, so I thought. Boy, she's just as juicery and sweet as they come. I never felt anything as warm as her skin on her neck in under those curly tails. That little move of her legs and her hips has already burnt my house down.

She didn't want me to be shoving the gas to her too fast. She tore out and left me here. I was one high-tempered fool, Rio, and I still am. I just got in such a big hurry, I guess maybe I threw the fears of the devils into her head. Like I thought that she was something too easy for me to roll over.

Well, I've mortally bitched up the works. Too dern-blame sure of myself—too certain about her. I shoved her so fast that she blew up in my face. I didn't let her petals take their time to open up. Gosh all razor blades, anyways.

I'll comb up and brush up a little bit, and pour out a

bottle of our best snake tonic, and make a little sashay around this town to try to run into a girl or two.

Boys, if I'm just half as fumble-fisted out yonder digging up my old Paw Jerry's mine as I was with that little Rina girl, I'll knock down that whole Chisos Mountain range and I'll be right down in under it when she falls.

Those curls of hers—she swings those curls around in the air to talk with—I mean, to help her talk to you. Her eyes snap fires that Hell Kitten's never did see. Hell Cat is a pretty girl in her own ways, quieter like, more like your mama, or like a teacher trying to help you learn some good sense.

Hell Cat's eyes would run big tears, though, if she had some kind of a little machine she could look into and see I, me, Woody, off down here rolling around with Missy Rina, as Papa calls her. Papa's pretty good that way, I mean, when he sees me going around red-eyed after Missy Rina, and remembers only back a few days ago, it was the same kind of a ruckus between me and Hell Cat. When it comes to the business of me and the girls, he says that on those private and personal and passionate grounds I am always my own boss. He says this stuff is just like getting hungry and thirsty or just like eating and drinking. I'm wondering what will happen between Helly and myself. If I dig out Grandpa's claim stake, say, and we sink down a shaft, and get a road built and a mine to going here in these Chisos Mountains, I wonder, then, will Helly and I get married? Will we come down here, or will I go back up there and live around Pampa?

No. No. I sure fail to love that Pampa town enough to want to live in it or around it anywhere. Oh, Helly, I can't beat her for a girl, a buddy, I know that. Helly Kitten could have a houseful of kids and make all of them a nice warm mama to look out after the whole bunch.

This little Riorina, though, she's just about six laps ahead of Helen when it comes to looks, figure, shape, build, fire. I wonder how deep I'm going to get mixed in with her. If it's not any more than eighteen miles from the Study Butte rock over to Jerry's old camp house, I'm fairly apt and liable to keep these cactus roots pretty hot back and forth. Any girl in this rockbound world as pretty as this prancer dancer that fired those two devilish eyes at me can have me tonight or all day tomorrow, or every day and night for sixty years. If I was married right now and already had a wife I loved and three kids I loved to death, this Riorina girl could pull me over into her little kinky curls any such a time as happened to suit the lights of her eyes. Right nor wrong is not in the picture. I see nothing in between me and the moon-stars but that shape of hers which can pull me to it, or can throw me down in this old bar ditch, spit on me, call me bad names, slap my ears, beat on me with long sticks.

She may be somewhere right this minute having a funny laughing dream of some kind about our little run-in down the road tonight. Or she might be, could be, crying at home on her pillow because I dropped the whole crate like I did, and broke every stick of hope there was in it.

Troublesome sleep is only a shade better, I guess, than no sleep at all. I never spent a night where my fever got this hot. I never saw a night in my life as crazy as this one. I saw everything twist and bend out of shape—old trigger springs, levers, screws, cogwheels, hot rocks, thorns, stickers, ropes, wild varmints, loud animals, dust storms, high winds, cyclones, head-rise waters, lightning and thunder and trees all hit and knocked to the bushes. I rolled over on Rio's blanket so many flips and flops. Wonder if Rio ever did roll any such a loco night down here on this blanket of his?

I woke up with four deputy sheriffs holding guns at my back. They took me to a little creosote-smelly office and shined their flashlights in my face. I heard them ask me, Where do you come from? How come you down here along this border? How much cash money have you got? It's against a few of our laws for you to be where you are.

The guns, thank heaven, turned out to be the little dry scabs over the cactus cuts I'd got last night trying to give Rio's blanket back to him. Well, there isn't any sleep for the wicked, no kind of rest for the red-eyed and bleary. Gotta get up. Can't just lay here and find your claim stake, can I, Jerry P.?

This is the big, big day, or was going to be, wasn't it? It looks like one awful little day if you ask me or if you don't ask me. I can't let this daylight kick Jeff's face in and wake him up while I'm around here. I gotta get myself gone. Get my little hind end to flapping out away from this truck. I'll walk over paddyfoot and easy, take a little peek at the others.

Hmmm. Sound asleep. Keep right on with your sleeping, men. Dream about it, go dream it out, find that little rocky hole where Grandpaw covered up his mine to make us all rich.

I'll just take one little thing, gents, just enough of your morning's dew to fill up my little flat pint. I can reach the fruit jars from where I'm standing, tiptoe a little.

Where'bouts can I run off and hide to pour my pint out? I never did know that a halfa gallon jar made this much noise jostling around.

Hey, here's a fine spot, all hid out in this clump of stringy bushes. Pull up a few little handfuls of these weeds under my feet, and I'll have plenty of room to kneel down here and screw this jar lid off.

Funnel. No dern funnel. Mouth of my flat pint is too little. Ohhm, yes, I'll take this big brown-green leaf here, like this, give it a twist around my longjohn finger like this, make a little angel's horn for the devil to blow. Stick the leaf down in the neck of the flat like this. Open it up a little wider around the top, like this. Tequila Cleo will tell you out of her own mouth that this greeny-brown leaf rot-gut slop is the best she's ever flopped her lip over. Ohhm. That's right. No'mm. I'm not going over to Cleo's pig house, am I? No'mm. Nawwp. Not on this day.

Whoa. Wait just one minute. What kind of a sound was that? Wait. There it comes. Listen. Closer, too damn close for comfort. Here, stob your cork back down in that flat, see, and get outa here.

I dug a hole in the sandy dirt and dog-boned my fruit jar in it, to get rid of it. Who in the devil was this barging in here to knock my playhouse down, anyhow?

My visiting friend turned out to be none other than Mr. Eddie Stone, his own self. He pushed his way into my same clump of bushes. He pulled up a few sprigs of sticker weeds around his feet, he kneeled down on the ground and pulled something out of the bib of his over-alls. I dropped down on my face and belly out of his sight and watched him through the limbs of the bush between us. I heard the sound of another fruit jar lid untwisting, then the sounds of something bubbling into a bottle.

Eddie twisted his jar-lid back on, whistled a tune under his breath, felt his good left hand along the dirt, and covered up a long, tall, brown, home-brew beer bottle. His little whistle came from pressing his tongue up against the roof of his mouth, and half talking, half whistling out the words: "She's promist me that she'll say Yessiree, that's good enuff for me, Sweet Jennie Lee."

Eddie's little whistle just nearly set my whole morning straight. But just then Papa walked out of the thicket with my fruit jar in his right hand, and Eddie's in his left fingers. He kept on walking past us, and told us, "I left your little bottles in the rat holes you dug to hide them in, men. But I have to take these jars back before Jeff wakes up and sees they are missing without plausible explanation. Well, see both of you tonight when you come back from your girl chase." Papa took off back towards the truck.

I walked back to the thicket and dug my pint up while Eddie scratched his out of the roots on his side.

I was oiling my tongue to tell him how I bashed up the works and chased Rina home as mad as a wet jaybird, when I heard the breaking of dry things. I turned to look. Just an early-bird Indian or Mexican walking the foot road to work the mine, I guessed. Soft, easy, barefooted walking.

Eddie said, "Oy, young lady. Come in. Squat down. Nice early mornin'?"

Riorina stood on the leafy bed, folded her arms, and looked our thicket over.

"Riorina, meet my cousin Eddie Moore," I said.

"I'm glad to meet you."

"Am I crazy, or did you change the colors of the spots in your pokey dotty dress?" I asked.

"Botha," she told me. "You crazy anda de spots arre deef'rant."

"Same kind of a dress, ain't it? Tear th' yaller 'un up? Er sum boy grab it an' run off with it?"

"No. You see, Addie, I tolda heem lasta night thatta I would put on my olda polka dotta yellow dress, anda thatta he be the bossa man, say where we go anda whatta we do today. I got to frand's house at night, I taka offa da olda yellow one. He boss de yellow one today, anda I, Riorina, bossa thesa parple one. Hey, Addie?"

I, me, couldn't think of anything to say right at this moment in history.

"Wouldn't you two boys lika to work today and maka se'nty fi'e sants apiece, no? Addie, you gooda carrpenta man? Builda t'ings?" she asked and looked at Eddie.

"Build what?" I asked her with my eyes down on her red leather moccasins.

"I am asking your boss man, Meestaire Addie."

Eddie stopped his laughing to tell her, " 'S all accordin' ta whatcha'd want me ta build."

"A wall anda de cellar. You get se'nty-fife sants every day wheecha you work."

"No work, no cents," I said.

"Shoota oppa de faiza, you teetha they fall out. Whatta you gon' say, Addie? I told Señor Charlie I had good job for you men."

Eddie sat up and looked thoughtful. "Ta be right truthful, Rinny Tin Tinna," he told her, "I was aimin' t' go shave myseff an' spruce up a speck 'r two an' take a big long walk around this Study Butte town, see if I couldn't mebbe scare up a little fun of some kind er 'nother."

"Ohh. Yas. *Sí, sí.* I cannot blame you for that. I woulda do de same-a t'ing, I guessa, eef I was away off fram my home, mebbe deeging oppa de gold around Cheecago. I woulda notta work, beelda any wall, deega no cellar, no. I would taka my leedle brown boddle in my handa; I steecka eet down eena my boozoom like you do, anda I ron see fella I like. I pulla heem off down de beega deetcha, I weegle, I jeegle, I no builda de walla for seecka mama, seeck baby. No."

"They's not no gold down under Chicago," I told her.

"How sick?" Eddie asked her. "This here mama an' her little wiggly baby?"

"Badda." She tossed her curls in the air where she sat to watch us. "Botha die thesa morning."

"Ought'r be nice an' easy folks ta work for," Eddie said. "You lyin' or just jokin'?"

"Both," I told them. "Truth ain't in 'er."

"Why you say thees?" she pried at me. "Why?"

"Lied to me," I told her. "Lied your little tongue off. Don't pay 'er a lick o' mind, Ed. She's a preevarrycater of th' worst waters."

"You de leezard"—she cocked her head my way—"leezard fram de salt water. I no lie you. Deeda not."

"Said y'z gonna meet me over atta cert'n spot when th' sun riz up this mornin', an' y' didn' do it," I told her.

And Rina told me, "How coulda you know so verra verra mocha whan you deeda notta comma de spotta, yourself? Talla me thesa, Meesterr Wizemon."

"Well, y'see, Rinner, I couldn't get away from Eddie here long enough t' run over ta th' spot we picked out."

"I can show you both nize job eefa you weel follow me. Eyekayy?"

"Where 'bouts, young missy?" Eddie got to his feet and we followed her down a path that twisted through the cactus and the brush. After a few minutes Eddie said, "I'll say this one thaing an' stock to it, Woodsaw: them is the prettiest curls that anybody ever did ask me ta foller in after."

I was flabbergasted to hear Eddie talk that way.

"Pertiest hind end I ever felt th' pleasures of chasin' down." I tried to be funny walking at Eddie's heels.

"Oh, you seely boys, seely keeds, won't you ever grow op lika beeg mann? Here, this way. Looka out for those thorns; they are planty lika knife. Follow, pleasa. Theesa trail."

"Ye're not a-gittin' tired of hearin' us men tell y' how perty ya look, now, are yah? Tell us th' truth."

"No, I am a-loving you forr eet. Now, looka there, where my finger ees. That leetle roof of that leetle house down over there, see?"

I looked down the hill to the roof that Rina was talking about. "Looks awful leaky to me," I said, and took a look at the weather at the same time. The sun clumb up in the big vacant blue pasture. If a cloud had stuck its head out so far this day, I couldn't see it. A cool haze was in the air. The wind was about half asleep in some weedbeds. Eddie saw me gazing around at the weather. "Hey, 'member how we froze our gash-blame han's jest about a week ago up yond'r on toppa them North Plains?" he said. Rina listened with her lips wet. It was fun to her to hear Ed and myself make remarks about this weather she had breathed and bathed in every day of her life.

My eye lost track of the weather, though, as I caught sight of a lady in an old faded brown speckled housedress walking up our trail from the house. Her thick-set head of dark, chocolate hair tossed as she pushed her hands against her kneecaps to give her more of a back-lift and leg-swing up the path. She looked fairly young as her face came closer. She looked puffy, tired, lazy, and hot, but I had the feeling she was acting a bit worse than the morning, the trail, or the sights of us could really cause. She rubbed her strings of hair back away from her cheeks and neck, as hot and sweaty as the lead-off woman on a cotton-chopping gang. She was lower built and wider in hip, thigh, shoulder, and face than Riorina, and could have passed off as a Japanese or a Chinese girl in most any chop-suey kitchen.

"'Allo." Rina bowed and did a little half-curtsy. "You arr outta moch too early for your own good. Why?"

"Oh, *buenos días*." The walking girl held her hair in her hands, and made a slight bow. "It is very early. Yes. I am leaving the house."

I stood back and watched the two girls as they shook hands. I heard by her first words that she spoke a fine fresh English, plainer than my own, Eddie's, or Rina's. A touch of Papa's braggery, but in a more shy and bashful way, always pulling her head back, eyes down, like she was begging your pardon, apologizing, explaining, and in such a quiet voice, it seemed like she was tippytoeing around a sleeping room full of babies.

"Anda why moosta you walka de hilla so early theesa morning?" Rina asked.

"I, I am going, on my way to find some men to work," the girl said. "You remember my wall and my cellar. I told you about it last night. I didn't hear any more from you, so took it for granted that you didn't find anyone. So now I'm going to try myself."

"Rina was jest a-tellin' me," Eddie started to talk. "'Bout th' job o' work."

"*Mis amigos.*" Rina pointed at Ed and me.

"Yeahhm," I said.

"Meestaire Addie Moore," Rina motioned. "He da bossa man."

"I am very pleased to know you," the girl nodded.

"Anda," Rina went on to bow and point, "Meestaire Wooda Shuck. Luisa."

"Glad to meetcha, Miss Luisa." After I shook her hand, I told her, "I am Mr. Eddie Moore's strawboss helper. I do all o' th' shoulder work."

While Luisa chuckled, Rina put in, "Eefa you ever want any beega brain work done, you joosta bring eet over to Mestaire Eddie. I have seen his work. I can say eet ees first-classa. Hah."

"I have always trusted your opinion." Luisa smiled off down at a pair of horny toads nosing under a weed. She acted like a high business lady and said in her soft way, "You have been very correct in the past, and I see no rea-

son to doubt your judgment this morning. Might I ask what
contracting company you gentlemen represent?"

I tried to think, but Eddie jumped ahead of me. He
jammed both hands down inside his overalls and threw his
chest out army style, then told her, "Th' Study Butte Mud
Slingers Company. An' me, well, I'm th' president of th'
damn place. Rina, here, says th't you got some celler holin'
an' some muddy wallin' th't ya aim t' have done."

"Yes. I do. I mean, I intend to. You see, Mister Stoner,
I do have the mud work, like you say, but, now, I just
haven't any money with which to pay you. Not so much as
the Study Butte Mining Corporation."

"Awwwh, bosh on them Minin' Crappysations; hell, most
of 'em is forty years behind th' times, anyhow. Take me an'
show me y'r mud job, womern. An' while we're a-walkin'
along sa dern peaceful an' quiet, Rinny, why do't you an'
Woody Hole, here, roll me up a nice big fat mama cigarette? Ya've gotta be doin' somethin', ye know, ta earn
yer cussed keeps." Eddie followed at Luisa's back, looked
up and down her from head to heel, and Rina followed
after Eddie, with me to bring up the tail end.

I thought I had spent several glad mornings back off
down the goaty path of my life, and always did pride myself on jumping up at the creaks of the day and running
out to feel the best I knew how. But, here, walking along
in back of Luisa, Eddie, and Rina, I felt like this morning
was more than just a fine day. It was better than the best
friend's howdy-you-do or hello. The stickers had jokes on
them, the thorns laughed at your skin, and when I looked
around at the old piley rocks they had electricity and all.

I jerked my tobacco sack out of my shirt pockets so fast
the breeze didn't see me. I fingered that crease down and
poured in the tobacco. I held it up over Rina's shoulder
and told her, "Here, I roll'd it, you lick it."

"Weeth mooch pleasure." She licked the paper, stuck it
down all around, and handed it up ahead to Eddie's lips. I
put a match in her hand, and she lit up the cigarette, saying, "I'm a ceegaratte girrl, leetle ceegaratte girrl. Ha de
ha de ha. Good, hey, Addie?"

"Fine." Eddie blew smoke back. "Best I ever did taste,
an' I'm a ole fagger from away back. Walk on. Lead me,
gals, t' this here work job."

Rina turned around to see what I was doing. I dropped
back a few paces and jig-danced on the trail as we walked

down towards Luisa's shack. I snapped my fingers across, around, and fancy in the air, doing my Charlie Chaplin loose-shoe shuffle. Rio's first signal had flared up and been seen. That cigarette. I got my foot caught in the long grass, fell, and jumped up to wink at Riorina to let her know, Cigarette, Cigarette.

Cigarette.

"Jist a-warming up t' go t' work real good," Eddie called out, rubbing his hand against his overhalls.

Luisa and Cleo's shack looked exactly like the dirt, the clay, the hardpacked sand, the looser dirts, the leaves and stems and blades of grasses about the place. Our side of the wall, the upperhill side, rose up not more than four feet to its eaves, and five and a half feet to the highest part of the single-slope roof. The grayish-yellow tint of the clay rubbed on the wall took on the same glint and color as the dry and greening things growing or dying around it.

Luisa led us around to the side of the house, saying, "Here, boys, here is the wall. My sister has gone to sell some goats, but she will be back this afternoon."

Eddie scrounched his face up like sour juice and asked her, as he walked to look, "Boys? Boys, did you say? I'm a-wund'rin', sister, jest how big does th' menfolks git where you come from?"

"Big as trees," Luisa told all of us. "And this little muddy-walled shack, gentlemen, is where I come from."

"Where'd ya ev'r go off to, ta le'rn how ta spit out sech good English?" I asked her.

"I went all of the way through high school, by working in the Indian Agent's office in Alpine. Yes, this is my adobe wall. My three boy friends got it started for me and built it up this high. You can see."

Eddie took a slow, sober look at the twenty-four sun-dried bricks laying end to end, but seeing that only the one single layer and line had been laid, he jammed both hands down in his pockets, stiffened up his back, and spoke down over the ball of his chin, saying, "Didn't git so very much of a start, did they? How many boy friends was it?"

"Three." Luisa played with her fingers in front of her dress. "They all had to go to work the crop for a few months. I would certainly like to surprise them when they come back and see my adobe room, all four of its walls, up to here, like this. Do you think, maybe it could be?"

"Well, if me'n my helper man was a-goin' to be aroun'

yore strip o' th' timbers a week er two, mebbe, but I don't see much of a chance ta git all four o' them walls up t'day." Eddie took a few steps up the line of bricks, then straddled them, turned around and paced back, and said, "Awful late start we're a-gittin' this mornin', folks, awful late. Where's th' bricks at, that you're usin'?"

"Yeah, where'bouts at?" I looked around.

Rina walked up the hill in the weeds and said, "They are here, piled op to dry, see?"

"You may use that big flat board there to carry the bricks from the stack to the wall," Luisa said.

"Look perty heavy t' me," Ed told them. "Much does one o' them bricks weigh?"

"These are eight by twenty-four; they run a hundred pounds to the brick. Between ninety-eight and a hundred," Luisa said.

"How many of them bricks d'ya s'pose one man can tote?" Ed scratched his head and fingered his ear.

"Two off us for eacha breeck," Rina told him.

"Gonna wear a lotta big blisters on that there board." I looked around the stack of muddy grass bricks. I shook my head and told them, "It shore looks like some kinda trap to me."

"Trappa? Pooff." Rina blew her breath into my left ear. She told me, "Ees notta thesa whole world a beeg trap? And ees everybody not een eet weeth us?"

And Luisa caught her chance to say, "Rio, I believe, would tell us that some kind of a trap comes in around us every day. We have to kick out of our trap, and have to push it down, and crawl on to the next trap, which, we think, is a little nicer than our old traps. I will try to kick my way out of today and its trap to do my work, to lay my wall for tomorrow."

I scraped my shoe soles on the ground, and nodded to tell her, "Smart girl, Luisa. I'm a-kickin' loose frum a blue jillion damn ole tangly traps, myse'f. Rio. Does sound like him talkin', don't it? Ya know Rio very good, Luisa?"

Luisa dropped her eyes down and told me, "He is known by everybody, Woody, up this side of the river and down the other side. You waste your words when you ask me if I know Rio. It is like asking me if I know the weather, the wind, the stars, or the moon."

"It's commencin' ta look thatta way." I knelt down to rub my finger along the muddy, manurey hay and grass dried hard in the adobe bricks. "Luisa, tell me, d'ya reckin ole Rio c'n read an' write? How'n th' name of heck does he cram sa much stuff in his head? Know?"

"No. I don't. Nobody seems to know." Luisa brushed a floating milkweed seed off her breast. She had broken out in a thin oily coat of sweat that shined on her skin. She twisted her jaw and lips a bit out of shape, and told me, "Rio will speak to you, or he will sit and listen to you speak by the hour. And this small bottle of whiskey which you are trying now to hide from my eyes to give to my sister Cleo, well, Old Man Rio could drink down three bottles like it and it would never slow him down."

I looked at the bulge of the bottle in my pocket, and tried to tell Luisa, "Naw, Luisa, I wasn't aimin' to hide it from ya, ner ta give all of it t' yer sister. Here. I'll sot 'er right here up on top o' this brick. I'll be th' bar man. An', well, y' c'n jest name yer drink. Hey, Luisa, wanta ask y' somethin'; dontcha thaink th't Rinny over there's th' pertiest girl—all th' way 'round pertiest girl ya ever seen? Hmm?"

"Very beautiful. Very sweet. Always full of some kind of fire and pep and fun. But no, Riorina is not so pretty as her mother. Here, hand me the bottle, and I will take it on the back porch and cool it in a bucket of water." She opened the screendoor. "This door sure needs an oiling bad. And a real good oiling, at that."

I stood back a ways and watched Luisa tiptoe to the water bench and put the flat bottle in a bucket that I could not see for the lower porch boards. I patted my foot and hummed to myself:

> Good oilin' bad,
> Good oilin' bad,
> Two bucka lube job,
> Good oilin' bad.

> Bad greasin' good,
> Yes, a bad greasin' good,
> Five bucka lube job,
> Bad greasin' good.

> That's what I need,
> Oh ho, yes, what I need,

Ten bucka lube job,
That's what I need.

Luisa walked out the screen door as easy as she could. She heard the last parts of my singing, and smiled, to say, "Oh, that is right, Rina told me last night about how good you could play the violin and sing."

"Gittar. I can't ev'n tune a fiddle up," I said. "And fer's me an' saingin' goes, heck fires, I jest rear my head back an' yell, er squall; 'tain't what ya'd call good, it's jest what ya might call, ah, loud."

"Cleo will play her mandolin for you, after a while. And you can try to play on our old guitar. Somebody left it here several years ago. I am anxious to hear you, after what Rina told me."

I spun around on my toe, snapped my fingers, and asked her, "What? What was it she said? I mean, 'bout me?"

"She told me," Luisa walked in a small circle around me, and brushed her feet with every word along the grass, "they you were just the man."

"Yeahm, jest th' man, man, for what?"

"The man that she has been looking for."

"Geewhizzerkins! Fghughmm! Yeah? Fer which?" My looks and stumbling tongue gave away my nervous feelings. "Lookin' for? Yes."

"Just the proper man to, ah . . ."

"Ye're strainin' my toes an' a-chokin' my naick."

"To build my wall for me."

"Aww."

"Rina likes you a great deal, for mixing mud."

"Fer drivin' me bats. I'd shore love t' mix her mud. I c'd eat her up on a stick. If I could jest only git th' chance. Thaink I might?"

"I would say that there is a good chance; that is, if you do not move too slow today. And if you can think of the right words."

"Womern, ye're lookin' at a man that cain't even thaink. I jest stan' here 'n' boil over lika hot tea kittle."

"Rina, I will say, is as fiery as the sun, there. Pay no attention to the way she changes from good to bad, and from hot to cold, from bitter to sweet. She acts this way even around her own family and around all of her girl friends, and around me. She has been playing with all the boys since her husband went away, but she gets afraid when the time comes. She promises all and she gives nothing. She really needs a boy friend that can break his way inside her little ring. Your music and your playing and your singing make her heart and her feet wish to break free and dance. She talked mainly about your cousin, Eddie, and how Rio spoke to Eddie in his sleep. She asked me if I would help. I told her I would be glad to try. We wanted Eddie to believe that I would like him, well, because he worked so hard in my brickyard. It sounds foolish to me, as it sounds partways senseless to you, and to all of us here. But Rio's mind and his words fly along on such a high mountain that he takes me up along with him. I see that it is helping one of us. I felt so good after. Rina told me the story last night. This is all I am asking—that all of us get to work at carrying these bricks to my wall. I don't care if we lay three or three hundred today, don't you see? I wish only to spend a few hours to get to know Eddie, and what kind of a fellow he is."

"Who was it made wimmen so wise in th' head?" I turned and ran up the hill to the brick pile, and told Eddie and Riorina, "Well, sir, Mister Eddie, I jest now signed th' papers. We're gonna lay these brick here till th' sun goes down fer a buck an' a haff. 'Tain't sa awful long off. An' Luisa is gonna pay us outta th' first gold dollar she finds a-rollin' up this here hill. Okay? Lemme git at them there cussed bricks, Rinnio."

" 'S awright enuff with me, Woody son, but who's gon'ta do what? Which job f'r who?" Eddie opened up his pocket knife to clean the fingernails of his withered hand. "I'm tryin' ta figger. I'm th' dern-gum boss, ain't I? Lemme see, lemme see."

"You go weeth Luisa anda help her to sprad the mud. I halpa Woody to carry down de breecks. Alla right?" Rina shoved Ed a step or two down the hill. "Here, Wood Head, halpa me to leeft thesa breeck down to thesa board. Leefta some onna your side."

"I'm a-liftin' ninety pound over here on my side," I told Rina. "I cain't figger what's a-makin' you groan an' grunt sa loud."

"Oahhhamm! I can gronta alla that I pleasa. Thesa are free mountains around here. Ughh! You sheefted de ninety pounds over here to my side. Keepa walkeeng, stannd op, I joost cannot carry de brreeck and you riding me down."

"I'd shore love ta try."

"Ughmm, ohhhmm. Shut oppa."

"If ya'd gimme a shot at it. Lift!"

"Ughh, ugghhmm. Don'ta maka me laugh. Ughhmm!"

"I got a little seven-inch grapey vine that'll make ya
laugh, an' grunt lots better th'n that."

"Don'ta maka me laugh. I will drop thesa breeck. Anda
than we will roll down thees hill joosta lak de olda deada
beelygoat. Oh, oh, don't! Don't teeckle me, pleasa, pleasa,
Woody; notta now, notta now."

"Rina, you're sech a perty little she-devil, them curls of
yores knocks me down an' stomps me in th' dirt. I'd like
ta bounce yore little fanny aroun' on this grass, Baby, jest
like a big joosie cactus apple a-rollin'. I don't know how
much gringo lingo you c'n unnerstan', Honey, but that's
how they'd tell ye, way back in them Oklahomer hills.
Boys up there'd go plumb hoggy wild if'n they c'd lay an
eye on any secha perty set of hips. I'd ought not ta let my
mouth run sa loose, mebbe. I'm drunk dizzy, Rina, an' I've
not had a drink o' likker this mornin'."

"I coulda not hear a word wheech youu said. My eyess
were on de breecka wall, anda my earrs were over there
inna de Slick Rock Gap."

"I'm a-lookin' fer another slick gap. Slippery Gap. It
ain't no covered waggin I'm a-wantin' ta skid in."

"We moosta notta let our words fly so crazy; eeta ees
not good for de work. Addie ees de new boss here today.
Holda your mouth shoot a leetle beet for Addie's sake. My
promise ees not to youu, but a my worrd ees to Rio. Either
you act decent anda worka your bast and holda backa
yourr tongue, or I run de hilla now anda you see Rina
never morre. Okay? Wheecha?"

"Work."

After a dozen of the bricks were carried and smeared
with wet clay to stick them together, Eddie told us, "We're
a-crackin' an' a-crumblin' too many. Hey, Luisa, have you
got a well rope 'roun' here? I jest now thunk up th' best
dern invenshion on th' Maixican border."

Luisa ran and came back with a rope. "It isn't exactly a
well rope, it is for roping goats and cattle." Then Eddie
sent her back to an old trash pile to look for a pulley. She
carried an old rusty clothesline wheel with a hoop eye on
it, and Eddie strung the lariat through the wheel. He
helped Rina to dig a hole with a tin can, shoulder deep,
and while she dug, with her ear to the ground, Eddie

pulled out a hammer and drove some nails into a long pole, through the eye of the clothesline wheel. Eddie bossed the whole job. He helped us to skid the long pole down into Rina's hole, and we pounded and tromped rocks, dirt, shaley slush, and loose grass all down tight around the pole. And we stood back with our hands above our kidneys to brace ourselves while we looked at one of the latest model lifting cranes in that entire river bed country. Eddie tossed loops of rope around each end of the lifter board, and told Rina and me, "Now, by doggies, you set a coupla bricks on the liftin' board, an' I'll stan' back hyere 'n' keep th' slack tight on th' rope, an' jest see whut happens." He dug the grass up with his shoe heels pulling backwards, and the two bricks lifted from the stack and swung through the air to where Luisa stood by the wall. Ed let the bricks down easy and nice, then he ran with all of us to lift them onto the new mud on the knee-high wall. We hugged one another, patted, kissed, bragged, and got our breath. Eddie yelled out, "Woody Man, me an' you's th' loader man an' puller man; now, which job d'ya want?" I told him I would be Mister Loader Man, since he'd won the green ribbon as our champeen puller man.

"Youu do de pooling, Addie," Rina waved at Eddie in the sun of the midafternoon.

"And Rina and myself will unload and smear mud." Luisa wore a smile as proud as the afternoon sun. She looked as dirty as the mud, and as happy, in a way, as the wind. "You have to be sure to line them up real good with our string here along the wall, Riorina; that is all of the trick."

At their lifting and smearing, the girls wanted to make Ed feel good, so they sung a little nonsense song they made up as they looked at each other and at Eddie and me:

> Eddie he fly high,
> Eddie he fly low,
> Eddie beedie pah de pooh pah,
> Hey, hi de ho.

Rina wiggled her hair in the mud on her bricks and sang one verse by herself:

> Kiss my Addie high,
> Kiss my Addie low,

> Itty bitty pah de poohpaww,
> Now thees wall will grrow.

Together again, they teased, flirted, and acted cute, to make Eddie feel like he owned the whole Rio Grande:

> Eddie he fly high,
> Eddie he fly low,
> Eddie beedie pah de pooh pah,
> Hey, hi de ho.

Luisa sang softer than Rina, but her words carried as far in either direction:

> I like Eddie low,
> I like Eddie high,
> Ootee booty pahm de poompaw,
> Build it to the sky.

Ed held up his hand to let us know that he was thinking of a verse, and to stop still and listen:

> Eddie like the bull,
> Eddie like the horse,
> Poom poom pooh de poohm boom,
> Eddie he the boss.

I knew I had to toss my verse on, or else to duck my head and go for home, so I thought, and sung out:

> Eddie smart like fox,
> Ed's smart like the flea,
> Jingle jangle dingaling ling,
> Ed is smart like me!

CHAPTER 15

FOOLISH GOLD

Our mud-brick wall was waist high on its lower end and neck high on its high end by an hour before sundown. The girls felt so good they giggled and chased each other around and around the wall while I kept my eye on the girls, the rising wall, and the weather. Ed said, "Looks mighty like somethin's gon'ta blow in on us," which is exactly what happened. A cold river of the upper airs tore off across the rock rims of the mountains to help us celebrate our adobe wall, and when this river of cold upper air spilt down along the river's bottom where our little hill and house stood, a scratchy fight started between the upper cold and the lower heats. The sun tried to be the referee, but the rocks didn't agree with the decisions the sun made, so the rocks chased the sun on out towards his new home. The breeze won a few dollars on the fight, got drunk on a vacant lot, and got to dreaming that he was a big stiff wind, and chased about the hills and canyons puffing under girls' dresses. All of the mamas and papas cried to see the wind out making their girls afraid, and the wind tried to cover up their crying and weepings. He tossed their teardrops up in the air and they turned into fancy glass beadworks which set up a great noise when a glass drop hit a rattly dry cactus thorn. The dagger weed broke the glassy drop into ten squillion pieces that melted in the last few tracks of the sun. Rocks dashed hailstones to bits; the bushy brush knocked others to splintereens, and others melted on the ground amongst the tracks of the rabbit, squirrel, quail, pheasant, turtle, lizard, snake, scorpion, and big tarantula spider.

The hailstorm blew on over in fifteen or twenty minutes, I judged, because it was fighting a losing fight around our hotrock volcanic valley here. If I was a hailstorm trying to get my first start, I would blow up somewhere in the skies and I'd roll myself and twist and wiggle, and ride the rods and the blinds, I'd hitch with my sore thumb in the air, I'd walk, I'd crawl on my achy knees, till I got to some place a few hundred miles up to the north. There you can catch the sun about half asleep in a cloud stack and rattle down on a lot more windmills, barns, tin-roof stores, buildings, houses, and water tanks, and with the same amount of hailstones you can thrash the daylights out of a whole herd of cattle out on the open pasture; you can whip the tails of a thousand wild, runny, broomtail ponies; you can make the studs snort and the mares nicker at the little colts crying in the hail. You can knock the tar out of farmers on their wagons, plows, tractor seats; you can whim-wham the devil out of their old straw hats and sweat-soaked Stetsons. You can raise a bunch of Cain on a car top, and throw hail big enough to knock deep dents in the shiniest car on that road; and as for the old rattlers, boy howdy, you can whop a hole in their old, raggy-taggy tops that will keep the owner and his wife and kids sewing and gluing and patching for the next six weeks. But, heck's pup, down here off along this old melted-up, runny-rock, lava-steaming Rio Grandio, about the best thing you can do, if you happens to be a hailer storm, is to catch a little handful of folks working to build a mud wall, and you can't sting much fear into them—but you can, like I'm telling you, if they're tired and dirty, and if the sun is nearly over the dog's hump, anyhow, you can cause them to look at one another and to call it quits for this day.

Trailing these two girls from the mud wall into their house, you, Hailstorm, might cause a guy like Eddie—an old veteran of many soakings, lightnings, and thunderings, and of those hailstorms that beat the high parts of Oklahoma and Texas down as flat as you see them there—you might cause a man like Eddie to say, "Is this th' best hailstorm you gals c'n drag out?"

Rina let Eddie walk in at Luisa's heels, and I was the last in line, but heard her tell us, "Eet hails here atta Study Butte only one time everry weenter. The verry day thata we peek out to try builda our 'dobe wall!"

We stepped inside. I saw the floor boards were laid and nailed no more than four inches off the ground. The side of the hill had been dug down and the dirt piled to make a level spot for the floor. Old blue wallpaper tacked onto the walls looked faded to the washed-out color of a pan of soapy, greasy dishwater. Under the wallpaper in some spots I saw a thickness of packing-box cardboard; in other places the wallpaper was tacked onto the naked wood, each tack nailed through a big tin washer the size of a quarter. A crooked door led into a second, darker room that looked like a sleeping room. The screen porch ran only half the length of the house, to stop halfway between its two southerly windows. There was a wide-open, free feeling about the whole house, like nobody tried very hard to keep out the weather, sun, wind, rain, mud, sleet, nor hailstorms. The house would certainly not keep out any human being that had the desire to get into it. I saw no locks, bolts, nor padlocks of any sort or size.

The things in the room could not have cost, all added up, any more than twenty dollars. There was a knee-high, flattop monkey-heater cookstove with a flat rock under each leg and an apple crate full of ashes beside the stove. I saw four flat pancakes on the stove, a granite pan of hot-stuff sauce, a lid lifter hung on a wire close to where the stovepipe ran up through the roof. There was no ceiling, no attic of any kind, just the weather, and you, and some old wiggly shingles. The shingles curled from the heat of the monkey stove on their bottoms, as much as from the heat of the sun and wind on the topsides. If there had been any kind of an attic or ceiling boards, nobody could have stood up in the room.

A woman's voice—a voice that rung deep and low—sounded from the direction of the porch, and I heard the screendoor open and close. A short lady with a mop of the bushiest, reddest hair I had so far seen, and wearing an old, white, lacy shawl, strolled in.

"Sister Cleo"—Luisa made the introductions—"these two men are friends of Rina's, and they came to work on our cellar and adobe wall. They have done a fine job. Woody, Eddie, this is my sister, Cleo."

"Glad t'meetcha."

I joshed at her, wondering how much of my English she could understand: "Lookin' aroun' here at all of uss muddy ducks, Cleo, I'm a-sayin' that you're th' best dressed one at the ball."

Cleo told me some words I couldn't make out.

"Cleo wishes to thank you," Luisa told us, "not only for building her such a fine adobe wall, but for telling her how pretty she looks. She insists that both you contractors remain here for your evening's meal and drink."

"Drink. Tell her I said yes," I said. "My belly's lined with solid cast iron, an' I'm a-gonna eat ya right out of a house an' home."

And Eddie told them, "Me fer th' guzzlin'. I c'd eat a dern volcano lizard if he don't eat me first. My belly thanks my mouth went outta business. Here's a little soparise fer ye, Cleo. Panhannle's best rotgut poison." Ed set his bottle on a nail keg in the floor. "This is fer ever'boddy. Cleo, you're ta be first. Shoot."

"Out on the porch it goes." Luisa walked past Eddie to lift his bottle up under his nose, then to swing on out past him with a prissy twist of her hips. She came back with my bottle, dripping from the water bucket.

"Woody's bottle ain't as good as mine," Eddie told her. "His is squizzed outta th' heads an' tails of a barrel o' snattlerakes."

Luisa touched the bottle to Ed's cheek, and asked him, "Now tell me, how does that feel to your hot skin?"

"Well, doggone my skats! Cool. Plumb cool. Wall, shucks afire, Cleo, this'll go down yore gizzer so slick an' so smooth that it's a gon'ta taste jest like ice cream combs. Okay. I guess th't you gals is got a brain er two workin' somewheres in yer head, at that. Roll me a cigarette, Woody, you 'n' Rinnie, here."

Rina licked the cigarette to hold out for Eddie while Luisa got a granite dipper of water from the bench on the porch. Cleo took the bottle and drank. She sipped at the water dipper and handed the bottle to Eddie. Eddie wiped his lips with the back of his hand, passing it over to Rina. Rina stood on the tips of her toes, shook her curls, and took a somewhat smaller gulp than Cleo or Eddie had. Luisa drank more than Rina, but no more than half the amount that caused Cleo to smile so proud over towards Eddie. Eddie teased at the girls as they went out to wash up at the wash bench, and told us. "Lookit them little ole bitty gals, now, jest look at 'em, wouldn't ye? Snortin' like they've done somethin' in their pants. Mighty awful proud. Hmmm. I took a lots bigger swaller th'n both of them did, heck, 'fore I's weaned offa my mammy's titty milk." He elbowed Cleo and told her, "Takes a long ole time, lotsa years of practicin', Cleo, y' know it, ta git to be very much of a expert likker-downer."

"Takes a big long time ta ev'n git you ta pass me that there jug an' water dipper," I said. "You'n Cleo does okay fer a coupla green hands, but quick's you'll toss me er han' me that there bottle, Eddie Rooster, I'll show ya a few of th' high, fine parts of this here manly art. I'm a-drinkin' this purely an' strickly 'cause th' doctor, he sez it's th' besst thing in th' world fer my wife's kidneys."

Eddie asked Cleo, "Say, which kind o' coal are y' burnin' here'n yer monkey stove? Antrycite er byetoomalous? Hard er, dang it, soft?"

Cleo made no answer, but Luisa talked into a handful of water in her washpan from the porch, "Roots. *Blurrble.* Very hard. Mesquite roots."

" 'Skeet? Hmmm. Shore does lay back up in there nice an' throws a right smart of heat off," Eddie said.

Cleo smiled bigger when Rina told Eddie through a mouthful of soapy bubbles, "Hard roots are allaways hotta, Addie."

I swugged in another mouthful of water and said, "I gotta hard root that throws off all kindsa heat."

"Yah," Rina laughed in a wash-rag, "wherre you keepa heem? Backa de truck? *Sí, sí, sí,* I have de leetle monkey stove, also, backa home, wheech ees verra hot sometams— sometams. Ha ha."

"Mebbe you 'n' me c'n do some work tageth'r, hmm?" I set the bottle and dipper down on the same nail keg Eddie had put it on before. " 'Hut d'ya say?"

"Plooh on you," Rina kidded at me. She sounded tough like a chunk of spring steel. "Blabbh on you."

"Burp on you," I told her. I wanted to show Cleo that Rina and myself had met long enough ago to be cussing one another in fun. "I'm a-wantin' ta warsh m'seff."

Luisa walked in rubbing her face in the towel. "If you want to wash before your supper, you will have to carry a couple of buckets from the water barrel, just around the corner of the house, here."

Eddie and I walked out onto the porch and picked up the two water buckets. As we walked towards the corner sniffling at the early night air, I asked: "Thaink that ya'll give that there Luisa gal a little bit of a try tonight, Ed-derookus?"

"I dunno. Been a sorta doin' some smellin' off up in that d'recshun. I guess this here's th' waterin' barrel. Y' know, Woody, if'n I had enough money t' jest buy you a big limozeen an' all, I'd jist hire you ta, ta stan' aroun' an' roll cigarootes up fer me. Dang'd if this'n didn't taste better'n snoose er chewin' eith'r one. Ya didn't see me chew ner dip ner spit all day long while I'sa layin' up them there 'dobe brick, didja, huh?"

"Nope. You done fine. But I'm sa shakey an' nervous, Ed, I couldn't hold my han' still enough right now ta twist up anuther cigarette, ner t' strike a match an' light th' damn thaing. My ole sinful blood's a-cookin' pure dynamite on an open fire. Cain't hardly git my wind. I'm a-thainkin' about layin' somethin' a whole lots warmer an' pertier th'n a dag-rattened old muddy brick. I gotta hold onta this here rim o' this waterin' barrel, 'y doggies, Ed, t' hol' myseff up from a-fallin' down yonder in that river sand. That little Rina has got th' two pertiesst—well, two per-tiesst of ever'thaing! I'm a-gonna try 'er one time, Ed, an' ya've gotta help me out with 'er. Gotta help me ta git 'er off ta m'self somewheres."

Eddie dipped his bucket down in the barrel and told me, "I reckon I could try to take that Luisa out fer a breath o' frash air an' a little stroll off down towards th' river. If it'd be of any real help t' yeh. I dunno, I jest took a perty big hankerin' today ta th' way that there Luisa does thaings. I could set down on some good grass an' jest set there 'n' cock my ears back, an' listen to that little Luisa woomern talk, talk, talk, an' talk 'erseff ta a frizzle. Good ta look at, ta my jedgment, in 'er own ways, ez yore little Reenio is."

I dipped my bucket and said, "Ya made us a perty good boss t'day on our little bricklayin' job. I reckon ya're still th' boss tonight about these gals; I mean, I'm a-throwin' th' whole thaing in yore hands. We'll not go back at th' truck till you say th' word. That ole whiskey of Jeffrey's is a-boilin' me aroun' sa hot, Ed, that I jest got ta grab a

gal onta me an' she's got ta run by th' loose name of
Reenio. Savvyo? Eddio?"

Ed set his bucket down on the ground to wait for me.
He said, "Well, I'll do all that a pore feller can. Here.
Light up my smoke fer me, th' dern thing's went out. I
don't feel like these folks is a-pullin' us aroun' ta git us
into no kinda trouble."

"Naw," I told Ed. "I feel like these people is on th' level.
Straight as an arrow. Couldn't make me feel no better a-
bein' as friendly as they are. They're not a-puttin' on ta
git our money, ner wigglin' fer us ta git our gold mine. If'n
I had 'leventeen big deep silver mines, an' forty-'leven a-
runnin' th' pure quicksilver, Rinnie could havvit, jest by
stickin' out 'er hand. That little sassy smile. Big thick head
of bobberin' curls. Heck fires, Eddie, if you 'n' me was ta
dig out a dozen mines, an' run up a big, thick bankbook,
and ease off down in here in a big, red, shiny sport job,
we'd be sa dam-blame afraid of ever'body that we'd pack
a pistoliver on our ass ever' steppa th' way, an' never git
ta knowin' how these folks c'n be sa dang-gone friendly.
Y'know?" I struck a long wooden match up to Eddie's
mouth and watched him suck on the slick end of his
cigarette. "Ain't that about right?"

"Righter'n a fox. Might be a dern good streak of luck
that we did roll down in here in our ole muddy common
labor clothes. These gals could be a trap of th' deadliest
kind. Ta git me an' you ta git all mixed up with 'em, see,
then throw th' hogs, an' dogs, an' brothers, an' menfolks,
an' lawbooks at us to git us loose from evert'thaing we've
got, er ever hope ta have. See that?"

"I see that." I blew a drop of spit off my lip. "I see that
an' plenty more. Rina an' Luisa, both of 'em, could bait
you an' me off out here in these dry weeds, an' just let out
one little squeal, an' we'd git a big long blade in both of
our backs."

"Worms wouldn't even come a-lookin' f'r us. Jinnies w'd
bray a time er two when they smelt of our ole bones. Me
'n' you's got too much ta lose, Wood Eye, to let a coupla
perty titties throw us over onta th' boney pile jest now.
Mebbe we'd oughta take off right this minute an' shake a
laig back over to Jeffrey and Charlie an' th' truck. But, I
jest don' know, Wooderow, I jest gotta different feelin',
somehow, about Rinny an' Luisa, an' Cleo, an' seems like,
well, I can jest pert' near hear that ole Rio feller noddin'

his head up an' down, an' up an' down, an' a-tellin' me an'
you th't they's nothin' th' matter with these folks here in
this little ole muddy matchbox of a house. Kinda funny,
I reckon 'tis." Ed spoke so slow and so quiet that every
word made my eyes open up to see a thousand other words
just like it. He seemed to be thinking of every step he had
ever taken in his life, to add up his whole life with every
new word. "I s'pose th't th' buzzards w'd be th' onliest
fellers ta really say how many knives has been found down
in und'r a little ole twig of cactus with a few rib bones
an' ankle bones layin' here 'n' yander."

"I'm a-bettin', bettin' ya a dollar to nothin'," I said,
"that th' folks aroun' Study Butte that don't speshially want
us ta ever find Paw Jerry's mine would make a line from
this mud shack back ta th' Panhandle oil boom."

"Mebbe a heap longer'n that. Rinnie an' Rio, an' this
here Luisa girl, are th' best friends we've made down in
here, an' neither one o' them'd squeak a peep ta put us
onta th' trail of that mine. Oh, they'd not run any knife in
our belly ta keep us from a-findin' th' dern mine, 'n they'll
help us ta git over onta th' Sammy Nail Ranch, but they'll
never lift a little fainger ta show us wherebouts ta go dig.
Papa Charlie an' yer Uncle Jeff is both back yund'r on our
ole truckbed ta study Claude's ole pencil maps. I jest want
you ta know that I know that we're both a-riskin' our
skins an' hides out here a-dickerin' aroun' with two sech
dang-burn perty gals. Me, f'r my own self, I'd say, 'Woody
boy, le's jump up an' scoot our fannies outta here, an' not
ev'n stay fer supper, n'r drinking likker, ner a-singin', ner
walkin' off down yond'r along that little ole river.' I'd tell
ya that, them very words, Woody. But it's like I told ya
'bout how much I'm a-trustin' th' words of that there ole
loud-foot talker, Ole Man Ryoe."

"I guess I risk my naick one way er th' tother'n ten
times a day," I told Ed, "fer some crazy thaing that's not
half as perty ta be with as that little Riorina gal. Th' way
she's put tagether an' stacks up jest knocks my eyes both
blind, Ed. I cain't see what I'm a-doin'; I don't give a hoot.
An' heck amighty, Lord knows, 'at's all I c'n do with a
gold mine when I git th' thaing all dug up, jist turn right
aroun' an' give it ta someone. It's a woomern back somewheres that makes ever' dern man run out here 'n' bust
his head wide open a-tryin' ta dig er scratch er claw some
dern fool kind of a rock outta these big ole mountains. If

'twuzn't Hell Catten it'd be Rina, an' if 'twasn't Rina, it'd
be Zinnia, er Bina, er Chorine Chorina—some blamed
female with a dern dress on. That was why Paw Jerry had
th' guts it takes ta roll down here through that ol' Slick
Rock Wagon Gap, jest fer 'is womern, jest ta dig down in
under alla these rocks around here fer a coupla years, an'
by doggies, turn right smack dab aroun' an' give th' whole
kaboodle ta nobody but his kids."

"An' them kids of his'n," Ed said, "whatta they know
about a dern rock? Paw Jerry c'd wiggle his ears an' smell
a chunk o' gold in seven miles of solid granite. Hell, I
couldn't feel a chunk of silver if I was suckin' it on th'
enda my tongue. It's sort of a stand-off here tonight, fer's
I can see—nothin' ta lose an' nothin' ta gain. These rocks
belong ta Rio's people, an' they keep a closer watch on us
than th' hawks does on th' chickens. That little Luisa
womern in there, if'n she took a good noshun, she c'd keep
me a-hangin' out aroun' these cactus daggers fer th' nach-
eral days of my life. I'm jist a-standin' here and a-tryin' ta
guess if she's gon'ta tell me ta go ahead on an' try ta find
Paw Jerry's mine, er give up th' hunt."

We carried our buckets to the wash bench and washed
our hands and faces, and threw our pans of washywater
out the screendoor. Eddie stepped back into the front room
and sat down on the floor with the others around a gray
wool saddle blanket. A stack of flapjack tortillas was on a
tin pie plate; Cleo's granite pan of hot stuff stood by the
side of the tortilla plate; a pot of coffee sat there with five
cups; and a tall waterglass held all of the tin knives, forks,
and spoons. A tin plate for each person, a salt and pepper
shaker, a long-neck bottle of hot, vinegar-soaked red peppers. One other pepper jar with a wider mouth held some
small green peppers not much bigger around than a broke-
off matchstick. The scent that came to my nose from the
steams of the pan of hot stuff, mixed in with the powdery
dry smells of the dust and dirt the house was made of,
caused me to break out with hot onion tears before I could
get to the table. I took this chance to get myself one good
fast look around this room. I guess the light from the lantern made things look a few shades dirtier and darker than
they were by day, but the lantern caused everything to
throw a wiggly shadow acrost its humps in the wall paper-
ing, and caused the Cross of Jesus to do a little shadow
dance with several white plastery Kewpie dolls; a few

flintrock arrowheads hung around by strings on nails, tin
cans sat around on little narrow shelves filled with rocks,
shells, jewelry, keepsakes, trinkets, and talcum powders.
Religious picture cards with some gold words I couldn't
make out, religious picture calendars with a new picture
that turned up every month, a few small prayerbooks and
Bibles. A few apple crates, lined with crinkly newspapers,
held all of the kitchen articles; three bead-top hatpins held
several curls of hair against the sky-blue paper. Some odd
pieces of harness, saddle thongs, buckskin strings, and a
pair or so of spurs were on nails up in the higher boards.
Another cutaway half-size grape crate was tossed half full
of shoes and fancy-work sandals. Three small-size handmade Indian skin drums, painted by hand, hung up along
a north wall two by four, and gave the only bright colors
the lantern's lights could find in this room. A large tam-
bourine with jinglers hung by the drums.

Luisa smiled and pointed out my spot on the floor across
the mat from Rina; and because of the oblong shape of the
blanket we sat two on each long side. Cleo sat down at
the end after I had got my legs crossed the right and
proper way. Rina and Luisa faced Eddie and myself, and
the pot of hot stuff seemed to be facing all of us at the
same time. Cleo gave a nod over to Luisa, and we all
bowed our heads down over the firebowl and blinked till
we cried as we listened to Luisa.

She gave thanks: "Our Father who gave us our mothers
and fathers, who gave us the beautiful sky and its rains to
make fruitful and to multiply our labors in our fields, we
bow our head to thank Thee now in this moment when we
take Thy food and Thy drink to our souls and bodies; show
us, Lord, with every bite and with every swallow, how to
rise up renewed in our works to help those who love us,
but more, how to help those that hate and fear us. Help
me to help the aged, Father in Heaven, and help me to
lift and give my aid to the crippled, my healing hand and
my word of God's love out freely to the sick, and a kiss of
relief to the fever of the dying. Make me with each sip and
bite wise in Thy secret and hidden ways; guide my foot-
steps to walk in the glory of Thy highest pathways; and
make us fruitful, O God, patient in our hardships and
struggles; and, Lord of All Saints, pardon and forgive the
sins of my loved ones and pass them quickly out from

Purgatory. May Thy Name forever rule my heart, my mind, my body, and my soul unto Eternity. Amen."

Ed picked up his fork and said, "Luisa, that's just about th' pertiest prayer th't I ev'r heard. Never was too much of a hand at speakin' no pray'rs, m'seff, but I shore wisht ya'd take me out here an' teach that'n ta me. I heard lots of pray'rs in m' day an' time, but that'n is th' best 'un my ears ev'r soaked in."

"I never getta tired of those words." Rina held out her tin plate for Cleo to fork a tortilla on it. "Didda you t'inka they was-a prettee, hoh, Meestaire Mud Chuck? Say?"

"Almost perty ez them curls of yoren," I told her. I looked down to see Cleo flip a tortilla onto my plate. I asked Rina, "Say, what kinda pancakes is these, anyhow?"

While everybody laughed as quiet as they could, Rina told me on the side, "Notta panacakes. Tortillas. Tor-tee-yahs."

"Torpedoes." Eddie tried. "I heard about them when I rode that troopship ov'r ta France. Tarpeeters."

"No, don'ta eata it yet," Luisa said. "Wait for Cleo to put some of her ice cream sauce on top."

"I use to work in a likker drug store fer three years," I told her, "an' I nev'r scooped up no icey cream that makes yer eyes run an' yer nose dripple a mile away, like this here brandin'-iron stew does."

I watched Cleo kneel over my way to spade a big pile of her bloody red chili con carne concoction over my tortilla. I saw out of my other eye that Eddie had lifted the dipper of water and the cool bottle of whiskey down onto the blanket. We all drank, but the two younger girls took no more than a small sip. I noticed Luisa eating, so I followed the rest.

Cleo shook the salt, black pepper, and the red-hot vinegar, and picked five or six of the little green matchstick peppers out onto the edge of her plate. She handed each bottle on to Luisa, Luisa to Rina, Rina to me, and I passed it to Eddie. Cleo chewed up one or two of her little green peppers and swallowed them by the time the jar got around to me. Luisa took three, Rina three, Eddie one, and, to show how hard my muscles were, how tough my tongue and my stomach was, I forked in and flipped out four. I tossed two of them back into my mouth and brought my grinder teeth down a few times with my mind on the nice, soft, tender, pretty colorings on Rina's skin. My mind left Rina's

skin pretty fast. It had to come back to the back end of
my tongue to see about a fire breaking out. I felt like my
ears and eyes, my nose holes, skin pores, air vents, portholes, and openings were all spewing and spouting with
blazes of acid and flames of blistery fire. My eyes ran
down enough water to float a holler log full of river rats,
but the tears didn't squirt in the right direction to kill out
what was burning in me. My tears fell down and down,
while my blisters and ashes and the fires of those two little
greeny peppers went up and up me. I couldn't see a face
around that blanket. Nobody I know. My home's not here.
Hey, see that head of hair down there burning up with a
peppery smoke? Well, I'm th' guy that owns that head of
hair. Hurry right on over with your bucket. I ain't got no
place to go, I'll wait. Two little old bitty peppers no bigger
than a January promise. I cain't spit 'em out, 'cause I done
went an' swiggled 'em down in my gut. Streak of fire from
my head on down. Huhhm? Whatzatchasay? Do which?
Huhh? Drink? Ya mean, me, drink what? Wheeeww.
Thanks. Yeahh. Muchablige fer th' dipp'r of waters, but
them waters just didn't cut out one little ounce of my
burnings. Scattered 'em. Made 'em hotter, an' a burnin'
me worser. Cain't jump up an' tear this house apart; that'd
spoil the whole evening. I cain't break my fist ov'r nobody's
head, that'd spoil the evening, too. I'll just stand up here
right real good and easy and walk off out here on the
screen porch, where I can take my hands and fan a few
little puffs of good fresh airs back inside my teeth an' jaw-
bones. Whooooeee. Wheewww. Ohhh. I cain't stand out
here all night an' fan myself.

Poets have sung and the sages have said that there is a
great, deep, broad streaks of sweet and tender sympathies
in the bloods of all our colors that draws us all together
here and melts us so close into one another that we find
an equal share of pleasure, pain, joy, and aching, all of
which makes me wish that they were only here to take
their fair share of this hell-fired burning out from around
my teeth, tongue, neck, Adam's apple, throat, eyes, ears,
belly, guts, my career, my standing, my background, and
my high reputation. But nobody but me is here to stand
up under all of these hot burny peppers. Well, hell, I just
can't stand here and let little Riorina think those two little
bitty greenish peppers are keeping me from the supper
blanket. How could I ever find old Paw Jerry's gold and

silver mine standing out here on this back porch like a snotty-nose sissy, missing out on my supper?

Back I go to the blanket row. I go back where the peppers grow, see the hot-pods on the blow, stumble around some peppery ground, and talk with the crowd at the pepper show. Maybe I can ask which way to go to find my trail where the gold mines grow. I've got to get back where the pretty hair wiggles. Oh, Rina, don't you know, don't you know, Riorina, don't you know?

Everybody laughed around the eating blanket so much they could not eat a bite. They had to hold their hands over their mouths, hold back their breathing, and shake their heads to keep from waking the baby up.

"Where'bouts ye been off to?" Eddie joked at me.

"How are things down south?" Luisa asked me.

Cleo's face was prouder than anybody else's in the room. She spoke a few low-set words, none of which I could understand. She went ahead to eat her supper before it got cold.

Rina ate, giggled, and snickered, "That ees thee best laugh I have laughed inna my life, frands; itta willa maka me livva ten years longer. I t'inka I can call you my Red Hotta Poppa. Ho ho. Ha ha."

"How's them torteeyers?" I asked Eddie.

"They're jest a little bit hotter th'n them there little greeny peppers," Eddie joked.

"Not so very much hotter," Luisa put in.

Cleo held the back of her hand over her mouth to hold back a loud laugh. She finished the hot-stuff on her plate and poured herself a cup of black coffee. She watched me dig into my tortilla, and told me something in her Indian dialect.

Luisa said, "Cleo says that the green pepper will get you ready for the chili sauce."

"Ready fer th' unnertaker," I told them.

"My people tella me"—Rina finished the last bite on her plate—"thatta ass long assa you keepa de leetle green pepper inna your moutha to suck, itta keeps your blood so hotta thatta you neverr can die. *Sí?*"

"It keeps your skin warm like a baby's." Luisa poured an old chippy blue-white enamel cup full to its rim, and went on, "And it washes your eyes out clean with your tears, and burns you so you dance like a four-year-old child, and helps your hand to feel its way to the treasure

in the lost rock. The pepper burns your eyes so clean that
you can see who is trying to help you, and who is trying
to hurt you."

"Here. Here. Gimme some more of them peppers."
Eddie took his third pepper and tossed it down his throat.
"More of 'em. More of 'em. I wanta clear my ole eyes up
ta where I c'n see if my ole pardn'r, here, Mud Dabber
Woods, is fer me er aginst me. Hey, Luisa, tell me one
thaing: how long d'I hafta feel around amongst them
sharp rocks 'fore I tetch my fainger onta my trasures?"

I poured my big double-size rusty tin cup full of Cleo's
black coffee, and used it to wash down my last two mouthfuls of hot sauce and flat cake. I drained the flat bottle
of its last drink, listening to see what Luisa would say to
Ed.

"That all depends." She brushed a lantern flier off the
breastline of her dress.

"Yeah? 'Pends on what?" Eddie rubbed his crippled
hand against the wool of the supper blanket to try to feel
the fuzz and the heat. "Y've got me guessin'."

"It depends on the people that you will find living
among the rocks. If you make them like you, all of them
will help you to find your spot."

"Which spot?" I asked Luisa.

"Thee spotta you are try for to find, silly," Rina told
me across the mat. "The spotta where your treasure ees
now hiding. Waiting, mabee. No?"

I looked as far back into the shines of her eyes as any
man would dare to travel on foot. It was, I guess, for a
longer time than I could notice. I had been trying all day
long to get a good straight look into her eyes, but she had
always shifted around, or turned them some other way.
Her face took on a look that told me, "Take a good long
look, man, go ahead and look; you worked hard today
on the brick job. You're a pretty nice *hombre,* yourself.
Take my eyes and look at them for as long as you desire.
It makes me feel glad and good to feel your eyes up and
down my body. I see some kind of an honest look, a
funny look and a crazy look, but, as I said, I see in you
an honest look. I don't think you are pretending or acting
for me, you wouldn't know how. You earned today seventy-
five cents from Cleo and Luisa; and from me, Rina, I guess
this good long look."

I felt so weak around my wrists that I had to use both hands to swallow my next mouthful of coffee.

Eddie scratched his wilted fingers with his good hand, and said, "I'm a-guessin' that if I keep on an' build enough mud walls, I might be able to make friends, huh?"

"A very good way," Luisa told him.

"Eddie's really a woodwork man back home," I told them. "He built up th' finest carpenter shop in his whole town, an' he jest used one hand ta do it. Little one-cylinder kerosene engine runs th' whole place. Jigsaw, copin' saw, bandsaw, sander, turnin' lathe, an' all."

"Whole works." Ed shook his head and filled his second cup of Cleo's coffee.

"A woodworker man? Really?" Luisa asked him. "Then, here, somewhere in behind this curtain . . . Cleo, where is it? Oh. Here it is. Maybe you can fix up Cleo's old guitar. Look. See, see how it's cracked here across the back end? The crack gets wider if you try to turn the pegs and tune the strings. See?"

Ed held the guitar on his lap and tilted it over towards the light of the lantern. "Hmmm. Yeahp-sir. Right in acrost here. Feel th' gap with my finger. Y'd hafta git a brace post, see, an' stob it aginst that there crack'd wall from th' inside. Spread th' gap good 'n' full of irony glue. Books 'er sumthin' ta weight it down, right lakky thatty. See?"

"It sounds all right." Luisa held her hands on her knees to stand and look down over Eddie's shoulder. "But there hasn't been a bottle of glue or paste in this house since I was born here twenty-four years ago."

"Ya don't have ta have iron glue, Ed," I told him. "Melt up that strip of inner-tube rubb'r, there, th't ye're usin' ta hold up yer shirt sleeves. Git it real good 'n' hot, an' then, swabble it on fr'm th' inner side an' sock y'r patch brace on like ya say. Twist up a shoestring clamp over th' back hind end, an' Cleo c'n tune 'er up 'n' saing us a few good songs th's she's got in 'er head."

Luisa found a tin can for Eddie and they stood over the monkey stove to watch and to smell, not just the one, but both of Ed's rubber armbands melt away to a hot black sticky stuff.

I walked out the screen door to look around for two thin, flat sticks of wood. Rina sneaked out at the east bedroom door and jumped out from behind the water barrel to scare me in the dark.

"Boohh. I am-a the davvil! I come-a for to taka you de home onna my knee. Hahh."

"Don't scare me sa bad," I told her. "I cain't hardly stan' up as it is. Hey, say, Mr. Devil, mebbe it's you that's makin' me wanta bite that there little Riorinnie gal on 'er left hind ear. Huh?"

"Mabby so. Mabby sooe! I trry maka de boys de girrlsa bite each other lots of times. But, I de Saytann, and I say you moosta show me how that you willa go anda bite Riorina, eef I feex itta for you."

I humped around in the light of the moon and picked up a flat board, which I cracked in two over my knee. I threw the boards up close to the back screen doorstep, and told her, "Well, Old Missy Devil, ya've beena chasin' aft'r me f'r a big long time. But I'll swear ta come in an' give myseff up if ya'll jest show me how ta bite that pretty little naick of that Rinny gal. It's a good thaing, Mr. Devil, th't you rubbed 'dobee mud all over yer dress, 'cause overalls like mine has got that same kinda mud all ov'r 'em."

"Mabby after a leetle while both of us davils can-a wash out our t'ings. Joosta where do you t'ink you willa bite thesa girrl, anda how hard?" She walked past me away from the watering barrel and looked off down the hill into the moon upside down in the Rio Grande. She took a seat on the grass. I heard her say, "We moosta make good use off our time while we leave Addie to veesit with Luisa for a while."

By the time that I walked up and sat down, Rina was humming a little song, half humming, half singing:

> Yip yip yip, anda toot toot toot,
> So, youu come-a down to the Study Butte,
> Lots off boys are gone galoots
> Because off thee girls at the Study Butte.
>
> Because off us girrls at thee Study Butte
> Lots off boys are gone galoots.
> Gone galoots, yes, gone galoots,
> Because off the girrls at the Study Butte.

"What was it y' said about us devils a-warshin' our duds out?" I tapped my knee and asked her. "Oh, I ain't a-gonna bite hard enough ta bruise 'er. I don't like that there song. Hushit. I'm not afraid of bein' no goner aloot. I'm a-kneelin' down right here."

Rina wiggled her curls on the grass and shook her face at the moon. She pinched her toes in the grass, and sung some more of her teasy words:

> The boys come brave anda they come cute
> For the foolish gold of the Study Butte.

I grabbed her by the arm and ducked her head down against the grass, joking, wrestling, and telling her, "Grrr, stoppit; I said stoppit, an' mean stoppit. Grrrff. Grrf."

> For the foolish gold off the Study Butte,
> Many boys arre gone . . .

"So, ya try ta tell me th't you're th' ole devil, huhh?"

> Gonne gallooff . . .

"I'll give them spidery curls th' best knuckle rubbin' they ev'r did feel. There, now, how's that? Ya satisfied? Satisfied? Hoosh 'er up."

> The foolish gold off the . . .

"This is fer goin' aroun' a-tellin' folks you're th' ole devul, tryin' ta rub y'r dress fulla 'dobe mud to look like th' devul, hoh? This'll teach ya. This'll make ya perty. This'll make ya wise. This'll make yer hairs curl; this'll make ya wise an' curl yer eyes. Y'r a-gonna lay right here till I hear y'r own mouth, 'y doggies, tell me th't I'm th' devul his own horny self. Talk it. Say it. Tell me, 'Howdy, Mister Devul.' Go ahead 'n' crow it. Stop yer laffin', an' tell me plain. Hello, Mister . . ."

"Hello, Meestaire Davill." She rolled her shoulders on the grass laughing at me. "I amma notta thee devill."

"You're Missis Devull."

"You are meesis davill."

"No, not me, you, you. Hah hah ha ha."

"Notta me. You. You de Meesyy Davill. Ho ho."

"I'm not th' Missis, Crazy Head, I'm th' Ole Man, Ole Daddy, Ole Stud, Ole Shaggy, Ole Man Rio Devul."

"I de Ole Stud-a Jackassa Olda Manna Rio Davill."

"Ohhh, Lordy."

"Ohh, Lorrdy."

"Both of us is devuls."

"Botha davills."

"Both all muddy."

"Botha beega moddy."

"I'm th' pertiest."

"I de prittiest."

"An' you're th' smartest."

"You de smarteest."

"I'm all muddy, an' you'll wipe me off."

"I all moddy, anda you cleana me offa."

"I ain't no gone galoot."

"No gone-a galoot."

"One little word jest to test ya out."

"Tasta me out."

"If you're th' Old Womern Devul—"

"Olda Wooman Davill—"

"Tell me where'bouts my grampaw's gold mine's at."

"How do I know? You haf to aska God. Your granda-father deeda not come-a to my place; no, he want op, opa de h'aven." She flapped her hands like a big bird caught in a snare trap. "Zoopp—lika theesa."

"Hey, Ole Devul Woomern."

"Yass, Ole Manna."

"Is y'r naick perty tough?"

"Lika de sanda leezaird. For why?"

"I'm jest a-gonna show ya, little nib er two, sorta how I'm a-itcherin' my pants off ta chew chaw on that there little ole sugar tit Rinny, in th' housse, yund'r."

"Notta so harrd. Ootcha. You willa break her."

"Ain't a-gonna gash 'er 'nough ta braing no blood. Jest sorta graze aroun' on 'er some."

"Ohh. Onna her wheecha?"

"Some. Some."

"Shee willa notta be so prettee verra long."

"One more thaing I'm a-wantin' from ya."

"*Sí sí, no no.*"

"If'n you're th' ole woomern devul, how's it come th't ya could look sa dern much like that Riorina gal in there?"

She pooched up her face and told me, "All of ussa davils can do it. It eees nothing. Nothing. We can look laka any wooman we weesha. Joosta de same as you can looka like de man. *Sí? No?*"

"Yeahh. I see now. How about Luisa in there a-helpin' Eddie ta glue back that there ole gittar of Cleo's? Is she a womern devul, too?"

"Cleo?"

"Naw, Luisa. I said Luisa. An' I mean Luisa."

"Luisa no davill. She angela. Angel. Cleo she de angel, also. I, me, Riorina, I de only she-davill thesa whole country. Me. Rina."

"I'm the onlyest he-devul up 'n' down this dern Mexico border. Bom bom. Y'r boosum makes a perty good drum. Mebbe, though, mosta y'r gentlemun friends don't whang aroun' on ya, huh, like I do, do they?"

"Ohh. I say, summa yes, summa no. My brootherr he breaksa me worrsa thana you. I maka you steecka your head inna de cactoos deetch lasta night—ha ha ha, he he he! Ha ha ha! Thata ees going to keepa Riorina laughing for my grandakeeds onna my knee."

I told her, "Quit a-laughin' sa loud; ever'body plumb clean on back ta where that ole truck is can hear ya. Sssht!"

"Noboddy canna hear me." She stood up to rub her face in the palms of her hands. "Noboddy except Cleo's goats. Tella me, Meestaire, issa Addie Stoney assa moch of the davill heemself assa you arre? Yas?"

"Naw." I looked at her. "He's lots more like Luisa."

She walked over to the east side of the house, just under the bedroom window, leaned back against the mud smeared over the wood, and said, "The moon iss assa bright tonight as itta wassa lasta night. Rememberr? Theese grass feels so gooda to my toes. Ahhmm. You forgeet lasta night, mabbe, hoh?"

I put my arms around her and kissed her to see how she would act. We pushed against the wall for a kiss or several, each time a bit hotter, a little wetter, a bit braver. She moved her hips against my belly until I forgot my name and address. I licked her neck, and sucked her ear, I ran my fingers up and down her back to play with her curls. I felt afraid that she might skip off down the grass and run away from me if I let my hands touch her skin under her dress. I felt my heart lumping along so big that my mouth couldn't speak a single word. My hands broke out with a cold fever of sweaty oil as I lifted the hem of her dress to touch her legs and thighs. She seemed to be moving and hugging, kissing, and breathing so fast that

she didn't even know or feel my hands under her dress. I
shook like a sick sheep, like a cactus limb in a dusty
blow. I rubbed her skin, I pulled her so tight up against
my overalls that we stuck, somehow, together. She let out
a little heavy breath of air that turned into a very happy
moan or groan. She tried to walk through me, to climb up
me, to dance, and to move, to skip across me. She kissed
me while she pulled me by my neck down onto the grass.
The seedling smell of the juice in the blades got up into
my nose and made me lots drunker than a drunk man. I
kept my right hand in under her dress, and as I chewed
and sucked her lips and tongue, I put my hand over the
nipple of her left breast, then across her bosom to the
swell of her right breast. I thought to myself that Rina's
breast was a good bit fuller, harder, if not any hotter, than
Hell Cat's. It could be, maybe, because Rina had no kind
of a brazzeer nor bosom band on.

I kept my hand against her skin to feel my way down
over her stomach to rub her hips, around and around,
and her knees and her thighs. She shook her face slow
and easy from one side to the other, and kept on rolling
the muscles of her lips to stick her tongue out more and
more for kissing. She seemed to be trying to lift her hips
and stomach up, somehow, up, a lift-up, a roll-up, to touch
the hairs of her womb against the fingers of my hands.
She opened apart her legs to feel my fingers play with her
till she got soaking wet with the juice between her legs. I
slid my finger as easy as I could till it was as deep as it
would go amongst her hairs. I felt like maybe she would
tell me to quit now, if I stopped kissing her long enough
for her, or for me, to catch a breath of air. I saw such an
easy, pretty, woozey, happy shine across her face that I
wanted just to kiss again, to lick my tongue around her
teeth, to keep my finger inside between her legs, mostly,
to keep watching that odd and curious smile of peace in
her eyelashes, and in around her curls. We both got lost
and tangled up in her curls, like a patch of some kind of
wild climby vines. Hot, sweaty, sticky, juicy, slickery, dizzy,
seedy, thorny, and out of our heads. I had no more of an
idea what to do next than Old Grover's cow at the bulling
pen. After a few more minutes, both of us woke up
enough to take a look around the hill. She shook her
head, blew her breath on her bosoms, and told me,
"Uummm, Beebee, thees feelsa so good. Uhhm. I weesh

we coulda do eet for alla night long. No. No. Let'sa stoppa. Let's quita. I willa malta anda ronn all down ov'r thizza grass. Mmm. Mm. Ohhm. Awwm. Butta, Beebee, Honney, don'ta—no, letta mee opp, letta me opp. I joosta want to see iffa my feeta willa take me. Gosha. Ooop. I no know, I know, I no know. Heyyp. Halloe there. Eesa thata stilla you, here, Mistaire Davill Man?"

I watched her get up onto her feet and shake her dress down around her legs, shaking her curls in their places, walking on the grass with her face towards the moon.

"Yeahhhp. Same ole devul feller. Same man. You? You th' same? Ya look th' same."

"Nohh." She took a deep breath in and out. "Nohh, I ama sorry to tella you, I cannotta say thatta I feel any worse, nor notta thee sama, butta, mabbe I feel beega boncha betterr, allaready. You better, worse, hoh?"

"Both. Better while we done it an' worser when we quit. I was jest barely gittin' started right real good." I got up and walked towards the house, brushing off my overalls and my shirt. "Where'bouts y' headin'?"

" 'Round to de door to look innaside. They willa be madda iffa we do notta come-a back in."

"My Little Johnny's gonna be lots madder," I followed her back, "if you don't let him come in."

"Leetla who?"

"Little John."

"Ohh. Anda whoo ees Leetla Jon? Does he know me?"

"Jest by touch. Long distance. Shore wants t' come in an' git warm by yer fire. Awful mad a-waitin' out here."

"Where are those two feedle steecks you putta here for Addie to glue onna Cleo's *guitarra?*"

"Right here in unn'r yer feet, don't step on 'em. We weren't talkin' 'bout no gittar. 'Bout Little Johnny havin' ta wait out here on th' outside in th' cold." I held her up against the screen of the back porch and tickled her legs and breasts like a long spider with hairy legs. "I'm a-waitin', Missy Devul!"

"Keesa. Keesa my eyes more so I canna see plain."

"Likey theesy. Huhm? Thissy, Missy?"

"Yessy. Tella me, why do youu lika so mocha to play anda to feel off my teeties? Long John? Say?"

"Hell's little jerrybells, don't ask me. My hand jest crawls up there 'cause my faingers wants t' do it. Does this hurt? Er don'tcha like f'r me to? I'm an ole devul an' a fast prospecter with a long shovel an' a slick pick an', well, Honey, I jest start in a-diggin', I guess, whenever I git up on a hill this perty an' warm. Say, tell me, Rio Reeno, jest about when's ole Big John a-gonna git his head in yore gate?"

She licked my lips a few times like candy and told me, "Maybe I will hava my door opan for Johnny tonight, tonight, after we sing some sangs weetha Cleo, and after she tells us a few off herr olda stories. Perhaps we willa ron way down over de riverr I show you, anda your frand, Mister Longa Johnny, he can come-a in and stay by my stove for assa long assa John pleases. Hokay?"

"Hokay. In we go. How's th' gittar glue job? Folks?"

I heard Eddie ask me, "How many fish did you guys ketch?"

The eating blanket was gone from the floor when I looked down. A cheap tin pan on the stove held all of our dishes to soak. Cleo dried each dish and put her tinwares up on the nails and shelving on the wall. I saw a little crayon picture drawn like a cartoon, with a girl in a flirty kind of a pose. I made out the words in the lantern light: "Cleo 1918." Some sort of a Spanish greeting, the name of some Mexican town.

Luisa handed the guitar over to me, asking, "Do you think you can tune these strings?"

I bored holes in the ends of the flat sticks I'd found, and unlaced my left shoe. I laid one flat board on the top of the guitar and the other on the bottomside, then laced my leather shoe string in and out of the holes till I took all of my slack up.

"I'm jest a-prayin' fer that there dern-gum glue t' take aholt an' growl." Eddie watched me slip the fancy red silk strap around my neck, and listened while I flipped the strings with my thumb.

Cleo nodded over my way while she took off her drying apron and hung the string over a shingle nail above the stove. She kept her best ear cocked my way while I ran a few free sample chords to tune up my finger joints. We all walked out onto the grass and away from the house.

"Well, folks," I told everybody watching me, "this's not th' world's champeen gittar brace, but it's right up amongst th' champs. Last jest as long's this here Mack Schmellin' feller."

Eddie said, "Better'd last longer'n that."

"I, for one, think Mister Smelling is very nice, and he will make a good world's champion."

"Hell, I could floor that there big sissy right here on this grass t'night with jest my one good hand."

"He does notta seema so verra popular weetha you, Addie; why notta?" Rina brushed her curls around Ed's overalls to walk around him. "My beega broother was op inna Fort Davis anda he said Max Smalling geeva someaboddy a beega knockout lika deesa, onna de radio."

"Both of us ladies are taking Smelling on our side." Luisa linked her hands around Eddie's shrunken arm, and kicked at the grassy blades with her moccasin toes. "Just why are you two men so much against him? Tell why?"

" 'Cause." Eddie let his tongue go free, "Jest b'cause he's a Heinie Hun an' a sissy bum from Germiny."

"You don't say"—Rina held Eddie by his good arm—"that you hate him for being born somaplaza, wheecha he cooda not halp. No? Meesterr Schmalinng has verra nize arms, verra beega sholders, nize deepa inna hissa chast, de tougha stummik, limber inna hiss back, anda queeck lika da cat onna his feet. I see heem sav'ral times inna de magazina, de paperrs, wan tam ina El Paso del Norte onna de moving screen. If I wassa de manna, or de boy, I t'ink I worka, I try verra hard, yas, to grow de beega halthy muscles, lika dees, anda de niza shape body like Maxie."

"I ain't a-knockin' on bein' healthy," Ed told the girls. "I'm a-wantin' to see ever'body ez healthy an' ez perty ez Luisa, here, Lord knows I seen my fill of broke-down wracks of humanns while I laid up on that there hospital sheet them sev'rul months. I jest met me a little Fransch wine girl, in th' mud of my tranch, oh, couldn't of been much more'n ten minutes 'fore that there big sixteen-incher cover'd us und'r. Looked a dang sight like you, here, Luisa; couldn't guess which's which if I'd meet th' both of yaz out here 'n this little streak of th' moon's light. It woulda been awright, yep-sir, if'n them god-dern bastardly Heinie Huns hadn't a seen me an' her caught down there 'n that ole hard gummy mud. Ya know what it was that I was a-tryin' t' ask 'er when them dash-gone bullets bustedd down on us? Ya know what it was?"

"No."

"What?"

"I kept a-tryin' . . ."—Eddie walked with slow, easy

steps that covered and uncovered the words of his thoughts.
The girls sat down a few feet away from the same water
barrel that had eavesdropped a few minutes ago on the
match of Riorina versus me. They listened for Eddie to
go on. "I kept tryin' my dead level best ta say, ta ask 'er,
'Hey, what's yore name? What didja say yore name is?'
Then, kerbluunng! Them Hunny Huns got a crack at us. I
didn't even have a gun on me, ner nowhere aroun' me. I
don't know if it makes y' much differnce one way er
another'n, Luisa, but ye're jest a livin' image of that little
wine-tub girl. 'At's why I hate them Heinies th' way I do.
An' some o' them same Huns is eggin' on ole Mussolinny
now to persecute them pore igner'nt niggers in Aferkee,
an' threaten ta make war on 'em. Ole Max Schmeller's not
over yonder tryin' to save a saingle fainger of one o' them
nigs, is he?"

Luisa took Eddie's good hand in hers and watched me
sit down over by Rina's elbow to thump a chord along the
strings of the old guitar. I heard Luisa tell Ed, "It would
not make good sense for the world's champion boxer to
throw down his gloves and rush over to Africa. Would it?
Maybe Mister Maxie takes all of his money and gives it
to people that need help as bad as those blacks in Ethi-
opia."

"An' just mebbe he don't. Mebbe he's too busy a-
blowin' his wad on one o' them high nosy dames, kind that
ya've gotta cram 'er hole with a thousand-dollar bill, an'
light up a big ha'f a doll'r seegar in 'er ass t' git 'er juicy, t'
git 'em warmed up fer a fockin'. I'd like to have seen that
colored fighter Jack Johnson get after that old Maxie. That
Heinie wouldn't be lookin' half as perty after jest about
th' first go-round with ole Jack. If'n Maxie was able ta go
out'n th' weeds with a woomern after that, well, she'd
shore have ta drag 'im out feet front'erds. An' if'n somebody don't knock ole Max's eyes outta their sockits, well,
I'm a-slippin' me a glove onta this here good han' of mine,
see, an' I'm a-gonna climb up in them dang-blame ropes
an' whang 'im back t' them Heinies where he come from."

"Anyway," Luisa said, "let's not fight tonight among
ourselves, not about prize boxers, not about the Huns, nor
the blacks in Africa, nor about anything else. Let's try to
sing and play and have fun tonight, just this one night."

Cleo had gone back to the house to fetch her mandolin
and the water bucket. As she came towards us, Eddie

jumped up and gave her a lift with the bucket. Then he stood up spraddle-legged and took a long bubbler out of his own bottle. Cleo took one as bubbly as Eddie's, handed the bottle down to me, and I sat it on the grass in between the girls' toes. Both took a good sip and both beat their bosoms with their fists to get the air to pump back into their lungs.

Cleo stood up to play a few warm-up chords on her mandolin. The silk rope around her neck was the same red color as the guitar strap. I crossed my legs and played a slow Spanish waltz in the key of D, sat back against Rina's shoulder, and listened to Cleo's mandolin.

Her mandolin sounded like it was a thickskin gourd, and was of the buggyback, big-belly, round-back style of several years ago. The ribs of light and dark hardwood around the soundbox were fancy carved, and the spaces on the neck were of a solid black ebony wood between the brass frets, and a patch of pure white mother-of-pearl was fitted into the black ebony fingerboard every few notches. The nice, quiet, slow-going, and easy way that Cleo tickled her strings with her flat pick, the way she kept her eyes up off the mandolin to look over our heads and the tops of the worried mountains, showed me that she put in an hour or more every day over the humpy back of this old mandolin. She played the waltz with a very plain rise and fall of the One Two Three, One Two Three, Omm pahh pahh, rhythm and beat. She swayed her body from side to side in an exact sway with the music. The words of the song she sang were such an odd mixture of Spanish, Indian, Mexicano, that their meanings missed my ear completely. I liked that low, deep, boomy outdoor, clouds, wind, blue-sky, sway and swell that she sang with very little hard labor. You felt like she had rocked about and sung so many days of her life that she wished and craved just to play along and to sing for the good of her own ears and own soul all night long.

The only thing that stopped the music was Rina's younger brother, who ran up the hill out of nowhere. As he stood in the middle of our little circle, I saw that he was the same fellow that had borrowed my guitar last night. He shook his face and his finger and jumped around as he told us, "You stayed too long."

"You mean me?" Rina asked him.

"And they are verra mad." He waved his arms.

"Madda? Weetha me?" Rina stood up to ask him.

"No." He told her, "Atta him. Woodabox."

I kept my seat and held the guitar, and asked him, "Who? How mad? What for?"

"Jaff he mad. You papa he madda. Botha madda."

"Bothie." Eddie rolled over on the grass to listen. "Hmm."

And Luisa asked, "Well, what on earth happened?"

"Jaffrry he tak troock. He drive 'way. You Papa Sharlie he go 'way weetha Jaffa."

"Baick up t' Pampa? God an' little whirlwinds," Ed said. "Big long walk from here ta Pampa. Six hunnerd miles, 'f not a dang sight more'n that."

"Did they tell ya where they was driving to?" I asked the boy.

"No. Notta oppa de Pampas."

"Where?" Rina asked him. "Make it quick, broother!"

"They drive Sam Nail's rancho. Get boy show way. Fram here twenty miles."

" 'At's better'n six hundred," I said. "What's you' 'n' me gonna do now, Eddyrooster? I cain't find th' way ov'r there from th' toppa this hill."

"Me neither. I'm lost like th' Woodchuck," Ed said. Then he asked the boy, "Is they enybody 'roun' here that y' know of, mean, that can show us how t' git over there? Huh?"

"Sí. Me." The kid looked proud like a preacher. "Me anda my franda. We take you de brush. Short way."

"Money?" I asked him.

"I no wanta manney," he told me.

"These wimmen owes me'n you a dollar an'a half, Woody, fer that brick wall. Give 'im that. Hey, Sonny, one dollar an' a half we got. 'Zat okay?" Ed asked him.

"Eyekay. Whan I bring my buddy—whicha time? Whicha place?"

"Right here." Ed tapped his finger to the ground. "First thaing in th' mornin'."

"Daylight? Or sun-op?"

"Daylight." I shook my head at his tennis shoes and stuck my finger towards the east. "Too early?"

"Oh no. I be here. I ronna backa now tella my buddy." He ran back down the hill and hit the clumps of bushes so fast that a cloud of alkali dust jumped up out from the weeds to follow him.

"Mighty fine brother there, Missy Rinia," I told her.

"How old of a man is he?" Eddie asked Rina.

Luisa watched the trail of tennis-shoe dust out through the weed patch and told Eddie, "Coming along twelve."

"Mebbe he c'n show me where'bouts ta dig out my grampaw's gold mine." Ed snapped his fingers. He looked up at Cleo with her potato-bug mandolin in her arms, and handed her the bottle of whiskey as he said, "Let's g'wan with our music, Cleo. Ta heck with them little brothers, ev'r dern one of 'em. C'mon, an' set y'rself down here an' thaw my back out, Luisa. I'm a-frozen up an' down my speenal column. Warm me. 'At's th' girl. Now, both o' you music makers, cut 'er loose, cut 'er deep. I wanta lay here'n jest bathe my soul in a whole big bunch of them there perty songs."

CHAPTER 16

TIGHT BLANKET

Cleo smiled down at the top of Eddie's head, and played one of the wildest songs I had ever tried to chord for. I could only see by the position of her keyboard fingers that she commenced in the key of natural C. C can be one of the driest, deadest keys on a mandolin, if you are in one of the early stages of courting the mandybox. Every early starter, beginner, and mail-ordering stranger in the RFD or thickly settled townships, drives a large number of honest workers to pack up and hit the road, rather than to try to live through this misery and earthbound insanity of the neighbor who is just now fingering open the C-natural pages of any book of music lessons. They go un-counted, seldom checked; the patrolman does not ever stick his head in your car, truck, jalopy window, to ask you what key it was that your neighbor used to drive you and your beloveds out and down this hard-job highway, look-ing for a place that's hard to find. No. They neither ask you if it was the drum, the saxtifone, harmonica, bones, voice lessons, tap dancing, violin, piccolo, piano, guitar, yodelery, or jaybird opera, nor try to keep any sort of an accounting of the particular kind of instrument that drove you, as I said, out and down. I, my own self, if I roosted

on that highest judging bench, I'd not strike out to make
an outlaw of any known musical contraption, nor would I
be so empty of heart as to make your practicing against
the laws. Nor would I walk out with my brand-new fountain pen to dictate to your conscience which musical key
you must do your frolicking in. I know this would be pure
dictatorship of the foulest, meanest, lowest kind. But if I
could think up some fair and honest way, say, to outlaw
that key of C natural for early beginners, amateurs, and
new commencers, I'll admit that, looking back down the
trail and track of headaches, throbs of fevers, high bloody
pressures, and such likes, which my friends and my neighbors dealt out to me and to my kinfolks, I'd call out all of
my cops in uniform and send them out smelling and
listening for harmonies, harmonics, tones, overtones, un-
dertones, and vibrations caused and given birth and rise
and shelter under the roofs and hideaways of that key
called by the common name of natural C.

There is where the whole rot and cankery mould gets
its germy start, its suckling, its growth, in the apple basket
of our entire musical world. But as I tried to keep in the
clear at the start, my C Key Patrolmen, my Key C
Troopermen, my C-natural Smeller Noses, my FBIK-C's,
my CCC-ers, would not be able to lay a hand on a champion such as Cleo, here, for the simple act of straying over
into the Key of C Straight. Cleo worked an hour or two
every day for years and years just to be able to take her
stand, and to stand her ground, over in that wilder, loster,
tangleweed world of Native C. She tossed it around so that
you could not tell that it was that deathy place of Soury
C. She kept all of the moans and groanings of Rattly C
choked out, covered up with other more civilized sounds.
She used her last two little fingers on her left hand so fast,
so self-certainly, so expertly, that the poison acids and
poison oils were downed, hogtied, hobbled, ear-choked,
and taken out of the musical tune, the same general way
that these acids and oils are char-soaked out of whiskey
and rum. She knew that many a fine talented champion
music-maker had been knocked out in the first round by
this luring, baiting key of Naked C. It was for our sakes,
for Rina, for Luisa, for Eddie Stone, and for my ownself,
that Cleo stuck her chin out, risked her very existence, to
take this worst of all crazy clays and to whip and to beat,

to pound it up into something that made sense, or made you feel good.

She used pauses to let the C key strike at her and miss. She used offbeats to kid it blind and to run it crazy. She played a tune that was full of lazy waits which wore the C out like a spider wears down a measuring worm. She swayed, feinted, shadowboxed, and weaved around to sap the strength of the killer key. And when it seemed most certain to fight its way up to her very throat, she let out a little yip, paused, swayed, possumed, acted dead, and the poor key, the Choker C, lost its breath, lost its wind, drooped open at its lower jaw till Cleo caught its dead weight falling, at which split second Cleo threw from the tops of the grass blades one long running back backbend shoulder drive that laid the ancient and honored Fighting Key down wiggly on the ground.

I was glad that Cleo showed such native human genius as to pick such a tricky, foxy, fast-moving, broken-time tune as she did to challenge this deathly C in. A waltz, a slow trot, a blues, any slow melody now or forever in the futures to come, can last no longer in that fishy, tramble-net key than a hard-head lobster lasts in a hungry pot. She was also wise enough to choose this kind of an offy beat, run and wait, dash and rest, push and pause tune which was followed by such an easy kind of a regular beat on the guitar strings. And even at the times when my guitar was voting solid C all the way across, Cleo used every doggy trick on the strings of her mandolin to beat down my solid row of C and to make her little mandy sound like a dozen folks out voting against the rotten C machine.

Luisa sang the next song as Cleo played with my chord-ings. I saw that it was pitched in the key of open D, which, being one of the finer and more respectable keys, gave Cleo the free and leisure time to join in with the words as Luisa sang them. An easier-going, more broadminded key, a more friendly and restful key, a key that has a clear character slate and a good reputation, a key that does not require strict patroling, close watching, but a key that can be trusted with your most sentimental valuables, plain old common D, it was another stroke of great genius on Cleo's part to pitch the song here for Luisa to play around with in such an easy manner. She kept her knees wide apart,

and held a hand on either knee, to sway from side to
side, to brush her hair and cheek against Eddie's as he
listened. The words were sung in some dialect of Spanish.
While Luisa and Cleo mixed up their words with the
guitar and mandolin, Rina leaned over into the center of
our circle, rubbed her curls against Luisa's hair, and told
us after each line what the words meant:

> There was a bigga strrong man . . .
>> da da diddle de, doodley, dummty,
>
> He come-a riding down my river . . .
>> toodle toodle de da dummlty
>
> On a horse so dark anda prettee,
>> yes, yes, yess,
>
> Anda he saw me inna my frront door
>> ta ta ta ta squeekerty squirkitty
>
> Anda he asks, canna he come-a to me,
> I said, yess, my door issa open,
> Butta, thesa reeverr flows between us,
> Anda your horse cannot swim so far,
> Anda my father's rope can't reach you,
>> daddle daddle jingle jingle
>> bring a rum pot when you comm,
>> bring a rum jug when you comm.

> He cried, "Thee reeverr's getting higher,
> My horrse ees getting hotter,
> Twist your curls into a silk rope,
> Girl, anda throw it over thees waters."
>> daddle daddle jingle jingle
>> bring yourr bottle whan you come-a
>> bring yourr bottle whan you come-a.

> I threw my curlie rope over the reever,
> Butta the waters caught tham halfa way,
> He says, splice your belly hairs on the roppe,
> Whicha I didda, than ita reached over.
>> daddle daddle jingle jingle
>> brringa beeg jugga rum whan you comm
>> bring yourr rumma jug when you comm.

> He threw his saddle rope to the waters,
> Anda he roped the hairs onna my rope,

I pooled hissa horse out 'cross thee reever
Anda my man hung on the horrse's tail.
    daddle daddle jingle jingle
    where's my rumma jug you didda brring,
    where's the jug off rum for me?

My bottle iss hiding inna my blankeet,
Where your father cannota see,
You moosta come-a innaside my blankeet
Iffa you wooda drink witha mee.
    daddle daddle jingle jingle
    thank you forr my jug of rum
    thank you forr my rumma jug.

I ask, show me to your blankeet, sirr,
Howw beeg may thissa blankeet be?
My blankeet itta coverrs thesa hills anda rocks
Assa far assa your eyes canna see.
    daddle daddle jingle jingle
    that's verra beeg jug off rum
    soch a beeg, beeg rumma jug.

So I want innaside hiz blankeet witha him,
For a day and a night, or more,
Anda I found theeza beega blankeet belongs
To the Study Butte Mining Store.
    daddle daddle jingle jingle
    soch a beeg long bottle off rum
    soch a beeg sleeck bottle off rum.

Howw did I learn thissa Study Butte blankeet
Coverred up all off my lands?
Forr one leetle dollaire an acre
Thissa whole world ees inna his hands.
    daddle daddle jingle jingle
    now the jug ees all inna me,
    now your rumma jug ees inna me.

Eddie rolled over on the grass and said, "Hmmm. Is
they any truth ta that there song? That there dollar-an-
acre verse of it, I mean?"

"Just as true, Honey." Luisa rubbed her shoulder against
Ed's cheek. "That verse is just as true as the other ones."

"Cleo says that she weeshed for us to sing thata verse

to see iffa you woulda know what ita means," Rina told us.

"Some kinda dern blanket, some kind," I said. "Sounds like an awful true song t' me. Awful big blanket. What kinda damn blanket is it? Anyway?"

Luisa told us, "It is called a blanket claim."

"Blankit claim?" Eddie looked around mad.

"Yes," Luisa went on, "on the first day of January every year the first person to get into the Office of the Clerk—Land Clerk—up in Alpine, can pay one dollar an acre down as a blanket claim; that means, to claim as many acres as he has dollars, say, in and around a spot where he thinks he has found a rich mine. You can tell the Land Judge that the regular size of the twenty-five-acre claim is not big enough for you to open up and to operate and to build a road to your mine, so you can claim more acres in the names of your blood relations, and you can lay down twenty thousand dollars, and lay a legal claim on twenty thousand acres of land where you think something might be found, and where you do not wish too many people crowding in too close around your mine. That is what we call down here, the blanket."

"Th' ole blanket." I shook my head. I combed down through Rina's curls with my fingers and said, " 'Tis a big blanket, one mighty big blanket. One helluva big blanket."

"Beeg enoff for youu, beeg enoff for me, beeg enoff for sixteen keeds, beeg enoff, mabbye, joosta mabbye, for to holda your grandpappa Jerry along witha us, ho, inna our bigga Study Butte Compannio blanketa. *Sí, no?*"

"My sakes a-livin' grasshoppers!" Eddie rubbed his hand over his hair, face, and eyes, and massaged the blood around the back of his neck. "Means th't we cain't dig out our own grampaw's claim an' file no papers on it. Don't it? Ain't that whut it means?"

Cleo climbed to her feet and carried her mandolin across the grass towards the screendoor. She bid us some sort of greeting in her native tongue, which Rina told us meant: "That is all of the stories I will tell for tonight."

Luisa looked towards the house. "Cleo is very odd," she said, "and strange in her ways. When she goes, she goes, and when she comes, she comes. She treats everybody nice and kind, but she is liable to just walk up, or just walk away, or no telling what, at almost any time. I thought that she would set down with us and tell us a few of her

true stories about these mountains, but she saw that our
song about the Study Butte blanket had given you enough
to think about for this one night. That is the way she feels
sorry for you, the way she goes off to cry for you; she always walks away somewhere in the brush to weep or to
cry or to pray for me, or any of her friends. She wishes to
be polite, too, and to leave us younger ones out here to
bundle up as we please. I never have seen anybody like
Cleo, except Rio. Rio is a fine talker, and Cleo can't speak
any English at all. In her Indian and Mexicano ways,
though, Cleo is a good match for Rio."

I took Rina's fingers in my hand and rubbed her skin
across the grass to tickle her. I said, "Wh'never I dig up
ole Jerry P.'s hundred-dollar-a-ton mine, I'm a-gonna pay
th' first half of it over ta Cleo ta play all our towheads to
sleep, baby, sleep. Y' know, Rinia, that there song about
th' blanket, an' th' rummer jug?"

"*Sí*. Why?"

"Th' dang song made my lips foamy. I gotta havva
'nuther littel titcha Ed's ole stolen whiskey."

Eddie drank ahead of me, then passed the bottle, saying, "Naw, no water f'r me. Brrr. Brrrm."

Luisa and Rina took their last sips out of Ed's home-
brew bottle, emptied it, and sat it in the middle of our
circle. I was chasing my big swallow with the dipper of
water, when I picked up the beer bottle to toss it away
over my shoulder, and to make a wish with my eyes shut.
Rina stopped me, put her hand on the bottle and told me,
"That will makka de good water boddle inna de morrning
forr Addie anda you."

Luisa said, "Unless you are a pair of camels, and have
kept it a secret from us."

"Hey, Luisa"—Ed was feeling his day's drinks by this
time, or, rather, wanted to act a bit dizzier, now that both
our bottles were emptied—"Luisa, wuzhit a, a jug kinda
like this here one, th't wuz roll'd up in that there blankit y'
crawl'd up in with that there feller th't y' roped frum
acrost th' riv'r? Same kinda glassh?"

"Nearly the same. Except, well, the jug that was rolled
up in his blanket was rum."

"Rumma jug," Rina told us.

Eddie told them, "What I'm a-wantin' ta ask ya is, who
wuzzit tolja 'bout that big muddy blankit th't covers up sa
much country? 'Zatta fact?"

"Yeah." I shook my head and rubbed my nose behind Rina's ear. "This might really toss a monkey wranch in our granpaw's mine, huh, Eddie Steever?"

"Jest who is it th't gits on th' innside of that Lan' Clerk's office door on th' firsst of ev'r January?" Ed asked the girls.

"Certainly not any of my people." Luisa talked with her eyes on the grass. "These muddy-hut Indians, or these mud-house Mexicans. They sure won't be any too quick to help you dig up your mine, and to lay down a big pile of your money to keep them away from your part of the blanket. Blame them?"

"Nawp," Ed told her, "I'm a-guessin' I'd do th' same blame thaing. I see ev'r fam'ly of Indyuns in about halfa Oklahomer git rooked outta them oil an' farmin' strips they was livin' on. Dope, likker—bayrummed 'em, lit 'em up, sceered 'em out, tricked 'em loose, stole 'em ragged, robbed 'em blind, gunned 'em, beat 'em, an' ev'n poison'd 'em, shot 'em, hung 'em, an' swung 'em. Indyuns is lots lower down, lots worser treat'd th'n cows er hosses, 'n' knock'd worser down now than them niggers is. Black c'n leastways go a little an' come a little bit like he pleases, but y' take an Indyun, biggist part uv 'em is tied an' roped down ta some county line, an' they cain't git acrost it till they ooze pure blood, ez th' ole squaw sez."

Luisa dug her fingernails into the grass roots and said, "So you see why none of my people here can push their way into that Land Office door with any dollar bills in their hands. And you see, also, that every stick of the brush is like an eye watching you hunt for your mine. It was either very good luck for you boys, or else very wise of you, to be so ignorant as you are."

"Ignerant?" Ed cut in.

"Who's ignorant?" I asked her.

"Ignorant enough," Rina laughed on my arm. "Domb enough to tella Rio joost lika that—snappa, snappa—that you are simply looking for a seelver anda gold mine. Ha ha ha. It wass the verra first word you said to him. Joosta lika that."

"First thing he asked me," I told them. "First thing I told 'im back. Was I mistaken or crazy?"

"Ignorant. Huhhm." Eddie hugged Luisa a bit closer. "Always knowed that I hadda certin cousin with th' wheels in his head runnin' backerds."

"Not one person out of ten thousand would just drive
down in our mountains and tell the first old man they saw
that they were standing nearly on the top of a silver and
gold vein their grandpa dug up, and had assayed and all."
Luisa shook all over laughing at us, and went on, "All
the white people who come down here to trap furs tell us
they're down here to take up an ore claim, and all our
miner bugs tell us they're down here to trap. But nobody
who's standing on top of a proven claim ever says, 'Yes,
we came down here to look for silver! How do you say
silver in Mexican?' That's the best joke of the year!"

"Yoo hyoo hyoo." Eddie mocked at me with Luisa.
"'At's a good one, awright."

"But that slip off your lip," Rina said, "was what made
Rio t'ink you to be some kind off an honest man. He
laughed at you whan he tolda me about you. He wanted
us to helpa you find your way over to Sam Nail's *rancho*,
where your grandpapa ran the cattles anda dugga op hissa
mine. Rio told me, I, me, Rio, remamberr Jarry P. varra
varra plain. Butta Rio, he say you coulda not find a rock
off silverr iffa your grandpapa was hitting you on your
head with it."

"Hummie yum." I tried to act funnier than I felt.

"The boys will take you tomorrow," Luisa said, "through
the brush and over to the old adobe house where your
grandfather put up a windmill and a watering tank. This
old house is where his woman lived and kept the boys,
three little boys. I forget their names. Sam Nail has not
been here long enough to know where your grandfather's
ore vein was located. So he can't help you in finding your
mine. He could make it harder for you if you make him
mad and he orders you off his land. See? So don't do a
thing to make Mister Sam Nail mad at you."

"Not a teensie speck," I told Luisa.

"I'll tickle his toes all night with a turkey feather if it'll
keep ole Samuel in a good humor," Ed told the girls.

Luisa went on to say, "There is an old colored camp
cook that found a tobacco sack of nuggets one day, and
he took down with laughing fits and ran back up into his
canyon. About twice a year some of us get a glimpse of
him, and we hear him laugh his crazy laugh out in the
bushes. We call him by the name of Old Niggerhead, which
is the name of one of the highest peaks of the Chisos
Mountain range there. All back across the east."

"Ole Niggerhead," Eddie nodded. "Gotta look 'im up. I'm jest's much of a rambly goat ez Ole Niggerhead ever was. I'm a slick-rock sticker an' a dagger-thorn nicker, myself. Ha ha."

"Ole Niggerhead is the only other living man along this border that knew your grandfather well—which canyon your grandpa herded his cattle in, where he branded, camped, where he cooked, and where he found that running spring of medicine water."

"Find that there britches-filler spraing, an' we, I c'n walk from that medicine-water hole ta th' clift Paw Jerry dug on," Ed said.

"If Sam Nail has the time, and if he likes the sound of your story, he will show you around to ten or fifteen of these dead-horse stinking springs of water. You can't expect to locate a mine by every spring, though," Luisa said.

"Shore cain't," Eddie agreed. "I'll run that there ole Niggyhead feller down, an' by doggies git 'im good an' souzled, an' he'll show me, I, Mister Eddie, where'bouts th' ore's a-hidin' out."

Luisa watched Rina and me as we stood up to stretch. She said, "If you find your spring hole and your mine, or no spring and no mine, that is a stretch of curious country over there where your old adobe house is. It is real close to the bottoms of all the mountains, close to the Slick Rock Wagon Gap, and you might find any kind of strange person over there: cowhands, sheepmen, hunters, trappers, prospectors, officers, hermits, tramps of all kinds, and even a few of the wet Mexicans."

As Luisa got up to walk along southeasterly down the path on the hill, I watched Eddie put his arm around her. Then Rina and I passed a few paces ahead of them, so I could only try to guess what went on between Luisa and Ed. I asked them, "What makes queer ducks like this here old 'dobe house sa much?"

"Wella, you see," Rina said, "that olde adobe ees de only house you can stop at."

"Who's there to stop?" I asked.

"Mexicans, Indians, averybody," Rina told me. "The only spring off gooda clear watter for ten or feefateen miles. Stove there, to cook. Averry wild animal comes there to drink the water."

"What's a wet Mexican, anyhow?" I asked them.

"A wet Mexican is a person that—how would you tell

him, Rina—that wades across the river without any papers," Luisa said.

"Which kind of papers?" Ed asked.

"United Estados ceetizen papers. *Sí*," Rina told us.

"Unit'd States cigarette papers," I laughed. "Hey, Rinnie, where ya pullin' off to? Helluva hill. I didn't know that grass was that slick. I'll be a wet Oklahomeran, if I skid off down yonder into that quicksand. I'll slide plumb over inta Old Mexico without a sign of a legal paper on me. Wet Gringo, huh?"

Rina hugged my arm and rubbed her curls against my shoulder. "We are going down to wash our t'ings. Anda your t'ings."

"Oh, mercy me," Ed said. "Down here'n this river's water? I ain't a-gonna wade off out'n that gosh-blasted, muddy slick, jest to warsh my t'ings, ez you call it."

"I can't walk close enough to you, Hon," Luisa joked, "with all of your dirt and dry mud pushing me back."

"Your duds is stiffer'n mine is," Eddie told her.

And Rina looked over her left shoulder to say, "This looks to me like our washing-macheena place, hey, Luisa?"

"The same outward appearance." Luisa rolled her eyes around and looked with her lips apart. "I thought I told my service boy to wash and polish my laundry trucks real nice, and then to drive them into the garage for the night. But, there they stand, all in a line, just as dirty and just as messy as they were today."

"*Sí, sí, sí*," Rina said. "Thisa moonalight she eesa too hot for those cars' paint." She turned my arm loose and danced around to spin her dress out like a thin-skin umbrella.

"I have a cash customer for tonight with enough dirt in his clothes to wash out for a month." Luisa spun away and over the grass from Eddie to whirl and to act a clown with Rina. She used her hands like a rich owner lady, and said, "I am ashamed to drive my truck over to pick up this laundry, Missis River Girl, and my customer has to walk from Study Butte to the Sammy Nail Ranch when the sun comes up in the morning. Would you walk over with me, River Girl, and assist me in picking up this bundle?"

The crackling sounds of the winter twigs and stems under the girls' feet, the whole muddy baked color of the river's mud, the dried-brick mountains, the sun-dried can-

yons, the gummy, sticky smells of root sap and resins out
of the weeds, all made both of them look darker, prettier,
riper, and sillier. Rina told Luisa, "I, too, like you, ama
on my way to peeck op an old dirty bondle of 'dobe mud."

Ed slapped his hand on my back and said, "Boy, Wood-
sucker, now's th' time ya need yer guitar. Where'bouts is
it at? Knock off a little tune fer th' gals to do their goofin'
off with music."

It was Luisa that sung out,

> Ohh, sweet by and by
> Sweet by and by
> We will have some clean clothes
> Sweet by and by.

Both girls stopped their circle dance to hear Ed say,
"This kerazy idjiot of a cousin of mine went an' left Cleo's
guitar back up yander on th' side of th' hill where we was
a-settin' down saingin'."

"Can't leave it there by that watering barrel," Luisa
told me. "Some of the animals will knock it down and
trample it. Yes, do go and bring it. We'll take fine care of
your kinsman, won't we, Riorina?"

I heard them laughing back in their brush as I ran at
top speed, full power, back up the fifteen little goat, cow,
chicken, sheep, dog, rabbit, and human foot trails that shot
off and wiggled towards the water barrel. I thought what
a dumb, empty-headed, absent-minded trick it was to have
left Cleo's guitar leaning here against this water barrel in
the first place. I strapped the cord around my neck and
picked a soft chord or two. Then I walked my way back
down towards the louder laughings, the joking taking place
in the brushy weed bushes on the Rio Grande's lip.

The bushes, most of them, anyhow, were making a
laughy sound. Female laughs from female bushes. The
male bushes made a fairly respectable groany moan, but it
faded out and turned itself into a little feathery tickling
cough.

I came to my same old spot in the trees where I could
smell the dank wet soggy grass and sunken woodbarks. I
heard, a few feet on my lefthand side, the laughs of the
girls once more.

"Eddie Roosterr." I called out easy enough not to let
the girls hear me. "Hey, Eddie Stinger."

"Mmm?" This drifted through the brush.

" 'Zat you? Eddieye? Ed?"

"Here I am. Down here. Looky down, down here'n th' itchery sticks. Here atcher feet."

I hung the guitar strap over a V-cut limb and took a step backwards to look along the ground. "How come you're down there?"

"Women. Naked women."

"Naked whiches?"

"Naked bitches."

"Dump'd ya here this away?"

"Jest like y' see me."

"What went with yer clothes—yer overhalls?"

"Naked women."

"Bunk'd ya down on these dry leaves like this? I don't quite catch it; I mean, jest don't see quite how."

"Don't try ta see; jist take a free look. Y' mean t' stan' there an' tell me th't ya nev'r did see no naked flesh before?"

"You had on yore thin army longhandlers last night, last time I seen ya."

"I ain't now. No shoes, no socks, no jockerstrop, not a damn thaing."

"Is that them I heard down there a-makin' that splash of a noise?"

"Here, here, anda here!" Rina jumped out from the brush at my back and shoved me to turn me around, then plopped a handful of soggy, wet leaves from the river into my face. "Iffa you are so itching to know how the air ees, I will soona letta you see for your salf. Luisa, halp me."

Luisa threw a double handful into my eyes, and laughed to say, "Here are a few nice little soap bubbles I had left down at my laundry. And here is some more for you. This makes it hard for you to spy on us naked girls, but, after a while, when it gets washed out clean, you can see much plainer."

"I schlubbhmzzkkr. Tha's all."

"Poosha, Luisa!" Rina fell down on her hands and knees at my back. Luisa shoved me for a nine-yard walloper. "Gooda worrk. Fine work, Luisa. Now, go to work onna his clothes. Some-a boys joosta neverr t'ink to changge their clothes, nor washa his face, nor nawthing. Us women always have to maka him t'ink about washday.

Luisa, keep a close eye onna that Addie over there. He may trry joompa halp his buddy. No?"

Luisa drew back a handful of mud towards Ed.

"I'm jesta settin' here," Ed said. "Not sayin' a dern dang word."

I kicked around on the leaves to make them think that I was putting up quite a fight against the undressal, but there was something I liked about Rina sneaking my clothes away, even if my eyes burned and itched with her stinging mud. Ed lent the girls a hand while they fought and wrestled me down the slope and skidded my feet on the ground. I knew I stood on a high grassy patch for a snap, then six hands and six feet knocked me somewhere out into the free air that sneaked over the waters to work our crops and railroads. I was wetter than any wet Mexicano, Indiano, or any other kind of an Ano. My soul was the only thing I could see in the upper spaces while I fell, yelled, whooped, and screamed, as both of my eyes were out of business and stung with mud. I went down into the water just as far as its muds would allow, and kicked and scrambled off the oozy, leafy bottom away from those old, cold graveyard sticks and waterlog muds. I shook my head at the surface and tried to see the three pushers along the weedy bank, but the shadows were too dark and the moon too drunk and spinnery. Laughs again, that was all I heard. Cackles, scroobles, chuckles, slappings, poundings, and yelps, ohos, ahas, heavy breathing, stumbling, rolling. The whole brush sounded like it was full of laughing parrots and laughing mocky birds. I swum on my back and washed my eyes with handfuls of water, then grabbed hold of a long brush root and pulled up as close to the grassy bank as I could. I heard the splashing of Rina and Luisa as they rinsed the worst of the sunbaked dirt out of our clothing.

Up the river towards the moon I could see a pair of old tangly water trees caught full of logs and limbs of a small drift. Luisa and Rina stood barefoot on the loggy limbs and swashed the dirty clothes around in the water. The moon made the old logs the same fishy color as their skin. I let my toes float up to the top of the water and drift downstream in the slow, mopey current. My root was muddy slick, but still holding. I splashed a handful of water into my hair and rubbed my face as clean as I could. Eddie made a running high jump and took a big preacher's

seat that blistered his rumps. He yowled in the weeds, in
the air, in the water, and going down and floating back
up to the top again. He swam upstream on his back,
spouted water, and told me, "Blooghh! Dear cousin, I never
did see no hand laundry th't operates quite as rough as
this'n here. D'jou?"

"Little rough," I told him. I never had seen Eddie do
any swimming before, so I paid close mind to how good he
handled his bad arm. "Hope they ain't as rough on th'
duds as they are on th' customers. Perty fair swimmin',
there, Cousin Edricks."

"Wimmin? They're pertier'n jist fair." Ed used his
crippled hand like a stiff oar to paddle up against the
current.

"Swimmin'," I kidded, "not wimmin. By George, cousin,
if I was ta grab up a handaxe an' slit yore skull open ta take
a good look at yore brain, all we'd git ta see would be jist
a big thick bunch o' naked females a-dancin' in an' out
like road-runners."

"Mebbe ya c'n tell me a little somethin' better ta fill my
brains up with."

"Nawp. Cain't think of nothin' no better."

"All we'd find in yores if'n we busted it open with a
ball-beam hammer w'd be jest, jest a little pair of Riorina's
tits, an' a coupla hips a-wigglin' like Mama's wild plum
jelly. Why ain'tcha out here swimmin' with th' wimmin,
Ladies' Man?"

"I'm a-layin' over here waitin' fer them ole logs, see?
I'm gonna jest lay up here'n draink the water see, as it
floats from her down here ta me. Shee?"

"I'm a-sheein'." Ed waded out and stood on the other
bank. He looked back towards the girls upstream, yelling
at them, "Yeehoo! I c'n always tell my gran'kids that I
hunted fer gold plumb clean over inta Ole Maixico."

"Might tell 'em plumb," I yelled back, "but y' cain't say
clean."

I lost sight of the girls for a minute, then saw each one
pick up an armful of our washing and walk away through
the brush. I trailed their laughs all down along in the
bushes to that same little spot where Eddie and myself took
a dobbing and a dumping and a stripping.

I heard Rina ask us, "Boys. Do you hear me? Boys?"

"Yeahhm."

"We're lissenin'. Talk."

"Luisa, she ees hanging your t'ings on-a thesa same place where you hong op Cleo's *guitarra,* savvy?"

"Savvy."

"Iffa you lose your heads tonight, see, you cannota remember thissa boosha here de broosha, eyekay?"

"Hokaye."

"We'll go look in th' first early daylight."

"Iffa your lose your heada so badda that you cannotta remember your name-a, please t'innk off thisa little boosha inna the broosha."

"Hey, gals, is they any of them there wild *banditos* out there 'n that broosha th' booshy?" Eddie joked and ducked his head to shake his hair back into a pompadour. "Looky good."

Rina put on a puffy frog voice to answer back: "Assa long assa your arre witha I, me, Riorina, nonne off thesa *banditos* willa beatta your head. I kissa thee *bandito* down onna de grrass, I poola de triggerr onna hiss peestola. Boom! *Banditos* arre alla gonne."

"Big girl," I told her.

"Verra verra beega." I heard her pound her ribs to brag. "My frranda, Luisa, shee issa verra verra beega, also. Beega inna herr hipsa. Here. Feel. Anda leestan. We arre botha so beeg thatta we wonder if the river issa beeg enoff to holda us. Say?"

"You girls come ahead an' take a chance. Dive in an' see me sometime."

"Here I amma." Rina splashed water enough over my head to strangle the words in my mouth. She came up to the top on her back, kicked her feet in my face to strangle me even worse, and laughed, "Thissa issa I, me, Riorina. I gass you know your name. Ha ha!"

Another chug of the water up the grass a few steps let me know that Luisa had finished her clothes-hanging, and had dropped in to see the fun. She shook her hair in Eddie's eyes, blinded him, doused his head once, then ducked him down as he tried to come up again. Eddie's words were no more than a gargling sound of spitty water choking in his throat. He just got to say, "Yurrpphm," and she pushed him back to the muddy leaves and rocks down along the bottom. Luisa took off up that current towards the drift of piled logs, and Eddie Stone was no more than a stroke or two behind the foam of her heels. She laughed herself out of wind trying to pull up onto one of the logs, and this gave Eddie his chance to catch up with her. I watched him drag her back down into the water to give her the same number of duckings that she had given to him. I swam out around Rina, then back over to my bank root again to give my ears over to what Luisa and Eddie were saying. Rina swam over to hold onto my root, but both our weights broke the root loose from the bank, which let us float in the moonlight down along close to the northerly bank with the grassblades tickling our noses. We kept as quiet as we could so as to listen, to try to catch the words Eddie said to Luisa.

In amongst all of our limbery floating, our lip licking, and our heavy breathings, I caught Ed's words.

"An' that ain't all," he told her. "You started this here duckin' war, then y' got th' worst end uvvit, see? You started that there oozeldy mud war, an' then y' got th' worst o' that. Ye've gotta work for me now, jest like any other new soljier th's lost a battle. I'm a-herdin' you right out here onta this perty little grassy spot, see, an' I'm a go'nta make you roll cigarettes fer me all night long till my duds gits dry at th' crack o' day. An' I'm a-gon'ta smoke yore cigarettes ev're step o' my way over yonder ta Sammy Nail's Rancho Grandey till I find me old Grampaw Jerry's claim stake. Hyee, heehh, he he he!"

Luisa was a good loser, saying, "Yes, but I have no papers nor any tobacco. And I don't know how to lick a paper with my tongue. Please, sir."

"Here," I heard Eddie tell her. I squeezed Riorina's hand down in under the waters, and shot my ears back again towards Luisa and Ed, to hear, "Here. I'm a-usin' Wood Chuck's terbaccy an' hiz papers, both. Y've gotta roll an' lick up ten fer me, and ten fer Woodypecker. Aw, here, I guess it'll jest about take me th' longest parts of th' night ta show you how to lick y'r blaimed tongue."

CHAPTER 17

LONG HAUL

Rina's little brother beat the daylight there. He ran up just as Eddie and myself were stepping off in our damperish duds. I shook and shivered so much I couldn't hardly look the boy in the face. I saw that he carried in his right hand a package, bundle, or long box which he set down on the leaves at my feet. He told me, "Good monning."

" 'Mornin'. See y' made it. Whatcha packin'? Where-'bouts is yer buddy at? Two of y', I was thainkin'."

"Fine big damn ole crazy mornin'," Ed said to the boy. "What's yor name when y' spell it right? Hmmm?"

"My name ees Leetle Davil, my seester says. She says I geeva you thesa feedle. Jaffrey gotta verra mad. He lefta thesa."

I told him, "Musta been awful riled up, ta drive off 'n' leave this. Where'd he leave it at?"

"In Manuel's house," the boy said. "My frand, Fernando, he papa sicka, he no halp me taka you Sam Nail *rancho*. Nobody ees at Cleo's house today, iffa you lika hotta coffee, say?"

"How long'll some hot coffee take?" Ed shook his pants leg and hobbled around to keep warm. "How much time'll we lose?"

315

"Wan hour we loosa. Cam olda house afterr dark." The kid tried to look as sober as he could. "Langa pull, eighteena miles, bot that ees lika de buzzard flies. We, us, we go up anda down thees way, sam lika leezard."

I danced on the dirt and leaves around Jeff's fiddle case. "I nev'r did need a cup o' hot scaldin' java half as bad as I'm a-needin' it right now, but if she takes a whole hour an' throws us over ta Sam Nail's after dark, I'm a-votin against th' damn coffee."

"Before today ees overr," Little Devil told us, "you are going to ask for somet'ing a leetle cool. Eesa this all you have to carry, joosta Jaff's feedle?"

We followed Little Devil out of our home in the bushy brush, on to the east away from Cleo's little muddy shack, on down the bird and animal tracks and trails. To make Little Devil feel like a big man, we let him carry Jeff's fiddle case. The morning was a fine one with darkly bright colors and an empty blue haze of a sky with hardly a sign of a cloud from horizon to horizon. What few clouds there were, we saw laying over around the top rocks of the saw-blady range of the Chisos. I dropped in back of Ed's heels to bring up the rear end of the line down the slope.

"Them big old mountains over yonder look awful perty, don't they, Eddie, th' way them clouds is pulled down over th' tops?"

"Yeahhp," Eddie told me. He struck his first match to the end of one of Luisa's cigarettes. "Shape o' them peaks ov'r yunder looks like Ole Man Ryoe's face, beddin' down with a whole big batch of wimmin' an' pullin' a big wooly nightgown an' flannely blankets all down aroun' their heads."

"Looks a lot like them there big puffs of 'backer smoke you're shootin' off back here in my face. Ya woodn' part with one of them tailer jobs, woodja? If'n I'm gonna walk, I gotta keep th' nickytine oozin' outta my skin holes so's them grattler skates won't chew me."

" 'Tain't customary." Ed walked at Little Devil's back as we left the hill slope and took up northerly into the first clumps of mixed, confused cactus limbs and leaves. The ground was clear and sandy, no loose grasses nor ankle-sticker weeds, just a carpet rug of pure, tannish-white sand. "But sence they's apt ta be more th'n jest th' one den of them cracklin' hooper snakes a-filin' up their fangers t' stob us dead, well, here's a smokey weed fer ya."

"Muchablige. Which brand is this?" I took the cigarette
and lit up to smoke. "Ya didn' off'r th' Littel Devil up
ahead no smoke. If y' insult 'im th' first thaing in th'
mornin' thissa way, he might lead both of us off up in
some blind canyon, an' starve our fiddle ta death."

"Hey, Leader Devul." Ed tapped the boy's shirt. "Care
fer a smooke? Fag? Siggy?"

"No, t'anks. I never didda smoke verra mocha. I cussa
so loud I don't have to smoke."

I asked him, "Who d'ya cuss at?"

And he said, "My seesster, Riorina."

I said, "I've heard of 'er."

It was Ed that asked him, "Where's Rinnie at today?"

He broke off a twig to nibble on, and told us, "She had
to go witha my papa mama work de cotton, Arrzeenia. She
backa some day. I stay my grandpapa."

I felt like asking him a thousand questions about Riorina,
but then I figured he was too young to understand much
about women, and there was no big rush anyhow, since
we had the whole day. I kept on putting one foot ahead
of the other till I got thirsty and asked Ed ahead, "Did'ja
braing that beer bottle fulla water, Eddie?"

"Got it here'n my assways pocket. Cain'tcha see th'
dern naick of it stickin' out?" Then he asked the boy,
"Where'd ya says Luisa an' Cleo went off to?"

Little Devil shook his head and ducked down to miss a
spider web, saying, "I deedn't hear."

"Hey, Wood Hoss, jist take a look at all o' them big
dern spider webs! Big as dang washtub! Jillionz of 'em!"

"That big black yeller-belly spider there ain't no slouch,
his self. Big's a Texas papershell pecan! Wonder what it
is th't makes alla them webs shine up sa perty an' sa
plain?"

"The dew in the sun," Little Devil told us. "You willa
see alla kinds. Spiders thatta fly onna the wind. Spiders
that have long wheeskers, lika theesa. I willa show you
one spider beeg enoff to catch a bird. Called tarantula."

I told him, "Reg'lar spider country ya got down here."

"If I was a spider, by heck," Eddie said, slapping a
handful of cobwebs off his cap, "this's th' very place I'd
head fer."

"I show you scorpions thissa beeg—beeg assa your
handa!"

"Nawp!" I blew some spider webs off the end of my

nose, "You keep yer stingin' scorpins—keep 'em! I shook
'em outta my duds twicet a day back in Oklahoma, big's
my fainger. I'm shore not a-itchin' ta shake out none no
bigger."

"I couldn't sleep of a night back in Clar'ndon fer the
sounds of them big ole four-incher santypedes," Ed told us.

"Our centipeed issa tan inch longa, anda he walka on
de dead leaf lika—ohh, sam lika burro."

Ed untangled himself from his fourth or fifth web of
the morning. "Them ole santypedes is got big sharp hooker
claws on 'em, like a chicken hawk."

"Yes. Twanty legs."

"An' when he crawls up over yer skin, all o' th' flesh
rots, an' y'r meat falls off'n yer bones. Wheewwee! Gittout
'way fr'm me, you dang ole crazy-headed santypeede, you!
Git! Skat!" Ed put on a shadow boxing show as he walked
along.

" 'S'matter, Eddyroo? Snakes in yer boots already?"

"They's not but three thaings, Woody, th't I cain't live
with. One's tarantulers, another'n izza stingin' scorpeen,
an' t' other'n's a gol-dern santypede. Wow! Boys howdy!
I'd a headed off back up inta Canady 'mongst th' bergs
an' th' icicles, an' slept every night with a nice big pile of
ice under my covers. But nobody didn't let me know 'bout
this here whole country down here bein' crawlin' wild with
tarantulers, an' scorpeens, an' great big ole santypeders
ten inches long. Ta hell with Grampaw's gold mine!" He
fought in the air as he walked along and felt the imaginary
varmints inside his overalls, shirt, and cap.

"Take it easy, Ed boy," I said. "Hell's puppydogs, if
ya'd a tore off up ta Canader, them big fangy timber
wolfs woulda been tossin' yore bones right this mornin'
over the cliffs ta them big shaggy polar bears. Me, I'll take
a chance any old day on a good pocketful o' tarantulers,
or cowardy scorpions, or a good tin plate o' centypedes
an' black coffee any old mornin'."

A red tobacco can dropped out of Ed's shirt pocket and
fell down lid open on the sand. I saw the other eighteen
cigarettes Luisa had rolled up for him. The cigarettes rolled
out of the can and Little Devil stooped down to help Ed
pick them up. Ed showed me one in his fingers, and said,
"Shape of 'em ain't sa much ta brag about, but th' papers
is shore 'nough licked together good."

Little Devil walked far enough ahead of us to miss out

on our talk. I took the chance to ask Ed, "Ahhmm, how'd ya make out las' night? Luisa?"

"I'm jest afraid th't I took a mighty big likin' ta that there little Luisa woomern, Wood Man. 'Fraid so, 'fraid so. How fer'd you drift off down that there river with Rinia?"

I pushed both hands down in my pockets, and said, "How fer? Ohh, we drifted all th' ways down ta the first sandbar."

"Maixico er 'Meric'n side?"

"Mexico."

"No passin' papers?"

"Nope. No nothin'."

"Out very deep?"

"Yeahhp. Deep's it goes."

"Some gal, that there Rinia. Perty as a dang pitcher."

"Yeah. That Luisa of your's ain't no ugly sight."

"Perty as Rinia is—jest perty in different ways, that's all. Wimmen's like this here Ryoe Grandy river out here, Woody; th' waters runs th' deepest where th' ripples lays the stillest. That there Rinia's full o' red-hot fires, an' Luisa, she's nice an' smooth, quiet an' easy-goin'. Man, I'da froze plumb smack ta death las' night, if it hadn't been fer that there Luisa a-thawin' my old bones out."

"What all did you an' Luisa talk about, if it's any of my affairs?"

"Man, sakes alive, they's not anything much we didn't talk about. She soaked ever' saingle word in, just like a sponge drainks water, just like them old hot sands out yonder. I run a gallon of pure honey all over her head. Wimmen eats them kindsa words down 'em like ham an' aigs. Know?"

"I've heard tell."

"I, funny thaing, didn't never believe that I c'd talk that good, Woody."

"You're lots better of a talker, Eddie Stew, than I, me, Woody, ever was."

"I don't know fer dead shore where my words does come from, Woody Eye, but, but I jest lay my mouth open a little bit, an' first thaing I know, I've said too dern much."

"You an' Luisa, ahhm, didja shake han's on any promise?"

"Yeahrpp."

"Sech as?"

"Such as, well, I'm gonna meet 'er ten nights from tonight on that same little spot, an' do some talkin'."

"Fast man."

"How did you do with Little Rinia?"

"Not good as you done."

"No? How come?"

"Aww, I dunno. Tried ta talk 'er outta th' idea she had 'bout traipsin' off acrost Arryzona ta make six bits a day snatchin' cotton bolls."

"Hmmm? But?"

"She had ta go. Figger'd she owed 'er paw an' 'er maw that much."

"Guess that's a fact."

"Told 'er that I'd try my damnest ta locate that mine, an' give 'er whole blame family a good job at decent pay, anyhow."

"I'm a-givin' Luisa an' her folks a job, too, doller an' a haff an hour straight time. Whole bunch of 'em."

"Riorina wrote an address down on one of my cigarette papers, where she'd be a-workin' up in Arizona, said she'd write me back if I'd write her first."

"Didn' do so bad, cousin. What're y' aimin' ta write ta Helly Cat Cliffman?"

"Gotta thaink up sumthin', sumthin' good an' sumthin' fast."

"Shore have. 'S best, though, write 'er an' git th' dern job over with. Spill it out on 'er apern. 'Twon't kill 'er. Hell Cat's too smart a girl fer that."

"She'll jest go ta that country barn dance hall an' snag 'er a feller an' fergit alla 'bout me. 'Tain't no easy job, though, Ed. You're gonna hafta help me out with th' words. You talk 'em an' I'll write 'em."

"Pull y' out all th't I can. Ain't a-sayin' how much that's a-gon'ta be." The tracks under the brush of thousands of birds and reptile animals kept Eddie's mouth as wide open as his eyes. He asked Little Devil, "Say, lead'r boy, ain't them awful big dog tracks?"

"Thot isn't any dog track. Thot iss a cat's—*sí, los gatos.*"

"That's a paw track, awright," I told Ed. "Damn thaing's big as my hand. I wouldn't be wantin' him up on my lap this mornin' b'fore brekfust. Mountain lion? Cougar track, L'il Devul?"

"*Sí,* mountain lion—cougar," the boy told us, walking on ahead. "They sneak across the river here where the water is notta deep. I have watched tham inna their caves inna thee Santa Rosa Cleefs. Lots off tham come to the canebreaks to chase the deer anda the rabbit anda to catcha birds."

"Ohhh."

"You no have ta be 'fraid. The mountain lion willa no come thisa way, because there are too manny rattlesnakes."

I brushed some more floating webs out of my hair and eyes, and asked him, "Hey Devul, what's that there noise I hear, out yonder thrashin' aroun' in th' brushes? Hearit?"

"Sounds like a whole herd of them big paddyfoots a-chasin' in after us," Ed said.

"Notta any beega *gatos*. Those are beega bonchez off birds flurring their wings. They are as loud as wilda ponies, butta they are only quails. They hitta their wings op onna the brusha, see, to leadda you fram the eggs anda the leetle wans."

"Be a hard job, men, ta gitta bead onna quail in all of this stickery brush. Shoot forty-'leven times, an' still miss 'em," I said.

"Thot issa why they fly here to live."

"Jillions of 'em." Eddie watched and listened. "I'd lots druther fer it ta be them quails out a-fannin', than to be that same number of long-fanged mountain lions."

Little Devil whipped up our pace to move along faster. After a while he stopped to wait for us, and pointed down at a rocky, dried-up sink hole about twenty feet across. "Here ees a salt lake," he told us. "Eet ees a leetle one, bot a beeg one looks the same."

"Dead-lookin' hole," I agreed.

"Eeet eesa not dead," the kid said. "Eet leeves anda grows."

"Grows?" Eddie looked around the outer rim of the dried, salty, needly crystals of a yellowish-white color. "This thaing's growin'?"

"I putta my steecks down—see, over there—three years ago. The lake ees seex inches beeger now on every side."

"How deep's it run?" Eddie reached down to run a handful of salt dust through his fingers.

"How deepa? Me, I no know."

Eddie crawled on his hands and knees to pat the hard top of the icy-looking crystal pond. "Hey!" he yelled. "It's a-crackin' down, boys! I'm a-sainkin' down! C'mere 'n' give me a hand. I'm a-goin' down an' down. Pull me!"

Little Devil grabbed one of Ed's shoes, and I pulled on the other one.

"Don'ta kicka."

"Ye're awready out, see?"

"I forgot to tella you thot eet eesa hard onna the top and verra, verra soft onna the bottom."

"I found that out fer my own self." Ed brushed his clothes off and said, "Let's be a-gittin' outta here."

The boy stood up on a pile of rocks to tell Ed, "Iffa thesa rattlesnakes hear you making soch a beeg noise, they will alla crawl outta fram their dans to see what ees going on."

Ed cleared his throat. He pulled his cap down tighter and said, "First damn snattlerake th't wiggles his tail at me, I'm a-snappin' his dang head off an' a-spittin' it back in his face."

A loud covey of quail flew out of the brush and knocked Eddie to the ground backwards as they sailed over his head. He got up, dusted himself off again, and took up the rear position in line as we walked on across a stretch of bareback, bony rocks.

The rocks were just as bareskinned and bony a few hours later at the little craggy place on a slight hump where Little Devil sat Jeff's fiddle case down on a benchy ledge. He told us, "Thiss ees where we do our eating."

"This here ole beer bottle of water's all th' eatin' we're gonna be doin'." Ed snapped his cap against his knee.

"Hey, Eddie," Little Devil said, "you flippa de feedle case open. Meester Woods, you come runna with me, thissa way. We backa soon."

I trotted down the grade after him, skipping over loose rolling rocks the size of your fist or your head, that lay on top of a whole young mountain of flints that never grew quite so big. I tried to see how the boy skipped along over the shifty flints. When I missed my longest leap and took a thirty-foot nosedive, I decided to just give it up. Little Devil walked over and told me, "You musta notta let your foot come down so hard on the rocka. Taka yourr foot offa joost before itta start to weegle. Hurry. We only have to go to those bushes down there. You savvy de preeckly pears?"

"Prickledy pears? Oh, yeah, but I couldn't eat 'em. Too many dagger needles."

He reached out his hands, played around with the thorns, laughed at me, and said, "We joosta peeck the apples, see, up there? Those red little things? Peecka them eassy orr they willa stinga your fingers. Oho, I be gladda whan I tella you tonight gooda-bye over at the Sam Nail place. You no know nawthing. Here, I peecka."

He loaded his shirttail full of the little red, thorny apples. Walking up the hill ahead of me, he skinned a few of them and sucked them. I had a hard job just to climb back up the hill. My pockets were full of the apples which, by the time I got back to Eddie, were smashed into a prickly heat sauce. The little needly daggers worked all into my shirt and overalls, and set fire to my skin all over my body.

Eddie motioned over the open fiddle case and said, "Well, chuck is on. This here fiddle case had six torpedoes inside it. What'cha got?"

"Cactoos apples," Little Devil told him.

"Daggerweed sauce," was all I could say. I laid all my bashed-up cactus apples on the rock by the tortillas. "Are they any good, Little Devil, when they're all squoosh'd up this way?"

"Joosta throw those leetle skins out, see, anda dippa the torrtilla down lika thees anda eata the seeds. Verra, verra good. You trry."

"Say, Devul," Ed ate and asked him, "who was it put them torpeders in Jeff's fiddle case f'r us?"

"Ohh, those weemin." The kid finished his last bite, "Cleo. Anda Riorrina. Anda Luisa."

I said, "Well, gimme th' fiddle case, there, Eddie Roo, I'm full's I c'n stick. Better be walkin', fr'm th' looks of that sun up yonder."

"I c'd eat down a barrel fulla them prickledy apples. Hate ta waste 'em. Walk aheadd on. I'll trot up an' ketch ye."

I trailed Little Devil around through some tall rocks the size of two story buildings and up a sharp, steep climb. "How fer'd we come this mornin' so fer?" I asked.

"Almost seven miles." He dug on up ahead, using his hands and feet to brace his climbing. On a flat path he sat down on his haunches, and said, "Anda thesa naxt 'levenn miles are the worst. We are betterr to wait for Addie."

I opened up Jeff's fiddle case and took out the fiddle to play an old dancy tune known as the "G Breakdown," yelling down at Eddie, "Don't git lost off, Ed! Jist foller the fiddle notes in amongst them rocks, an' ya'll find th' right way ta crawl."

Little Devil stood up and looked away towards the Chisos. "Hey, looka where I point. See, thosse blankeets of clouds are going op, anda you can see a leetle patch off the snow there onna the north side off that mountain. We call eet the Slick Rock."

I looked where he pointed. "Shore is. Tha's a bed o' snow, all right. Looks awful funny, don't it, ta stan' hyere 'n' look down in th' valley an' see sa much volcano ashes, 'n' look on up a bit of a ways an' see all that big ole canyon full o' snow. Where'bouts does th' snow's water run, back off down th' easterly side?"

"No. Itta feeds your grandfather's reever. Rougha Run."

Ed walked up at our backs to put his arms around the boy and me, just as the kid said the words "Rougha Run." Eddie said, "I've heared Paw mention that Rough Run Canyon a million times. Where's th' actshul canyon?"

"There ees no Rougha Run Canyon."

"No kind of a canyon call'd by th' name of Rough Run?"

"Do you see over to your lafta hand, a leetle to the north off that snow?"

"Yeah, I see."

"That leetle valley goes across fram the north to the south. We samtimes call that de Rougha Ron Reeverr. Eet goes in witha thee Terlingua Creek after a few miles. The waters run verra verra rough. The river beda she never getsa more de eight, ten feet deep inna de rocks, and never more de honderd feeta wide til she get down near Study Butte. We samtime call thot whole river bed the Rougha Run Valley. I wade, climb uppa down that river many times. No canyon."

"Okay! Valley, then. Grampaw Jerry's silver vein's somewheres near th' head of it." Our flat path took a steady, slow upgrade for the next few miles, and was very easy walking. The long, slim ridge that our trail was on was too big, really, to be called a hill. In any flatland country this hill would be called a mountain. Here, bellied up so close to the western shanks of the Chisos range, and to the upper humps of the Christmas Mountain range, a few miles to our north, our hill was a fine walker's hill. I wished to my soul that my grandpa's mine was on this very hill. There was just enough magnet rock in the melts of that hill to tickle the irony flakes in my blood veins. It lifted my face up on a beeline with the farthest horizon.

Little Devil braced himself atop a pile of rocks and pointed his hand north and easterly, to tell us, "Iffa you wish to see your old adobe house, stand up here anda look."

Eddie scrabbled up, looked, and said, "Clear as a crystal. Mmmm, mmm. Looks jest like a clay matchbox to me. Mount up here, Wooden, take a free peek."

I wiggled up alongside their elbows and saw it. "Makes a real perty sight, if ya wanta know sumpin'. How many rooms?"

"Two."

"How fer's it down to th' thaing?" Ed asked.

"Four, fi' miles. Queecka walka."

"I don't see our ole truck nowhere down there 'roun' that 'dobe."

"Truck jest could be drug in aroun' on th' backside of th' derned house, in under that there little ole scrubbery shade tree. Fair-size cottonwoods jumpin' up there back of th' house, ain't they, Devull?"

"Yiss. There is a fine water spring there. All of the animals fight to drinka that water. Let's be moving. Mabbe you peopul have de breakdown inna de trock. No?"

"Could shore be." We trotted along down a slow, easy, curving slope on the path. After about a mile, Little Devil told us, "Look down there to the southa. That issa the rancha house, the *hacienda,* off Sam Nail. There, down where you see thosa bigga trees. Eet iss only about three more miles over to the old adobe. Ron fast. I beata."

"Whut's alla them piles of color'd ashes, as if trucks'd dumped 'em out?" Ed asked.

"Volcano creestals, or samt'ting."

We trotted along the flat bed of a valley, coming, every fifty or a hundred yards, to a roundish-topped stack of these crystals. Each stack was a clear, salty, bright color, shiny in the sun. Each looked to be from six to twelve feet high. A pile of yellow, a mound of snaky green, several shades of orangy colors, as well as purply blues, red, sandy and chocolate browns, and umber, with all their grays in betwixt and between. Around each mound of glittery crystal was tough iron grass. I noticed several goats and cattle nipping all around at the grass. Little

Devil slowed it down in order to give me and Ed a good chance to look things over.

"Hot lookin' damn-blame thaings," Eddie said. "Look like they're jest right frash out of some big oven somewheres, don't they? All sech perty colors, to boot."

"Looks like somethin' from some other world," I said. "All crazy."

"They grow oppa."

"Grow?" Ed asked. "How?"

"Joosta poosha oppa fram de ground."

"How did they come to be such perty colors?" I asked him.

"Aska the son, notta me."

I did ask him, "What're they good for?"

"For maka de peepol comma look, aska seely quastion. We comma fasta trippa thissa day, sí, no? You two fella gooda fast walkers. I say we ron bigga race fram here oppa to that old adobe *hacienda,* hoh? Go, sheepy, go!"

Little Devil ran along a cattle trail till he hit a road which was new enough, at least, to make good fresh dust fly. We panted after him. He rounded a sharp bend that led through a half a mile of the thickest brush we had seen on our long haul today. He yelled and jumped, waved his arms around, skipped, jigtrotted, and leaped from side to side along the ruts till he dodged down under an old stretch of barbed-wire fencing. He shot his dust up once more as he ran from the old fence up across a cleared and trampled yard to the rotted-out south door of our new mud home.

Ed pulled a sneak on me as I got stuck in the barbs, and beat me to the door to win second ribbon. To be good and late, to have some excuse for losing the races, I poked along and acted like a crippled cow with a sad limp. I yelled ahead to ask, "Any sign of 'em? 'Round out'n back there?"

"Nope. No see."

"There eesa not anybody innaside. Joosta de olda stove whicha eesa stilla warm. Oh, bot thot old stovve itta never does gitta verra cold. Here ees a leetle poppydog. Hey, look! You can't sleep inna this east room."

"Why not?" Ed stuck his head in the door to ask.

"Because it issa alla full oppa with Mister Nail's beehives."

I walked in at Ed's back, asking, "Bee which?"

"Buzzeldy bees has done went an' jumped our cussed claim," Ed growled.

"Helluva lookin' damn stove, hain't she? Legs all flew to hell an' busted. Them flat rocks does a fair job holdin' up its belly. Wonder if yer pa an' Jeff was here an' gone on back to Pampy, an' left us here in the Rough Run Valley with nothin' 'cept a squally fiddle an' a busted cookstove with a few little warm coals in it."

"Mebbe the bees stung 'em out," I told Eddie.

"No," Little Devil said, "iffa they wass here, they would leava some cans, some tire tracks. Bot outside I see nawthing. Mabbe they turna troock back atta Study Butte anda drive back to Terlingua. Hey, puppy, tella me, didda you smella anybody come here inna de bigga, bigga troock? I see. You weegle your tail, no. I theenk I call you Pedro."

I looked the room over, and said, "Wiggy wiggle. I jest wonder where'bouts I heard that before. I know somebody that c'n outweegle you, little Pederokus. Hey, Devil, wonder who nailed them ole rotten boards up over alla them windows?"

"Sam'body."

"I'm a-rippin' them boards down. Keep out th' sun, keep out th' breeze, keep out th' nice, perty scenery." I shoved my shoulder against the old one-inch pine boards nailed onto the southerly window. "I wanta see out."

"Whan the bigga cougar lion cams tonight, I woulda be verra glad for to see some more nails inna those boards."

"Cougar comes?" Ed dusted the north wall with an old weedy broom of oily bush tied and wound with shoestring bark. He reached up along some cracks towards a few spidery webs, and asked, "Where?"

"Here. To the yard."

"Which yard?" I asked him.

"To thisa water spring to fight offa the skunk."

"Skunk?" Eddy swept the ash-covered floor with strokes of his broom not quite heavy enough to move any of the ashes in either direction. "What'n th' name of heck's pups would a dern skunk be a-doin' out here a dragassin' aroun' in my privet yard?"

"Drrinking." The boy sat on the floor to hold his puppy on his lap. "Waterr fram thot spring. Out where you willa carry your buckets off water frram."

Eddie circled the room. "That dern-blame water c'n turn

to volcano crystals 'fore I, me, Prospector Moore, lugs any damn old britches-down waters up outta that spraing."

"The stink water ees not inna thot spring. That ees the besta spring of clear water inna all off these mountains. Where you walk away, Meester Woodbox?"

"Jest outside ta git away fr'm th' racket." I walked out. "Looks as how ya've already called th' border boys down on us, Eddie! We've gotta nice little Plymouth sedan out here, 'bouta 1930 model, ta deal with. Jist one man. Ahemm."

I leaned back against the south wall to look up and down the medium-sized gentleman wearing a Johnny B. Stetson white hat, nice-fitting pair of tight corduroy breeches, and mail-order cowman boots, who walked towards our house with a bow-legged gait. I spoke, "Howdy do."

He touched the wide brim on his hat and spoke. "Good day."

"Nice day we had."

"A very likable day this one was. It's nearly gone." He walked up to shake my hand and to tell me, "No, I don't happen to be, as you say, the officers. Nail is my name, Sam Nail. Your name is?"

"Woody. Glad ta see ya."

"Mister Woods. I the same. I heard you fellows raising a bit of a good time here in the old adobe, so, being on my way to mail a few letters at my box, figured I ought to come over and tell you where to trap."

Eddie and Little Devil walked out with the puppy under their feet to shake hands with Mr. Nail and tell him their names.

"We ain't a-trappin'," Ed said. "We're grubbin' a stake."

"Prospecting, then?" Sam asked us.

"Tryin' ta spot an ole claim that my gran'paw, Jerry P. Guthrie, located right in through here somewhere, oh, back along about the year of 1902."

Sam smiled. "Oh, I see. Way, way back there! Well, these rocks are certainly full of something that ought to do somebody, somewhere, some good. Two trapper boys packed out from here this afternoon early."

"The fire ees warm inna the stove." Little Devil chased the dog around over the yard, and asked Sam, "Didda you see any troocka drive op thisa house yesterday or today?"

Sam grinned at the puppy and said, "Nope. Just saw those

trapper boys drive off. They left that little doggy here. I can't use him over at my house; my wife is hatching off some broods of baby chickies. You need a good smart fighting watchdog? Keep him. Keep him. He'll make a noise when the cougars come to sniffle in at your windows, here."

"Thanks. Seegaratte?" Eddie said. "How's th' minin' laws run down in here?"

"Not much to them. I can't keep you from digging on my land, because this whole country down in here, three whole counties, are set aside under a special mining law that gives you the right to come in here and to dig. One eighth of everything you dig up belongs to me, and the smelter takes that for me. I have picks, I have shovels, I have bedding, quilts, blankets. No canned goods, but I can keep you in all of the meat you'll need. These rabbits around here, you can whistle them up into your skillet if you just hold your lid open and keep it good and greasy. Same with squirrel, quail, pheasant, turkey, wild guineas, deer, goat, and antelope. I strung a flagtail deer up in that little wooden house out back of here for those two trapper boys to eat on, but they left out before it bled very good. You boys are most welcome to knife that deer up and fry him. I dropped him just up there along that high slick rocky cliff just about this same time yesterday. He's a good, fat, sassy, fresh flagtail, right enough. All kinds of turnips, okra, radishes, peppers, and salad greens, that grow all over my house and yard over there, almost wild; you're more than welcome to come pick, pull, and dig. If you want to send mail, leave it in my mailbox and it'll go out. I've still got to drive my daughter's school tutor over the pass tonight, so I'll see you gents early bright in the morning. Good day."

Sam climbed up into his car to wheel and to whirl away to the northward towards his tin-plated, hand-painted, red-flagged mailbox on a section-line road about a good mile from where we stood to watch him.

The two trapper boys had left a few chunks of mesquite root, old limbs, and odd firewood stacked by the front door, on top of which Eddie and I threw a few woodsticks we rustled from the brush. We filled Ed's brown beer bottle with water in the cottonwood spring while Little Devil and Pedro smelled out a dozen various shapes of claws and tracks for us. We traced the trickle of the spring water a

hundred yards to the north, where it spilled down a twelve-
foot cliff of pure sands and ran along the bottom of a gully
wash ten or fifteen feet wide, for as far as we trailed it.
The steep, sandy banks on both sides, the tracks of barefoot animals the size of my hands and fingers, caused us to
run back to the adobe to put our looking tour off till daylight got brighter. We filled up our pockets with forty or
fifty hunks of quartzy rock with webs of dark ores spread-
ing out in different shapes, and brought them back to the
house. We could hardly wait to find out more about them,
specially whether they was valuable, so we stoked up the
fire in the old stove and put a dozen ore chunks on top of
it to heat, to see if gold or silver would melt out.

It was away along after dark that we heard voices in the
distance and ran out and down the rutty road to meet the
old dim lights of our old T truck. The motor was taking a
vacation and a rest, and so were the two rear tires, which
had caused Jeff and Papa to pay an Indian fellow to hitch
two heavy-meated, long-eared desert burros onto the front
end to pull the truck up to the side of the adobe bee house.
I could see they'd had plenty of trouble.

CHAPTER 18

BIG VISIT

Pedro barked as he chased Little Devil down the old road
to meet the truck. They piled into the back and Pedro
barked even louder and gladder to stick his nose out over
the endgate to sniff at wild eyes which watched him from
out in the dark.

I hoped Jeff had got over being sore at us for goofing off
to work with Luisa and Rina and leaving him and Papa to
get the truck over here—though after all, they could have
waited for us. I trusted Jeff would be so glad to get here
that he'd forget about yesterday. I hid his fiddle in the east
room under the beehive boxes.

I heard Papa ask Jeff out by the truck, "I, ah, do you
think there's any use to try to do any work on that motor
tonight, Jeff?"

"It's that magneto brush," Jeff said. "Be a hell of a job
in broad daylight, much less after dark. Hey, Muler Man,
how much do we owe yore booroes fer pullin' us? Ye
goin' t' drive back t' yer place tonight, er bun'le in here
with us?"

"My burros need four pesos. I sleep here. My road essa
verra dark."

"How much is four pesos?" Jeff asked him.

331

"Two. *Dos dólares.*"

I heard the harness buckles unsnap and fall to the ground. Papa and Jeff walked in the door with both arms loaded with bedding. Papa looked like an everyday mechanic coming in from his job, greasy and dirty. He asked in the low flicker of the light from the stove cracks, "My, my, where have you jellybeans hidden your lantern?"

"Make y'seff mizerbul," Ed nodded over a double handful of his ore chunks. "Take a seat. Don't make any too much noise, though, 'cause I'm right in th' middle uf some awfurl big prospectin'. Ain't got too much time to waste on trampy visitors. I'm a-cookin' off my first batch of ore chunks."

"Us ladies' men don't need too much of a light, anyways, to do our jobs by. You bums got good money to pay f'r yer beds?" I asked them. Then I said, "Don't walk sa heavy ov'r there, Jeff, ye're a-shakin' our meltin' rocks off of our stove."

Little Devil and Pedro stayed out in the yard to talk to the driver of the burro team.

Jeff tried to jar the floor under his feet with a heavy push of the soles of his shoes, and the dirty ashes were so loose on top that they slid away and he sat down hard on the floor. He jumped up looking fighting mad and I could see he had had a rough day with all his troubles and worries about the truck and having to pay the burro skinner two dollars, on top of me, I, Woody, and Eddie taking off like we done.

Jeff swiped his hand acrost the top of the stove, telling us, "This is no hangout fer grubbystake hoboes, boys, sorry! This's th' main sher'ff's office. What's all o' these dad-rotted ole black smokery sooty chunks o' rocks here? Off'n my stove, off'n my stove lid! I'm aimin' fer ta boil my belly up some good old spring-water coffee! You damn nugget bums, gitcher grabblin' goldern ole smoky soot rocks off'n th' top o' my coffee stove, please!"

As Jeff pushed out the door to shake his bedding in the night air, I told him, "We live here just th' some as you do."

"Ahhh," Jeff shot back at us, "I'll take th' whole crazy shebang of ye—c'mon out 'n' jump me. If that truck'd fire on two damn cylinders, I'd load my stuff up on top of it an' drive off 'n' let ye lay here. C'mon."

Papa trotted out of the house and stood back rooster

fashion, barefist style, wide-legged, flat-footed on the dirt by Jeff's feet. Before Jeff could drop his bedroll on the ground and throw up an arm guard, Papa shot three or four short trippy hammer six-inch ear jabs to Jeff's head. Jeff ducked backwards, winding his arms about his head like the blades of a haysickle, so as to knock Papa's fists upwards away from his ears. Jeff felt a hard straight wagon-tongue jab in his belly button. He took another one an inch on up higher, over his solar plexus windbag. The next drive that Papa laid in caused Jeff to throw his jaw open for air. Two lefty bare-knuckle hooks found that jaw of Jeff's hung open.

"Why, you didn't even find me. I thought, at long last, I'd discovered a good serious sparring partner. Here, now, I've come at you entirely too fast. Let's slow it down, let's stop dead still and start all over," Papa said.

We all stepped out to lean back against the adobe wall in the light of the early moon to see the exhibition of fistic arts and cultures. I told everybody, "Papa's breakin' a bone in his fingers every lick he lands on Jeff. Hey, Jeff, you're up a perty bad tree ov'r there, if y' ask me."

Jeff could not guess how serious Papa was. To show that the whole boxing match was good-natured, he joked, "Heck fires, Charlie, I'm not a-wantin' ta skin ye none. I nev'r did study them boxin' less'ns like you studied 'em. I'm a bett'r hand ta wrastle ya down th'n I am t' box with ya. Le's wrastle it out. Huhh? I'm half out o' wind. Wrastle?"

"You wrestle and I'll box," Papa told him. "I've not even started to breathe good yet. Don't hold back. Let's go. You wrestle, bear hug me, choke me, strangle me, rooster me down, butt me with your head, do anything you want, and I'll stick to my jabs, crosses, uppercuts, and hookers, dear brother, half-brother of mine. Come on."

Jeff shot out a long hard poke that covered six feet in the night air, landing solidly to the offside of Papa's nose. He threw a similar haymaker up from his kneecaps. The third came from Jeff's lower left hand, an uppercut which Papa did not look at. Papa tilted his head one quarter of an inch away and the pull of Jeff's longshot threw his whole body out of balance with the world. Papa caught his fist in Jeff's rib while Jeff's feet were an inch off the ground. Jeff came towards Papa beating his fists in the wind like a frailing machine, but there was a loophole somewhere which our naked eyes could not see. He was so out of wind that it took him a few moments to shake his head back straight, or to recall why he came down here to these mountains in the first place.

"Enough for tonight? Or do you want to see how I do when I use both of my fists instead of just the one you saw?"

Jeff spoke as he regained his footing and sat down in the doorway to rest. "It's a good thing we're just a-playin', Charlie—good thing we're just a-playin'. I c'd still jump up fr'm here an' break ever' bone in yore body. Just a little short on wind, that's all."

"You can arise at your own convenience, sire, and come at me in any manner best suited to your build and character. I will be very pleased and highly glad to furnish the bones, any time that you feel the desire to try breaking a few." Papa did a little shadowboxing. "Arise and shine."

"Too winded," Jeff laughed. "Gimme a little minute er two ta git a lungfulla air, an' I'll crackle yore ole naickbones like it was one of Aunt Maude's fryin' chickens."

"You ain't a-runnin' in none o' them old boomer town whores now, Jeffyroo," I told him with my hands jammed in my pockets, "ner roundin' up no doped-up jakeyleg gambler."

"Don't blab your mouth off so smart." Papa walked back a few steps, rubbing his bruised knuckle bones in his palms. "I just happen to be the most scientific whore-jailer that Jeff has encountered this far in his career."

"It's them little old bitty two-dollar fines, Wood Hossie, that brought our ole T truck out here, that brung us off down here with a few beans in our guts. I used my pay an' fees ta feed my wife on, an' ta board an' keep yore old daddy here on, an' to pay th' bills fer five er six females of yore close relatives. Go ahead an' take their old, dirty dollar bills back up them old blind stairs steps, if you want ta pay 'em back. I use them dollars to make a lick er two more sense than them old whores off down in them flea-bit flats. You've ben a-pokin' at me this whole trip, this whole month er two, Woodrow, an' it's got to stop."

"There are higher ideals, and many higher flights of human horse sense than your words reflect, Jeffseefus." Papa looked at Jeff's bedroll on the dirt. "But, as the days pass, these more noble ideas will take the form of conversation between us. However, for tonight, Jeff has told us a very understandable and conceivable point of view. He has given us several fine and good reasons for his blunt, straight, direct way of acting, dealing, and coping with the problem of, Who maketh best use of our legal tender?"

I tried to show Jeff that my feelings had risen a degree to the warmer side by wrestling with him in such a way that he threw me off my feet and onto the dirt on my hip muscles. Eddie danced out and squared off to stick out his best hand to dare Jeff to grab ahold for a squeezy pull. I was down on my knees when Jeff took a spill with Eddie, laughing. Little Devil was saying, "Eddie, you bigga strong. Maka Jaffa doompa downna. Ha hah. *Sí* no?"

The muley burro driver said, "Surre t'ing." The pooch hound, Pedro, snapped at something in the dark towards where the burros made a scared snort. A few twigs and pebbles crackled, and we saw a big whitish cowman's hat bobbing up in our direction.

"Finest time in the world for exercise." It was Mr. Nail again. "Night air even makes me wish to join in on your good times. Of course, I'm far too brittly in my joints for that sort of thing, but I always feel young again when I see people enjoying some such a good game as yours, here. Howdy, all."

"Folks, this here's Mister Sam Nail," Eddie said. "Mister Nail, meet Jeff, our best fiddle sawyer. An' Charlie, Jeff's whole brother, almost. Mule driver out here'n th' dark; his name I nev'r did git ta hear."

The fast Indian Spanish name missed my ears, but Mr. Nail shook hands with everybody around.

"I brought you fellows a long-blade knife to cut your flagtail up with. Pocket knives are not much *bueno* for a deer."

"Men, I'm a tellin' ye fer a fact"—Jeff shuffled in his tracks—"I'm so long-gone an' empty-gut hongry th't my mouth is a-mailin' post cards, picture cards of sumthin' ta eat, away off down ta my vacated belly. Han' me th' butch'r knife. Thanks. Whereabouts have ya got any flaggytailer hung up? Lead me."

Sam Nail showed Jeff and me how to cut a ham leg off the deer in the little back shed. There was no east wall on the shed, and the deer swung by a wire to one of the rafters. Papa helped Eddie sort his ore chunks back up on the window ledges, and set a few of the rocks around a warming skillet on the stove. Little Devil and the burro man carried some cases, plates, and bedclothes off the truck

and into the room. Little Devil showed them how to take
a few of the beehive boxes and to use them on the floor to
raise our pallets up out of the dirty ashes. Pedro trailed at
everybody's heels, and acted as brave as he knew how,
sniffing at each can they opened, and smelled into Papa's
granite mixing pot as he stirred up a frying batch of cornmeal mush.

I carried the deer leg in the door as Jeff walked in talking to Nail. The burro driver took the longblade knife out
of Jeff's hand and sliced the deer ham down on a beer
case. While our noses, eyes, lips, and ears moved towards
the fresh-killed meat, Jeff stepped outside to take a look
around over the truckbed for his panther fiddle.

Papa asked out the door, "Looking for something special, or just for the fun, Jeffie?"

"Lookin' fer m' red fiddle case," Jeff said, "B'dern if I
c'n see hide n'r hair of it. You seen it? Anybody in there
seen m' fiddle?"

"I've not seen it at all, not even while we loaded the
truck back at Study Butte," Papa told Jeff. "Have you
found it yet?"

"Hmmm, funny damn thing." Jeff threw the few little
things around on the bed of the truck. He leaped down,
rummaged in the cab, tossed out the cushions, lifted the
hood and looked over the old dead motor. " 'Tain't down
hyere und'r th' damn truck, hmm. D'ja carry mye fiddle
in th' house jest now, any of ye? Mmm?"

"Hummh-uhmm." I shook my head around the room.

The jinny tramp shook his old raggy clothes and motioned, outside, *"No música, no música."*

Little Devil shook his head, "I, me, Leetal Davil, no."

Jeff butted his way through the room to run his eyes
around in every corner. He kicked cases, boxes, bedrolls,
and beehives hard enough to turn them about, but easy
enough to appear in a good humor in front of Mr. Nail.
He stumbled out the door backwards and tossed things
topsy-turvy around the truck. "Ahh, Charlie, when'd y' see
m' fiddle last? Say?"

"Sitting so nice and pretty up in the corner of Estrella's
house. I've not seen it since you and Woodrow played
there night before last, Jeff." Papa fried his cornmeal mush
patties in the skillet.

Jeff yelled in from out in the yard, "Y' mean t' say, th't
I took yore ole no-good guitar, Woodrow, an' loaded it on

th' truck sa damn careful, an' left my fiddle a-settin' there 'n that corner by their wall?"

"Crazy trick," I told him, winking around.

"But it looks that way to me." Papa stacked his mush patties on a hot tin plate by the stovepipe, took a few slices of meat out of the burro driver's hands, and looked around the walls to see if he could spot the fiddlecase. "It sure must be back at that other place. Too bad, too sad."

Jeff walked in and took a seat on a beer case, too tired to say a word. He grumbled out, "No wife, no womern, no 'Eenie gal, an' no fiddle, hmmm. Hard t' say which'n I'm a-gon'ta miss th' damn mostest."

Eddie puffed a whiff of dust off a rock, and told Jeff, "Yuhhp. If I'd lose my ore rocks hyere an' m' womernn, both, by gravies, I'd feel jest as bad as you do. Rackon. Yander goes th' pertiest web of black silver powder that I've seen in some long time. Woodyrock, see this? Hyere, ov'r here by th' lantren light. See? See?"

"See, shore 'nough." I followed the end of Ed's finger down the crackly sides of his whitish-clear crystal quartz rock. "I ain't sa keen on th' webby black silver—I mean, I'd pass that on up ta keep a-trailin' down that showin' of purple flaky gold. Crisscrosses th' silver sa many times that ya'd lose th' gold if ya went aft'r jist th' silv'r, see?" Ed hung his leather sack on a wall peg, struck a match between our faces to light up the quartz rock, and looked at me with a sly eye, to joke, "We got two of th' toughest depaties in this whole S O B town, right here at our backs a-droppin' their ears on ev'r dern word you'n me sez."

Sam Nail, weaving about on an upside down galvanized bucket, smiled at our joshery, and asked us, "Ohh? Well, which two are deputies? Those two pistols hanging up there on that gun belt, I believe, they do look somewhat well polished. Deputies? Ahh."

"I've been an office man for several years." Papa forked his meat in its juice, "Jeff, here, has been on the forces up in Gray County, oh, for several years."

"Well." Mr. Nail looked at Jeff's boots.

"Six years. Yes sir. Charlie here, he quit, about a month 'r two ago. I jest took a litle vacayshun, ta run off down hyere 'n' see 'bout this mine of my paw's. How good, how close did you know Jerry P., Mist'r Nail? An' his wife an' his kids?"

"I knew your Uncle Gid lots better than I knew Jerry.

I knew Gid when he had to kill that bull rustler up on the streets of Alpine, yes, sir. Gid owned the One Oh One land then, you know, and Jerry rode herd for him. Of course my house was not built yet, when I met Jerry. I was down in here looking this land over to try to take up a grazing lease on it, saw Jerry and his family camped here in this old adobe. I shook hands with him, spoke to his wife, patted his kids on their heads, but just that one day."

"That was my head ya was a-pettin'," Jeff told Sam.

"Well, well, sakes a-living! You did jump up some!"

"Mama jerked me up by th' red of my hair." Jeff rocked on his beer case to whip up the good humor. "I was hopin' mebbe ya could inform us just a little bit more, Mist'r Nail."

"I don't know very much. I wish I knew more. I wish I could take you by your little finger and lead your feet right out to the spot where that claim is staked. Or was it staked?"

"No," Papa told Sam. "No. It never was, not legally. Paw wrote his name on an old piece of paper and wired it around a flat rock, but twenty-eight years has worn that paper out."

"Antelopes may 've ate it off the wire. They do sometimes. Well, that makes the picture a considerable bit foggier, doesn't it? Any other markers to go by?" Mr. Nail played his fingers like drummers against his knees. "You know of any? Speak right out with me, men, I want you to find not one mine here on my place, but sixteen of the things. I get my eighth out of all of them, and I can't chase you off my land, by state laws, so let's open up our collar and tell each other all we know. I'm here to help you dig that mine out from under the floor of this house, if that is where it turns out to be."

"They's an ole medicine-water spraing right real close," I said to Sam.

"Well, now, how close?" he asked us.

"Thirty foot," Eddie said.

Mr. Nail talked up, "Very good. Thirty feet from a medicine spring? Mmmm."

"Between ten feet," Papa told him, "and a hundred; we don't know for certain. A kid held Paw's horse while he took a drink. Paw walked back and found the kid pounding on this tough chunk of backbone rock, see, and knocked off a chunk and sent it in to the smelter at El Paso. Showed up one hundred dollars in silver and ten dollars in gold to every ton."

"That would reverse itself after you dug down ten or fifteen feet." Sam smiled around. "Run you a hundred in gold and fifteen or twenty in silver. Dollar's worth of copper in every ton."

"How'd you know whut them papers read?" Jeff shot an odd look at Mr. Nail. "Huhm?"

"All of this cinnabar silver does that trick, and all of this around here is the cinnabar. But this here spring of medical water, that isn't going to be any too easy to walk up onto."

"Why?" Eddie asked him. "Why ain't it?"

"I ride across over a dozen of those old springs every day, boys, and I know how they are. They dry up on you. This one will bubble up and trickle for a year, or for a month, and then it goes as dry as the dryest bone on these sands out here. If your pa was here, no doubt, having his good eye for rock and ore formations, as well as knowing the odd kinds of tricks these medicine springs pull, he, his own self, might have to walk for a solid month just to retrace and to track back to the little spot. Without him here, I'd say that you men had ought to come well prepared to spend six months or a year to track your story down. The eyes that find our mines, men, are the eyes that start looking, and looking, and just never do stop, or, I ought to say, just take the looking fever, and never can stop till they find their strike. Any of you boys know mining, prospecting, rocks, ores?"

We shook our heads No.

"Well, then, I trust that you are going to be good friendly neighbors, because I think it will take you the best part of six to eight months to run down your tale. It has a good solid sound to it. Most grubstakers' tales have a tinny, imitation ring to them, and the bugs and worms eat big holes in the stories, but I say that your story, at least, does sound logical." While Sam spoke, I watched our lantern light play on his freckledy face and hands. I saw that he was of a lightish red complexion, slightly lighter of hair and skin than Jeff, built up more along the bony lines of Papa. "But, then, your story sounds like the Cathedral Mountain Bandit—very true and very hard to find. How is the deer coming? Smells like it's nearly ready to gnaw on."

"Cathedral Mountain Bandit?" I asked him. "Who's he?"

"Story goes, he robbed all of the gold candlesticks and altarpieces out of several cathedrals over in Mexico. He waded the Rio Grande, and he drove wood pegs to the top of that mountain. He hid all his gold, several pack mules of it, back in a cave, and then he took out every one of his wood pegs as he came back down the facing of the cliff. That is the reason we call that mountain the Cathedral."

Papa stacked out a slice of meat and a fritter of mush on our warmed-up tin plates, and handed each plate to a reaching hand. He said, "If we fail to find our father's claim, which we are more than apt to do, then we can bend our efforts to scaling that cliff and carrying home a truckload of that church gold. How high to the top of this hump, Mister Nail?"

"Cathedral Mountain is close to seven thousand, the Christmas Mountains are up to over fifty-seven hundred, Hen Egg five, Niggerhead a bit under five, and Slick Rock is a bit over the four mark." Mr. Nail shook his head as Papa offered him a hot plate. "You boys are emptier than I am. I've got a woman and a daughter back through the brush here, that are going to pound a skillet on my nut if I fail to come home in this next half hour to eat. I'm hungry and your corncakes look like you know your business, but I have to stay hungry, see, in order to make my little girl happy. We never do cook deer meat any more at my house—just got fed up and tired of it. The Indians come in and fry some deer once in a while, but I've just about forgot how it feels in your mouth."

" 'Fore ya go off, Mister Nail," Ed said, "I'd like ta sorta git cleared up in my head, is the any sech place down here as th' Rough Run Canyon? Little Devul, here, was a-tellin' us t'day th't this is call'd th' Ruff Run Valley—no setchy place az th' Rough Run Canyon."

"That is just about exactly right. Unless, of course, if you want to call the bedrocks of this Rough Run River by the name of a canyon. I wouldn't call it a canyon, but I have heard a few Mexicanos call it the Rough Run Canyon. Most of us call it the Rough Run River Valley. Why do you ask?"

"Our maps call it th' Rough Run Canyon," Eddie said. "Glad ta hear some other folks use th' same name."

"If we lost out on our loosey-bowel spraing an' our Ruffity Run Canyon, both, by dammers, men, they wouldn't be 'nother damn thaing ta hang around down here fer," Jeff told the bunch.

"Clearly the Rough Run Valley is the same place that Claude called the Canyon," Papa reassured us.

"That old colored camp cook that found the sacks of pure nuggets, Old Niggerhead, he could take you and show you the very spot, but we just get a short glimpse of him jabbering and laughing to himself, oh, about once a year, somewhere in the cactus," Sam said. He got up, stretched, and made his way to the door. "So, I don't suppose that old Mister Niggerhead can do you so much good. If you happen to hear something out in the stickers laughing and talking like fifteen people at a dance, that will be Old Mister Niggerhead. But, since he can't help you, not for the next few days, at least, let me try to help. I live just down this south road here where you came from today, and my gate takes a little quick jag off to the left. You can't see my house from here, but my daughter's cooking will take your nose and lead you there. So come around. I can't help you much, but I can't hurt you any. I'll try to drop in on you tomorrow sometime, don't know just when 'twill be, I've so many jobs and things to do. Even if I do fail to show, don't let that stop you from knocking on my open door any time, just any time at all. 'Nighty-night."

"Awful sorry th't ya won't git ta hear Jeff's fiddle howlin' t'night, Misser Nail," I joked at Sam as he walked away. Then I yelled as he got farther away towards his car: "Jeff traded it fer a drink of that muddy shack whiskey ov'r at Studye Butte, an' he's a-tryin' ta make us b'lieve th't he lost it. Ha ha."

A chunk of corn mushcake hit me on my forehead. Jeff grinned and spoke out the window boards after Sam Nail, "If y' come back in th' mornin' an' find a little runty, no-good guitar-plunker scattered all around th' house in little pieces, ya'll know what happened. You got my fiddle hid out some'ers, Woodrow, an' y' know it. Why'n't y' ev'r stop yore damn infarnal lyin', anyhow? Git it out here. Fast."

I asked Jeff, "How'n th' holy heck d'ya 'spect me ta git it out fer ya? I cain't reach my hand out plumb from here back t' Estreller's place. Hey, Poppy, wher'd we warsh our dirty plates at, humm?"

"I haven't found any dishpan, nor carried any dishwater from the spring. I really could not say," Papa told me.

"Letta Pedro licka tham gooda clean, than ruba some sand inna tham inna the morrning." Little Devil walked around to get all of our tin plates, which he set down on the ground outside for Pedro to lick. "I taka your plata, Misterr Jaffa."

"Y' taka nothin'. You help'd Woodrow t' hide my fiddle. You'd oughtta try your derndest to be my friend, Little Devul. I got alla th' guns in this here crowd. Like to shoot guns, humn?"

Eddie blew dust off a few of his mineral rocks on the south window ledge, as he spoke, "Save yer guns to kill frash meat with, an' I might put yer nose on th' scent of yer fiddle. Don't git crossways with Little Devil, 'cause he's about the best friend that ole Jeff haz got in this house t'night."

"Little Maixican Devul. That's a good name fer 'im, he's dev'l'd me ever sence he's been here," Jeff said. He got up and walked the floor to meet Eddie by the window, "If ya know where my fiddle's hid out at, boy, y'better speak it out, an' plain."

"I jest know it's here'n Texas, somewhere," Ed said.

"I didn't even leave it over at Mannywell's."

"Y' most squirtenly did," I said.

"Dang shore did," Eddie told Jeff.

Papa looked over Ed's shoulder at the row of ore rocks on the window ledge, and told Jeff, "If you did leave it over there, Jeff, somebody will bring it over in a day or two, surely."

"Them Indians'll peddle it fer groceries," Jeff told us. "Damn best little fiddle I ev'r did have. I'll just have ta pick myself up tonight an' walk eighteen mile plumb back t' Study Butte. Cain't even wait fer th' sun to come up. Boys, 'atsa helluva tramp, fer a man with feet as blistery as mine is tanight."

"A rather long footback journey it would be," Papa nodded.

I asked Jeff, "What'd ya say, if I toldja th't somebody here in this very room has done packed it over here fer ya? Hmmhh?"

"I'd say they done me a mighty big favor." Jeff looked away towards the Study Butte trail through the westward wall. "A damn big favor. I'd haul out a brand new dollar bill an' fork it over to 'em, who ev'r 'twas."

While Jeff unfolded a dollar bill from his deep pouchy leather snapper pocketbook, Eddie told him, "Y' c'n do yer forkin' right over ta that there Littul Devul. He toted it down ta th' river this mornin' where me an' Wood Knot was a-warshin' out our clo'es. Fulla tortillas. Fork th' froggyskin."

"I'm a-forkin'. Clothes? River?" Jeff mumbled as he passed the dollar over to Little Devil's fingers. "I don't git it."

"Tortillas?" Papa bent over towards us. "Who on earth put tortillas in Jeff's fiddle case? Where is the fiddle hiding?"

"Luisa anda my seester." Little Devil stuck the dollar bill down inside his pants to keep his belly warm. "Anda Cleo. Those girls."

Papa whistled a quiet, easy little tune under his breath, and turned around to feel the rocks getting red hot on top of the stove. "Ahhemm. How did your clothes get so dirty all of a sudden, so quick like?"

"We laid some 'dobe mud wall fer some ladies." Eddie stood up, squared away and told them. "They paid us a dollar 'n' a half."

"Apiece?" Jeff asked.

"Betweena them." Little Devil smiled proud. "Anda they gave the money to me for to showw tham the way over here."

The mule skinner laughed and slapped the ground with his hands. Pedro waggled his tongue as fast, almost, as he wiggled his tail. He put on a big dog smile and looked proud for the boy.

" 'Ja ask them gals while they was a-warshin' yer clothes, where 'bout y' could find Paw's mine at?" Jeff asked us.

I took Jeff's fiddle case out of its hiding hive, and said, "Paw's mine? We, ah, we was diggin' fer somethin' else right at the time."

"On deep mud bottom." Eddie grinned and scratched. "Them gals said we couldn't find yer paw's mine if'n it was shoved in our faces. 'Speshyully if we don't do our dang-blamedest ta make friends with folks aroun' here."

Jeff looked inside his case to see if the tortillas had left any stains or smears. He frowned and flipped the strings. He played "The Soldier's Joy" and "Ragtime Annie," "Chicken Reel," "Old Dan Tucker," "Sailor's Hornpipe," "Devil in the Woodpile," "East Tennessee Blues," "The Tennessee Wagoner," "The Mississippi Sawyer," "The Bully of the Town," "The Bed on Your Floor," "Sail Away, Ladies," "Back Up and Push," "Ida Red," "Ida Blue," "Whistling Rufus," "Greencorn," "Brown Ferry Blues," "Blue Eyes," "Brown Eyes," "Brown-Eyed Boy," "Leather Boots," "Leathery Britches," "Billy in the Lowland," "Grow Big 'Taters," "Skip to My Lou," "Loveless Love," "Cackling Hen," "Coming Round the Mountain," "Hound Dog Do Bay," "Possum up a Gummy Stump," "Nine Hundred Miles," "Memphis Blues," "Riverboat Gambler," "Roving Card Shark," "Old Aunt Rhodie," "Chicken in the Breadpan," "Gals in the Grapeyvines," "Trouble in Mind," "Poor Boy," "Reckless Rambler Hobo," "The Baggage Car Ahead," "Budding Roses," "My Little Darling," "Wheat Seed in the Cyclone," and a few others which nobody asked for, and nobody could think of the names of, just snatches, parts, chords, scrapings of the bow hairs, flying of the rosin dust that powdered the fiddle strings, Jeff's workshirt, his knees bouncing, his feet tromping, and braver flakes of homeless rosin that fell down to sleep on the old ashery floor.

I played along with him, to get out of the job of unrolling and fixing our bedrolls up on the beehivey boxes. I just know personally that Jeff fiddled to try to jar some hard secret dirt down out from those sawblady Chisos humps over there on our east elbow, about three miles. It was a good night for the fiddle to go deep and do good. The brush stood still, the stickers heard every fiddle note, and the cattle, the oil derricks, the oil truck drivers, the planters, the reapers, the spotters, the weeders, all the way back up north to Irenie's pillow passed the music words along.

Jeff fell down onto his bed with a thick coat of sweat on his skin, slipped his pistol holster close to his right ear, and lay down with a yawn that was louder than his panther fiddle. I sweated out a letter to Hell Cat to send next day from Sam Nail's mailbox. Then I passed out on the north bed by the wall. The mule skinner slept out on the cushion of the truck cab. Pedro and Little Devil slept next to Jeff, with Papa and Eddie bundled up asleep in the midsection of our four-passenger bed, stretched to five and a half. I dozed off into such a quick sleep that I only heard the first two or three snortings of Jeff's snores. It was those three snorts that chased me to sleep so fast. I wanted to run away somewhere to get away from more snores, but there was no place I could run, fly, melt, vanish, evaporate, nor otherwise retreat nor hide away from the rattly shakings and screakings of Jeff's worried snartling.

I ran my feet to the lands of my dreams, the dreams of rest, the hopes of peace, the visionings of haunted spots where my soul could lay down and fall back to listen to the chemical dances of the music still ringing in the dreamy rocks, but the snortings, the coughy sneezlings, the chortles, grumbles, the senseless words, pitiful whines, gurps, guggles, gurglings, the noise always found me like a playful dybbuk devil and stuck dagger thorns into all of my dreaming about rest and sleep. I ran as far as I could, and decided to dream my way back to the adobe house again. Maybe I could push my way over onto the middle section of the bed and find just one short yawny stretch of good sleep. The snarling followed my thought. I felt so bad gone that I jumped up and yelled with both hands over my face. Pedro, the pooch, and me were the only ones awake. He had been having bad dreams, too, from Jeff's snorings and mumblings. Poor little poochie. Crawl over here by my side of the bed. You've got a right to whimper and whine, poochie, with someone making such wild animal sounds. I'll sit up here against the wall and let you lick me on the hand. Here, poochie hound.

Look at Jeff's mouth there, hanging so wide open. But, funny, the sounds are not coming out from Jeff's mouth, are they? Huhmm? Crazy? Where else could such a snartly noise be coming from, anyhow? Such a sound couldn't come out of Papa's ear, could it? Eddie's not snartling a beep. Dead asleep, whole cattle camp. There it is again, Whoochy Pooch. Not coming from under the bed. Not snorting down that old stove pipe.

It comes in from that window. Papa locked and barred our front door when he turned in. Window. Hell of a place for a snartling sound to be coming from this time of the night.

Breathe in at your nose with your mouth open. Now, blow it back out your lips, ahrrchrr bllrrhh, arrh bllrrhm, and you'll have the right kind of snort that snuffled all around those old loose rotten boards over our south window. Like a horse goes when you hold an apple up to his nose, only, well, only I never did hear of a horse that went barefooted. No such of a thing as a paddyfoot jinny, nor a pillowfoot burro. Take a pretty huge burro, anyhow, to stand up on his hind legs and sniffle up as high as the very tippertop board on our window's blind. Down again on his all fours tiptoeing easy around to our east open window. That east window isn't boarded over, and the blinds are open. I saw the moon through that window while I walked in this room an hour ago to get Jeff's fiddle out from under these beehives.

I can tell by the scrape and shuffle of those big padded claws that the night smeller is now standing in the loose wooden framework of that eastern window. I can tell by the way this little poochie pup tucks his tail between his legs and shivers here on my lap on our covers, yes, that Mister Padderfoot is getting too close for good bodily health. He must be closer than that, now, as I run my hand along these stiff hairs quivering on the pup's back. Rub your tongue over my head, little poochie, and tell me how scared my hairs feel to you. What could be making those bee crates rattle together any such a way as that? Is that his feet on the dirt floor of that east room, or his hips rubbing dry mud off the wall in there? And that sound, that thommp, thommp, thommping, is that his tail beating the dust on that floor? Or could it be this thing bumping around here in my neck, jumping around in my throat, this big hard knot that chokes my words out and down?

"Hegheyegte, felarsthsszz! Wwaakkee uupp!"

Mister Fourpaws heard everybody snort and shake their heads as I tried to shake them and wake them up. He thought we were a whole big family of his lost kinfolks, by the sounds of our grunts and groans, mumblings, waking up half asleep. I shook the bed as hard as I could, since my voice got lost off out through our east window somewheres.

"Heyghffte, fellerzthsszz, c'monn, shake it up!"

"Harsha marrahh? Hmm?" Jeff blinked under his covers.

"Wuzza matt'rr?" Eddie asked me.

Little Devil popped his eyes open like a tree owl, and asked me, "Huzza wroonga? Ohhhe. Bigga veezite? Ankla

Charrlie, wake oppa de eyyesa, we haffa samme cammpanio. Bigga veesita."

"Big what? Leave me alone. Get that dog out of my face. A big what?" Papa shook his head under his covers.

"Gotta big visit." I shook Papa's bedroll on my hands and knees, whispering to keep from making our visitor mad at us. "Big somethin', anyhow. Wake yerse'f up. Hurry. Jeff, here's y'r pistol; hey, right here. I'm a-usin' this'n."

Jeff took his pistol and flipped the cylinder with his thumb to check the bullets for a full turnaround. "Where- 'bouts at?"

"Listan, inna thata rooma."

We gave one ear and lent the other one to the dusty padded scrape of the visitor's feet. Ed's eyes rolled in exact timing with the peem, pomm, poomm, of the poundy tail. Little Pedro made the first move towards the hive room, but only as he heard the window framing screak under the weight of the going stranger. Outside our burros were braying and stamping and the driver was shouting. I slacked my pistol hammer back against my thumb and followed the tail of our little poochie hound, each of us about as nervously shaky as the other one. Jeff pushed his shoulder against mine in the east room door, and clicked his pistol for action.

Eddie held the old leaded .22 bolt-action, single-shot rifle as he listened by the cookstove. "Mountain lion. They go 'round stealin' whiskey stills, an' a-slittin' joogler veins. Tha'ss him, 'round th' north corner!"

Jeff tiptoed back to the west room. "He's in after that there flaggytail deer out yunner on that rafter. Back shed. Take that gun barrel outta that window, Eddie, that littl' measly twenty-two'd jist rouzzle 'im up."

"Dead bead right on 'im." Ed sighted out the north blinds. "Nawwp, he's in th' meat house, now."

"Your old plugged-up rifle would feel about like a weakly bee trying to sting that thick hide of his," Papa told Eddie.

"Listen t' 'im shakin' that ole smokey house! Sonuvagun! Lemme draw down on 'im with my pisstal." Jeff pushed Ed away to gouge his revolver through the boards. "Cain't see 'im near as good as I c'n hear 'im. God dern, thievin', meat-stealin' basterd ta hell 'n' gone, anyhow. This

forty-four'll blow ye. It'll spade a hole in yore guts bigger'n
Skinny Granny's warshpot. Sneakin' sonuvabitch!"

The little poochie pup ran all around the room, smelling,
sniffing, whimpering, crying, and digging in the ashy dirt
to bury his nose and his head. Little Devil picked the dog
up in his arms and rubbed the cold shivers out from his
hairs, saying, "Jaff! Jaffa! No, no, no! Don'ta!"

"I c'n blow that whole damn smokerhouse plumb up
yonder ta th' Slick Rocky Gap. Here goes."

"Iffa you joosta hurrta himm, he willa drop thot deer,
anda he willa come knocka this house alla down! He willa
fix you so thot you can never find your mine. Letta himma
havva thisa deere. Letta himma taka thisa deer home for
hizza leetle babies. Sam Nail willa shoot another deer for
uss, a bigger wan, a better wan. Save your boolets for his
papa anda his big brother." The boy patted Jeff on the left
arm while he talked.

Jeff kept his eye out through the cracks of the boards.
"Big which? Big who?"

"If you wound him, then he will drag himself home to
his cave, and send his big brother down tomorrow night to
attend to you." Papa took a northernly peek out the blind-
ings. "By gollikers, just listen to that rumpus he is kicking
up out there. Listen to that, would you?"

"I'm lisshenin'." Eddie moved over to test the bar across
the front door. "Sounds ta me like he's a-jerkin' that there
whole rafter down. Whole dern meat shack."

"Boys," I shook my head, "J'st give a liss'n ta them ole
rusty nails a-squeekin'. He's a-shakin' that whole meat
shack jest like it's made outta tisshy payper. Let 'im have
that raw meat, Jeffseefus, if he wants it that bad."

In the first early daylight just before sun-up, we found a
pot of coffee the Mule Man had made before he went
home. We walked around the meat shack to see what was
still holding it together. I heard Eddie tell Papa, " 'Taint
got but two sides, now." And Jeff spoke to the brushy
bush, "I cain't figger out what'n th' name of poker saints
is a-holdin' th' dern place up." I took a few looks at the
disjointed pile of lumber, at the ham-leg that still swung
down from its wire, at the saggy slabs of hand-axed
shingles, the drunky sway of the entire building, and said,
"I can see, at least, where th' rest o' the deer used ta hang.
I wonder where 'bouts Little Devvy 'is at this mornin'?

Seen 'im? Here's his littel poochie hound a-smellin' alla
'round."

"What's that piece of string there around that little
doggy's neck, Eddie? Catch him, hold onto him. Here, I'll
cut it loose, since you'll not wear any collar while I am
your part owner. Here is an old piece of brown sacking
paper." Papa broke the string from around Pedro's neck.

"Letter of some kind," Eddie said, patting the dog.

"I'm all ears," I told them.

Papa stroked the pup as he read the words, "Deere
Amigos. I hav to go. I can get My Munny from the girls.
The Dollar and the Hallf. Make pedro Feel goodd."

CHAPTER 19

THORNY DAYS

This little old sun-dried adobe brick house was the only home we had. The feeling that Jerry P. and his wife and three boys had built it with their own hands set all kinds of older feelings free to go and come around the place. The truck stayed parked out close to Jerry's old blown-down windmill, but his watering tank was gone. I felt a million questions rise to my throat as I looked around in the clearing that first early morning. I answered as many questions as the other men asked me, but all of us, at best, could shoot only a longshot guess when we tried to kill and bleed one of the real answers.

With Little Devil gone away, little Pedro took after all of us to lick, sniffle, rub, bark, run circles, act brave, and perk up his ears at everything that wiggled out in the brush. He followed our tracks and our heels over to Sam Nail's house on our first morning. A well-worn road and a few good footpaths took us around Sam's house on all nine sides. I looked in his screeny south porch and could see the Slick Rock Gap out the window set low in his north wall. I yelled, with Jeff, Papa, and Eddie, in at Sam's door and a few of his windows, but all stood wide open, unlocked, unlatched, unbolted, and unbarred, with not a soul anywhere about.

"We'd ought to lock Sam's house up fer 'im," Jeff said. "He's run off some place an' fergot ta latch up." We scattered up and down the little low valley to see Sam's barn, manure piles, windmill, trough, his wild-growing garden, grape vines, and honeysuckles that rubbed bellies with his sunnyflowers. I scaled up a steep slope of a half-size mountain out west at the back side of Sam's house and filled my jumper pockets with a few chunks of white rocks. I picked up a few more around an old dried-out yellowish water stain. Each rock had enough blackish tracing of powdery dust in it to be all silver and half gold. A hundred yards north I hit another dried-up trickle and pulled down several hundred pounds of hard flakey shale with the knobby end of my little ballbeam hammer. I could hear Eddie pounding on a harder fishback somewhere down the canyon. The tall parts of all of the Chisos family lay over on my east not more than two mile away, and their rock cliffs threw Jeff's words, and Papa's, too, back up clear to my ear.

"Hey, Eddie," I yelled out. "This'd shore be a perfeckt dern spot fer Paw's mine. C'mon up an' git a few samples of this here crystal rock in yer pockets!"

"Cain't come," Eddie yelled back up at me. "My pockets is draggin' me down."

"I cain't ev'n budge, mine is sa full," Jeff cackled out somewhere on the side hill.

"Let's pull out for the house," Papa called to us, "and dump our samples. We can come back to see Mr. Nail later on. We ought to walk over to that Slick Rock Gap, anyway, today, to get our sights and levels. That is where Paw hauled his family in. Claude's maps begin with that Slick Rock Gap. It's about six miles."

"I couldn't drag six blocks," I laughed down the weeds, "not with all of this load on. No wond'r Grampaw Jerry always rode aroun' here on a pack horse. Smart man. I'm a-hittin' out fer that sheepy trail, an' I'll meet ya back at th' house."

We emptied our pockets at the house, then stuck a few cans of sardines in our clothes and struck out north for the Slick Rock Gap. Papa carried Claude's pencil maps, Jeff a pistol, me a pistol, and Eddie the old sidewiping

.22 rifle. Papa's police patrol hightop shoes had leather soles which slid so bad on the flat rocks and rolled so much with the loose flints that he slowed all of us down to a crawl. Jeff had on his officer walkers, too, and stumbled only a few feet ahead of Papa. Eddie moved so fast in his brogans with gummy rubber soles that he hit his ankles too hard against the fireball ends of the dagger weeds, with their sheaves of sharp-toothed, pointed green blades. My rubber soles flew around over the flatrock and caused me to take too many chances. Where the high sticker brush missed us, the dagger weed gashed our ankles. Every step called out a word of cursery at the sting of the prong or the lay of the slope. I never looked and saw the whole four of us up on our walking feet at the same time. One was always down from a slip, a slide, a fall, a rolling rock, a rattle, a buzz, or some other curious sound that scared us —always down with something. Four miles in rough country is a good hour's walk, but we walked two hours and a half before we crippled into the mouth of the Slick Rock Gap.

"That's jest whut she is, a slicky rock gap." Ed put his hands on his hips and looked up the sides of the narrow pass walled with rocky cliffs. "I c'n see now whut Jerry used to mean when he'd tell us we'd need a dang good pair of chaps down in here. My ankles is both swell'd up like I was bit by a mad spreadin' adder."

We stood and laughed till we got so weak we fell to roll on the solid rock floor of the slick-sided wagony gap. Our old bundled and ragged clothes were stuck full of burrs, nits, stickers, tickers, seeds, haystems, and grassy blades. Papa's old reddish fedora hat, Jeff's face in under the brim of his old, sweated-out cowboy beaver hat, Eddie pulling the bill of his leather cap. Rocks baggy in our pockets, old pliers, wrenches, hammers, string, nails, hand picks, ore samples, pulling us more out of balance and twisting us all out of shape. It was Papa who said, "We never will run short of something to make us laugh."

This touched pretty hard on Jeff's tickly rib. He stumbled backwards to sit down roughly on a little pile of skiddy cactus. "Ha ha ha. Ho ho ho ho. Is this th' way folks finds gold mines? Le's try ta stop laughin' long enough ta find Paw's mine. Yee hee, yee hee, hyoo hyooh. My belly's crampin'. I cain't laugh no more with alla these here rocks in my pockets."

"Nuggess, folks calls 'em. Map sez, stan' up right hyere in th' middle of th' Slick Rock Gap, an' take a dead level beeline righte due south. Hmmm. That misses our 'dobe house jesta 'bouta haffa mile." I took a squint and then I spied Eddie climbing up the slope to the west cliff of the gap, and while Papa and Jeff squinted and pointed, argued, and measured over Claude's pencil maps, I went around the end of the gap and climbed up the slope to the tip top to meet him. I yelled down to the bottom: "Yeahhp! Git a lot better bead on it from up here!"

"This is just about all that we can do here," Papa called up to me. "We had better walk back in the direction of that high gravelly hill to the west there, where Claude's map says his pony fell down with him on the way from the mine to the house. Hurry, Eddie and Woodrow."

"I'm a-takin' me a short cut back down, Ed. I'm a-climbin' right off down th' slickery face of this cliff. Bettin' I'll beat'cha down. Ever'body else in this derned bunch is a sissy an' a mamma's boy to boot." I climbed off over the oil weeds and iron grass down onto the fifty-foot face of the rock.

"Whuzza matter with ya, carrazy? You silly idjiot!" Jeff waved and yelled from down on the ground. "Monkeye, baboon, idjiot!"

"You'll never make it!" Papa sung out to me. "Now isn't that a foolish trick? Those rocks are sliding loose, and you've lost your handhold. You cannot get down, nor up, either one. Are you trying to kill your poor old father out of pure fright, boy?" Jeff ran up the slope with Papa at his heels.

"Stuck?" Eddie looked down the shiny rock at me, as I grabbed my last handful of shaly, loose, rotten rock. "Hmm?"

Jeff hit the top of the cliff and said, "If you ain't a funny looker stuck down there, I'll eat yore hat."

"I ain't got no hat." I kicked my feet and felt around with my fingers on the crumbly rocks. "Ner no handholt, neither one. Fellers bett'r shore cook up somethin', an' cook it up fast. Alla these rocks here's rotten an' a-shalin' off."

"We've not got no lariat with us." Jeff kneeled on the grass to look down on top of my head. "No bedsheets to tie t'gether."

"Wait." There were tears in Papa's eyes, "Here. Here is

my coat. For God's sakes, I hope those rocks hold him till
we can tie something together. Here, Ed, your overalls
jumper! Knot our sleeves together—yes, and your woolly
shirt, Jeff, it will take all we've got, and the good graces of
several saints, to reach down where he is before those last
few rocks go. Just listen to that old cliff shale away,
wouldn't you? How would you like for your grandpaw
Jerry to see you stuck for your dear life up there on the
face of that cliff—down there, I mean, young smarty?"

I looked up and down. "Ruther that he'd ketch me here,
th'n down yonder on that rocky floor. Ya hurryin'? This
junk's a-flakin' down all over my head. Cain't toe onta 'er
much long'r. 'S been good ta know ya. Hurry app!"

The fall of their jackets and shirts caused my last little toe-
hold to turn into loose dirt under my shoes. I kicked my
way out as free from the cliff as I could, and grabbed my
handsful of drygoods as I kicked. I took a good wallop of a
bump when I swung back again up against the rock facing,
and the friction of the homemade rope showered all kinds
of deserty mountain objects, roots, twigs, rocks, grasses,
goat droppings, as well as a few odds and ends that fell
down onto my head out of their pockets. They walked
back away from the gap and got my feet to walking
straight again on livable sod.

All my way back to that high hill of loose gravel where
Claude's horse fell down with him between the mine and
the house, I heard myself called by every name, referred
to by every bad label in the book. I walked along a good
bit more mindful of those daggery pointed, ankle-stabbing
weeds, too, nearly to the gravel hill, before I even so much
as let out a sound or a noise.

Claude's Falling Horse Hill was the highest of the loose
gravel ridges. Papa walked along the barbwire fence line,
and aimed his eyesight down the posts, saying, "Yes, this
fence does line up with the adobe camp windmill and
watering trough, except that the trough isn't there anymore, and the mill is knocked over. The map's miles are
often three, and the quarters are often a whole mile. It's a
pity we can't do any more today, but that sun is so low and
so shimmery that I can't see anything."

"Hey, Papa, Jeff." I called them to a halt. "Remember
what th' kid told me'n Ed yessterd'y about the Rough
Run Valley? By doggies, th' way that last light o' th' sun's
a-crankin' up ag'inst them Chisos cliffs yunner, ya c'n

gitcher las' good look of th' day off down inta th' whole
Rough Run Valley. Heads up ag'inst them cliffs, see, then
down past our mud 'dobe house, an' right around this
hyere hill to yer south, see? Gits t' be perty fair size 'tween
here'n Stoody Butte. Runs off down t' th' Terlingua Creek
a few miles on south and west o' Stoody Butte."

"It's all the same," Papa said. "I'm positive of that.
Your Pawpaw could call these three or four miles between
this gravel hill, see, and Sammy Nail's crystal rock ridge,
a canyon. It looks big enough to be called a whole valley,
all right. Did you ever see the sun pull so many pretty
tricks in all your life? Just watch the way that pure solid
burning flame of gold shoots off around over those purple
blazing mountains and hills. Everything actually shimmers
and dances where the hills and the slopes come down together over there, see? Yonder? Your old Paw Jerry knew
a pretty place to run his cattle, and to do his crawling
around, all right, all right."

Back around the house a bit after sundown, tired out,
sore, cactus-pricked, seedy, high-tempered, short-humored,
we gobbled a supper down—pork and beans, sardines,
vanilla wafers, cornmeal fritters, crackers, water, black
coffee. We filled up every flat surface in our front room
with sample hunks of rock. Then we filled the east beehive
room, then the windowsills outside, and the fenders of the
truck, the truckbed rims and edges, then back along the
hardpan dirt all around the four outer walls of the house.
Jeff fiddled some, but not as much as he did last night,
and I was too knocked out to follow any more on the
guitar.

The second morning got us up for coffee and mush
cakes with some sorghum molasses. Jeff and Papa cut
pieces of rubber tread out of an old wore-out truck tire
and hammered them onto the soles of their shoes, while
Eddie and myself scoured out around in the bushes to
knock down a rabbit for supper. We saw rabbit roads, we
saw black and red ant highways as wide as your two hands,
running out along the dirt among the roots of the cactus
brush. After five or six shots apiece, Ed put a hole in a
nice fat bunny, about half grown. I asked him, "How'd ya
manage ta hit 'im, close yer eyes, 'er sumpin'?" And Ed
laughed and told me, "Nope. Y' gotta be an ole soljier an'a

dead shot. An' y' cain't shoot where he's a-settin', ye've got
ta fire where he's a-gon'ta be."

Back at the house, Papa felt the rabbit's hide, said he
had a disease, was too warty, and tossed him out by the
meatshack for Pedro pooch to eat.

Jeff took his pistols out in the thickets and blasted five
or six shots to come back with a jack, a good bit bigger
than ours, but he was too badly burned with powder, too
badly torn apart by the forty-four bullet, and so Jeff carried
this one out for Pedro at the meat shed.

We tried the other side, the west slope of the Sam Nail
ridge this trip. Two hours through tight brush and up slick
cliff slopes put us there. Two hours we spent crawling all
around the stains of an old dried-up water spring in a V-
shaped crevice in a fishybone rock. Jeff took a ten-foot
spill which sprained his kneecap out of socket. He gave his
sample rocks to the rest of us to carry back home in the
prettiest colored sunset I'd seen down in here so far.

The third morning, Eddie nailed some rubber tiring on
his shoe soles and cut the rest of the tire up to clamp on
around his ankles, his shins, his knees and thighs. Papa
stepped out in the west thickets and fired two twenty-two
cartridges to come back with a fresh grown mama rabbit
with no warts, no worms, no ticks, no poison, no smallpox,
no distemper, no open runny sores, no nothing. Pedro
wagged, barked, danced, sidestepped and hopped, but this
one flipped into the grease of our skillet, and made each
one of our tinplates five or six pretty fair-sized bites. Pedro
still got the bones, which lasted him lots longer than the
meat did in our guts.

We split up this day. Jeff and Eddie took off over the
west gravel hilly slope to see if the mine could be any
farther to the westward. Papa and me started east to comb
around the bottoms of the Chisos cliffs, but we got off
down in the slicksided canyon, its sandy floor pock-marked
with big paw prints, that was the main highway up to our
cottonwood spring. Well, for two hours neither one of us
could see the sun, which, like it or not, petered out when
we were about five miles back in the general northwesterly
direction between the Slick Rock Wagon Gap and the
highest tops of the Christmas Mountains. We got back a
good hour after dead dark, but Jeff and Ed were another
two hours dragging sore-footedly in to fall down on their
faces on the ashy dirt floor, too tired to undress for the

bedrolls. A hot coffee knocked both of them to sleep till the rise of day the next dawning.

It was not till the upper sky got light on this fourth day that our frequent arguments about whose ore rocks were whose came to a head. Puppy Pedro had sniffed our hand oil on nearly every sample rock, and when our eyes were turned, had nosed them around. Several rocks had been misplaced, and nearly every rock moved and scattered. Even our highest-hid ones were tampered with. Jeff was afraid that human hands had helped little Pedro do some of his mischief, so we sent Papa to the rabbit thorns again with his rifle, while Ed, Jeff, and me screwed a pair of thick iron lock eyes onto the front door, on which we swung a heavy padlock in the sun. Papa's cottontail gave the four of us enough energy to scatter again to line up some more of Claude's old letters with the dots he had smeared on his pencil maps. We scattered to try to bring family gossip and hearsay, dreams, hunches, inspirations, guesses, blind grabs, dark pinchings, old memories, visions, ghosts, spirits, signs and signals, tales and stories, truth and lies, facts and superstitions, all in line with Sam Nail's fences and the mud sides of our adobe hive house. Papa traveled with me again to stab at the same Chisos cliffs, and we steered clear today of that royal sandy gorge we'd got so lost in yesterday. We hit more thicket stickers than we banked on, which cut our distance in half. We came to a high round knobby rock, as big as a brick building, as round as any hen egg, or bird's egg, which we took a look around. After a short rest, Papa walked on ahead of me to see if he could get any closer to the starting place of the Rough Run River, which was not on Claude's map anywhere. Claude's Rough Run Canyon ran the south and opposite way from the sandy gorge, so we crossed this off our maps and our minds, along with nearly everything else. I yelled up to where Papa had walked into some berry vines, to tell him, "Well, looks like ever' day that passes we mark somethin' else off'n our map. Coupla more days an' we'll be markin' th' whole mine off." But Papa was too far ahead of me to hear me, or to answer back.

I saw a man in a woolly shag of old clothes walk out from the vines up onto a rock about as big as our T truck. He stood with both arms folded across his belly, legs wide apart, and had all the looks of some kind of an iron man. If he moved an inch either way, I failed to see it. I left

off the trail along which Papa had gone, to work over
where my new friend stood watching me. I walked past a
desert jackass with a high load of roundish, barrel-shaped
cactus strapped onto her back with leather strings which
twined in and out of the pegs and holes of an old-timey,
home-made wooden pack saddle. The pack jinny stood so
still that she didn't raise a squeak from her pack nor her
saddle. The man stood a good bit stiller than the burro. He
kept his face and his eyes on the top of my head, and his
gaze glanced off in a beeline with our camp house. His
blanket hung down from one of the knob ends of his
saddle, but the rest of his clothes hung down from around
him in a grey, greasy rag bundle, a little bit like Rio had
worn.

This was a younger man, lighter and redder of skin,
with long knotted cords of a dirty blondish red hair, faded
blue-gray loose-fitting pants tied on his belly by a hair
thong, a pair of braided open-toe sandals, a fairly new
greeny flannel shirt with black stripes that criss-crossed to
make squares. A silver dog-leash chain fell down on his
neck where his shirt collar lay open for air. I looked him
over plainer as I walked on up to face him, to say, "Hidey
do. Nice fine day." If my words reached his ears, he did
not allow me to notice it. I remembered Rina's words of
advice, and went on to tell him, "Down in hyere tryin' ta
locate an ole silv'r mine, my bunch is. Awful perty we'ther,
thank so?" But the particular kind of rock which his face
was carved out from did not care to make any changes in
its looks right at this time. I figured that I hadn't spoken
up plain enough, so took a deep breath, and said, some
louder, "Gran'paw's mine. Prospector. M'gran'paw, not
me."

I saw some kind of a hurt look, a pitiful damp look come
into his eyes. He licked his lips and swallowed, but no
words leaked out from between his teeth. I watched his
pitiful expression fade into a fiery, a hateful, a frowny
scorny look which he shot out at me, and on back towards
our adobe house. I looked back in his eyes as deep and as
long as I could for a minute or more, and I could hear
several years of lost words back in his eyelights. I blinked
and rubbed my eyes, yawned and stretched my arms, and
asked him, "Ahh, mebbe you'd know Jerry P? Savvy, Jerry
P? Grampaw, Prospector? Gold mine? No? Yes?"

He lifted one pointing finger towards one of the fresh

barrel cactus jugs on the dry grass, and let his eyes go down where he pointed the one finger. He kept both arms folded, both feet molded onto his looking rock, and watched me pick up the cactus in my hands. I saw the top seedy part had been cut away, and felt a gummery juice soak my fingers while I took a quick glance back at his pair of heavy silverwork earrings. He watched me lift the cactus to my lips to drink a few mouthfuls of the milk. The rubbery, gummy juice did not come from the milk on the inner side, but stuck all around the places where the outer wall had been chopped and scarred. The rubbery gum was a good bit sweeter than the juicy milk, which had a touch of the bitters about it, but around on my taster and tongue the gum and the juicy milk tasted mighty fine, like more.

I wiped my lips on my sleeve and put the cactus barrel down between his feet. I squinted off into his eyes again and nodded, "Thanks, thanks a lot." As the breeze tickled his forehead with a few bangs of loose hair, he lowered his eyes in a look of shame down at my shoes. The look of shame got full of tight wrinkles when he twisted his eyebrows once more back towards the house, a mile and a half to our west, at my back. The calves of my legs felt burny with dagger points broken off under my skin, the water of my kneecaps turned away to a simmering stewpot of hot lead in the lost piles of salty peter halfway in between the outskirts of purgatory and salty hell. I foamed out with a coat of salty sweat which matched the color and flavor of the sweat drops that bubbled up across his neck and face. I tried to comb my hair with my fingers, but my hands wiggled so shaky I only smeared more adobe dirt down across my forehead. I nodded with my mouth wide open and full of bubbly spit, then I backed ten or fifteen steps down around the rolling rock slope till a climp of weepy cactus weed waved its arms to rub him out of my sight.

My head and my eyes buzzed with odd noises as I felt my way that mile and a half back to the house. Who was he? What did he want? Why did he keep so still? What went wrong? What made his eyes get so wet and his face turn so wrinkled with that worried look of shame? Why did he let me drink his cactus juice? Was he deaf and dumb, or was it just that he didn't speak my English? My brain was a pile of hot rocks in a rain of a thousand wonderings. I boiled up with a fever heat by the time I'd walked up to run my hand over the shape of the old T truck in that front yard. Nobody home, yet. No sign of anybody. I'll feel around the house here and take a look at some of our sample rocks. These mountains feel like they're good pals of mine, and the cliff rocks laugh like they know me. I scoot my shoe toe around on this ashy dirt around this north wall, and I feel just like an old clod of dirt walking along.

You old cottonwoods down around that animal spring are watching every track I make. I watch your leaves fall, and your seeds float and scatter, yes, the same as you keep such a watch on me. Think I'll go in the house and flop down for a quick stretch on those bedrolls. Well, Little Poochie Pedro, where did you trot from? What are you shaking your hip so glad about? Where is your tongue running away to? Your face and eyes look smiley enough for three poochie pups. I wish I was just about two thirds as flippy as you look right this minute, Little Poocher. Heymm. What is this? Our brand new second-hand padlock is all beat up; it's all scarred up, jerked loose, thrown down and stomped around in the dirt. Looks more like an ore sample than it does a nice, respectable, friendly padlock. More like an old rough chunk of rusty copper ore than like any kind of a law-abiding padlock that I ever did see. Screws just the same, jerked out and gone. Who in the deuce do you suppose took a notion to do that? Mister Sam Nail told us that this house belonged to us while we stayed here. He said that we could stash our stuff here. This land belongs to Mister Sam Nail. Sam owns the homestead rights, the grazing rights, the mineral rights, the oil and gas rights, and all of the other rights, I thought. Ohh, just a stumbly outlaw. Mexican, maybe, out here on a blind staggery drunk, full of crazy snake medicine or tequila or something. Which reminds me, I wonder if they left any of our belongings in the house? I better push in and take a free gander around. Besides which, I'm shaky, and almost snaky, which gives me a perfect right, with everybody gone away, to uncap a jar of that whiskey hid in the hive room, and to drink myself a good long hot scorcher just to revive some of the old signs of life in my empty vacant shaking hull of a body.

Scrreaak. Scrraacck.

Squeek, damn you, you old rusty hingey door, you. If I was half as old as you are, damn you, I'd squeak too.

"Good afternoon."

I jumped a few paces across the room to say, "Hhuuhh?"

"Fine afternoon. It is only me, old man Sammy."

"Humm. Scyared me at first. I see ya had ta bust yer way in. Eddie nailed up that east window few days back, aft'r that whijjymakallit drug off our deer—yore deer, ruther. Well, we oughtta been smart enuff ta give ya wunna th' keys ta fit th' padlock. Damn fools, I guess. How'd ya vote right now, Miss'r Nail, on a good stiff slug of our bug juice? Hmm?"

"Thank you. Here's to your grandpaw's old hard pick, and to that big sheet-iron mine you are going to erect very shortly in close sight of my house down there. Brryymm."

"Thanks." I took a heavier drink. "Be needin' all th' good blessin's th't ya can send our way. Hyere's one more, Peedro, ta you an' ta alla yore hairytail pups. More, Sam?"

"Plenty for me. I have to drive my daughter's tutor over the pass for home tonight."

"Well, hyere's ta yer daughter. Hey, tell ya what, I'll give you my key ta th' padlock, so's y' can git in a little bit easier naixt time. Here." I drank a long tall dipper of water, lit up one of the cigarettes that Eddie had lost from his shirt pocket, and tossed my padlock key over onto the bedroll where Mr. Nail sat to watch me.

"No trouble for me." He looked at the puppy scratching. "I didn't break your padlock. It was a family of these wet Indyuns. They stopped off to cook a meal and to wash up some, then they headed on up for the crop country."

I squatted down on a beer case, and said, "Left out perty fast, didn't they? Cain't ev'n tell they've been here. Don't lose yer key there."

"I'm not picking up that key, boy, nor that padlock, either one. You take your padlock and your keys and toss them back up onto your truckbed out there. You're not in the padlock country now, Sonny. You are down here in another world, down in another canyon of life that runs like a different world from yours up there on your lock-and-key streets. You did not find any sign of a lock nor a key around my house over there, nor around my sheds, nor around my barn anywhere, did you? No."

"Shore didn't, at that."

"That house is a few years older than you are."

"Shore don't look ta be."

"Yes, many, many years older than you are, Sonny boy.
And it would have been smashed to the foundation stones
the first sixty days if I had screwed and bolted my doors
and my windows under the weight of a lock and a key.
There is not three days that pass hand running that some
family of these Mexicans or these Indians doesn't stop in
to make themselves a meal. They come in, they use your
pots, your pans, your cupboard, your stove, your water,
and your grub if they have to. And, if they do use your
grub, you will find something of an equal value down in
the middle of your linoleum when they get done and you
get home. I have been stuck a dozen times in my life over
in the rocks and the brush some place or the other, and
have been able to save my very life by making my way
to some such a house. It is not a joking matter—down here
it is a matter of life and death. If I had found your house
locked up tight with food, and drink, and life itself just in
there through your door and your window, believe me,
Sonny, I would smash your doors and your windows down
to the very dirt under my feet."

"Guess a feller would, at that."

"It is like the old ruling down in here that I can break
down your fenceposts and burn them to cook me a meal
on, and not a judge in the land can lay a hand on me for
doing it. I've broke and burned a few, too, in my hard
travels."

"I burnt up a couple of footbridges, m'self," I said.

"The quickest way in this world for you to get this adobe
house pushed in over your very head, son, is to try your
hand at screwing your padlock back up there on that door.
You tell your people this when they get here, I'll be gone
on home. I think that your bunch, by and largely, means
to do right. It's my fault, in a way, for not telling you
when you first pulled up here to camp. This house, and
every other house from El Rancho del Sol to that Oak
Canyon Ranch, down past the Oh Two Ranch, back on
past Study Butte, and on along the border there to Terlingua, and on up seventy more miles to Presidio, and
another seventy miles back north to Alpine. This is it—
this is the law and the ruling of this open mining and
grazing and homesteading country, and the law of the
Indians, the Mexicans, the whites, and every other body of
every other color. I know of two or three homesteaders

that built up houses down here under tight locks, and—
well, I can only show you the dust and the dirt now piled
up on the foundation where the tight-locked houses used
to be. I certainly do not wish to make enemies out of these
folks that come and go down in this country."

Before I could make Sam any kind of an answer, Papa
pushed in at the door with the busted padlock in his hand.
Seeing the open jar of liquor on my beer case, Papa said,
"I thought I heard some one in here speaking English. You
gentlemen appear to be having quite a long and loud dis-
cussion. I heard you all the way back to the spring. This
crazy-headed son of mine, Mister Nail, just takes fits of
some sad kind, he just walks off away from you, out in
the dark, back at the Study Butte, and up on the face of
that Slick Rock Gap, and now, today, less than an hour
ago, he simply stops following me through the brush out
past Knobby Rock, and, bingo, I look around, and cannot
find him to save me. Funny son."

"Funny country. Funny world." I shook my head. " 'F
you'd seen what I seen out yunn'r in that there bushy
brush, dern me, you'd stagger inta th' first house y' could
find."

"A ghost of a dead cow? Another deer-stealing catamount? A two-headed gopher? A snake running backwards? Three bears making ant hills out of beeswax, maybe? What didst thou see?"

"Seen an' Indiun. Indiun carv'd outta solid granite."

"A dead one?" Papa paced the floor tossing the rock up
like a ball. "Was he dead?"

"Nope. He was alive as me an' you, 'cept he was made
out o' solid iron. Didn' stir, didn' wiggle a hair, didn' shake
a lip, didn' move a toenail. Gimme a big drink out of a
cactus jug. Look'd awful bad worried 'bout sumthin'."

"He had a very good reason to worry," Mr. Nail told us.
"That padlock you are holding there in your hand, Uncle
Charlie, and this key laying here on this bedroll blanket.
That is what your Indian friend was worried about. I was
just telling your son that we don't make a practice down
in this part of the world of locking our doors and our
windows with a night latch nor a thumb bolt, much less
under a padlock."

"Oh ho, oh ho." Papa took up the jar with a damp lip
and a curious eye, saying, "That sounds entirely logical to

me, Mister Nail. I had not heard about any such an open-range law, but there is something high and fine about the idea. I, for one, am in perfect accord with the whole idea of a world of wide open doors, windows, chimneys, flues, shutters, and portholes. Here's a toast to the land where the paddylock does not rule, where the brassy key and the skeleton key is not the boss, and where no iron bolt nor latch keeps out from decent shelter the nightly wanderer, the daily comer, the seasonal goer, the traveler in dire straits, in serious circumstance, in lonely solitude and an empty stomach, in the left-out feelings of paining misery which cause the warmest heart to turn cold, brutal, mean, and destructive towards property as well as the person. You mean to say a family of people broke our padlock any such a way as this? Mister Nail, it makes me feel good and glad all over."

Sam smiled at the puppy dog smelling his boot as he stood in the door, to say, "I feel better since you two fellows agree with our padlock ruling. How do you suppose the other two boys will feel about it?"

"Ed'll be okay," I said. "Ain't sa shore about Jeff."

"I think I can cook up some way to make Jeff see the point. If you tell us, no padlock, I guess that means, no padlock." Papa hid the jar back among the crates of the hive room. "If that is your word, it will have to stand."

"You tell them in no uncertain terms"—Mr. Nail tapped the wood on the door facing—"that padlock must not go back on. You will find every article of your belongings thrown out in a pile, if you screw that lock back on."

An hour after dark Jeff and Eddie dragged in with four eatable rabbits. Papa watched them unload their sample rocks from their pockets, as I watched the rabbits and asked them, "How'd ya come ta down sa dern many of 'em?"

"All good young fatties, too," Papa said.

Ed puffed his chest out prouder than any paid soldier to say, "I run up alongside of 'em 'fore I whack 'em. I tickle their funnybones ta see how nice an' fat they aire, an' if I like th' feels of 'em, I whackle 'em."

"Whackle?" I asked him.

"A new technique, surely. We will get a copyright and a patent on your whackling. How does it operate?" Papa moved the rabbits around on the floor with the pup nosing in the hairs.

"Knocks 'em down." Jeff lined the top of the stove with ore chunks as big as peas, marbles, poolballs, and fighting fists. "That's whut he does."

"Knocks? How? With what?" Papa pushed the dog back.

"With dern rocks." Jeff smelled, felt, rubbed, looked at one of his baking rocks. "That Eddyroo c'n throw a rock jest like a damn bullit. I wore my arms both plum t' a freezle, boys; I knock'd up half o' them bushes betwixt hyere'n Study Butte. Nothin', not a damn thaing."

"Ain't never seen a man knock no bush up," I joked. "Hey, Father Charlie, tell these rocky-thrower men th' latest news."

"Sam Nail paid us a visit. He says it's against the open-door law of the miners and cattlemen to keep a padlock on that door. A family of hungry Mexicans tore it off, cooked a meal, and went their way. Sam says do not try to put the lock back on."

Jeff jumped across the room to touch the screwholes in the old wood, and to say, "He told us a damn lie, then. He told us that we c'd unload our stuff in here'n this damn house. Sed it c'd be th' same as our own house."

I rubbed my shoe on Pedro's nose and said, "Same, 'ceptin' fer the paddylock. Poocher, ya'd like ta try ta stretch yore belly aroun' all four of them rarebits, wouldn't ya, hey?"

"I ain't got nothin' worth a-havin' on th' truck er here in th' dangburn house neith'r one. Lock er no lock, I don't give a big rat's ass," Eddie said, seeing some ore samples he'd collected on top of the stove.

Jeff sat down in the door with his back to us, breathed and sighed a few heavy breaths, rubbed the puppy's ear, and said, "Little preachy hound, by damn, ye're th' smartist one o' this whole damn bunch. Who's gon'ta stay here at th' house ever' day an' stan' guard ov'r our b'longin's? Sam Nail ain't no stranger off down in here like you'n me is. Hell's titties, half o' these here Messicans an' dirty Indians helped ole Sam build up that house an' barn of his'n. Other half of 'em knows 'im by his walk an' smell. We ain't got no friends down here, men, ain't nobody that knows me er you either one, ner gives a big damn about us. If I cain't lock up my doors like a sensible human, an' know that my fiddle an' pistols an' clothes an' stuff's not a-goin'ta git stoled, well, I'll jest hang around this house ever' day till I c'n git my ole T truck ta runnin'. I'll throw my crap an' gear up on it, by God, an' smoke outta here. I still got plenty enough gas to put me ta th' first pump. I'll pull outta here jest like I pulled in."

Papa laughed a quick snort in the cups of his hands.

"I c'n wipe off that magneto brush in a half a day's hard work," Jeff bragged to the moon, "an' smoke out from here under fifty horsepower. I damn shore ain't a-beggin' th' company of a one of yeh, neither. If y' sneak a ride on my backbed, I'll be a good sport an' try not ta see yeh. Drug me off down here ta chase aroun' all over this hellhole of a lost damn world, anyhow. Talked me outta th' best flurkin' deputy's job on them Upper Plains. I knowed whut it was we was a-drivin' off inta! I knowed all o' them little ole penny pencil maps of Claude's couldn't set our feet down on Paw's claimstake. Gosh sakes, I can make m'self ten er fifteen dollars ever' night back aroun' home with Irene, a fiddlin' aroun' at them places. If that truck'll jest sa much as roll me part o' th' ways tomorra, I'll crawl, I'll walk, I'll steal, beg, an' borrow my way on inta Pampa."

"Far as I'm concerned, padlock or no padlock," Eddie said. "I'm a-stayin' right here 'th my monkey stove, an' my ore sample rocks, an' my smokin' tabacker, an' my flea hound."

"And my ole smeary, dirty pencil maps." I walked across the floor to sort some of my samples up into lines of different colors. "An' my good cottonwood spring of water. An' my little tangly-headed Riorina. Pickin' dern cotton over in Arizonie."

"And my Rough Run Valley Canyon." Papa hung the rabbits on a pair of wood pegs with a hole punched through all four of their ears. He chanted up along towards the ceiling, "And my Rioe Grande river, and my old Paw Jerry's living wish and his working hope for all of us children, and my verbal promise to Paw there on his deathly sheet. I'm only sorry you had to be away from Irene on this trip, Jeff, both of you so fiery and so freshly wedded."

"I'll be gone by this time tomorra night. Soft talkin's notta go'n'ta slack my speed none." Jeff walked out and away towards the cottonwood spring, calling back in the night: "I'll be gone, dern it, gone!"

And the sun and the moon closed our fourth day.

Papa cut and fried Ed's four rabbits on our fifth morning. Jeff did not show for early chow, so I stacked his rabbit pieces on a tin plate of corn fritters by the stovepipe to keep warm. Ed fished Claude's pencil maps and letters out from Jeff's coat on a peg, and we took to the sticker brush for the day. Papa turned over a flat rock along towards noon, and got a bad sting from a little wormy, wiggling snake. Eddy pounded the snake with a fork of a limb as it wiggled away in a piling of loose leaves. Nobody knew what breed the snake was. Papa said, "Looks like a little old baby ground rattler to me. Too young to have any rattles yet. Little devilish dickens has a pair of really sharp fangs, and, look, my finger looks exactly like you had punched two little bitsy holes in the end of it, there, with a pair of redhot sewing needles. The way my hand is drawing up, Eddie, it appears like you are going to have to show me, show your old cripply Uncle Charlie how to knock down rabbits with flint rocks left-handed. I can actually feel the poison ooze back out at those holes every time you suck it real good and hard."

"Splatteewwhh!" Ed shot a big blob of bloody poison spit out of his mouth. "Whowwee. Yowwee. Man, I can taste it planty—you don't have ta tell me 'bout it."

"How does the flavor taste?" Papa watched Eddie lean against a rock to vomit. "Like wild bully honey?"

"Bbiitterr! Blotterr. Greeny stuff'sh all in aroun' my teeth. Bllaahhpph." Eddie pounded his chest with both hands.

"Swaller it on down," I kidded him. "Little good clean snake juice is a fine meal this time of th' day. Downn it, gulp it, swaller it—aw, don't waste it. Looky at Little Pedro smellin' where ya'v spit it out. He's a-thainkin' 'bout lickin' it up an' drinkin' it. If'n a snake is a-gonna stop me, men, that little ole thing down there ain't him. Heck, I'm a-hopin' it'll be a nice big six-foot rattler skattler. This little baby of a thing here, he's too brownish, too reddish, an' his head's too little ta be a ground rattler. Copperhead, I'm a-guessin'."

"Whatever be his breed and tribe," Papa gritted and squinted as Eddie sucked some more, "I can swear and avow that he is an early riser and a quick striker. And if he'd not been squashed back in under that rock like he was, he could have coiled up better and hit me harder, cut me deeper. It's all up my arm, all up and down here, like hot fire and stinging bees—like a whole nest of hornets daggering me at the same time. If you was not sucking and spitting so fast, Eddie, I would be paralyzed down there on those dried leaves. Ohhmmhh."

"Yohhmm," Ed said. "Here, Wooden, you take over an' sucky tit fer a while. Warrsheephh."

I kneeled on the dirt and wiped Eddie's spit off a bit, but the touch of my sleeve made Papa squirm so fitful that I said, "Well, hell, Nellie's drawers, Eddiereefer, yore spit cain't be no worser 'n th' copperhead juice. Here goes somepin'."

"It's not paining me like it was. Suck as hard as your jaws can pull for a few drags, and then I think we can walk on. It's not any more than a good big bee sting, now. Does it taste anything like a milk shake, son?"

"Tastes jest lika beer mug full carbolic acid. Blughh! Ya know how carbolic acid tastes, don'tcha? Yeahhrrummh! If y' don't know, I cain't tell ya. But mebbe we'd oughtta git up an' go back ta th' house an' pour somethin' on it, huh?"

Papa shook his finger easy, folded it into his other hand, and walked on. "No. We can't find our mine by going back to that house."

"Wonder whut Jeff's gon'ta do?" Eddie said. "Think he'll change his mind?"

"Not this time, I'm sorely afraid," Papa said.

"I don't believe that ole T truck'll take anybody anywheres," I told them. "Nobody."

Papa glanced past his finger, and said, "If the truck doesn't take him, Jeff will get up and walk. He's too sore at these cactus daggers, and he feels badly about leaving his good county job, and most naturally, craves and itches to be back with Ireenie. How do you boys feel about staying down here on our own without Jeff's truck?"

"Nice, perty country down in here." Eddie slapped his hand on a roundish rock. "Nice, perty place ta be. I'd ruther be down in here a-lookin' fer somethin' real good, then ta be back up at home a-livin' off'n my cripple penshun."

I said, "I was nineteen years old, men, 'fore I ever laid

eyes on that ole battered-up crate of a truck! I was nine-teen years old 'fore I ever laid eyes on those mountains! I 'spect ta stay here till I'm fifty!"

We pushed on towards the Slick Rock Gap.

CHAPTER 20

THIRSTY NIGHTS

Jeff was gone when we walked into the 'dobe house at sundown to look around. All three of us looked the truck over before we walked into the house. I said, "Ya can see that Jeff tried his best ta fix that magneto. He dug up th' dirt in under that ole truck as bad as twenty chickens out there scratchin' aroun'."

Eddie looked our lineups of sample rocks over, emptied his pockets of the day's pickings, and said, "I see he's wrapped up a fried rabbit an' taken it 'long with 'im— left these other three stack'd up hyere'n these tin plates on th' stove. Look aroun', men, an' see what else he's taken an' left with us. Mebbe fergot an' left his fiddle case— nev'r know."

"He would not do that." Papa took a look at his stiff, drawing right hand in the beehive room. "No siree, Bob. Jeffseefuss might leave one of his arms, or one of his legs here, if he positively had it to do, but he'll hang onto that fiddle case for dear life. He used that for a suitcase."

"He left that ole lead-loaded skywinder of a twenty-two hangin' up here on th' wooden peg." I stood in the room and turned around and around. "I feel lots bett'r now, men. He didn't take more'n a han'ful of the sample rocks with 'im. And our grub boxes haven't even been titched. Ahheemm. Hhmm. I see that we've got comp'ny. Visitors."

A big, broad man covered over with the dirts of many trails walked in at our door, the outer brims of his wide flop hat scraping the door facing on both sides. I heard screaks of new, creaky leather boots as dirty and as dusty as his jacket and his hat. A tight-fitting pair of breeches too small for him in the legs and the belly were unbuttoned all down the front and in fact held up only by a thick, hand-rubbed leather gun belt with a saggy-down holster swung down from each hip. I could smell dirty, sour sweat and gun oil all across the room.

Eddie's lip shook as he said, "Gg . . . Gg . . . Gg . . . G'day."

The big man touched his fingers to roll his eyelids, and told us, "Thee day was good, but now, she iss gonne."

Papa carried our last full jar of snakey whiskey out of the hive room, saying, "Thank the Little Angels that Jeff did not have room in his fiddle case for this. My snakey-chawed fingers are going to receive a portion of this from the inner side to combat that snake poison. Ummhumm! Oh, well, *buenos días,* or as they might say on the back streets of Amarillo, 'Howdy you do?' I can fairly well see what kind of work you do. Welcome home. I never did know that pistols, or gunbelts, or hats, or men ever grew up to any such a size as this! Welcome to our dusty home. Care to wash up for some fried rabbit? Oh, a little snifter of this lizard tonic, perhaps, with me, here, and with my family?"

"I am a pore dusty releegiouse worrker." He shifted the weight of his body from boot to boot, touching his fingertips easy to the gun handles. "Ande these arre mye prrayer books."

He leaned back against the south wall to roll up a brown paper cigarette from a quarter-of-a-pound bag of loose dry-flake tobacco. "I see that you arre trappers, trapping for some gold lika my badda tooth. Hey yaye? Orr a leetle bitta de seelavaire, mobbe, lika my belta bockle? Hey yaye?"

All of us nodded up towards his hat. I said, "Heyaye."

"Man th't's big as you air," Eddie grinned, "takes about two gold mines fer ever' tooth, hi yi?"

Lighting his cigarette, his first puff choked the whole room with the smokes of many dry leaves. He joked back at Eddie, "Me? I beege? Nawwehh. I leedle boy! De man backa where I come from grow oppa verra *mucho grande*."

"Wouldn't part with one o' them there shucks, wood'ja?" Ed lifted a finger toward the triple-size sack. "I gotta light off one in self defense! Hmm?"

While the man tossed his tobacco and papers to Eddie, Papa said, "I failed to get your proper name."

"Nama?" His face broke away to a smile. "My mothaire calls me Little Red Sondown."

"Little Red Sundown." I looked across his face. "Where did you learn to speak such good English at?"

He looked more out the door than at me, while he said, "Ennglizza? Ohh. I learn whanna I ussed to worka in thee bank."

"Bank worker, hey?" Papa nodded. "Might rightly be that you possess a considerable knowledge, then, of silver and gold, in the rock as well as in the, ah, in the coin?"

"Gantlemans," he said to all of us, "all thot Redda Sondown knows about seelvaire anda gold, ees whan I poota my hands down inna both off my pockeetsa, ande find nawtheeng. I have some frands outta in the broosh who arre verra tired anda thorsty anda hongry. They wait for me to aska tham to comme innaside. Hey Yaye? No?"

"Any frienda yor'n is a damn good friend of mine. Axe 'em ta come in. Axe 'em." Eddie peeped out the blinded window.

"What on earth are they waiting out in the bushy patches for?" Papa set his jar on a beer case. "Tell them to get themselves in here out of that night dampness. Go tell them."

And while the screek of his gun belt faded out in the dark with his boot heels clumpity clump, I shook my head at Eddie and Papa and said: "I'm askin' ya, men, jest what kind of a bank job d'ya s'pose he held down?"

"I'll betcha that he don't let them gunbar'ls of his'n git any too cold." Eddie kept looking out at his blind crack.

"Looks more like some kind of border-patrol rider," Papa said. "Officer of some kind. Hush your noise. Here he comes back with his friends. Just hold your nerve, men, and try not to lose your heads. Remember, the best bet when you get into a tight corner with people of this kind, is just to keep cool and calm and collected. Let me do most of the talking. And, remember, for your own sake, be as nice and friendly as you can. That is certainly the biggest size tobacco sack I have ever seen, and I happen to be an old and heavy smoker. You'll have to get Woodrow to roll you your smoke, Eddie Stone; that little old stinger snake knocked my fingers out of commission. I can see them out in the yard, but I can't count how many are in his bunch. Remember, boys, for your poor old Papa Charlie's own sake—for all of our own good—for everything that we stayed here for, don't pop off at your mouth and start any kind of an argument with these fellows. Those two automatics that he wears backwards in those holsters . . . somewhere I've heard about them. Automatics backwards . . . that means he draws them cross-handed, like this, hand over hand, across his hips."

I watched at our door as the talking outside picked up a good bit louder. An old, gray woman crippled her way in, and an old man just as gray held onto a clubby walking stick in her hand. Little Red helped them in by touching their elbows, and by speaking to them in a soft, kind voice. Next in walked a boy close to nine, his little sister around seven, along with an older girl in her late-looking twenties. A man about Eddie's height and build came in last of all. They all had on rag-sack clothes, except for the old lady in her hand-knitted shawl and colored jacket decorated with hand-made lace. All of them dropped raggy bundles down on the floor, bundles the same dusty color as their hair, faces, and skins. The old man wore the worst rags of the bunch, and all of their shoes, sandals, moccasins, and even their pants legs and skirt hems had the smells and the sounds of sloshy wet shoeleather, the waterlogged odors of a flavor akin to the deadly rot of caskets in quicksand, rotty-bark coffins, the silkery satins and velvety gases that drifts from the cement graveblock. Our old lantern made this hard to see, but easy to smell.

The boy and the girl touched our walls, our sample rocks, our window blinds, stovepiping, stove, grub boxes, bedrolls, with the help given them by the nose and tail of little poochie Pedro. Their mouths opened up as wide and as big as their eyes as they trailed the pup into the hive room. The older man and girl took slices of goat's meat out of their bundles and unrolled three or four quail from pieces of paper. Papa gave Red Sundown the whiskey jar to drink from, then he poured two smaller drinks into some tall, skinny pepper-sauce bottles for the old couple. Our skillet fried them up a quick batch of Papa's salty cornmeal-mush patties, warmed up a few chunks of leftover rabbit Eddie had knocked over with rocks, and fried their smelly goat and sweetlip quail alongside our old singing coffee pot. Papa talked about this and that to the whole family, but their names, their words or any of their business we could not understand. Eddie ran to the spring for a fresh bucket of water. Their eyes lit up towards my old guitar on its strap and peg. Papa opened up a tall can of evaporated milk and poured two cups, half water and half milk, for the boy and the girl.

I asked them, as I stuck a few long, slim sticks of desert root into the stove, "Ya wanta hang yer ole wet clothes up here on th' wall pegs?" As I watched the older couple took seats on our beer cases, and the younger man and lady hung their things up on the wall pegs. I went on to sniffle over the stove and ask, "How come y'r duds ta be sa wet? This little ole monkey cooker stove throws off lots more heat than ya'd thaink. Where'bouts y' say ye've come from?"

The boy in the dim-lit hive room laughed out. "Not anny place. We deed not say. No."

"No place?" I twisted my neck. Then to make it funny, I laughed and said, "Ha ha ha. That's where I come from. No place. Mebbe we knew one anoth'r back yonder at Noplace, hey yay?"

Papa spoke up to say, "That is a fine place to come from. I think every one of us here in this room came from that same place, that no place."

The little girl carried a tin plate of meat and mush cake over to where Little Red sat on his packing case. Red patted her on the head and told her that she was a nice, fine, big, pretty lady. He kicked his boot toe against one of their dirty, raggy bundles and said, "Thiss wan does notta belong to uss. Itta belongs to samboddy inna your tribe."

Eddie sat his fresh spring bucket on a case, looked over at the bundle, asking Red Sundown, "Huh? Whattaya mean? Which'n?"

"The green wan." The young boy spoke for Little Red.

And like a little lady, the little sister said, "Green lang tam ago. Wan tame."

"Ohh," Red said, with a mouthful of supper, "I found itta op inna thee seat off yourr troocka."

Everybody in our bunch walked over to look down at

the bundle. As Papa tried to undo it with his snakebit finger, Ed pushed him back away and went to work on the knots. I told them, "Why, dog my skats to th' dickens, anyhow, folks, that's th' ole greeny blanket that Ole Man Rio left a-hangin' on our truck post."

Papa rubbed his hands in his fingers, to say, "Jeff had it down on the ground to roll around on, I'm guessing, while he tried to jerk that flywheel pan off and get in to take a look at that magneto brush. Know anything about fixing cars, any of you folks?"

"Enoff to know thot your trobble issa not in your magneto." Little Red shook his head. "No magneto."

"Wher's th' ailment at?" Eddie grunted. "Heaviest goddern bun'le I ever tried ta budge. Mmmm. Jeff must have tied it up fulla solid cast iron, er lead blocks . . . somethin' th't sticks ta th' ground arfull heavy. Consarn my ole gran'ma's hide, men. Looky hyere. Looky hyere."

Papa smiled and pooched up his lips. "Jeffey Seefuss's gun belt, two holsters, twelve forty-four cartridges, and one of his pistols, his left-hand one. I be doggie! I be dog! He stuck one down in his shirt and left this one here for us to find after he got real good and gone. Hand it up here to me, Ed. Hmm, well siree. I be dog! Here, Woody, catch it. Oouch! My snake finger hand is just so stiff that I can't hold it."

I made a fast grab, but the gun fell out of my reach. Red Sundown had it spinning around on his fingers, thumbs, frontways, and back, around like a spinnywheel, aimed it, cocked it, let the hammer back, down, clicked the trigger spring, boxed the magazine open and spun it around with his thumb, to the right and back to the left, puffed a few grains of dust off the handle and barrel, and clacked the chamber back in its place. "Verra fine. Verra good gon. I say, oh, savantee-five dollaires, no? Butta, why thesa Jaffa fella leava you witha only seexa bullets inna, anda seexa bullets outta, lika this?"

"Run back ta see 'is new wife. They haven't been married long." Ed hung Rio's blanket back up on a peg back of the stove. "Blame 'im?"

"Jest didn't bring enough bullets 'long with us. If we fire a bullet a week we'll have enough ta last us f'r three months." I tried to sound entertaining.

"I have a forty-four." Red squinted up along the pistol

barrel into the lantern. "I willa be verra glod to let you haf
about wan dozen, mabbe, yiss?"

The old lady elbowed him in his ribs. She spoke in a
lingo I couldn't understand. By her eyes and her nod I
knew she was telling him to hurry up and eat his supper
because it was getting cold.

Red Sundown flipped his hat back with his finger, tossed
the six shooter over into my hands, and spaded the rest of
the food from his plate into his mouth. He clowned and
acted like he was running an eating-and-coffee-drinking
race with everybody in the room. He finished his third cup
of coffee at the same time the others got through with their
first. He asked me to take my guitar down and play. I
sung all the words that I could remember to "Work's All
Done Next Fall," "That Eastbound Train," "Pretty Boy
Floyd," "East Texas Red," "Joe the Wrangler," and
"Roundup Time" . . . just bits and snatches, old words my
head had picked up and halfway forgot about. Then I sang
"Utah Carlos," "Goin' Back to Mammy," and "Bacon in
the Fryin' Grease Nine Days Old," but somehow without
Jeff's fiddle in there to back me up, to smooth over my
mistakes, and to fill in my nervous gaps with panther
squally harmonies, I couldn't sing my very top-shelf best.
Papa walked the waters on some of his finest bully bluffing
bass, all chanted in that clowning, sour, minory Indian,
Negro, whiteman harmony of his, which, I imagine, sent a
few tribes of wild brush yelpers back with tucky tails to
hide ashamed in the stickers. Eddie sang a word of most
songs, but sang along too much on the same melody notes
which I sang. Everybody frowned at Eddie's bad guesses,
but at its worst, it tickled our greasybones, and we ran the
smelly-nose varmints back to the weeds again with the
harmony of our laughing.

The man in the corner behind the stove took the guitar
and sang one in his Mexican tongue. In the pauses between
the words, Little Red Sundown stretched his feet out full
length on the floor, thumbed his gunbelt, and told us the
meaning of the words:

> I was born inna Mezzeeco
> Wherre the cactoos grrows
> Ande thee prettee girlls blow.
>   Wet feet arre wet, *sí, no,*
>   The drry feet arre drry.

I builta my housse fram sun-drry mud,
I deega my crops offa maizey corrn,
Mui hands arre blissters harrd like rocks.
 Wet feet arre wet, *sí, no,*
 The drry feet arre drry.

My landalord grabba my three *centavos,*
Ah, I scratcha his nose and spill wan drop blood,
Hizza dog, hizza cat, hizza tail kisser jommp onna me.
 Wet feet arre wet, *sí, no,*
 The drry feet arre drry.

I hearr bigga cottone Arrezonna needsa me,
I hearr bigga peacha Caleefarrnie needsa me,
I tella my fomliee we walka, ron, crawl de fieldsa.
 Wet feet arre wet, *sí, no,*
 The drry feet arre drry.

The patrrol wass drronk, anda thee guarrd wass blind,
Whann I waded my Rioe Grrande,
For trry to feeda your moutha I de badda creeminal.
 Wet feet arre wet, *sí, no,*
 The drry feet arre drry.

Little Red Sundown sat up straight, swallowed hard
lumps, and blinked both eyes, while his bundle friend
thumped along and fished all through the puddle pools of
his memory for words that seemed to be washing in and
out like a hunk of lost seaweed, or like another civilization.
The slow, rubbery way that they held their words longer
and shorter, gave the fingers on the strings and the looks
on our faces, our high and low feelings, plenty of time to
operate. I heard Papa on the edge of his bedroll say, "Go
ahead. Think of it. That is fine."

Ed tapped his good fingers on his leathered hand, and
said, "Don't leave me stuck hyere'n th' muds of this Ryo
Granndey. Saing me som'er up th' country."

I shook my head without saying anything. Then the
Guitar Thumper Man smiled around and nodded, "Ahh,
sí sí sí. Yiss yiss."

And Red Sundown took over his old job of translating
the words back to our ears in fairly sensible English:

Policeamun he taka me oppa de joodge,
Joodge he say I de badda *bandito,*
I sayy, iffa I no picka thissa crrop, joodge,
Than, joodge hee starrva to death.
   I sayy, weta feet arre wet,
   And thee drry feet arre drry.

He shippa me back de Mezzico in de boxa carr,
I wade riverr backa five, seexa times,
I picka de fruita, livva de crrap houssa.
   My wife she die naxta trrip
   My brother he die naxta trrip,
   My sisterr die de roofa trrock naxta trrip,
   My dogga die nexta trrip,

Ohh,
Tella me, tella me
How canna you eat yourr nexta bite,
Whan you know my fomily's blood
Is onna your plata,
Anda their crying and their weeping
Inn thot tin can you arre opaning?
   Wet feet arre wet, *sí, no,*
   Anda yourr dryy feet arre drry.

   Arre yourr toes wet or drry, *sí, no?*
   Arre yourr toes wet or drry?

The words and their slow and minory tune had brought tears to every eye in the room a good long time before the song was over.

Papa wiped his eyes with the knuckles of the hand the little snake had bitten under the flat rock. He winked around to try to find some word to say, and found a few, "Ahhmmhm. That sure is a pretty song."

"Tells th' real facts." Ed's eyes ran just as wet as his lips and tongue. "By doggies. Shore does."

"Where'd ya ev'r hyear that song at?" I asked him. "I always bummed aroun' an' picked up th' saddest songs I c'd find ta learn how ta saing 'em ta th' gals. Where'd y' git such a sad'n at?"

"My peepol sing all kinds off sadda ones," the older girl bowed her head and told me. "They sing so many sad ones beecause, oh, so many bod t'ings happen to maka us feela lika crry. Orr sing sommet'ing fonny mabbe to wash the sadda t'inngs all away, swooshy swoosh, lika dees, lika dat."

"I hate thosse old bad sadda t'ings." Her youngest brother's face and eyes were as shiny and hot, as puffy red, as her own. He stamped his feet in the ashy dust and went around the room, saying, "I hate tham. Blahh. I hate to hear tham. I hate, hate, hate, hate, hate all off thamm. You can crry because you lovva tham, anda I willa crry because I hate tham."

"Anda I am going to sitta here anda laugh, laugh, laugh atta both off you." Red thumbed his gun hammers. "For crry lika leetla poopy dog atta thissa songa."

"Anda, Misterr Smarrt"—the girl shook her finger towards Red's nose—"I willa follow you to yourr lady's grave, anda I willa loffa loffa loffa while you cry down de flowerrs ona thot dirrt."

"I hearrd you talka to those olda flowerrs inna yourr pockeetbook, anda tella tham thot you willa not stoppa tilla you have showed all offa your peepol how to wade crossa thissa river. Thotta whan those officers cam after you, you willa taka seex off tham witha you." The boy waved from the north wall of the room towards Red Sundown. "Yahh, yahh, I know."

After quite a little wrastle, Red undressed the boy and younger girl and tucked them down to kick the covers in the center of our bedroll. The boy did not stop his yelling till Red took off a silver spur and laid it on the pillow at the boy's fingertips. Red took his right-leg boot off, pulled his woolly stocking over it to make a dolly for the little sister to sing and talk to sleep. It was her singysong jabber talking that droned her brother off in a big new dream on a planet of silvery spurs. After a few minutes of soft talk around the ashy box, Red reached over onto the bed and took his dolly boot and silver spur back to put them on his naked foot again.

While our backs were turned, the older girl undressed by the north edge of our beds and crawled in. Papa threatened to give Red Sundown a few bad samples of his artly science of bare-fisted bloody bruises if the old couple, the two kids, the older sister, did not roll up in our quilts for the night. "You men, you two jacks, you can sleep up here on this roof, or here on this monkey stove lid, or crawl off in under a wood chunk or a cactus root, for all that I care." He waved his cripplely fist at them. "But these older folks, and these young squirts, are going to keep good and warm, right here in this bedding roll. And the first one of you that does not sleep here in the warmth, I'll give your Big Red such a trouncing with my bare fists that he'll not have strength enough to pull either of his two guns out of its holster on me."

Red smiled at Papa's roughshod way of being sociable. Red eyed all of us around the stove while the old couple grunted down into their night of sleep. He patted his leather jacket on both sides of its fancy fringework, and joked, "I havva two morre peestols herre, Grandpappa, anda you don'ta have any morre fists beside those two. Hah hah. But I know whan I am leecked, so I do wheech-aver you tella me. *Sí?* Hey, look how prettee those hotta rocks arre gitting there onna thot stove lid, huhhm? Avery colorr I see de rainabow. Why you maka tham hotta lika these? Hoehh?"

Ed's bad hand rubbed the stovepipe as he said, "We jest heat 'em up thissa way ta git right real good look at how them there shadders, them webs, them cracks, an' them tracin's of stuff runs all around inside of 'em, there, see? See this'n hyere? Looks lika pure solid streak o' silver chasin' out acrost it, an' all down in yunder through th' cracks of it? 'Sides that, wall, I figger that my ole gran-paw, Jerry P., his own self, an' his wife an' his kids ta boot, het up their skillit an' Dutch oven, an' their sample findin's—rocks, crystials, an' quartzes, an' deer's meat an' hot biskits—twenty-some years ago, right, by doggies, right hyere on top o' this little ole monkey cooker stove. Savvy?"

Standing on his boot toes, Red sobered his eyes, looked down at the red hot rocks, and said, "Thot issa all verra good, this t'ing hassa been here joosta 'bout lika you say, twanty-sam't'ing years. I cam ohhe, tan, fiffateen years, anda she stay here thisa same spotta. Iffa you lika for see what issa inna thee rocka, you taka him framma de top de stove, and a pile him alla round in onna thee flames off thee fire. I take thesa wan, I taka offa thee lidda, see, boomm. I droppa herre onna top de flames. She gitta mocha hotterr there, she gitta so hotta she willa turrna purre millky white, white lika thee clear cleanna glass, and thee leetlea shadows off thee ores innaside, theyy show op moch plainer, see?" He showed us how to heat the rock twice as hot while we listened and watched him place a few more stones inside the belly of the monkey heater. Before he stopped talking, he smiled in the light and flares of the flames and said, "My father, too, knew avvery leetela rocka by his owna name. He knew avery leetela rocka by its touch, anda by itsa feel. Yiss."

"Same way th't our Grampaw knowed 'em," I told Little Red, "by their shape, an' tetch, an' like Ed told ya, by their names, an' by their nicknames. Did you happ'n ta ev'r run onta our Paw Jerry, down in hyere, Sundown?"

"No," Red told us. "I wish I did, but I didn't."

"Just a wild chance that you would have," Papa told Red.

"I heard other peepols talk off him, and talk abouta his wooman, anda they wass never won bad worrd said about tham. Itta was alla good. Which has made some few peepol halpa you allaready so farr." Red watched the ore chunks turn whiter, clearer, and shinier.

"Alla our own folks always did say that Jerry could make a hard rock like him, an' a cold flint turn off an' be friendly."

Red lifted his two spare pistols from under his jacket and hung them upside down on two nails in the window boards. He slapped his hat off the back of his head and his throat choker held it swung between his shoulder blades.

Red's guitar-playing friend was a quieter fellow, a deep-running thinker, a slow smiler, but at the same time warm, limber, and friendly enough to talk along, to repeat things we said, to nod his head and agree, or to frown sideways and disagree. I just did not know a word of his language; it sounded like such a rocky mixture of the windy muds both to the south and to the north of the Rio Grande. Red took time to make the fellow feel at home by listening to him, and telling us what he said, felt, thought, and hoped in general. He told a short story which Red nodded along at, then tongued his lips at.

"Cain't savvy a derned word o' what he's a-sayin'," Ed said as his eyes followed the slight wiggle of Red's two automatics on the nails back of the Music Man's head. "Not one derned word of it."

"Has a fine sound to it." Papa took a fresh drink from the fruit jar. "You men, here, take a swallow. These rocks out here are full of snattlerakes and tarantulas, as I so regretfully discovered this very day."

Red drank, passed the jar to his friend, and while the Singer Man got quiet enough to partake of the spirits, Red told us, "My *amigo* tells me thot he has heard thot old campa cook, Neegerhead, say crazy t'ings planty times, you know, ronna oppa anda downna inna thee brosh. Anda Olda Neegerhead woulda laugh and talka, you know, about how he always wass a loose rocka man, he always digga inna de loosa rocka. Olda Neegerhead woulda yell, anda laugh, anda scrream out atta your Oncle Jerry, anda teasa Jerry for allatime digga de bigga hard rocka. 'I picka oppa my tabacka sack fulla, my pockeets alla fulla, in de loose rocka, anda Old Oncle Jerry gits lost sammaplace down in hiza harda rock.' My *amigo* here, he tellsa me, Olda Neegerhead wassa thee only man whicha saw yourr Oncle Jerry anda hiz wife Ollie, anda their three boys every day or two while they built oppa thisa house here, anda stayed here those three years, savvy?"

"They's been lotsa folks tell us about that there old Niggerhead nugget finder," Ed told Sundown. "But most of 'em talk like they don't git a glimpse of 'im more'n once 'er twicet a year."

"Therre issa not a man now living thata Old Man Neegerhead willa stop anda talk with. But therre arre two off thee weemen whicha he talks to whan he sees tham. One wooman issa Meestaire Sam's wife, over here, anda thee other one issa overr by Study Butte, anda I t'ink herr name issa Cleo. I seena him saveral times out talking crazy de broosh piles. Butta he see me, my bigga hatta, my gons, an' he ronna downna de sanda joosta lika de rainawaters. He maka planty friends off mine afraid, friends I taka crossa thee Rio." Red acted out his words as he talked.

"How long have you been guiding and escorting your parties of sightseers and tourists, and damp-leg crop workers from Mexico, Sundown? I suppose you know those mountains over yonder fairly well by this time, no?" Papa asked him.

"I halpa bigga bonch 'Mericanos gitta frram theesa bank over to the Mezzico bank, also. I halpa Indianos, anda Mehicanos gitta fram thisa bank to thatta bank. I don'ta care which bank. I work thiza bank bizniss now, ohh, I say thirty years. I thirty-three tonight. I starrt inna atta thee same tam my papa mama teacha me how to hold onto your fingerr anda wade. I learned how to wade before I learrned how to walka verra good. I coulda swimma before I coulda crawla."

"That is the kind of a banking concern you work for?" Papa rolled a cigarette and laughed as he blew his spillings across the stove lids laying open. "A bank? Ha ha ha. Yes, thick-skulled Charlie they ought to call me. I see it now. Ah ha ha ha. You deserve another slow and sociable slug out from the friendliest depths of this old jar of graveyard juice. Here, banker, drink."

I wiggled my finger like a toy clock ticking, and laughed my eyes full of ash dust, whiskey fumes, tobacco flakes, and other things drifting around and about in our room, trying to say "Bank to bank. Yyahh hyahh. Best 'un I've heard since my old Grampaw Jerry was a pup. I cain't laff no more, men, my belly band's a bustin' loose on me."

Papa shushed his finger against his lips to get us to keep a bit quieter. Eddie chunked a few more sticks of hard root in the mouth end of the stove, and shushed the same as Papa. Red kept on laughing in his stove corner, so I flumped the open strings on my guitar as it swung on the peg, and whispered a little verse of the old-timey talking blues, that went:

> I was jumping with my wommern
> On the stinkwater bog,
> Both of us was jumping
> From swamp to swamp,
> She didn't quite make it
> From bank to bank.
> We splashed sour mud
> Fer an hour and a haff.
> > Snakes Eyes,
> > Dirty Naick,
> > Blue Pot.

This was one of those tickleboney nights, a night when any old thing is funny enough to laugh at. We tried to think about the folks trying to sleep in the bedrolls. We tried to hold back on account of the late hour. None of us wanted to laugh loud enough to scare the cottontail rabbits and the flaggytail deer too far out of gun range. We did not wish to pull Sam Nail out from his bed up here to order us out of his Rough Run Valley. We did not crave

for the big paddyfoot cattymount to tiptoe up and tear our
meat shack down for its bloodstains.

I scratched my dandruff in under my fingernails and
tried to think up some kind of a real extra super funny
verse about Little Sundown, which, I hoped, might even
cause him to unstrop his .45s and hang them up on a third
and a fourth nail. I flipped my thumb over the strings and
thought up the words to say:

> My hat looks dusty,
> But my boots are new,
> My gun is greasy,
> And my fingers, too.
> If ya got any riv'r wadin'
> Which ya gotta have done,
> Yell for Big Little Red.
> I'll come onna run.
> > Sunup.
> > Little Red.
> > Moondown.

When this did not cause the laugh I expected, I scratched
the knee of my itchy overalls, and told the entire gathering,
"Well, I reckon yer jest a little bit too laughed out, anyhow."

Little Red froze up stiff by the window boards. He
apologized to me, "Sorry, Currlie, I was notta lissening to
my fonny songa. Sshh. Sshh. Did I hear a squeakie leather
sound outta there? Didda you hear?"

"I was not listening," Papa told him. "I can hear almost
any kind of a sound when I let my ear get out in that
brushy bush and walk around in this crackledy moonlight."

"Not me." I shook my head.

"Let's march out'n take a little gander aroun'." Ed slid
Jeff's loaded six-shooter down in his hip pocket as he followed Little Red out. Red was telling Eddie, "Here, walka
with your backa op close against the walla. Do not whoop,
anda do not yell. No sillee business. Walka onna your flat
feet and a push your shoe down slow anda hard."

"Okay. Gotcha," Ed whispered at Red's back. Papa
stood with his eye through the window boarding to hear
Eddie ask Red, " 'Spectin' anybody?"

"I sosspect averybody." Red's words fell down in a low,
clear whisper. "Thot iss how I maka my living."

I heard no more words, only the scraping sounds of boot heels, hat brims, gun butts, breeches against the walls of the house. Then even this left my ears, and I knew that Eddie and Red had stepped out to make a wider circle through the paw-track trails in the dagger bushes.

At the same split second when Papa stepped over to puff out the light of the lantern, the Music Singer fellow brushed out the door barefooted with both of Red Sundown's spare pistols in his hands. I could hear no sound from his bare feet, so I had no idea which way he had run. The moon that sprayed in at our open door and windowblind cracks was the lightest thing I could see. Our monkey-stove fire crackled brighter than ever. And as my eyes got used to the shapes of things in the dark, I could hear at my back the bothered, worried, troubled tossings of the folks in the bedrolls, trying to sleep. The curious lead and zinc gray of the ashes on the dirt floor turned a light, dancy color, and all of the boxes, cases, shoes, bundles, piled clothing, beds, and sleepers looked several shades darker. My ear did not hear the panting of the little Pedro pup, so I knew he had outrun Little Red and Eddie out there to snozzle around those cactus roots.

Papa motioned his hand back for me to keep still, not to make any foolish move or sound. I stood over the stove and kept my eyes on the half dozen white-hot ore chunks with their tangly shapes of darker powders running through the center of each one.

Papa's eyes traveled back to older things and times while he listened through the walls. He asked me, with the monkey stove between our faces, "You afraid, Wood Jugger?"

" 'Fraid o' what?" I asked him. Then I looked at our stoveful of white-hot rocks, and told Papa, "I'm borned of th' blood of ole two-fisted Charlie, an' if he was ever 'fraid o' anything, nobody never did see it on his face. But I ain't a-feelin' what ya'd call none too brave, right at this p'rticular minute. You?"

Our words had to be kept down in a slow whisper so as not to wake up our nightly sleepers in our beehive bedrolls. Our whispers sounded almost like regular street-corner talk, but they were still whispers. And in this way, Papa went on to tell me, "The way that Red Sundown fellow ran out of here, well, I guess I am what you could call afraid. The only earthly time that I really feel afraid of anything,

Wood House, is, well, like right now, when I can't see what it is I'm afraid of. When I got it out here in front of me so that I can lay my eyes on it, I'm never afraid of it anymore. I wonder where they've all gone off to. I can't hear a single sound outside, can you, sonny boy?"

"Nothin'." I shook my head. "Not a danged sound. Funny."

"I always want you to be, Wood, just as solid on your two feet as those rocks there getting hot. Just as solid as a rock."

"Which'un ya mean? Ain't no two of them rocks there alike. Some of 'em a lot solider th'n others. Ain't it funny th' way them rocks heat up an' look sa different—I mean, when they go ta gittin' hotter?"

"They are just like people, Wood boy: when things go to getting hot for them, they all change their stripes and their colors. They all try to tear their hearts and middles open to tell you all about their souls. People are that same way. When it comes your time to stand up and be assayed by the rest of us, you will be just exactly like one of these old ore rocks. You'll say, 'Oh, please don't judge me by my old rough, knotty, mean, and ornery outer looks. I've got lots of good things down closer to my heart, my center . . . closer to my middlings. When the going gets hot, then I turn clearer, so that you can see the good things, the better things, the golds and the silvers, the real things deeper down in my soul. Please don't judge me by my old, rough-looking, ugly outer sides. I am like this mountain here: my outer things are ugly to see, easy to find, but my better things are deeper down inside me, harder to see and slower to find. Every person on this earth is the same as me. My finest parts, my most valuable ores, are all away down so deep in my centers and my middles that it takes a good bit of digging and scraping, and a good bit of hearing and firing to find them and to run them out in the fires of your hearts, to mold them up and to mold them down into their best shapes and forms.' "

I shook my head up and down while Papa talked to me. His words sounded like the last words any father on earth had a chance to pour away into the listening ears of his boy son. There was nothing else for me to do, except to stand there and to shake my head up and down to each word that he spoke to me.

"Some people, Woody son," Papa kept on, "are like

this largest rock here. They look the best on their outer sides. They have big wide shoulders, a big loud voice, and a certain way of making you think that they have the real thing down in their pockets. But when the fires get extra hot, and the going turns off double tough, then they're perfectly willing to take their full share, without going through the melting oven to find it."

"Meet up with a big herd like that. Craves ta wear th' pertiest shirt 'thout ev'r layin' a finger on a cotton boll. They mus' be somethin' crazy inside of my head, Papa; I cain't rest my head at night if I don't work myself good 'n hard all day long. I guess, mebbe, th't I'm jest about like a few drops of quickysilver . . . jest cain't never find me no kind of place to rest till I fall down an' soak away somewheres in th' dirt."

"A real smart rock," Papa dropped his eyes down, "I guess, can be as loose and as itchyfooted as you are, and as lay-downy lazy as all of us are at certain times. That Jeffseefus brother of mine, for instance, when he is in the mood and the humor, will dig and chop, hoe and cut, lift and carry, roll and tumble more work out than all of the rest of us here put together, with our runty shoulders and our old crippling fingers and our dried-up arms. He grunted, and moaned, Woody boy, at the harsh country we've met down here hunting this claim. Maybe so. But he was the best rock in the fire, even with his human faults. We lost our best man when Jeff walked away."

"Well," I argued back at the stovepipe, "they's not a fiddler now drawin' breath in this world that can git th' lonesome howls and squalls out of a fiddle box that Jeffrey can. Me, I'd walk these here dang devil-horn cactus mountains fer th' rest o' my natcherl days ta be able to hear Jeff saw down acrost them straings th' way he drags 'em. Sets my whole blame soul on fire. But Jeff cain't never make up his mind 'tween his gun an' his fiddle. Good-bye, Jeffie Seefius, good-bye fer a while. See ya in Pampa one o' these days."

"You are a good mile or two off in your reasoning," Papa argued back. "It wasn't his gun that Jeff loved more than his fiddle, Wood. It was that new little wife of his. It sure is not Jeff's true nature to love to paste your head with a gun butt; he hates that a good bit more than he will admit. If he goes back to his new wife, then, you see, he is forced to go back to his badge and his gun belt. He fibs to us, Woody, to try to make us believe that he loves his law force job. He left his gun belt and one of his six-shooters out there rolled up in Old Man Rio's green woolly blanket. He'll have to pay out forty or fifty dollars on a new gun and holster belt the very minute that he walks into that office to go to work. Why, Jeff hates that old creosoted law force office, Woody, so bad that it goes plumb against his grain to fill out the forms in the docket book when he brings you in to charge you with whatever it is."

"Wasn't a guy in Texiz th't was any happier than Jeff seemed to be back before his deputy job, in th' days when he was a-fiddlin' 'round ta make 'is livin'," I said to Papa, "but after he got to knockin' off that good money in wages and fees an' all, well, he jest didn't strike me as being so happy. That's all I know."

"The trouble is, Woodrow, that people still think those good old prosperous days are coming back, and that the Panhandle oil field is going to open up bigger than it ever was. Shoot a monkey, that field is closing down tight as Burke Burnett, Seminole, Cromwell, Smackover, Slick City, the Black Bayous, or back to the Pennsylvania Hills. The stores are locking their doors every hour up there. People are hitting the road just like we hit it, Wood, to get up and to get out of there, to go anywhere to find more fields to wildcat and pipe away. I'd ten times rather spend my next few months right down in here, where, as your grandpa said, we could locate his mining claim and make all of our families and all of our kinfolks independently rich. We certainly couldn't rest any easier up there with the women-folks. It will take plenty of rough climbing and hard thorn-ing, Woody, and a full many a daggery day and thirsty night to find Paw's claim stake. Do you think you and Eddie Stoner will able to muster the perseverance, endur-ance, fortitude, and dexterity to stick it out?"

"Out an' in, both," I half laughed. "I'm a-stickerin'. An' I'm perty shore 'bout Eddie."

"I feel glad that you aren't afraid, Woody. But, then, you never was afraid of the Devil's Uncle Fudge."

"Took a little nerve outta yore big pile of it," I told Papa in the firelight. "I didn't always like th' things that you broke yer fists about, but I shore did like th' way that ya laid yer ears back an' waded in. I never did see ya git afraid of anything that drew breath."

"I'm frightened right now of what Eddie and Little Red

are going to find out there in that brushy bush. I'm scared, too, for these folks here trying to get a few blinkers of sleep in our blanket rolls. I'm worried about what could . . . what might happen to all of us if the border patrolmen step in this door and find you and me here with all of these wetbacks. I'm not mathematically certain as to the length of time it would take for us to discover the whereabouts of Paw's mine through the tempered steel bars of a Mexico border calaboose," Papa told me, looking from side to side, worried. "Hah. What is that? Sshhsshh."

Out in the open yard, in the scrapey clatter of several boots and shoes, I heard Little Red Sundown speak out in a voice that glanced up off the tallest cliff rocks. I took a look out at the door, and saw Eddie dancing the drunk staggers around and around the truck. He pounded his crippled hand on an old tin pan and sang out in a voice loud enough to match Little Red's:

> If ev'r I git my gold mine sunk,
> Roll away, wagon, roll away,
> Trap fer possum, coon, an' skunk,
> Roll away, wagon, roll away.
>
> Didn't she roll 'em, Daddyo?
> Didn't she jiggle 'em, Daddyo?
> Didn't she winkle 'em, Daddyo?
> Didn't I trap 'er, Daddyoo?
>   Didn't I trap 'er, Daddyoo?
>   Didn't I trap 'er, Daddyoo?
>
> Gun so rusty it won't shoot,
> Roll away, wagon, roll away,
> Settin' my traps at Studyo Butte,
> Roll away, wagon, roll away.
>
> Didn't she roll 'em, Daddyo?
> Didn't she jiggle 'em, Daddyo?
> Didn't she winkle 'em, Daddyo?
> Didn't I trap 'er, Daddyoo?
>   Didn't I trap 'er, Daddyoo?
>   Didn't I trap 'er, Daddyoo?

Red out-yelled Eddie for a time, to say, "Hey, Trrapper Man, hey, Curley, stop oiling your traps. Brringa your

guitarra out onder the moon anda play some. Play for my
buenos amigos, Misstaire Patrolman Fella. Com and I willa
show you my dance of the Little Red Sundown."

Papa shoved me out the door with my guitar strap
around my neck, and came after me with the half-gallon
jar holding the last few ounces of our Panhandle whiskey.
I saw, beyond our truck and lit by the headlights of their
patrol car, two men wearing new-looking cowman's rig-
ging. The younger and heavier of the two patrol officers
would weigh on a cattle scale nearly as much as Sundown.
The other man was slimmer and about fifty years old. They
were looking at Eddie and didn't see us come out of the
house. Red slapped his bare hands against his leather
breeches to keep time with Eddie's pan pounding. I noticed
that Red's automatics had been undone and ditched, along
with his gun belt, and I knew he was trying to divert patrol
officers so they wouldn't find the wetbacks in the house.
Ed and Sundown were acting as much like drunken trappers as they could. Sundown sang in time with Eddie's
trapper song, over and over, "Daddyo, Daddyro, Dad-
dyoooe!" He kicked up such a whirly storm cloud of dust
that the two well-dressed patrollers walked around the
truck, laughing and wise-cracking as they leaned against the
radiator. As Papa and I walked up to them, I sang along:

> Didn't she roll 'em, Daddyo?
> Didn't she jiggle 'em, Daddyo?
> Didn't she winkle 'em, Daddyoo?
> Didn't I trap 'er, Daddyoo?

"Hello there," one of the patrolmen told me. "How's ya
stock o' furs, boys? Got many nailed up on th' dryin'
boards?"

"You gents left yer car lights on," Eddie put in hastily.
"D'ya always leave 'em burnin' that way?"

"Your engine ronning, too?" Red hugged his arms around
Eddie and me. "You 'fraid mebbe she freeze op, no?"

I passed off a speck of time by saying: "I shore do wisht
our old jalopy wagon here'd set an' idle as nice an' as fine
as yore motor does."

The elder one rubbed the truck as he told us: "I can sure
sympathize with you, having a breakdown in the middle of
God's Vacant Lot."

To draw the noses of the two officers away from the

door of the adobe, Papa set his fruit jar down on the loading end of the truckbed while everybody stood around.
Papa motioned with his hand at the T model.

"I just got back from hauling a double load of furs up to
Fort Davis in this gasbuggy, men," Papa said. "She ticked
along fine until she pulled up about a half a mile from
here. If you upholders of the public good had come along,
like you should have, you could have roped onto my
bumper end and pulled me up here into the yard. As it
went, you came a day late, costing us boys here exactly
four pesos, which we paid to a burro driver. But here, take
a free sample of snake medicine, gentlemen. This is the
last few ounces in our possession. The doctor ordered it
for my snake-bitten hand." He showed the officers his stiff,
swollen right hand.

"Little ole ground rattler, down in unner a warm rock,"
Ed told them, nodding. "I sucked th' p'izen. Blahhmm!"

The heavier of the pair drank first and said, "Tastes a
lot like home-brew whiskey to me, which is highly unlaw-
ful. See what you think, boss."

The other drank and made a wry face. "These fellers
must have squeezed that ground-rattler juice into this jar,"
he said. "Here—hold your finger up under my flashlight,
old fellow. Hmmm. Two fang marks, all right, at that.
Look there, Puny. See those? Your fingers, those knuckles,
look to be as stiff as dry leather, Pop. Hurt much?"

"Like a whole armful of stinging bees," Papa told him.

"Positive you're not hiding any more such medicine
bottles as this one here?" the older officer demanded. "Is
this the only jar you have? What about us taking a little
look-see in there around your camp house?" He walked a
few steps away from the truck, and fingered his gun butts.

"We're not even able to use that camp house tonight,
Officer." Papa spoke out as the fatty fellow, Puny, drank
the last finger measure and set the jar down to tiptoe after
his leader man. "It's all full of stinging bees."

"Full? How do you mean?" the slim deputy said. "Wait
up for a second, Puny! Stinger bees? How come?"

"Jist come a-swarmin' and a-buzzin' "—Eddie acted
twice as drunk as he felt—"and flewed back home."

As the patrol men stopped to listen, Red Sundown took
a long step towards a cactus bush, where his friend stood
straddling, I saw later, the guns and gun belt.

"*Si, sí,*" Red called out to the officers, "alla de bees

swarm back to de hives in de house, chaseeng their queena."

I talked up: "Awful bad humor, them there bees is in. There's not enough honey drippin's left in them hivey crates ta feed 'em a decent meal on. All of 'em madder'n a wet hen. They're in there a-stingin' one another ta death —blue jillions of 'em, jest b'cause they's not enough drops of that there ole dried-up honey ta stay alive on. Least-ways not fer so many millions of 'em."

The older deputy tiptoed to the blinded window to shine his flashlight in through a crack between the blinds. "Yummmm. By jinkers, pardner, th' room is stacked fulla beehives! They've swarmed back into 'em."

The heavy fellow took off his hat to peer in gingerly. "Bees does the damndest things," he said. "Hummm. What do you know, boss?"

They stepped back from the window and the boss tiptoed around the cabin. We stood around the truck and watched him step towards the front door. I held my breath. Then I heard Puny say, "Them damnable bees, boss, will buzz out of that door and they'll stick all over you and sting you to death!" Puny fell back towards the truck as he warned his superior. "I had my pants full of them one day in our cow lot. That was twenty-two years ago, and I still take to stinging whenever I let myself think about it. Boss, please! For your own wife's and kids' sake, let's pile in and light out for home."

Just then Pedro howled in his sleep inside the house where he was snoozing in the beehive room. Puny rubbed his ear. "Listen, Boss!" he said. "I hear something that doesn't have any bee sounds to it. Sounded like a mountain wolf er cougar."

"There is nothing in the house, fellas," Eddie called, "but just those bees. Go in an' take yourselves a good look around. Just those bees."

As the head officer backed away a few steps with both hands on his gunhammers, Eddie joshed out, "That there panther is 'round out yunder back of th' house."

And I said, "He tore our meat shack down the first night we was here, an' drug off two flagtail deer that Mister Nail hung up fer us ta eat on. This here big visitor, he comes 'round here ever' night ta lap up them ole bloody carcasses we toss out fer 'im. He acts generally perty friendly after he gits his belly full o' new blood. Ah, where'd you gents say you was a-mooverin' off to?"

As Papa saw them slam their car door and speed up their motor, he yelled, nearly as loud as a meaty shack catamount: "Don't rush away, men, without leaving us your new address. Ha ha ha!"

The car jerked off into the moonlight, to steer itself around in a bend in order to switch off onto Sam Nail's main line. As the car whipped around, the fatter of the two traveling passengers tossed a flat, cob-stoppered whiskey bottle out on the dirt. I outran Eddie because he stumbled over a loose mesquite root, and grabbed the flat.

Eddie and I got back to the truck about the same time. I held up the bottle. "Heck fires, men," I laughed, "we can tear off out here 'n' get snake-bit five er six times on this here pint!"

CHAPTER 21

SOLID MEAT

We stood out back by the meat shack after mush, meat, and coffee next morning, telling Red's friends good-bye. We joked about what big-shot trappers we had been, but our words felt heavier as Papa squatted down to hug and kiss the boy and girl. I noticed that Papa's face twisted into all kinds of pain when he shook Red by the hand and said, *"Adiós, amigo."* All of them held their bundles and walked off down into the twelve-foot sandy-bottom canyon that Papa and me had followed the wrong way for one whole day. The sandy dry creek ran down so deep that it hid the tops of their heads and the sad parting smiles on their faces. Their footprints mixed and melted in to run with the claw and toe tracks of hundreds of wild animals.

This was the way that we started our sixth day here in our adobe beehive house on the Sam Nail Rancho in the Rough Run Canyon Valley of the Chisos Mountain range in the bendings of the Rio Grande on the track of Paw Jerry's mine.

Ed rubbed his leather railroad cap and looked off towards the sandy gulch of the departing family. He asked Papa, with a low-swung jaw, " 'Smatter, Uncle Charlie? Lose one o' yer laigs er somethin'?"

"I feel that way, Ed." Papa stepped up onto the rickety meat-shed floor and looked out where their heads and bundles had gone. "How does it weigh down on you, Ed? Wood?"

Eddie told us, "I stayed in that there Army long enough ta learn how ta keep my eye sockets dry tellin' folks goodbye. Them folks of Red's is th' real natcherals, I'll say that."

I patted the little poochie Pedro between my shoes. "Take a dead man ta tell them kinda people good-bye an' ta keep a dry eyeball at th' same time," I said. "I never will fergit how them folks looked when they walked in there at our front door last night."

"When Uncle Charlie shook his fist at 'em, an' made 'em undress an' lay down in our bedrolls, I'm gon'ta be seein' that run in my head till my ole grayback head quits its runnin'," Eddie told us. Then he asked Papa, "How come ya ta blink yer eyes an' grip yer teeth sa bad, Charlie, when ya shook Red's hand good-bye jist now?"

"Yeah." I wrastled and played along the ground with the pooch, and told them, "Jist a-fixin' ta ask y' th' same question. I saw them big ole drops o' tearjuice tricklin' down."

"Red gripped my knuckles a little too hard, I guess." Papa rubbed his left-hand fingers over his right knuckles in the warmth of his old fuzzery shirt in the upcoming sun. "Sure did shoot my right arm and my shoulder full of red-hot needles. Hyaummhh. I'm just leaning up here against this old wreckedy meat-house wall, men, waiting to see what in the sam patch is going to hit us next. Ooetchh. Ohhmm."

"Little ground-rattler friend is still givin' yo troubles," I said. "Want me ta run out fer Sam Nail an' git 'im ta come haul y' over some'res ta th' doctor? Huhhm?"

"Never sucked out alla that there dangburn poizen," Eddie said. "Shore'd better'd git it over to one o' these here towns ta where a doctor c'n git a look at it, Charlie. He must've hook'd them little ole needle fangs in ya lots deeper'n we figger'd." Eddie walked over and looked at Papa's hand. "Looks like it's painin' th' devul outta yer whole arm here. Is it?"

"I can't climb the rocks this morning with you boys." Papa moved his right fingers in the air. "You make a run over and check all around those Horse Trough Spring cliffs without me. I'll stick here around the house and be the watchdog, and I'll be the camp cook, too. I can't be your waterboy, because my fingers won't grip that much of a load. I may so much as twist up a new barkweed broom and give our *hacienda* the sweeping of the century, you can't ever tell. You go without me. You'll see."

The Horse Trough Spring cliffs lay a good three or four miles due east, close under the top rims of the Chisos. Eddie worried all day long about Papa's snakebite. I dropped our bottle of drinking water as I tried to climb a slick-face cliff to check Claude's maps with the humpy bumps of the rocks. One page of the maps blew out of my hand and it took us the better part of an hour to crawl down some steep granite to get it back. We found as much trace of Paw's mine on this day as we had found on the worst of our other zero days.

Eddie crawled along a flat footpath to take a look inside a two-by-four cave about a hundred feet up the facing. I stood on a high rock over across a dried-out water gulch and watched him crowd into the little cave. I could see no more than the bottoms of his shoe soles, but I could hear him scream bloody butcher and yell for help. A pair of cave eagles clawed his leather cap, his jumper, and his overalls into shreds of wild threads. He took a bad pecking and a wing beating before he was able to squirm out of the cave backwards. I heard the pounding and his bawling for help, but I fell down into the dry gulch when I tried to jump across to drag him out of the hole. I threw three or four poolball-size rocks at the pair of lovely birds, but my rocks hit Eddie's rumps and legs instead of the eagles. Eddie sat up to rub his face and head while the birds took a few circles in the air to peck at him. He left his tough leather railroader cap somewhere back in that cave. I teased him all the rest of that day, and for a couple more days, asking him, "When are you going to go back to that cleaning shop and pick up your cap?"

Back down at the adobe house again, we found Papa soaking his fist in a gallon bucket of simmery water. He made Eddie and me eat a fish and corn-patty supper while he kept on heating his hand in the hot bucket on the stove. He said that Mr. Nail's daughter had left the fish and a letter addressed to me. Papa did not eat, he told us, on account of he had nibbled all day around the cookhouse. We guessed that he did not eat because his fingers cramped so bad.

"Who's th' mail from?" Ed watched me across our packing cases and tin dishes, " 'F t'aint no big dark secrit?"

"Yes, who?" Papa kidded.

I tore into the letter, saying, "As if ya didn't awready know. Y' read th' name an' address on th' envelope. Yahh."

"Rio Rinnie?" Eddie pooched his mouth.

"Venus de Milo?" Papa shook his bucket. "Humm?"

"Missie Hell Cat Cliffman." I read the first page, the only page there was. "Hmmm."

My dear W.W., Jeff, Uncle Charlie, Eddie Stone, and all:

Yours of this date received and contents noted. Each time a boy friend comes into my life, I love to save and to keep all of his lover's notes. I keep all of his puppy-lovey mash notes. I keep all of his letters, the hot kind and the cold kind. When he chooses to drift or to drop out of my life, I borrow my mother's scissors and I cut his notes and his letters up into small pieces all different shapes. I put these pieces into a handmade pillow cover as tight as they will go, and I let my next sweetie lay his head down on all of my pillows when he comes to court me (while mama is to the movie show). Remember????? Your notes and letters are now cut up and stuffed into my fifth pillow. They are clean, nice, safe & sound there. Do not worry. I hope that you all find your gold mine and get rich and nasty real soon. I am proud of you for telling me about your new girl, Rio Rina. She sounds like lots of fun. Red Cruthers and I are getting in our share. I see your folks the same as ever and they all feel lonesome to see you, so write to them often. They are all well. Cleda had the mumps on one jaw but got over it in a few days.

> Much love
> Your friend
> HELEN
> (C.) (?) (?)

I took Riorina's address out of the tobacco can on the window ledge, wrote it onto a blank envelope, and wrote my new address in the corner, W.W.G., Mudwork Jobber, c/o Mr. Sam Nail, RFD, Alpine, Texas. As I started to walk out to Mr. Nail's RFD box to post Riorina's letter, Papa wiggled his fingers in his water can, and closed his eyes to tease me by saying, "Riorina de Gonzalez, General Delivery, Tucson, Arizona. Mmm. Did I guess it correctly?"

I held my breath and told him, "Yeahp. Tha's right. Anything ta say 'ginst 'er? How's th' sore finger?"

"The finger, the same as all sore fingers, feels very sorely." Papa screwed his face up in a twist of pain. "But this simmery water is mortally drawing my pains out through my fingernails. It's hard to bear the hot water, you know, but I sprinkled a half a box of salt down into my bucket, and I can feel it doing the trick. No, son, I have nothing at all against you. I'm not holding anything against your new girl."

"Got any letters ya want mailed? Boxes? Crates? Packages? Fur coats, diamond rings, filled-up money belts, gold sacks, deeds, titles, legal papers, marriage papers, any kind o' damn papers?"

"Not this week." Eddie grinned. "Them gol-blasted eagles grabbed my papers an' money, both, up yonder t'day, an' flew clean off with 'em."

Papa rubbed his left hand over his right elbow.

"I sent one letter back by Mr. Nail's daughter," he said, "that arrived in Mr. Nail's box for Jeff, from Irene."

I walked down the gentle little west slope through the sandyroot bushes and tracks that lay in between the old mudbrick camp house and Sam Nail's mail box. The plants, mountains, bugs, and birds, in the high colors of the sun going down, took my old breath out of me, somehow, and gave me a breath of new-found air to draw, to taste, to feel from my head on down to my toes. The tin mailbox looked like a friend.

I walked slow back to the house, and asked Papa through the wooden blinds of the south window, "This girl, ahmm, this daughter of Mister Nail's, how did she look?"

"She looked pretty enough to eat," Papa told me through the window boards.

"Most of the girls are pretty enough ta eat," I laughed back.

"For a twelve-year-older," Papa said, "she was a jim dandy."

"Little bit on th' young side," Eddie said. "Tenderish."

"Twelve, huh?" I walked over towards the truck, speaking up louder, "Drop around here in a coupla years an' ask 'er if she'll marry me. I'm a-settin' my traps right this minute ta ketch me a female womern from this here Rough Run-Rio country. I'm a-gonna knock off about six er nine boys an' girls an' each 'em how ta walk an' climb an' fight eagles an' ground rattlers, an', by goshy, dig up that mine of Grampaw's, an' fifteen others a whole lot deeper an' richer. Y' been messin' 'round tryin' ta fix this old dead truck with yer snake-bit han', I see by the tracks. That's jest one hell of a god-dern crazy trick, 'f ya're askin' me."

"I was merely tinkering," Papa hollered from the stove.

"Hadn't oughta try nothing heavy, Charlie," I heard Eddie warning Papa, "till them fingers limbers up some."

"I guess it was Old Man Rio, in th' flesh, his own self, that crawled down in here around on th' ground, an' unscrewed all o' these bolts ta drop down this magneto flywheel pan. Red Sundown told me he suspected the worries wasn't nowhere in that mag brush, anyway. Red said all we gotta do is ta whittle out some little hardwood pegs an' pound 'em down in t'wixt th' coil an' th' coil-box, see." I climbed up and flipped the dead coil under the dashboard as I talked. I saw Ed step up to watch me, while Papa stayed inside to keep his fingers in the salty soak. "See here, like this."

It was just at that certain split millionth of a second when the sundown melts into the dark that Eddie leaned bareheaded in over the steering wheel to ask me, "Coilbox? Okay. But did Little Red Moonshine tell you how ta make this here firecrate pull up 'n' outta here on four flat tires?"

And the dark caught both of us nodding our heads up, down, yes, no, maybe, I don't know, I just didn't think, I guess I forgot about that, I just didn't, I mean, I guess I'd ought to be shot.

Papa stayed at the house to take care of his hands while I climbed with Eddie on the seventh high and holy day. Papa wound some small-gauge cotton rope around Ed's jug, which made us a fine water bottle. We filled our jug at the cottonwood spring, then kept to the low brush all day long. Papa kept Claude's maps at the house to study over them some more. Eddie and myself walked this day on a hunch, on hearsay, on a word or two of gossip, to

look out for an old, handmade water dike. "A little dam
that raised the water up along about knee high to the
standing cattle," as we had sometimes heard Jeff recall to
us. "That spring of pure medical waters fed down into
this watering pond above the dam," Jeff would say. "Those
medicated waters, to judge by their smell, could be bottled
and labeled as a Cure for What Ails You, and sold, and
make more money, maybe, than Paw Jerry's claim at a
hundred dollars a ton dug."

Sam Nail's own daughter had told Papa yesterday that
there was only one such man-made water hole in her
whole valley, south of ours, all the way down from her
house to the Rio Grande. Oh, well, our newly cut rub-
bertire shoe soles were still holding out. What's a few more
steps, a few more puffs, a few more grinds, a few more
cliffrock pulls; a few more thousand stickery limbs, dead
roots, coiled snakes, scared birds; a few more blistered
hands and feet, and daggered ankles? Eddie and me could
make it. We did make it, like we had made everything
else. And we found the same as we had found in our other
walks, falls, and tumblings—exactly nothing. No trace. No
track. No trail. No smell, no nothing. Ed stood on the
measured spot where the medical pond ought to lay, kicked
some loose dirt, and told me, "Paw Jerry's spirit must be
testin' us out to see who's gon'ta be th' last one ta cave
in an' fall down."

Just as we kicked our shoe toes around again in the
general direction of home, I told Ed, "Paw Jerry is makin'
us earn our money, ain't he? Well, don't much blame 'im
fer that. I don't like nothin' if it's too danged easy t' find.
Hmm? You?"

"Nawp. Reckon I don't. Still, didn't take you none too
long ta get worked in with Riorinny back over yonder at
Study Butte. You shorely didn't have ta dig down any too
long ta find her. Seems like ye've tooken a right smart a-
likin' ta her."

"Yeah, but Eddie, you're lettin' it slip your brains completely that I had ta dig an' smell an' bark an' scratch an'
sniffle, an' hunt, man, fer nineteen an' a half of th' gad-
blamedest, blindest, craziest years 'fore I was able even ta
find that Rio River, an' that Study Butte."

Tickling his nose in his fingers, Eddie said: "Man, you
don't know whut it is bein' lonesome an' crazy, an' cravin',
an' lookin', an' a-frothin' an' a-boilin on yer insides ta

look out in front of ya ta see th' woomern that's cut out
for ya. I can't tell ya how bad it was a-burnin' me down,
Woody, 'fore I met up with Luisa. Fact is, I'm supposin' ta
go back over an' see 'er again, round about a couple days
from now."

"Looky," I pointed from the top of a little rising knoll,
"ya can see the top of Sam Nail's house an' his windmill,
an' on over ta our 'dobe house. See yonder? Ah, Ed, jest
wanta ask ya . . . how d'ya feel about Grampaw's mine by
this time?"

"They's not no more places to go look." Eddie wiped his
crippled hand across his forehead. "These here old weed
seeds mortally itch a man t' death, don't they? I be dawg'd!
Little old muddy house looks jest about like a dang-burn
matchbox settin' over yonder, don't it? I know that we can
find th' mine, 'er leastwise, I feel like we can. I shore ain't
itchin' off my britches, Woodhead, ta go back an' tittysuck
aroun' Maw an' them. Let 'em draw my sixty-five forty
ever' blame month. Let 'em mail me down five, ten, or
fifteen of it. I could git by down in here on jest next to
nothin'."

Walking some more in the low bush, I said, "I'm feelin'
th' same way as you feel, Ed. We've done used up th'
maps Claude drawed fer us. Cover'd ever' spot that anybody could tell us about."

In the high stickers, I heard Ed sneeze and say, "Covered
some of th' places twicet an' three times."

"Th' way we give away a few little extry groceries here
an' yonder, Papa won't admit it, but I know we've run
plumb out. Papa won't say nothin' 'bout his bit hand, but
I know that he's gotta be 'round a doctor fer a coupla
weeks 'fore he's gonna be able ta move even one finger."

"Awful bad hand," Ed said. "He's gon'ta have ta go
back up home 'round his folks."

"How're ya figgerin' on gettin' back over t' Study Butte
where y' said ya'd meet Luisa?"

"Strike out an' walk, I 'magine." Ed straightened up his
back and shoulders like a soldier who'd got his second
wind. " 'Twasn't more 'n eighteen er nineteen miles over
here; 'tain't no further th'n that back. I'm gon'ta try my
dad-gumdest, Wood, ta try ta git Luisa ta help me figger
out some way ta stick down in here. Gon'ta git 'er ta help
me set a trap line an' run it. If Mama'll send me jest five
dollers a month on th' dot an' on time, an' if I can sell ten

er 'leven worth of hides an' skins ever' month, I could stick down in here till my kids jumps up an' finds that there mine some o' these here days."

"Time," I told him, "time's what it is goin' t' take. All kinds o' time. Slow, long, easy time. I don't even need them old crazy maps of Claude's. I done got all o' that stuff down right here'n my head . . . Our old rich money-baggy Auntie Greenseed might toss about a dozen fifty-dollar gold pieces ta help us go in an' buy th' best damn string of claw-tooth traps in th' whole flurky state of Texas."

"Yeah, an' your old Pappy Charlie would go plumb loco pocono," Ed told me. "That'd hurt him lots more'n a little old sissyfied thing like a ground rattlin' snake. My own mama wouldn't send me forty-seven cents a month, if'n she knowed I knocked my hand on that there Greenseeds' door ta beg fer help. We'd have ta cut Auntie Greenseed in on ever' truckload that shoveled up outta that mine. Line of traps would be th' best way ta stick here."

I kept quiet for the rest of the way. We found Papa working on the truck's coil-box when we got to the front yard. He was sitting on the sunny south running board and rubbing one of the flat metal flipper points around over a flat sandy rock on his knees. Ed was in a little more of a joshy mood than I was. The whole house, yard, bushes, broke windmill, cottonwood spring, truck, everything about the place, looked like a good reason to hang down my head and keep still. Eddie joked and said, " 'Bout a ride with ya inta town, there, Mister?"

"I just can't afford to slow down long enough to pick you men up."

Eddie fanned his elbows around, and said, "I got a car-load of skins ta sell fer spot cash in Pueblo. 'Taint too far away from Denver town, is it?"

"I wouldn't know." Papa kept sanding. "What panther cat grabbed your tongue today, Sir Woodrow? Lost your vocal cords?"

"I'm jest a-keepin' my mouth still," I told Papa, "till I hear some talkin' outta you guys that makes a little streak o' sense."

"Upon which topic, now, do you wish to speak, or to hear your father speak, son?"

" 'Bout a lotta stuff." I paced up and down close to his knee.

"The stuff, as you label it . . . is there any other plainer name for it in any of the books of knowledge and wisdom? What might you wish to speak about?" Papa nodded his head clowny and sidewards.

" 'Bout them there fingers ye're usin' there." I looked at his knotty knuckles holding onto the things in his lap. "Them there fingers, about which you've not spoke one single horse-sensible word in th' past three or four days."

"What about them, son?"

"What about them groceries all a-runnin' out? That pork 'n' beans? Them sardines? Them crackers? That side of sugar-cured bacon? Them dozen cans o' cream? All ya've got left in yonder is a half a sack of cornmeal an' three or four pounds o' coffee, god-blamed ole chickery, pea-berry coffee. An' did ya open yer mouth about it when th' ten pounds o' sugar give out? No. Y' didn't. Y' know damn good 'n' well y' didn't. Tryin' ta make it look like everthing's okie doakie, when ya know damn good 'n' well we're gon'ta hafta live on black coffee an' cornmeal mush, an' fried rabbit, all o' the rest o' the time that we're down here?" I kept up with my pacing as I talked.

"Y've not been as honest as ya could, Charlie," Eddie told him, "about them there old swollen knuckles of yores."

Papa's face broke away into a melting run of tears as he asked us, "For Good God's own sake, men, can't I be the judge as to how my own two hands feel? Why, you didn't dwell under the false illusion that those eatables would last us forever and for all, did you? I dare say that our Paw Jerry and his wife and his kids would call our victuals a grand and glorious feast of some kind."

"Paw Jerry an' his wife'd talk honest about 'em," I told Papa. "Shore, a broke-off matchstick can taste like a big meal if it's all that you've got, an' y' don't try ta make it look like ya've got some more somewheres. Me an' Eddie, here, decided that we cain't let ya stay no more, Papa. Yore fingers, there, an' your whole arm an' shoulder're too swollen up, too stiff, too bad of a color, ta let y' stick down in here sa far away from a doctor any longer."

Papa sanded, and said, "Is that not a sweet consideration? How did you two decide to transport me to this medical doctor? All that any medical doctor would tell me, after putting my five dollars in his vest pocket, would be, 'Well, Mister Charlie, my advice to you is to go home and soak your fingers down in some hot salty water, as hot as you can stand it.' And I've been doing that here on our monkey stove. For nothing, for free."

I told him, "You always was a hard man to drag to a doctor."

"I'm not against doctors, and I do not hate a doctor." Papa worked at his sand-smoothing job, looking down. "I simply get mad when I get myself inside a doctor's office. I am not mad at the doctor, I am sorely peeved at the thing that sent me there—like a good bare-knuckle fist-fighter, a sharp knife blade, a pistol butt . . ."

"Like, mebbe," Ed put in, "a little wormy baby-sized ground rattler?"

" 'At's it," I said.

"Ground rattler. Ground rattler, hell." Papa sanded the coil spring around faster as his temper moved up hotter. "That ground rattlesnake did not bite your finger, he bit mine. I know, boys, I can feel my own finger a good deal better than you can. I know that the pain is leaving it. I am working here, am I not? I am holding this coil spring, am I not?"

"By them colors of yer swollen fingers, Charlie, I couldn't even tell ya which was which." Eddie touched his good left-hand fingers onto the coil spring, and told us, "That blue steel spring an' yore stiff skin is both jest about th' same dern color."

And I said, "Yeah. One's jest as purple as th' other."

"An' jest as dern-gum stiff lookin'," Ed said.

"No stiffer, Sir Eddie," Papa said, "than your dried-up right hand."

"Papa." I shook my head.

"And the worst that can possibly happen to my hand and my arm has already happened to yours, Mister Eddie boy son. You still get around over these sticker hills. You still work at your carpenter shop back home."

"Reckon I do," Ed admitted.

I shook my head sidewise, No, No, and said, "Papa!"

"I apologize, Ed. I am asking your pardon. I should not have let that slip." Papa bit his lips. "I will gladly allow you to wash my mouth out with soapy water, if you wish."

Eddie swallowed a hard smile and said, "Save yer soap. Warsh y'r boots with it. I like it whenever ya talk about my shot-up arm, Charlie. Hurts me lots worse when y' keep sa still an' don't even talk about it."

"My snaky finger feels a great deal better, too." Papa watched Ed's left hand rub up and down the jumper sleeve over the shriveled, bony knots and humps. Then he said, "I mean to say, when we drag it out here into the open air and talk about it."

"Hmmmmhh." Eddie touched his neck.

"It'd make me feel ten years younger"—I shuffled along with both hands down in my pockets—"if you'd be a little truthfuller 'bout yer hands. Go ahead on, talk. They's plenty of open air all around here. Talk it out."

Papa's head hung down when he spoke. "The open-air truth of the matter, men, is this: I am not any good to you any longer."

"I rolled an' squirmed on my hospital bed fer more'n twenty months, Uncle Charlie, an' groaned I wasn't no more account ta m'seff er t' anybody else. But I found out th' hard way that as long as I'm a-suckin' wind—long's my blood's runnin'—I'm a whole big bunch of good ta somebody, someplace. Mebbe they's a doctor somewheres over yunder at Study Butte." Ed patted Papa's knees. "An' mebbe we'll not have ta haul ya six hundert miles back up ta Pampa t' git cured up."

"Pampa?" Papa broke down crying. "Pampa? Back to Pampa? Oh, not all the way back up there! Oh, you both are so right, so right, about my fingers. That fiery sting has burned me worse than a thousand red-hot sewing needles, all the way up over my knuckles, my wrist here. My elbow and shoulder bone feel exactly like cast-iron locks on a concrete graveblock. I can't wiggle my fingers out of this position here around this old sanding stone and steel coiler spring. They're locked and barred. My whole arm is locked and barred. No good any more. No good to you boys any more. Just a dead saltblock weight around your legs. Just a bundle of dead, flabbery old gray-haired blood and bones around your necks. Ohh, boys, I don't want to go back up to Pampa and pile around on the folks any more—not any more like those months when they all nursed me back to breathing life. I wanted more than anything on this earth to stay down here, to keep on with our looking around. I did so crave and hope that, if we did have to leave for good, sensible reasons, I could be the last one of us to tell this Rough Run good-bye and fare thee well."

"I wished that same thing." I put my hand on the back

of Papa's neck to rub. "Th't I could be th' last one t' leave it."

"An' th' first one to come back, I wisht." Eddie kept on patting Papa on the knees. "Me 'n' Woodrow's been tryin' ta think up some derned cussified way er systum er scheme ta make us enough dern money ta keep us in grub an' gunwaddin' whilst we tried ta go on a-lookin'. Huntin'. I figgered that we might put us in a big line of traps, an' live off th' fur an' skin money so's we can keep on a-diggin' around."

"We've not even got five dollars, boys." Papa wiped his tears on the back fingers of his left hand. "It will take every penny of five hundred to buy a ring of good steel traps and a few months' grubstake."

"How about lettin' Sam Nail come in fer a share an' puttin' up th' cash ta stake our grubbers? Hmm?" I asked them.

Papa threw his hurt finger in the air and hopped up onto his feet, crying. Squinting and hopping around the truck, flipping his fingers to limber them, to flow the blood through them, he cried back at us, "If Sam Nail gets one-eighth for holding the school lease on this land, and we give him another eighth for staking us to trap lines and groceries, Sam will already come in for one fourth part, one whole quarter. No, no, no! fifty times—no, no, no! I'm dead set against such a sell-out of all that Paw and the rest of us have worked and dragged ourselves hungry and ragged for, now for these twenty-nine long, hard years. Let's go back to Pampa. Let's walk back, catch rides, crawl or cripple back, any way to get back. You boys have lost your minds entirely and completely. I can get a few dollars by going around knocking my old burning knuckles on the doors of members of our family."

"Yer hands wouldn't last past many doors," I said, pacing the dirt, "stiff 'n' full o' greenerish damn poison th' way they are. An' besides, Papa, they's not six of our family that has got enough ta buy snuff an' tobacco with, let alone to pass out to us to trail back down here a second time to track down nothin'. We didn't chop off no sample chunks of Paw's mine yet, if ya recall, ta show our laughin' kinfolks what'n the hell they'd be layin' out the good bucks for."

"Wouldn't pick up enough coppers ta fill th' bottom

linin' of yer ole, dog-eared fedora hat, Charlie," Ed told him.

To make his fingers feel a little warmer, Papa eased his bitten hand down into his overalls pocket, saying, "I intend to find this mine, boys, without any professional money lender coming in to gobble the best part down—I mean the juicy gravy, without doing a stitch of the work of locating or developing it. I can still see a nice beautiful picture in my head: the mine buildings, the slaggy dumps, the shaley pile, the open shaft, the truck road, and all of our houses built alongside. All of us, all of our relations, dressed up in fancy boots and duds, riding all around to do our jobs for today. Kids out there skipping all around. I am telling a few of them how long and how hard a climb it was before we found it. I can see Ed building a new building—an adobe-walled place, where several of our Indian and Mexican friends help him, at good pay, to bottle, to label, crate, and ship to all parts of the sickly, crampy, constipated world, his guaranteed Britches Down Medicinal Waters. But I just never could see Mr. Sam Nail, nor any other man, or woman, for that matter, standing there on the highest stack of our shaley dust, and saying, 'I own one fourth of all I see here, and I own one whole quarter merely because the lease papers and the bank account were in my name because of a little, lousy, measly five hundred dollars I let these fellows use for six little, pissledy months.'"

"I'd much rather have three-fourths of the mine, than not ta come out with anythaing at all," I told Papa.

Papa made me no answer. He kicked the dirt with his toes and listened to Ed say, "I reckon this'll be jest about my last day around here, Charlie."

"Last day?" Papa asked him. "What are you talking about?"

Ed kept his running-board seat and told us, "My last day of this perticaler mine hunt. I'm a-headin' back off over 'cross yonder ta try my goldingdist ta ketch myseff a wife. Study Butte."

"Studio beauty," I told Papa. "Name of Luisa."

"Luisa?" Papa nodded back. "When did you make that connection over there? Pretty swift operating."

"Onlyest thaing that's slow about me," Eddie said, "is my money. I jest feel like I can dig out lots more over at Study Bee than I can dig out around Sammy Nail's."

"Wish I had yore chance," I told Ed. "My gal went off ta help 'er folks make a little crop money ta do 'em this winter. Hey, mebbe all of us can work th' dam-burn crops an' make enough ta come back an' smell around some more. Huh?"

"Crops, hell," Ed said. "Charlie's hand wouldn't last down th' first long row. Starve ta death a-workin' them crops. Big string of fur traps. Tha's what this here outfit needs worser'n anything."

"Ed," we heard Papa break in, as he leaned on the radiator, "half of the boys in this world are just on the cliff-rim of pure insanity, trying to make a big stack of gold chips before they go and face into a woman. You can always tell your kids and grandkids, that I told you to grab onto your woman first. Make your fortune, be it good or bad, be it richly or poorly, together with your woman. I say grab your girl while she is still young and pretty, and while your own bony joints are bendy and not screakery. I've watched a hundred men try that single route alone, and take my word for it, they always do come to a crack-up. Some kind of a tailspin. And you could say, all because they courted too slow and never did tackle onto their right pardner. I certainly will not stand in your way, Eddie Stoner. I'll go back. I'll go with you, Woody, back up to Pampa."

"You'll not go back with me," I told Papa. I kicked the spokes of the left front wheel. "I'm not headin' out that way. I'm goin' up yore brushy trail as far north as Alpine."

Papa touched the wooden box of the coil he had been working on and asked me, with worried eyes, "North to Alpine? And then where?"

"West, that's where," I told him. "West from Alpine two hundred 'n' sixty-nine miles to a little spot in th' road by the name of El Paso—El Paso del Norte."

"Through El Paso, you mean?" Papa tapped the brass cap of the radiator. "And then on out west of there to wait around that General Delivery window in Tucson until you hear somebody call for the mail that belongs to Riorina de Gonzalez? I can stand out by the side of that Pampa highway as good as any of you young squirts—that is, if you do decide to follow that girl to Arizona. And your old papa will kiss you good-bye and wish you good luck, the same as I just this minute wished for Eddie and Luisa."

"I, my own self, never did think that I'd ever even think

about marryin' off inta Mexican blood, er Indian, either one, far's that goes." Eddie caught sight of the little flipper spring on the dirt where Papa had let it fall. He picked it up, blew its loose dust away, and went on, "But, by juniper juice an' by grassyhoppers, I'm shore gon'ta switch my tail over ta Study Butte an' ask that there Luisa womern, 'fore she runs off 'n' gits all tangled up with some dang-gum sheep-trail man er cowboy. Dern-gum smooth filin' job ya've done here on this here point, Charlie. Think I'll screw th' tap back on it, an' shove its coil-box down in there with th' rest o' them. Hey, fellers, I'll push this here coil back down in th' box here, now. I'm flippin' th' switch on. Wham! There!"

I watched Ed's retread shoe soles kick around outside the cab door while he laid along the floorboards to replace the cleaned coils. I moved both my ears in the late afternoon sun rays, and pooched up my lips to say, "Mmmhh! Hear what I'm hearin'?"

"Spark sings like a tree frog!" Papa nodded. "Give the crank handle a swift twist, Wood Son boy. I'm tugging over here on the choker wire with all five of my best fingers."

I could hear Eddie grunting on the floor timbers under the driver's wheel. I turned the crank over to its slip-in position and lifted it over a few times. Papa's choke wire opened the lungs of his carburetor to sing a steamy kind of a song to fit in with the buzzing songs of Eddie's magneto as the blue spark jumped down from the flipper spring to swing onto the long, slim-jim carbon post. On my fourth or fifth spin of the crank handle the spark flew and the blue smoke blew.

Papa patted his better hand on the open bottom side of the carburetor to tell it, and us, "There's not an easier starter than that in the Ford Motors factory line this afternoon. Well, I will be digged! Just look at that."

I lifted both sides of the hood while Papa laughed out with big tears in his eyes. I heard Eddie holler up from his floorboards: "I can ride over an' git myself married, an' by gollikers, ride back over here 'n' find Grampaw's mine. Yessir, dearly beloved, before that old sun can set itself down over there on th' tip top of that pretty Study Butte rock mountain. Yippee!"

"And," Papa spread his feet wide and stood proud, "for me, I can ride in the latest fashion all those six hundred miles back up to Pampa to get ready and set to drive right back down here again as quick as I've raised up the money green."

"Carry me up ta th' Alpine crossroad"—I felt the radiator getting warm under my fingers—"an' carry Papa on back up ta th' folks at Pampa, an' lemme ketch a big, long ride in anythaing that's got wheels on it on into El Passyo. I'll see how much dough I c'n raise up when I uncork my mouth an' tell my grubstake troubles ta my old, rich, moneybagger Aunt Patsy Greenseed."

Papa jumped up onto the driving seat, threw down the hand brake, shoved the clutch pedal down, drove around on the hardpan dirt with four flat tires kicking gravel. Eddie rolled around about the floorboards with his hands out the right side and his feet dangling out on the left. I jumped up onto the back bed as Papa whirled his next circle, and braced my hands against the top of the cab.

Papa yelled, cursed, shouted a wild song above the roarings of the motor, and the rattles of the screaky Model T. I could hear Papa's words flap around the side of the cab: "Seven flat tires, Aunt Patsy Greenseed! Eight flat tires, Aunt Patsy Greenseed! Nine flat tires, Aunt Patsy Greenseed! Ten flat tires!"

He drove twelve or fifteen miles an hour in his circlings, then steered it headlong and straight into the easterly end of the south adobe wall. Ed rolled out and down along the ground to bump against the wall. All of us yelled as loud as we could to try to drown out the noises of the crash against the mud wall. I heard the motor spin hot and fast enough to keep the hind-end wheels digging down in the dirt, which pushed the nose end, radiator, front wheels, the fenders, and even the motor itself, with jerks and goathead pushes, against the old sunny-brick adobe laid wall. I jumped off and skinned both knees on the small rolly rocks, to run and stumble clear of the truck. I saw Papa duck out of the cab and limp in at the front door.

I dragged my bloody knees in through the door just in time to hear Papa jump from the four-foot east window ledge down onto the softer ground on that side. I shoved and pushed my way through the beehive boxes that he had jerked down to block my trail. I called to him out through the window, to where he was chasing away in the cactus brushes: "Papa! Papa! Hey, Papa! What—ahh—wheere'n th' name of hell d'ya think y're runnin' off to? Pappaa!"

I heard Eddie out there in the east yard somewhere,

talking to himself, to Papa, and to me through the window: "Gad-rattled silly trick ta pull, if'n ya're askin' me what I think about it! That there damn-derned Charlie has gone jest as buggy as a damn peach-orchard boare hog."

"See any track of 'im?" I stuck my nose out of the window. "What did he do?"

"Nawwp. He's run off out here in this brambley brush, that's what he's done. I seen plumb smart fellers break down, Wood Head, over yonder in France, jest th' same way that yer papa jest now done. I guess I run perty hog-wild a few times my own self."

I walked out the front door because my knees hurt too bad to make any east-window jumps. I listened to Eddie a minute, then said, "I shore didn't expect old Aunt Patsy Greenseed ta make Papa pull any kind of a stunt like this."

"I tolja a time er two how it'd hurt 'im." Ed's eyes went down around the weedy track by the cottonwood spring. "Y' could of went on up ta see Patsy without rub-bin' it all over Charlie th' way that ya did do. Could of told 'im ya was on yer way over ta Tucson ta look aroun' that there post office, jest th' way Charlie said."

"D'ya s'pose he's gonna come back? Papa! Pappaa! Heyyhh! Come outta them burrs an' paper yore chin. Hey John, Lost John, my six men, come outta them bushes an' shave yore chin! One, two, three, spells out goes you two, me three, him four, her five, she six, it eight, ham nine an' aigs a dozen—an' a dime apiece, an' lather yore jaws with my best grease! Papaa! C'mon in home! I see ya out yonder a-shakin' that sticker limb." I pounded on the fender of the truck cooling down. "Pappaahh!"

"Better'd come aroun' out here in th' bushes." Ed walked in among the branches where we guessed Papa had run. I ran back to the bushes to the north and walked along, listening to Eddie call out, "Hey! Hey! Hey, Charlie! Charlie! Uncle Charlie! Come back to this house this very damn minute! C'mon back here. D'you hear me?"

I fought and pounded the branches as I walked along, cursing and calling, "Papaa! Papaa! Don't act like a damn fool! Have you gone plumb crazy on us? Papaa! Papaa! If you can hear th' sound of my voice, come on back. This ain't no damn way ta settle an argument. There's flies, there's lizards, there's catamounts, an' scorpions; there's spiders, tarantulas, centipedes, an' wild buzzards

out here'n this blame ole stickery brush. Mebbe I'll not go
knock on th' door of th' Greenseeds after all, if ya'll walk
on back here an' stand up'n talk about it like a man. Papaa!
Papaa! Ya'll starve clean smack smooth ta death out here
in these crazy old wild bush brushes. Come on back—
back!"

After passing Eddie a few turns around the house, I
climbed up on the old wreck of a truckbed and leaned
back against the sideboard to shake out my loose shoes and
to try to think what to do next. I heard somebody walk
up across the yard, talking, listening to Eddie as they got
closer. Sam Nail and Eddie looked over the end-gate at
me, while Sam spoke to say, "Well. Which did you find
to be the stronger, the truck or the house?"

"House," I told him.

"Won't take more'n a coupla days' fixin' ta git that there
wall back up in pretty good shape," Ed said, looking
around. "This here ole truck, though, is gon'ta take a big
jackin' up an' a brand new truck run down in under it."

Sam said, "It will require time and patience."

" 'Tain't gettin' none o' my time nor patience," I told
them. "Me, I, Woodrow, I'm glad ta see th' damn-dern
thing wrecked. I was afraid there for a while that I'd be
havin' ta climb up on th' damn outfit an' ride 'er back up
over them humpy rock roads 'tween here an' Study Butte."

"A big worry is off your mind, I suppose," Sam kidded
us. "But you don't necessarily have to go back through
Study Butte to get back up to Alpine. It's more than forty
miles closer if you go right back up here due north through
the Slick Rock Wagon Gap, past the Oak Canyon Ranch.
Nobody from around here ever drives through Study and
Terlingua to arrive on the scenes of Alpine. Eddie just now
told me that you made your father angry about something,
and that he ran off away to the laughing daggers. Right?"

"Daggers, I guess, but I didn't hear much laughin'," I
said. "I told Papa I was goin' ta borrow a few hundred off
o' my rich bankin' Auntie Patsy Greenseed, ta use fer a
grubstake, y' know? An', well, he got his pride hurt, I
reckon, an' took off in a high lope ta live around in them
dagg'r thorns like that ole crazy laughin' camp cook—
what's 'is name? You know 'im."

"Ole Buggerhead." Eddie nodded.

"Niggerhead, we call him," Sam said. "I have lost my
head one or two times about such things and tracked away

mad as all fire out to weep on the dewy thorn. But I came back to my house and to my woman before very many lost hours elapsed."

"Ain't no womern fer him ta come back to down here," Ed told Sam. "There's jest not much I can think that a man would be drawed back to here—I mean around this here place. Charlie's womern lives jest about six hundred miles back up yonder to th' north of here—jest a mile an' a quarter in on this side of th' Northerly Pole."

"How long," I asked Ed, "d'ya think he might stay gone?"

"Not a bit o' dern tellin'." Eddie shook his head, chin down. "Maddest ever did see Uncle Charlie in all o' my born days."

"Oh, I believe he will be back. It will take a little time for him to get over his pride. He will be back." Sam tried to make us feel good.

"Not's long as he can peek up out o' them bushes an' see my fires smokin' here'n th' monkey stove," I said. "Not's long as he sees my damn crazy bushy head aroun' here. I'm gonna pull up my chips an' pull outta here first thing in th' mornin'."

Sam listened, then said, "I cannot bring him back, or I surely would. I cannot give you a lift north towards Alpine. I happen to be driving my State Senator back over to Study Butte in about an hour. He is looking this land over to make it into a national park."

Ed said, "Boys howdy, I'd give ya my best left arm if'n ya'd gimme a lift over yonder with ya. I've got a little bizness over at Study Beauty I've shore got ta take care of, tanight."

"What's th' name gonna be, of th' park?" I asked Sam. "Can ya dig out a gold mine in a park?"

"Big Bend National Park," Sam said. "Or some such. The surveying has already been done for it. Why, yes, I don't see any reason, Eddie, why we could not make room for you on our trip to Study Butte. We will be leaving out from my gate in about one hour. If you are all ready by then, off we'll go." He hadn't answered my question.

"I'm already ready," Eddie said. "Make ya very mad, Woody, fer me ta take off this away on ya?"

"Nawp," I told him. "I'm pullin' outta here th' first thing in th' mornin'. Sam, you can have this ole wreck

truck ta pay ya back fer the damage to the wall an' the
favors ya've been doin' fer us."

I walked into the house with Ed while Sam drove for
home in his car. Ed washed his face and hands, combed
his hair, and asked me, "Ya don't feel like I'm pullin' out
an' a-runnin' off on ya, do ya, Woodseed? 'F ya want me
ta stay around here till ya find Uncle Charlie, er till he
comes back, I'll not ride with Sam over ta see Luisa.
Huhmm?"

I sat on the edge of the bedroll pallet, and watched
Eddie get cleaned up. "Ya can find Paw Jerry's mine lots
quicker with Luisa than ya can without 'er. Only thing
worries me, Ed, is how you an' me'll stay in touch with
one another. You've not wrote nobody a letter in seventeen
flat years, so I'll not expect ya t' write me one."

"I ain't gittin' my old hide any too clean." Eddie rubbed
his face and chin red and white with his left hand. "But
reckon I can git cleaned up a good bit slicker whenever I
pull in over at th' homemade hand-run laundry. Yeahp.
Ain't such a good hand at writin' words down on paper
sheets. I'll make ya this promise, though, Wood Eater—
let's see, now, ahhmm. I'll write a postal card with yore
name on it an' I'll swear ta tell y' how I come out with
Missis Luisa."

"Be fine." I stood up to rub my face and eyes and to
lean on the door looking out south towards the Chisos
humpbacks. "If ya do make a hitch with 'er, an' if ya do
start huntin' fer th' mine some, 'course th' first thing I'd
wanta do would be ta run back down here 'n' help ya.
You 'n' Luisa gonna try ta borry any grubstake money fer
an' eighth? Wonderin'."

"Be none of that." Ed poured and drank a cup of black,
painty coffee as he stood by the stove to look at our old
chunky pieces of sample rocks. "Our kinfolks an' relatives
already makes too many dadburned eighths. Luisa's folks,
too. Be no more come in if I c'n keep 'em out. Cuppa
cawfee? Buggy juice?"

"I'll drain a cup with ya, since y've drug me to it." I
walked to the stove and asked him, "Whatta ya s'pose we'd
best do with all of our crapperitus, here—beddin' an junk?"

"Junk's right." Ed poured my cup on the stove lid. "I
didn't bring nothin' much down here. Pocket knife, pair o'
pliers, old crooked screwdriver. I lost my pocket knife up
yonder at th' damn eagles' roost, where they peck'd my

clothes full o' holes, an' flew off with my leather mechanic's cap. Leaves me without nothin' 'cept my pliers an' old bent screwdriver. Luisa done said she'd be willin' ta start off without much. Gon'ta build us up a mud-brick house an' start up from th' ground, ya might say. Dirt."

"Y' ain't a-layin' too many hopes over there on that there Missy Luisa gally, are ya, Eddie?" I drank my coffee, looking around the room. "Huhhm?"

Ed walked up and down on the ashy-dusted floor and said, "No more'n you're a-puttin' down around Rio Rinnie. Aw, say, Woody Tree, where'bouts would ya like fer me ta mail that there postal card to you at? Th' Greenseeds', er th'—th' Gonzalezes?"

Instead of telling him which name I would be in care of, I asked Eddie, "Jest in case I wanta drop a card off ta you an' Luisa, ah, how'm I gonna address th' name on it?"

Out the door I saw through the southern bushes the little dust cloud that followed Sam's car as it pulled up a hundred yards away to honk its horn for Eddie. He looked out at the car, saying, "I never did learn how ta blow little words up an' play around with 'em like yer Papa Charlie does, Wood Houser. I never did learn how ta say good-bye very good, Mr. & Mrs. Eddie Stone Moore, General Delivery—by gummers, an' by dern—General Delivery, Study Butte, Texas. 'At's all. Be a good Wood Chopper. I'm a-runnin' so's I'll not keep th' State Senator boilin' too long."

I stood in the door and tried to think of a little joke to make Eddie feel good. My eyes caught a glimpse of Rio's old greenery blanket on the wall peg in the room by my guitar. As Eddie walked to the car, I leaned a bit out the door and called to him, "Hey, ya gotta buy me a dime hamburger an' a green bottle of soda water whenever they open up this here Big Bend National Park!"

Ohh. That is right.

I didn't tell Eddie where he could write me that postcard, did I? El Paso or Tucson. The Greenseeds' or the Gonzalezes'. Devil of a trick to pull. Yonder goes that car pulling out. I acted like a fool idiot, not even going out like a man to wave good-bye to Sam Nail and that state man.

I ran out to follow the car as it drove away down the rooty, rutted mesquite and cactus road. Their wheel dust choked my words in my throat faster than I could yell them out. I slipped my ankle sideways in the deeper sand, and stuck every kind of a sticker into my clothes as I hobbled along, limping and yelling in the car's smoky dust. I yelled, "Eddie! Heyyhh! Eddie Stonerr! Not at El Paso! Not at th' Greenseeds'! No Greenseeds!! No, no, nooo! Not at th' Greenseeds'!"

In the shifty plays of windspray lights of the prettiest sundown so far that my eyes had seen, I turned the bones of my other ankle so bad that I stumbled and fell to the tracks of the tires of Sam's car on the rooty road. I pushed myself back up onto my hands and knees, blew the dirt out of my face, mouth, and eyes, and shouted at the dust cloud the way their car had gone: "Tucson! Toossonn! Gonzalezes'! Dammit ta hell, Gonzalezes'!"

After the sounds and rebounds of all the echoes had gone, I saw that the sundown had gone the nightgown trail. My hands and my fingers felt the first chilly winds of a darker night as I rubbed them on my face to clear my eyes. I had no way to know how long I had lain down there hugging the shapes of the bumpy tire tracks.

I felt my way around the room for a match to light the wick of the lantern on its wall peg. To show these crazed and ghostly shapes of things here in the dim flickers of our monkey stove's coals, I yelled at everything in both of the rooms: "Tuussonn! Gen'ral Delivery! Gonzalezes'!"

CHAPTER 22

LAUGHING NUGGETS

I piled a bellyful of root chunks into the stove so the flames could make the room a little brighter. The lantern tried its best, but the stove had a woodysmoke smell which felt better to my nose than the old sooty, keroseny odors from the burning wick. I felt too nervous to go to sleep, and made my plans to stay awake all night and watch the shadows jump and fire flames play. I poured some water and fresh grounds into the coffee pot and listened to the simmering song of the runaway vapors.

I heard every kind of a wingbatter, belly crawler, foot walker, hoof beater, claw scraper, sneaker, peeper, and peeker, that you ever saw or heard tell about. If I told you that every mover's sound had a voice all its own, that would be the truth. A rubby limb, a draggy dry leaf, a windy thorn, a rattly rock, the cooling sounds of the old truck's motor, crackles from twigs and roots, shufflings of things I could not see in the east beehive room, the ashes and the dirt getting older along the floor. A dagger thorn would sound like Mama asking me to come home and take a warm bath. A bushlimb scrape would sound like Papa asking me not to borrow money on the mine. The creaking of the wood braces out in the meat shack was Jeff asking

me to come on up to Pampa and be his guitar-picker
around at the ranch houses. Irene, Skinny Granny, George,
Roy, Uncle Robert, Helen Cliffman, each spoke to me in
their time and turn. Then I could hear two of them, three,
or a whole crowd of them, speaking about me to one
another. The good things, the bad things, the medium
things about me. Laughs we laughed, old tears that all of
us cried about each other. Each person told of how I, myself, had caused him or her some pain, grief, misery, hurt.
Other faces, heads, forms, and shapes crossed over my
lands, each one asking me its one or forty questions. Eddie
asked me to keep in touch with him. Old Man Rio asked
me to shake his blanket out in some water and hang it up
on a limb in the sun to dry-clean. Riorina pointed at me and
asked me questions about her and about her people.

Why did you hurt me like this? Why did you do this and
this to me? Are you always so crazy in the head as this?
Tell me about this. I watched you when you did not even
know I was there. Almost all of the talkers, askers, goers,
and comers mentioned something about the mine. If you
do get to be the big rich owner of that mine, how will you
use it to make things better for my folks and me? How?
How? I am asking you, how and how?

I drank my coffee to the bottom of its cup, shook my
head as hard as I could, but still all of their faces, eyes,
hands, fingers, questions, words, hows, and whys kept
crackling out in the open, wild bush.

I took down my guitar and sat on a beer case to pass
away the time, and could even hear their voices boom up
at me from out of the round sounding hole under my
strings. I played soft-finger style chords for a good long bit
before my words turned loud enough to sing: "Well, it's a
hard road, dead or alive. And a hard road, dead or alive."

As my words got plainer, I forgot for a while most of
the voices asking their courtroom full of questions:

> Well, that new sher'ff sent me a letter,
> And that new sher'ff sent me a letter,
> Said, "Come up 'n' see me, dead or alive,
> Come up an' see me, dead or alive."

> Yes, he even sent me my picture,
> And he even sent me my picture.

How do I look, boys, dead or alive?
How do I look, boys, dead or alive?

I am sorry that I cain't come, Sher'ff,
I am sorry that I cain't come, Sher'ff,
Dead er alive, no, Sher'ff,
Dead er alive, no, Sher'ff.

I gotta go see my little sweet thaing.
Gotta go see my sweet thaing,
Dead er alivve, yes, Sher'ff,
Dead er alivve, yes, Sher'ff.
   It's a hard road,
   Dead er alive,
   And a hard ole road,
   Dead er alive.

I heard a sand-and-gravel voice somewhere at my back say, "It sho' is. Hahd road. Dead an' alive."

A black-skinned man with a cut, scarred face, healed-over cuts across his neck, his hands and arms, stood in the door to nod at me. His eyes weighed and checked every inch of me and my overalls, from the top of my head to the soles of my shoes. I saw that he wore a pair of torn, patchy overalls that looked to be as raggedy-taggledy as his face and arms, a shirt as dirty and torn as his lips and mouth. He stood there on a pair of bare feet which had the most cuts, bruises, scars, heals, open sores, and scabs that I had ever seen on any woman or man dead or alive. The ashy, dusty dirt that covered him over was of the same grays and bluish tints as the Chisos Mountains and the Rough Run Valley, the Rio Grande from bank to bank. His eyes stood half open, not pop-eyed but wide-eyed, and he moved his eyelids at the same slow, stiff gait and speed with which he moved one or two of his rocky clay fingers on the rags of his pants legs. I knew at my first glance that he had dust and dirt on his head and shoulders that was years older than me, this guitar, this old sunbaked brick house. I felt like those overalls of his were just a few days older than the covers of crystal-like dusts from hill to hill. He was all shoulders and hands. His hips and stomach did not even fill out his overalls around their belly line.

I jumped up to my feet and tried to grin at the man. I told him, "Ahhmm, shore is. Yeahh, come in. Coffee up."

"Uhm. I juz' cuhm mozely t' git thiz hyeah bahck t' yuh." He tossed Eddie's eagle-torn leather cap down on top of our bedrolls on their bee crates. "Buhlongz hyeahh, don't it?"

"Cousin of mine. Moved on over ta Study Butte not much more'n a good hour ago. He ain't a-comin' back this way. I never could keep a hat er a cap on th' top o' my head, myself. Why don't you take it 'n' wear it? I cain't keep it on. Here, I'm gonna rustle up a cup o' java fer ya. Ya look like y'r needin' one bad."

"Wal suh, if'n you is fo'cin' me, I guesses I'll make roomer nuff in my belly tuh 'hale it in. I thank yuh juhsta same, but I nevuh did see no hat er cap that's 'bout ta stay on top o' my head in th' brambly bushes where I goes. My ole pahck mule's ears an' 'er skin, both, is all ripped an' skint full o' holes, but then, that little ole leathuh cap wouldn' do 'er so much good, neithah. Tastes like *lobo*-lapperin' coffee, awright, suh."

"Been through lotsa stickery brush, that there coffee has. I didn't quite git yore name?"

"Nig'head." He rubbed his hand over his kinkery hair.

"Niggerhead?" I tried to laugh, but slipped away to a sober, frowny grin that stuck on my face. "My name's Bushy Head, Wood. Bushy Head Woody. Fuzzy Rug, they call me. Ha hah."

"Folks does give folks some teh'bul funny handles t' use foh names. Hyuhh, hyuhh, hyoohh." He shook the whole house with a deep bullfroggy laugh. "Tell me, Mistuh Wood Bush, how's come yuh heah all by yo'se'f? By ya lone-some?"

"Come down here ta try findin' a lost mine my grampaw dug inta. Four of us did. Three of 'em split off already. Lef' me here ta beat my brains out a-worryin' 'bout this ole wreck truck out here, an' about all o' this here junky crap that y' 'see a-layin' 'round all over th' floors. Ya need any beddin'? Know anybody needs any?"

"Noehp, sho' don't. I guess I packs th' bes' blahnket made out yannah on toppa that ol' mule's back." He took a seat on a packing box by the stove. Looking down at the coffee grounds in his cup, he went on, "That ole Lizzie-flea out heah sho' did bus' its head up ag'inzt Ole Man Sam's 'dobeh wall. Whowwhh!"

"Shore did," I told him. "My dad got sore an' run th' truck inta that wall jest a-hellin' it."

"How juh make 'im so mad?"

"Told 'im I was a-headin' up ta El Paso ta borry some dough offa some of our wealthy kinfolks. My aunt, Patsy Greenseed."

"Evahbudy knows 'bout Missis Greenseed. Nevah did know 'fo' now thut er frunt name is Patsy. She slid out th' stakes fuh mo' than a hundehd of 'em t' come down 'roun hyeah t' look foh stuff, awll kinds er stuff. Gol'. Si'vvuh. Quicksi'vvuh. Chem'kulz. Oiul. Made 'erseff a bagful. She staked 'um down hyeah when her family laughed and called her *loco de poco*. Time was when Missis Greenseed own de Hund'ed an' One, 'long wid de One Two. I stood mony's th' time, son, op top o' some cliff rock, look one huhnd'ed mile an' see nothin' but Greenseed's lond. It wasn't th' gol' an' th' si'vvuh, nor th' stuff a-runnin' in them rocks, thut made yuh aunty alla that, son. Noep. It was two thangs, th' cattle, an' the oiul."

"I ain't seen more'n forty cattle since I been 'round here," I said. "An', fer's oil wells goes, I didn't see a single dern derrick so fer, yet."

"Don't use a tall high derrick down 'roun' heah. Oiul runs too shallow. Them litta bitty tripod sticks runs a pumper cable up'n down that hole, thisa way." He made a loophole with one fist and stuck his finger in and out, up and down, like a cable pump. "Yeahp, mon. Don' need no derrick ta suck all o' de oiul out from down in unduh dis cuhntry an' Mayxeco, too. Mos' uh de tripods lays up nawth an' wes' o' heah. Cain' see 'um hawdly stuck down in da bush. Tha's wheah yo' aunty an' her husban' got mos' all uh deir kale."

"I jest ain't sa much of an oil man, don't reckon. Strikes me, I did see a flock er two of them tripod sticks. I was figgerin' 'em ta be some kind of a riggin' ta rope an' tie an' brand an' butcher cattle an' sheep an' stuff. I guess I got born'd inta th' music bunch, an' the miner crowd." I looked around at the lines of sample rock in the room. "An' I cain't ev'n tell one rock from th' other'n 'round here in this very room."

"Findin' raght smaht uh music on thuh gittah box jus' when I walked up. I'd swap off right now, an' giv yuh alla thu laughin' nuggets yuh could pack back home, if yuh'd show me how ta flimp them music strangs an tuh lay muh mouth wide open an' t' saing 'long with de box fulla music. Han's uh mine is way an' gone too crippledy stiff on me." He clawed his fingers in his lap to show me what he meant. "I done hit suh many dagger weeds yuh nevuh could count how many I hit."

" 'Long've ya been down in here, say?" I tried not to look at him any too straight, since I did not wish him to think I was passing judgment on him. "Good long while?"

"My ole man an' pappy brung me off down this place, oh, few dayz aftuh I stuck my head outta mammy'z ole belly. She fall down on a fevuh blanket an' pass 'way befo' I'ze up big 'nuff t' walk around. My pap, I nevuh know. Indians raised me all around da cliff-rock an' de broosh. Three kinds uh blood runnin' in me, heah. Dozen blood. I don' know. I wuhk 'round evuh cow camp yuh evuh did heah 'bout. Cook's boy. Cook's helpuh. Chuck-wagon chow hand. Chuck-wagon cook, full-fledge."

"How d'ja come t' quit yer cookin' jobs?" I asked him. "Mebbe y' bumped inta my grampaw in yer day. Jerry P. Guthrie?"

"I sho' done that, ahright. Sho' did. 'Roun' about a cuppla yeahs, yeah an' a hawf."

I turned around and about, slow and easy, trying not to appear to care any too much. "Nearly ever' day? Er jest ever' oncet in a while?"

"Evuh day, most about. I nevuh did know any too much 'bout his wife an' kids. I had me a puhty half-Indyun gal out 'n th' canyon, yonnah. I seed th' wife an' t'ree boys, spoke evuh day I seed 'em. I helped Jerry's family mix 'n' lay up these 'dobe bricks heah 'n th' wall o' this ole house. Helped 'um set up that win'mill out'n th' back yahd. Played a time er two wid th' t'ree littul boys. Nevuh could 'emembuh whut dem t'ree boys' names was. Jib, Jab, an' Paul? Jib, Jab, an' Paul. Harh harh harhh. Wife's name slips muh mind, too."

I saw that the man had a quick way to break his words off into a fast, easy laugh. It was where his words got stuck that his laugh began, and, when he could not call any word to speak about his thoughts, this laugh stepped in to take things over. I knew that he used this same laugh to show that he knew a good bit more than his face and words told. His laugh was the dirt which he used to cover up and hide away all of his deeper, higher, and richer places back in his heart and mind.

" 'Twasn't Jib, Jab, an' Paul." I shifted and shuffled around on the floor. "It was Gid, Jeff, an' Claude. Gid

an' Claude stayed back up in th' oil fields. Jeff married onta
a right perty black-headed gal, an' he come down here ta
dig Paw Jerry's mine up, an' he ankled all around th'
stickery, dagger-weed fer a while, then he flapped 'is wings
an' flooped back up north t' his new-found wife. M' cousin,
Eddie, lost 'is right arm over in th' war; he took off tonight with Mister Sammy Nail ta ride over t' Study Butte
t' try t' marry 'im a gal over there, if she'll have him."

He told me, "I ahready knowz 'bout how yuh Pappy got
mad an' to'e off out in th' brush."

"You? Ya seen 'im?"

"Truck wrack 'n' th' hull t'ing."

All I could say was, "I be damn."

Niggerhead went on, "I wawk'd 'im down, tawk'd
some wid 'im. Tried t' git 'im ta come back heah t' this
house. But no, he sez, he cain't an' he couldn', he won't
an' he wouldn'. Give me a littul messidge tuh tell yuh, er
else I nevuh woulda stopped in heah in th' fus place."

I bit my lip. "What was it that Papa said? Message?"

Niggerhead swayed on his crate as he thought, and told
me. "Yo' Pap, fonny feller, head hard's a dam'able jinnie
burro. Talked tuh me in a chant an' rhyme."

"Riddle?" I said.

"Riddull. Yeahhmm. Mobby tha'z whut you'd cawll it.
Ohhe, ho ho ho ho! Riddull." He slapped his legs with his
hands and moved from side to side on his box. "Plainest
riddull I evuh seed up tu this time. Hyahh hyahh! Oh hoo!"

"Went how?" My words did not carve into any very deep
rock. I was full of sticky coffee and weakly feelings.
"Yeahh? How?"

" 'Dubbul X, Dubbul IZZ,' ahh, dubbul, dubbul, ahh,
ahhh—"

> Dubbul X, Dubbul IZZ, Dubbul O, V, STOVE,
> That rock ain't hahd if yuh digs wid LOVE;
> Iff you takes any grubstakah in,
> I'm commin' wid my gun when I comes ag'in.

"He'd cert'nly do that all right," I told Niggerhead. "Did
Papa tell y' where'bouts he was a-goin' to?"

"Green County, bulieeve he said."

"Gray County." I looked around the room as I paced it.
"That's up north an' east from Amarillo, there. Where we
come from. Yeahm. D'ya think he's got much of a shot,

Niggerhead—I mean, much of a damn chance ta make it up through all o' that damn bush brush alive?"

"I'd say he'd have a good chance. He'll catch de train at Alpine. I'm sho' layin' my laughin' nuggets that yuh daddy'll make it. Smaht man. Hard head."

"Laughy nuggets." I scratched my ears to say, "Man, if you did show 'im th' best trail an' roads, an' if he does make it on up yonder ta Pampa in fair shape, fer yore riddle message an' fer yore tellin' 'im how ta git up there, I'll shove ever' last single one of these here nugget rocks all around this whole room over inta yer lap. I'd shove a jar of whiskey over ta boot but we drunk it all up. I'll toss my old music box over inta yore hands, fer a gift, fer a present, jest to show ya I'm yer friend. Swear I will. Swear it with my open han' on top o' yer head. Cut my heart out with a cactus dagger if I lie t' ya."

Niggerhead stood up, put his cup down on the stove lid, and said, "Yo' nuggets cain't laugh at nobody, mon, they ain't got 'nough real stuff in theih backbones tuh do much laughin' at noboddy. Keep 'um tuh buhn holes in yuh own pants. My packmule kicks up an' lays down when she ketches me loadin' her saddul wid anyt'ing less'n twen'y-two er -t'ree karats, loose rock stuff. She's jus' 'bout like me, uh, uh, she's a full-blood loose-rock lady, herself. Harh, harh, harhh. Ho."

"Yer lady mule"—I tried to be funny—"was she 'round with ya on th' day th't ya helped Paw Jerry ta dig out his first chuck offa th' backbone of that there cliff-rock?" I wasn't sure he'd done that, but from what Sam Nail had said I thought he might have.

"Jerry?" He walked around the room to keep his eyes off of mine, and on the odds and ends of things around the floor. "Me? Him an' muhseff? Wheah'd yuh undig that co'pse frum undah?"

"Relatives."

"Bettuh'd quit a-claimin' kin tuh anyboddy which tells yu that I was a-lookin' at 'im that day." He spoke slow, with deep breaths, walked spraddle-legged around to touch his fingers with a sly grin of pity to the rocky samples from our pockets. "He wasn't keepin' no camp cook at dat time. Juz' a-brandin' a stray uh two, heahh an' yonduh. His boys'd done already driv' evuh wall-eye in 'is herd out thru' th' Slick Wagon Gap towards th' deepot. His misssy was a-doin' evuh bite uh his cookin'. Jus' him, jus huh, an' just' deem t'ree boys. Me an' my squaw dug up a whole half a mount'in o' loose rock that ve'y day, that ve'y same week, unloosenin' a whole wagonful of loose-rock stuff. She took down wid sech of a laughin' spazum that I throw'd water, an' duht, an' evvuht'ing else in huh face jus' tryin' tuh shake 'er back ta 'er right seneses—tryin' tuh shake 'er outtuh that wil' crazy laughin' spazum."

"How'd she come out?"

He rubbed his face in his hands as he said, "Jerked loose o' me 'n' fell. Six hundu'd foot. Shaley grav'l. Still a-laughin'."

"Perty bad."

"Mon, I couldn' take a breath. I tore out 'cross th' brush tuh tell Jerry's fam'ly 'bout 'er. I busted in heah at this do'. I tossed a tobaccuh sack down heah on th' flo'e. I got so stuck full o' cryin' an weepin' that I tried tuh dry muh eyes up an' make some soht uvva joke out. I tried ta laugh so's I wouldn't skeer Missiz Jerry an' thuh t'ree littul boys. I wuzn't gonnuh tell Jerry till I got 'im out 'n th' house. I go stahted laughin', laughin'—some kind uvvuh laughin', laughin', laughin', crazy laughin'. Jerry an' his wife an' kids—yass, I knows—figguh'd I'd tore in ta rob 'em outuh th' sample chonk they done knocked off. I tried tuh say a funny joke, uhh, yass—tried tuh tease Mistuh Jerry."

I walked about and said, "Hmmm."

"Hard Rock Jerry. That's the nickname I called 'im. Hard Rock Jerry. Hyuhh. Hyuhh. I call 'im Hard Rock 'cause he was alwiz uh-razzin' me up an' down 'bout me a-bein' a loose-rock man. Always a-stumblin' 'round the sissy rock, easy rock, an' loose rock. Hyuhh hyuhh hyuhh. They all guess'd me tuh be uh-turnin' outlaw on 'em, see— uh-bustin' in this do' tuh rob their sample an' go jump on thuh claim an' dig it up. It wuz when I seed his missiz grab up th' pickaxe handle that—well, I dropp'd a li'l ole nugget er two down heah on this flo'e, an' I streaked back out 'cross th' brush a-laughin' back tuh wheahh muh wummun slid an' fell. I pick'd huh right up'n muh ahms, like thiz, an' I walked all around uh-laughin' at her two nights an' a whole day 'fo' I even let her feet drag an' touch down on th' groun'."

I told him, "Well, Niggerhead, I'm sorry ta stan' here an' listen ta sa much of a hard-luck tale as yores is. Ya might not be much of a man ta beg people ta go round

a-feelin' sorry fer ya. I've heard so much about ya an'
now, well, I'm awful glad ta git th' whole thing straight.
I heard you was th' last livin' man on earth that knows
where Paw Jerry knocked off his chunk at. I don't guess
they's a livin' soul now that knows how ta walk an' lay
'is finger on Paw Jerry's mine."

He paced faster back and forth, saying, "Yuh heah'd
about me? Oho, yuh did heah about me, hoh? Wall, did
yuh evuh heah 'bout anybody evuh takin' me by my fingah
'n' takin' me ta tetch it up ag'inst th' rock tha's got all o'
th' good stuffs in it? Nosuh. Mistah Hahdwood, they's not
a livin' mon that's gunnta reach ovuh an' take yuh by yuh
finguh 'n' lead yo' nose out heah an' rub it up ag'inst any
rock thet yo' grampappauh, Jerry, dug out by his own
hand."

I sweated some damper under my shirt, and told him,
"They's not sa very much I can say, 'cause I know yer jest
exackly right. Ain't nobody ever gonna hold my finger an'
stick it down in th' puddin' fer me."

"If yuh let 'em stick yo' own finguh up in thut honey
hole, mon, they'll stick it in theah own mouth an' lick th'
spittle off." He spoke towards the southern mountains, the
hot rocks rising back towards the Santa Rosa range, there
some thirty-odd miles across the Rio Grande. He shook
his fists above his head, spun and whirled on his toes with
the ups and downs of his words. The catamount meatshack robber had to stay hid out in the weeds with his
tail pulled tight in between its legs, during the spell of time
that Old Niggerhead growled, roared, snorted, walked, and
sermonized.

I stood close by the stovepipe and my guitar on the wall,
with my shoulder blades jammed up stiff against the hand-
smeared plaster. For any two men to try to move about in
this house the way this man moved in this room would
have caused a worse wreck than Papa when he steered our
old T truck into the south wall. I could see the flame of
our lantern wick dance, shimmy, quiver sideways, grow
little, blow out as thin as a lost gunshot, as the old glassy
globe wiggled its hinges with every breathing word this old
fellow of the stickerbrush spoke. My throat was like the
lantern globe, my words were like the wicky flame, rattly,
scared, out, gone.

"Po' ole Jerry. Hiz littul ole sampul tested an' assayed
uh hunduhd dolluhs tuh th' ton. One hunduhd si'vvuh an'

ten mo'e dollahs gold on top. Yass, yass. Why, son, boy, my ole sleepy-eye mule out yonduh in th' yahd knows fohty plazes thut runs bettuh than hunduhd dollahs for a ton o' diggin'. My little heaty bitch dawg thut follus me 'round knows wheahbouts some fish-back rock thu'll test out ten times bettuh'n yo' Jerry's hunduhd. Mon, I wouldn't tetch my hands down on top o' no rock thut's not a-gonna spill out 'round 'bout six, eight hunduhd in under th' dug-up ton. I can walk my laigs no mo'n a mile uh this heah ole bee-sting house, an' titch my hands down on stuff th't'll run me six hunduhd dolluhs on a hunduhd pound of it."

I shook all over. "Perty fair pickin's. Perty laripin, perty ever'thing."

"All o' th' stuff we done dug'd up out o' thiz ole Mothuh Earth has been ugly up tuh this day. 'S made puhtty peoples tuhn out 'n do ugly stuff, all kinds o' ugly stuff. When I looks 'round muh head an' sees th' mean ways folks treats one anothuh 'bout uh few shovelfuls o' gold 'n' silvuh, son, I stands an' I wunduhs whut I evuh does want tuh stay on livvin' fuh, jez' ta keep my eyes on uh-lookin' at 'em do so ornery."

"I ask m'self them same questions," I told Niggerhead. "I ain't dug out no answers so fer, in my nineteen-twenty years."

"I been uh watchin' it, boy son, all uh my nacher'l days, ta see how dirty folks treats one another after that ole fevuh greed sets in on 'um. Lickin' the hay an' duht off'n an ole cakey cow's assyhole's a nicey nicey bizness compared with starvin' an' beatin', an fightin', an' shootin', an' killin' each othuh. Dawg eat dawg, hawg eat hawg, evuh man fuh his own belly-gut, an' tuh shimmy shammy shit wid yuh own skin an' bone, yuh own kinnyfolks, friends— evuhbody's bit wid it."

"I shore ain't 'sputin' yer word there," I said.

"Some of yo' peopuls, Mistuh Headdawood, has got tuh luhn thiz wun littul easy lesson. I mean that, jez' 'cause yuh come off down heah widda rig o' pretty clo'es on, an' wid a fatback money pouch stickin' out wid papuh dollars, an' yo' ass on thuh cushion of yo'e big rolluh wagon, that this don't make yuh any bettuh'n me, heah, inside my old dag-gered-up ovuhhalls." He watched me part of the time, and part of the time he talked and motioned as if I was not even there to hear him.

"I ain't a-burnin' with none of them fevers." I touched

the stovepipe with the back of my hand. "But I'm damn shore aimin' ta try ta remember ever word of it, Niggerhead. My overalls here's jest about as whackled-out in th' ass end as yores is. An' my nugget pouch is flatter'n this here damn stove lid, here. I ain't got no nuggets, an' hell, I've not even got a pouch."

"Thuh pouch in buhtween muh laigs wuhz thuh pouch I done most o' my thinkin' 'bout, 'way yonduh long time fo' I evuh did git up tuh be any nineteen summers an' winters old. Jest ta pump thuh girls up 'n' down wid my long leathuh pouch. Mebbe you's thuh same hot nature as I always been. I got up a littul older, then, an' I come around tuh burnin' up wid fires o' holy hell, mon, ta fill up my ole leather dollar pouch. I learnt later on thut a mon cain' be no full growed-up mon till he gets both o' his leather bags fill'd up, an' keeps 'em fill'd up."

"Yeah, that's jest about right."

"In thuh commin' of thuh sun, in thuh mawnin', thuh eyes o' thuh brush gonntuh see Mistah Haywood walk out up thuh nawtheas' trail tuh look around tuh try tuh find somebody with a bag full o' good money tuh len' yuh some tuh drop down inside yo' grubstake pouch."

"I ain't a-gonna take in none o' them one-eighth wheelers." I pushed back tighter against the wall. "Not even a one-sixteenth. I'll borrow money an' pay it back at interest, but I ain't a-gonna sell out no set part of th' diggin'. Only ones that I'm cuttin' in on th' tonnage will be th' folks that helps me hunt an' locate th' claim, an' pick 'n' shovel it, an' blast an' fire it, an' dig an' haul it, an' stuff like that."

"Yo' pappy wuhd sho' like to heah yuh speakin' dem wuhds," he told me.

"If Papa had of waited here in this room jest about one minute longer," I said, "he coulda heard me say those same words, word for word."

"No suh"—Niggerhead wrinkled his wrinkles—"if yo' po' ole daddy would uh stood hyeah right now, yuh'd try tuh say bad wuhds tuh deal 'im pain, an' tuh lay up mo' misery on top'uhn his ole head. Yuh knows dat. Yuh knows it. Yuh knows dat's what yuh'd stretch yuh guts ta do tuh 'im. Yuh'd be mean wid 'im. Yuh'd say p'izenn wuhds in hiz eahs. Thuh p'izenn o' greed's done come a-settin' in on yo' cup, an' it's a-foamin' an' a-sizzlin', an' a-splaishin' up ovuh de sides. Yuh's too big of a coward ta stan' up 'n' say any of yuh divulish mean wuhds ta me, 'cuz yuh's shittin' in yuh pants 'fraid o' me. 'Fraid uh muh looks. I wants yuh tuh be sca'ed o' me. I dresses up like dis so's my patches'll keep yuh sca'ed o' me. Yuh knows I'ze gotcha bowels on thuh move."

"Well, I—that is, naturally, down here, dark night, and . . ."

"And." He grabbed my words before I had finished playing with them. "And, yuh knows thut I knows, if I was ta tuhn muhse'ff inta—say inta yo'e ole wearied pappy standin' up heah snake-bit, stiff-j'inted, all sickly, head achin', yuh'd not try tuh say some littul bit of a wuhd that'd make me feel one inch bettuh; yuh'd sling th' wuhst an' thuh meanest dahm wuhd at my head thut yuh cu'd scrape up tuh sting muh soul wid."

I slid down the wall onto the floor, rubbed my hands over my face, and told him, "That's right. Ever' word th't y' say cuts inta my damn warty hide like a red-blade knife. I did git afraid. Got nervish an' shaky, an' I took sick with a bad case of th' quick tongue. Go ahead an' rake me ov'r th' ashes."

"I hain' got thuh time tuhnight tuh ston' hyeah ovuh yo'e guilty bones an' give yuh ah hot wuhd lashin', much's I loves ta poke muh stinguh intu yuh. They's six, sevuhn, mountains a-waitin' fuh my ole callis'd feet tuh mount up 'um tuhnight 'fo' mawnin'. It's a-gon'tuh make mah sweet soul drapple down wuth big honey tuh see yuh lay heah 'n' shake thuh shimmies an' mess in yo' sissy pants, an' cry 'til yuh tears wets down all o' them ashes down heah on this ole dirt flo'. Yuh done a puhtty fair job o' makin' folks like yuh, back yonduh at th' Tuhlingua Mine, 'round Study Butte, ovuh heah from ovuh yondah that eighteen miles. Don't yuh see, po' son, po' flinthead boy, that yuh pawpaw had his heart an' his soul ovuh on thuh real folks' side, an' if yuh did take in a one-eighter, er mebbe a one-fou'ther, mon, youh'd not evun be yo' own soul's boss no mo'? Lunyticks! Give me a prize warm bed fulluh gila monster lizuhds any ole day o' thuh week. It wusn't jest yo' few families o' friends an' kinfolks yo' paw was a-stondin' up foh. It was evuh single one o' them livin' eyes out yondah lookin' up an' down at yuh. Tha's whut made 'im wrack that ole truck like'n he did. And made 'im run an'

jump out o' this east winduh an' run off in tuh th' brush
wid thuh littul Pedro puppy followin' at 'is heels."

"I guess, I reckon that's what become of our little
poochie, all right." I kept my face-rubbing position on the
ashy floor. "Hmm. Sniffed off at Papa's heels."

"If dat littul puppy had 'uh stuck heah an' a-been yo'e
frien', I mighta helped yuh tuh lay hands on yuh paw
Jerry's hill 'bout ten uh fifteen yeahs ahead o' time. I'm
jest afraid thut my good feelin's went mostly along wid
thuh littul dawgie's nose in buhind yuh pappy's heels. I
wouldn' lead Eddie tuh no place; he's way gone too wushy-
washy an' too ignuhnt 'long wid it. You's too young an'
hot-headed, an' ain't got none o' thuh real feelin's 'bout
nothin—not rocks, not hills, not mines, dawgs, uh not
evun 'bout livin' wid folks."

"Guess I tore up somethin' that was worth lots more'n
this ole 'dobe wall, er that ole T truck Papa wracked. What
if I go ta Tucson an' marry that girl, Riorina? Woodja help
me, then?"

"No. Yuh cuhd marry half a dozen guhls up un' down
this heah bo'der river, an' I'd nevuh give yuh one littul
finguh's help."

"But th' mine claim belongs ta my Grampaw Jerry. Folks
did tell me that you's th' only livin' human that seen Jerry
knock off that sample rock. It's his, 'cordin' ta law. He
never did have it registered in his name, but he did have
it analyzed an' assayed."

"Puuhh! Yuh wants tuh sho' 'nuff know thuh truth 'bout
how many eyes was a-watchin' Jerry whilst his hammuh
picked off that littul chunk? Not one, not a couple, but a
coupluh dozen uvvum. Hah! Whenevuh we git th' minerul
laws fixed up jest right, my folks is gonnuh reach down
an' dig up a coupla hunduhd mines twicet's rich as yo'e
Paw Jerry's. Gold. Silvuhh. Diamonts. Tuhquoise. Rubies.
Emeralds. Chemicals. Minerals. What yuh tawkin' 'bout,
mon? Who buhlongs tuh what? Which rock's mine an'
which hill's yo'en?"

" 'Cordin' ta law, it belongs ta Jerry P."

" Cordin tuh whut laws? Whut law? Whose laws? Mon,
jes' wawk yuh feets out heah in 'mongst th' rocks, an' yell
an' holluh up tuh them cliff-rocks, an' ask 'eum, 'Hiieey,
Mistuh Mountain, whose mount'in is yuh? Whose is yuh?
Who does yuh buhlong tuh?" An' the ole mount'in, it's

gon'tuh think yuh tuh be sa crazy in yuh top-knot, it's gonna take evuh one o' yo' crazy wuhds, an' t'row 'um right back in yuh face, an' ask all thuh othuh hills and rocks and weeds around, Whose? Whose? Whoosse?"

This is where Old Niggerhead slapped his pants legs to laugh at me in my corner under the lantern. His laugh and his pant-leg slapping made enough sound and noise to wiggle lanterns on the wall pegs around at the Four Big Ranch Houses. He tossed his head, laughed up and down the floor for a trip or two each direction, then laughed out at our unlocked, open southerly door. He laughed across the front yard and laughed his way to his mule in the waiting bushes. Two times around that house he laughed in circles. All of the rocks, hills, weeds, and cactus brush laughed on his shoulder and back towards where I sat.

The fire stove and the lantern both burned out while the moon took a running coyote laugh at me. The animals that I heard scream and startle in the bushes—I knew, I felt it —they were each one laughing because they felt glad to see me go. The stars laughed themselves to the floors of the sky, then the sun crew came along to laugh where the stars still pointed at me. I did not move from the stove corner till the sun was already frothing its mouth and foaming under its flanks in the yard.

It was the laughy ore chunks all around our room that laughed with the laughing nuggets cold on the stove's lids, which wakened me to the sounds outside of a young lady's voice calling, "Hallo! Hello! Anybody at home?"

I pulled myself up onto my feet and stood in the door. I saw a young girl, around twelve or thirteen, that I took to be the daughter of Sam Nail. She wore a tight slipover sweater, a brownish woolly kind of a skirt, hair in a flurry with the hurries of the day. I told her, "Howdy. Nobody much here. Jest me."

"I have a postal for you." She put the card into my hand. "If your name is Eddie Stone Moore. My father had to stay all night last night over at Study Butte with the state men. So this makes me the mail carrier. I'm not so good at it as my father is."

"Lots better." I read Eddie's card. Part of the lower words said: "I am just afraid you will have to make a trip back up here, Ed. The Govermint Man will not pay us your pension check. You forgot to fill in the right papers when

you changed your address. Your Sissy, Mom & All. Love
to J., to C., to W.W., & All."

Sam Nail's daughter had started to her saddle pony
waiting by the wagon trail road to her house. I called her
after she had mounted to her saddle, and she rode past the
door, asking me, "Isn't it a good card? Do you wish me to
take it back to the sender and have them write you a
better one, plainer, easier to read, or something?"

"This'n," I told her, "it's, ahh, for my cousin, 'steada
for me. Eddie Stoner rode over ta Study Butte las' night
with yer daddy. Eddie shore oughta have this here card,
though, 'f they's any way ya can git it over ta where he's
át. 'S about his soljier's pension."

"I will get it over to him, don't you worry." She took
the card and stuck it down into her back pack-saddle bag
while her pony stamped and whirled away to trot her
away towards home. "Sometime today, I don't know just
when. Today, sometime."

My rubber-soled truck-tire shoes walked as quiet as the
sky over to the wall peg to get my guitar strap over my
shoulder. I looked at the room and the room felt cold. I
looked at the bedrolls and their quilts and blankets looked
cold. I took my last two sample rocks out of my overall
pocket and threw them across the floor. I never will know
the exact reason why I hated the looks of those blankets
and bedrolls the way I did. I looked at the dead, chilly
coffeepot by the stovepipe, and it hit me harder, some
way, than a fist, your club, your brass knucks, your gun
by either end, its pounding butt or its fiery mouth barrel. I
stumbled to my hands and knees three times trying to back
my way out of that door.

An hour through the brush, two hours along a north
trail, another hour up a blown-out wagony rut road, set
my feet and my truck-tire shoes back in the middle of the
Slick Rock Gap, which lays close to eight miles towards
the north pole from Sam Nail's ranch place. I set my
guitar down on the same rock footing where Papa, Jeff,
and Eddie had pulled me down from the face of that cliff-
rock, on our first day with Claude's old penny-pencil maps
blowing in our fingers.

I took my first good long backwards look while the
whistling of the breeze and the sporting of the winds yelled
at me louder through the suction of the Slick Rock Gap.
Sam Nail told us that this wagon trail out of here to the

north towards Alpine would save us more than forty miles of daggery walking. I commenced trickling tears down both of my cheeks as I turned my face away from the Rough Run Valley, the Hen Egg, the Chisos, the Christmas Mountains, the Saw Tooth, the Santa Rosas, and the Niggerhead.

I commenced to walk along past an old sign, scribbled on the fan of a blown-down windmill, which said, "Rock Canyon Ranch, 15 mis.," with a little wiggly ground rattler arrow shooting towards the ranch. I commenced laughing at my own silly self as I flumped my guitar in a crazy banging which made no tune nor sense. My bangy laughing echoed back down in both my ears while I walked my first few steps on through the Slick Rock Gap.

I laughed so loud that I had to drag my feet like a cripple. I was thinking of something so funny that human words, human songs, can't quite run and catch it. Papa, and Jeff, and Eddie, they pulled me up that shaley rock cliff there, not down it . . . not down it.

Up it.

I'll skip Tucson and the Gonzalezes this trip. I'll head on back up to Pampa and make friends again with all of my relatives laughing at me. I'll save up, all of us will put up, and we'll make another stab at this country down in here. Maybe, maybe that little pretty, peachy, big-eyed, curly-headed Riorina will still be down here when I come back with a little more sense. I made so damn many mistakes on this run, I . . . I couldn't stand up and look her straight in the eyes. Hyooee. Hyooee.

Papa and the gang, ha ha ha ha. They did not, most absolutely did not, pull me down off from the rotten rock up yonder on that cliff-rim facing. It was not down it.

Saved my damn, no-good, crazy neck up there. But they didn't pull me down off of that rocky face. It was up the damn thing. Up the damn rocks.

With all of their clothes tied together, pulling together, to save my two-bit, wild-ass, no-good, nitty-witted neck. But it was up it.

Up it.

> Lots of good boys are goner galoots,
> Gone galoots, gone galoots.
> It ain't th' gals at th' Study Butte;
> It's th' Foolish Gold in th' mountains' humps.

I just hope this one hope this morning, which is, I want to hope that Eddie Stoner is having better luck, or at least just as good, down along the muddy pool with Luisa and that Rio Rattler River, and with Ole Man Rio's greeny wool blanket somewhere around.

Carlos Castaneda

With TALES OF POWER now available in a Pocket Book edition, one of the most popular authors of the twentieth century completes his journey into sorcery.

"We are incredibly fortunate to have Carlos Castaneda's books..."
—The New York Times Book Review

_____80676   TALES OF POWER $1.95

_____80498   THE TEACHINGS
                 OF DON JUAN $1.95

_____80424   JOURNEY TO IXTLAN $1.95

_____80497   A SEPARATE REALITY $1.95

Available at bookstores everywhere, or order direct from the publisher.

- -